CALIGARI 3D
TRUESPACE2
MODELING

CONSTRUCTION KIT

CREATE YOUR OWN
WORLDS WITH
CALIGARI
TRUESPACE2

WAITE GROUP PRESS™
Corte Madera, CA

DAVID DUBERMAN

Publisher • Mitchell Waite
Associate Publisher • Charles Drucker

Acquisitions Manager • Jill Pisoni

Editorial Director • John Crudo
Project Editor • Laura E. Brown
Technical Editor • Alexander Enzmann
Content Editor • Carol Henry
CD Coordinator • Dan Scherf
Copy Editor • Deirdre Greene/Creative Solutions

Production Director • Julianne Ososke
Production Manager • Cecile Kaufman
Production Editor • K.D. Sullivan/Creative Solutions
Senior Designer • Sestina Quarequio
Designers • Karen Johnston, Jil Weil
Cover Illustration • Adam Rogers
Production • Carol L. Bowers, Mona Brown, Ayanna Lacey, Chris Livengood, Gene Redding, Mark Walchle

© 1996 by The Waite Group, Inc.®
Published by Waite Group Press™, 200 Tamal Plaza, Corte Madera, CA 94925.

Waite Group Press™ is a division of Sams Publishing.

Printed in the United States of America
96 97 98 99 • 10 9 8 7 6 5 4 3 2 1

Library of Congress Cataloging-in-Publication Data

Duberman, David, 1952-
    3D modeling construction kit / David Duberman.
        p.   cm.
    Includes index.
    ISBN 1-57169-029-8
    1. Interactive multimedia. 2. World Wide Web (Information retrieval system)
    3. Computer graphics. I. Title.
    QA76.76.I59D83   1996
    006.6--dc20   96-32757
                                                                   CIP

DEDICATION

This book is dedicated to you, the reader.
May you take this baton of knowledge and run with it forever
through the visualized fields of your imagination.

Message from the
Publisher

WELCOME TO OUR NERVOUS SYSTEM

Some people say that the World Wide Web is a graphical extension of the information superhighway, just a network of humans and machines sending each other long lists of the equivalent of digital junk mail.

I think it is much more than that. To me, the Web is nothing less than the nervous system of the entire planet—not just a collection of computer brains connected together, but more like a billion silicon neurons entangled and recirculating electro-chemical signals of information and data, each contributing to the birth of another CPU and another Web site.

Think of each person's hard disk connected at once to every other hard disk on earth, driven by human navigators searching like Columbus for the New World. Seen this way the Web is more of a super entity, a growing, living thing, controlled by the universal human will to expand, to be more. Yet, unlike a purposeful business plan with rigid rules, the Web expands in a nonlinear, unpredictable, creative way that echoes natural evolution.

We created our Web site not just to extend the reach of our computer book products but to be part of this synaptic neural network, to experience, like a nerve in the body, the flow of ideas and then to pass those ideas up the food chain of the mind. Your mind. Even more, we wanted to pump some of our own creative juices into this rich wine of technology.

TASTE OUR DIGITAL WINE

And so we ask you to taste our wine by visiting the body of our business. Begin by understanding the metaphor we have created for our Web site—a universal learning center, situated in outer space in the form of a space station. A place where you can journey to study any topic from the convenience of your own screen. Right now we are focusing on computer topics, but the stars are the limit on the Web.

If you are interested in discussing this Web site or finding out more about the Waite Group, please send me e-mail with your comments, and I will be happy to respond. Being a programmer myself, I love to talk about technology and find out what our readers are looking for.

Sincerely,

Mitchell Waite

Mitchell Waite, C.E.O. and Publisher

200 Tamal Plaza
Corte Madera, CA 94925
415-924-2575
415-924-2576 fax

Website:
http://www.waite.com/waite

CREATING THE HIGHEST QUALITY COMPUTER BOOKS IN THE INDUSTRY

Waite Group Press

Come Visit

WAITE.COM

Waite Group Press
World Wide Web Site

Now find all the latest information on Waite Group books at our new Web site, **http://www.waite.com/waite.** You'll find an online catalog where you can examine and order any title, review upcoming books, and send e-mail to our authors and editors. Our FTP site has all you need to update your book: the latest program listings, errata sheets, most recent versions of Fractint, POV Ray, Polyray, DMorph, and all the programs featured in our books. So download, talk to us, ask questions, on **http://www.waite.com/waite.**

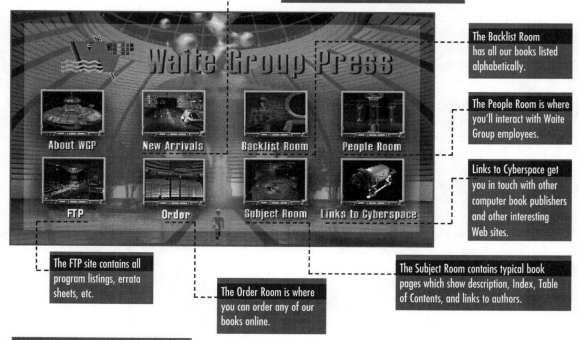

The New Arrivals Room has all our new books listed by month. Just click for a description, Index, Table of Contents, and links to authors.

The Backlist Room has all our books listed alphabetically.

The People Room is where you'll interact with Waite Group employees.

Links to Cyberspace get you in touch with other computer book publishers and other interesting Web sites.

The FTP site contains all program listings, errata sheets, etc.

The Order Room is where you can order any of our books online.

The Subject Room contains typical book pages which show description, Index, Table of Contents, and links to authors.

About WGP · New Arrivals · Backlist Room · People Room
FTP · Order · Subject Room · Links to Cyberspace

ABOUT THE AUTHOR

David Duberman has been active in computer graphics and writing about computers and software for 14 years. He started in computer journalism as the technical editor of *Antic* magazine, a monthly magazine about Atari 8-bit computers. Other magazines he has edited include *The Atari Connection, AVID* magazine, *Video Toaster User* magazine, and *Morph's Outpost on the Digital Frontier*. He's contributed articles to *3D Artist* and *3D Design* magazines, and has written a monthly 3D graphics column for *Morph's Outpost*. He has written several software manuals, including the user manual for Caligari trueSpace version 1. He also has written and published several popular books of tutorials for 3D applications, including Impulse, Inc.'s Imagine and Newtek's LightWave 3D.

TABLE OF CONTENTS

CONTENTS

8   THE IMPORTANCE OF LIGHTING 195

9   MATERIALS PART 1: BASIC SURFACE ATTRIBUTES 221

ACKNOWLEDGMENTS

First and foremost, thanks go to Roman Ormandy, without whose vision the marvelously user-friendly program that's the focus of this book wouldn't exist. As well, I recognize the invaluable contributions of trueSpace2's key developers: Bruce Walter, Peter Starke, Michael Plitkins, and Roger Hagen. Thanks and kudos also to the gang at Waite Group Press, including helpful acquisitions manager Jill Pisoni, efficient project editor Laura Brown, content editor Carol Henry, who ably assisted in toning down my penchant for pedantry, and Dan Scherf, who did yeoman service helping to put the CD-ROM together. Last but by no means least, thanks to all of the members of the Internet trueSpace mailing list, who were an endless source of inspiration.

INTRODUCTION

There's no getting around it: The 3D graphics field is incandescent today, and is rapidly approaching the state of white heat. Thanks, in part, to the success of such cinematic phenomena as *Jurassic Park* and *Twister*, in which many of the most impressive special effects were created with 3D graphics software, and *Toy Story*, which was entirely computer generated, companies are pouring millions of dollars into developing 3D graphics for everything from TV shows to the Internet, and anything else that previously used 2D imagery. The entrepreneurial and artistic opportunities for 3D graphics specialists are burgeoning as never before, and there's no end in sight.

Because of their ability to crunch numbers so rapidly, computers are ideally suited to the math-intensive task of creating 3D graphics. People have been using them for that purpose since they first became available. The first 3D computer images were created as non-moving wireframes on primitive vector graphics displays with large mainframe computers. At the time, this could only be accomplished by entering programs in the form of painstakingly created punch cards. Even a simple image took a long time to calculate and draw. Thus, early on, this form of artistry was limited to the technical elite.

Then, about 10 years ago, with the advent of relatively low-cost, high-powered 16-bit computers with superior graphics capabilities, such as the Atari ST and the Commodore Amiga, 3D graphics embarked on its rapid journey into the popular realm, and colorful solid-rendered 3D stills and animations began to be commonly incorporated into such varied media as computer games, commercial and fine art, and undergraduate-level scientific visualization.

Today, the man and woman on the street have ready access to desktop computers that are many times more powerful than the original super-expensive room-sized machines, with advanced displays capable of truly photo-realistic images. Certainly the field of 3D graphics applications has come a long way as well, with artists being able to construct scenes of impressive complexity by merely pointing, clicking, and dragging. Still, the user interfaces in most of these applications are far from intuitive and require weeks—even months—of training for the artist to be able to achieve the desired results. One of the biggest problems is the fact that the user must deal with three-dimensional objects in a three-dimensional space, all of which can only be seen on a two-dimensional display.

Shortly after the introduction of the Commodore Amiga, a young visionary named Roman Ormandy conceived a 3D graphics application with a revolutionary user interface that overcame many of the perceptual and cognitive boundaries between the artist and the virtual 3D space inside the computer. He went on to start a software company and develop the program, which at its inception was named Caligari. The Caligari program went through several iterations on the Amiga platform, and then, in 1994, moved over to the PC and Windows, renamed as trueSpace. While many new features have been added over the years, the basic interface has remained true to Roman's original conception. Now, with the introduction of trueSpace2—the subject of this book—and the recent drop in price, one of the most advanced and intuitive 3D graphics applications in existence is readily available to almost anyone with a Windows PC. (With this book, you get a free demonstration version of trueSpace2 that provides full functionality for 60 days after the initial installation.)

Nothing is perfect, though. In an ideal world, anyone with an interest in realizing an artistic vision would be able to sit down at a PC equipped with a 3D graphics program and immediately begin to create wondrous images straight out of his or her imagination. We're still a long way from that point, though. As intuitive as trueSpace2 is, many of the program's finer points require demonstration and explanation before the user can truly perform this sort of mind-to-computer transfer. And that's the *raison d'etre* for this book.

The best way to use this book is to proceed through it from beginning to end, working through each step-by-step tutorial in turn while reading the explanations of the various principles at work. Then put it aside and continue to work with trueSpace2 to advance your knowledge of and familiarity with the software, taking advantage of the additional informational resources described in Appendix A.

Here's a brief roadmap of the beginning of your (hopefully) never-ending journey through the world of 3D graphics with trueSpace2:

Chapter 1: 3D Graphics Basics

This chapter discusses some of the special attributes of 3D graphics and provides an overview of using 3D graphics applications. It then covers some of the career opportunities available to you as a 3D artist.

Chapter 2: Introducing the trueSpace2 Interface

This chapter shows you the specific concepts and paradigms used in the program interface, including the menus, icons, and the 2D views into the workspace.

Chapter 3: Quick Start Tutorial: A Guided Tour of Major Features

This chapter offers a step-by-step hands-on introduction to some of trueSpace2's most important tools. You're shown how to create and modify an object, change its surface appearance, render a still, and then animate the object and render a video.

Chapter 4: Navigation: Getting Around in trueSpace2

This chapter demonstrates the tools for changing the point of view in the workspace, as well as modifying an object's position, orientation, and size. Here and in following chapters you'll learn, thanks to trueSpace's non-modular operation, how navigation can be integrated effortlessly with other functions such as modeling.

Chapter 5: Basic Modeling

This chapter introduces you to trueSpace2's object primitives (such as a plane, a cube, and a cylinder), which can get you started in 3D modeling with a minimum of effort. You also get to know the other basic building blocks, including polygons and text, as well as how to use functions that form 3D shapes from polygons.

Chapter 6: Advanced Modeling

This chapter covers trueSpace2's more sophisticated object-creation and 3D editing functions, such as the application of standard navigation operations (move, rotate, scale) to parts of objects: vertices, edges, and faces. Then you learn about object deformation, which lets you manipulate a shape as if it were made of putty and can be applied to animation. Not to be neglected, the amazingly useful 3D Boolean operations let you carve 3D shapes out of each other and combine them in a number of fascinating ways.

Chapter 7: Utilities and Edit Tools

This chapter shows you how to use a versatile set of less-often-used but handy modeling-oriented tools, such as axis adjustment, which determines an object's rotation fulcrum, as well as Quad Divide, which increases an object's mesh resolution, allowing for greater control in deformation.

Chapter 8: The Importance of Lighting

This chapter offers a wealth of information on the different light source types available in trueSpace2, including how to use shadows and how to adjust a spotlight edge, or penumbra. It also contains a tutorial that shows you how to create a visible spotlight beam for an ultra-realistic special effect.

Chapter 9: Materials Part 1: Basic Surface Attributes

This chapter introduces the different ways of changing an object's fundamental appearance, including setting of such attributes as color and shininess. It also demonstrates trueSpace2's Paint tools for applying materials to objects or parts of objects.

Chapter 10: Materials Part 2: Advanced Surface Attributes

This chapter shows you how to add visual interest and realism to your 3D scenes by using image mapping to apply pictures to your object surfaces. You'll also learn about Material Rectangles, which let you apply images to specific parts of your objects "decal-style."

Chapter 11: Animation

This chapter explains basic animation concepts and then teaches you how to create movie magic in the context of trueSpace's remarkable animation capabilities.

Chapter 12: Rendering

This chapter talks about and demonstrates the distinctions between standard non-real-time rendering and trueSpace2's 3DR real-time solid rendering mode, and covers by example the wealth of options available when rendering objects and scenes.

Chapter 13: VRML Authoring with Pioneer

This chapter shows how to use Caligari's Pioneer, which lets you build navigable 3D worlds on the Internet's World Wide Web, using the revolutionary new Virtual Reality Modeling Language.

Appendix A: Additional Resources

This chapter gives you specific contact information for many places in print and on-line where you can get help, inspiration, tips, advice, and lots of free software such as utility programs, 3D models, and images for texture mapping.

Appendix B: Tools Quick Reference

This chapter provides a handy, comprehensive illustrated list of all of trueSpace2's functions, with each one's icon and associated keystroke (if any).

Appendix C: Using trueSpace2 with Other Programs

This chapter describes how to incorporate trueSpace2 output into various programs. For example, you'll see how to output rendered scenes with alpha channels containing transparent backgrounds, for easy compositing in programs such as Photoshop. You'll find out how to edit your animations and add sound with Microsoft VidEdit, available free on the Internet. Also, you'll learn about some special programs for making 3D landscapes and custom outer space backgrounds (both are included on the CD-ROM that comes with this book), as well as nifty explosions.

In closing, one of the most important things to remember about 3D graphics, especially with a program as powerful and versatile as trueSpace2, is that you don't have to be able to draw! No classroom training or experience in traditional media is necessary; all you need is the desire to learn and create. Once you've mastered the tools, with the help we offer here, you'll find yourself producing breathtaking images with relative ease that you might never have previously dreamed possible. You can do it!

ABOUT THE CD-ROM

3D Modeling Construction Kit comes with a companion CD-ROM that contains the book's tutorials as well as sample 3D models, animations, textures, and utilities for 2D and 3D creation. This section briefly outlines what's on the CD-ROM and how to install each component to your hard drive.

trueSpace2:

A 60-day trial version of trueSpace2 is included in the \TS2TRIAL directory. This version of trueSpace2 will not save individual objects or scenes with a resolution greater than 320x200.

Tutorials:

The tutorials outlined in the book can be found in the \TUTORIAL directory.

Cyberprops:

3NAME3D has provided twelve 3D models for use in your modeling projects. They can be found in the \CYBERPRP directory.

Landscape Maker:

This utility creates landscapes you can use in your 3D modeling. The author of the program suggests installing it directly into the trueSpace2 directory.

MediaPaint:

Did you ever want to change something in your animation or video without remodeling or reshooting? With MediaPaint, you can actually edit the animation or movie file. A save-disabled demo version for Windows 95 and Windows NT is provided on the CD-ROM in the \DEMOS\MEDIAPNT directory.

Model Masters:

Model Masters has provided twelve 3D models for use in your modeling projects, as well as an unlockable catalog of objects (see ad in back of book). The sample objects are provided in the \MOD_MAST\FREEBEES directory.

Painter 4:

This is a natural media painting program for the computer painter who likes the look of paint on paper. A demo version of Painter 4 for Windows 95 can be found in the \DEMOS\P4INST directory on the CD-ROM.

Pioneer:

Take 3D modeling to the Web by using Pioneer, Caligari's VRML authoring and browsing program. A 30-day trial version is provided in the \DEMOS\PIONEER directory on the CD-ROM.

Textures:

In the \TEXTURES directory, you will find textures that come from The Waite Group's *3D Modeling Lab* by Phillip Shaddock.

Universe:

If you want to use a star field background, Universe can generate one for you. Universe for Windows 95 and Windows NT can be found in the \DEMOS\UNIVERSE directory.

Videos:

In the \VIDEOS directory, you will find Windows AVI files.

Installation

Installation can be accomplished in Windows 3.x, NT, or 95. Please use the installation instructions for your particular operating system. The instructions assume you are at the DOS prompt, your primary hard drive is C, and your CD-ROM drive is D. If these drive letters do not correspond to your system, please substitute accordingly. Table I-1 contains the directory and setup filenames for the programs on this CD-ROM.

Table I-1 Directory and setup filenames

Program	Directory & Setup Filename
trueSpace2	\ts2trial\setup.exe
Universe	\demos\universe\unisetup.exe
MediaPaint	\demos\mediapnt\setup.exe
Painter 4	\demos\p4inst\p4demo95.exe
Pioneer	\demos\pioneer\setup.exe
Model Masters	\mod_mast\mm_3dck.exe

Windows 3.x and NT

In the Program Manager, select File, Run, and type in your CD-ROM's drive letter followed by the Directory & Setup filename found in Table I-1. For example, if you want to install the trueSpace2 trial version, select File, Run, and type the following in the dialog box:

```
d:\ts2trial\setup.exe
```

Then click the OK button. Follow the onscreen prompts to finish the installation.

NOTE for NT users: You will not, of course, have to install any of the Win32 components to make your programs work.

The tutorials, CyberProp models, and sample videos can be copied by launching File Manager and dragging the appropriate folder to your hard drive. If you want to copy the tutorial files to your hard drive, launch File Manager and click on the icon representing your CD-ROM. Select the Tutorial folder and drag it to the icon representing your hard drive. Follow these steps for any other programs you wish to copy.

The author of Landscape Maker suggests installing it directly into the trueSpace2 directory. Assuming you installed trueSpace2 into the default directory \TRUSPACE, run File Manager and select the hard drive where trueSpace2 resides. Click on the TRUSPACE directory. Click on your CD-ROM icon and then click on the DEMOS directory. Now click on the LANDMAKR directory. Control-click on LANDMAK2.EXE and LANDMAK2.HLP and drag these files to your hard drive icon.

There are three VBX files and one DLL included with this program that you need in your Windows system directory to run this program. Select the hard drive where Windows resides and click on the WINDOWS directory. Now click on the SYSTEM directory. Click on your CD-ROM icon and then click on the DEMOS directory. Now click on the LAND-MAKR directory. Control-click on VBRUN300.DLL, CMDIALOG.VBX, GAUGE.VBX, and THREED.VBX, and drag these files to your hard drive icon. If for any reason you are prompted to replace existing files, click No.

Windows 95

Double-click on your computer's icon and double-click on your CD-ROM's icon. Find the program you want to install in Table I-1 and continue double-clicking until you reach the setup program. Double-click on the setup program and follow the onscreen prompts to finish the installation.

For example, if you want to install the trial version of Pioneer, double-click on your CD-ROM's icon. Now double-click on the DEMOS folder. Double-click on the PIONEER folder. Locate the SETUP.EXE file and double-click it. Follow the onscreen prompts to finish the installation.

The tutorials, CyberProp models, textures, and sample videos can be copied by dragging the appropriate folder to your hard drive.

For example, if you want to copy the tutorial files to your hard drive, double-click on your computer's icon and double-click your CD-ROM's icon. Drag the TUTORIALS folder to your hard drive's icon. Follow these steps for any other programs you wish to copy.

The author of Landscape Maker suggests installing it directly into the trueSpace2 folder. Assuming you installed trueSpace2 into the default folder TRUSPACE, double-click on your computer's icon and double-click the hard drive where trueSpace2 resides. Double-click the TRUSPACE folder. Double-click your CD-ROM icon and double-click the DEMOS folder. Now double-click the LANDMAKR folder. Control-click on LAND-MAK2.EXE and LANDMAK2.HLP and drag these files to your TRUSPACE folder.

There are three VBX files and one DLL included with this program that you need in your Windows system directory to run this program. Double-click the hard drive where Windows resides and double-click the WINDOWS folder. Now double-click the SYSTEM folder. Double-click your CD-ROM icon and double-click the DEMOS folder. Now double-click on the LANDMAKR folder. Control-click on VBRUN300.DLL, CMDIALOG.VBX, GAUGE.VBX, and THREED.VBX, and drag these files to your Windows System folder. If for any reason you are prompted to replace existing files, click No.

1

3D GRAPHICS
BASICS

1

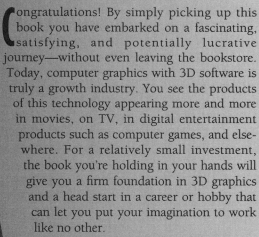

ongratulations! By simply picking up this book you have embarked on a fascinating, satisfying, and potentially lucrative journey—without even leaving the bookstore. Today, computer graphics with 3D software is truly a growth industry. You see the products of this technology appearing more and more in movies, on TV, in digital entertainment products such as computer games, and elsewhere. For a relatively small investment, the book you're holding in your hands will give you a firm foundation in 3D graphics and a head start in a career or hobby that can let you put your imagination to work like no other.

This book is about learning how to create 3D computer graphics using Caligari trueSpace2. In a series of step-by-step, illustrated lessons, it covers modeling, surface modification, animation, rendering, and much more. A demonstration copy of trueSpace2 is provided on the CD-ROM included with the book so you can follow along. Creating 3D worlds on the Internet's World Wide Web (called VRML) is also

3

discussed, using a provided demo version of Caligari's Pioneer program for VRML authoring. But before starting the hands-on lessons, let's find out exactly what 3D graphics is all about.

DRAWING THE LINE, DIGITALLY

Historians are reasonably certain that early humans drew pictures before they learned to communicate with written language. In fact, the alphabets we use today are derived from simple iconographic images. Our need to express ourselves graphically is almost as basic as the need to eat or breathe. But today's specialized society has most of us convinced that we "need talent" to draw or that it takes years of training and practice to be adept at visual expression.

Thus, when photography came along about 150 years ago, it captured the enthusiasm of millions. People were excited by this medium because they could create realistic images without having any drawing skills, satisfying the deep-seated need for picture making.

Today, photography is commonplace. You can buy a disposable camera for a few bucks and shoot away without even having to load the thing, but you're limited to making images of things and people in your environment. And let's face it: Unless you're traveling or are a new parent, most of the resulting photos are pretty boring. But the new medium of 3D graphics lets you create "photos" and "movies" of almost anything you can imagine, thanks to recent advances in the state of the art of the personal computer.

Why did you buy a computer? Maybe for word processing, for doing your personal/business budget with a spreadsheet or financial program, for keeping track of stuff with a database, for using e-mail, or perhaps for playing games. Probably, like most computers, your PC came with a simple drawing program that you dabbled in, but got frustrated with. Or maybe you're adept at producing two-dimensional artwork and want to add depth to your images.

You may already be aware that there's no more power-hungry type of software than that used for 3D computer graphics. You may have heard of or experienced the user-hostile nature of some hard-to-learn programs. Most such programs require constant practice to implement the arcane command structure. But if you bought your personal computer within the last two or three years, you've got a remarkably powerful piece of equipment, and most of the time you're probably using only about 10 percent of its power.

Now, thanks to trueSpace2's user-friendly interface from the inspired folks at Caligari, the problem of the steep learning curve for 3D graphics programs is mostly done away with. Once you get to know trueSpace2, even if you stop using it for a month or more, when you come back it will be as familiar as if you had used it yesterday.

WHAT IS 3D GRAPHICS?

3D graphics is sometimes called *virtual photography* because you can design highly realistic scenes as well as scenarios that couldn't possibly exist in real life. And you can use them to generate still images and movies without any equipment other than a computer. You don't need special "dedicated" equipment such as cameras, film, darkroom equipment, props, or actors. But 3D graphics is more than that, because you can create your subjects before photographing them. In many cases 3D graphics is more like virtual filmmaking, without the outrageous star salaries, because of trueSpace2's animation capabilities.

What many people like best about 3D graphics is the feeling of absolute power and freedom to create worlds as realistic or as fantastic as they can dream up, to populate them with animated characters whose behavior is totally up to them, and then to travel about, exploring at will with no restrictions. The term *godlike* is often associated with this most versatile of crafts; few of us haven't coveted omnipotence at one point or another.

USING TRUESPACE2 FOR BUILDING 3D WORLDS

Unlike some programs that force you to switch between modules to build your 3D scenes, trueSpace2 lets you do everything in a single virtual workspace or "studio," depicted on the screen in true perspective, just as you see things in the real world. There are five stages to the process of creating 3D graphics in trueSpace2:

- Modeling

- Scene setup

- Creating and adding materials, which is akin to "painting" your virtual 3D objects

- Animation setup

- Rendering

Some argue that planning is an important additional step that should come first—indeed, for professional work, planning is crucial. But trueSpace2 is so user friendly that when you're learning the program's basics, it's easy just to jump in and experiment. That's what this book is about. As you come to know trueSpace2 and the process of creating 3D graphics, you'll realize that your intuition is the best tool for harnessing your artistic impulses and imagination.

Modeling

You start by creating three-dimensional objects using a multitude of program tools. The easiest way to get going is with *primitives*, which are building blocks that you add to the workspace with a single click. The six available choices are cube, cylinder, cone, torus (a doughnut-shaped solid), plane (a flat square or rectangle), and sphere. These objects are arrayed in the trueSpace2 workspace in Figure 1-1.

Like all objects in trueSpace2 and most other 3D applications, objects are made up of interconnected *polygons*, which are flat shapes with three or more sides. This method of construction is called *wireframe mesh*.

Other object-creation tools let you make polygons in any shape you desire—including text—and bring them into the third dimension using techniques such as *extrusion* and *lathing*. In addition, trueSpace2 gives you very powerful sculpting tools, called *deformation* and *Booleans,* for fine-tuning your objects.

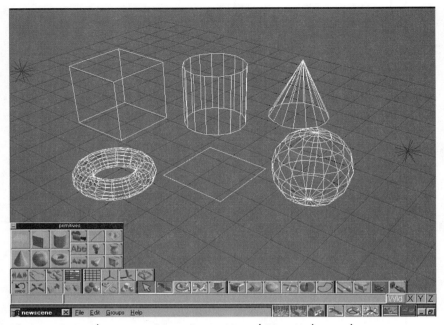

Figure 1–1 The six trueSpace2 primitive objects in the workspace

Scene Setup

Once you've created the objects that are to make up your scene, you need to arrange them so they make visual sense. For example, in an office interior, the chair should go behind the desk, the filing cabinet should be against the wall, and so on. Because you're working in three dimensions and can view the scene from any angle and position, you want to set the point of view that best presents the scene to the viewer. The trueSpace2 *navigation tools* let you move, rotate, and resize your objects in any of the three dimensions. Another similar set of tools lets you position and rotate the "eye" with which you're viewing the scene, as well as zoom in and out—all completely interactively.

Materials

Part of what makes our world such a visually appealing place is the fact that every type of object (including a human body) has its own set of surface characteristics. Some objects look flat and colorless, others are bright and shiny, and many have complex textures and/or colorful patterns. You can re-create this visual variety in your 3D scenes with trueSpace2's *material creation and painting tools*. You can set such basic attributes as color, shine, and transparency. Using texture mapping, you can apply patterns and images to object surfaces. In Figure 1-2, different materials are applied to the six primitive objects to give you an idea of the variety of available options.

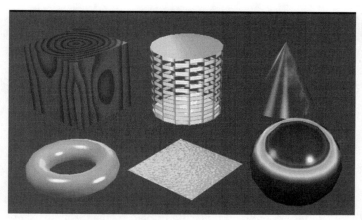

Figure 1-2 Primitive objects with materials added

Figure 1-2 shows materials applied to entire objects, but you can also apply materials to individual object polygons. In addition, you can also apply "decal"-style textures to objects anywhere on their surface.

Animation Setup

Now we enter the fourth dimension: time. With animation, you can bring your scenes to life using a method called *keyframing*. It's simply a matter of figuring out when you want something to happen, going to that frame, and using a navigation or other tool to make it happen. Then the program uses *tweening* (from "in-between") to create smooth transitions between one *key* and the next. You can keyframe object positions, rotation, size, and color. You can even make objects change shape by animating deformation. What's more, materials can be animated in a number of ways, making object surfaces seem alive. Once you see how easy it is, you'll be hooked!

Rendering

The final step in the process, called *rendering*, involves turning your wireframe meshes into solid objects. It's how we went from Figure 1-1 to Figure 1-2. In trueSpace2, you can render a single object, an entire scene, or a full animation with one command. The process is pretty much automatic, but you have substantial control in terms of options—reflections, shadows, a special effect that simulates fog, and more. Moreover, trueSpace2 uses a limited real-time rendering technology, Intel's 3DR, to let you work with solid-appearing objects that help you anticipate the final outcome more accurately than wire-frames do. As you'll see, 3DR has some limitations, but it can be useful nevertheless.

Rendering is the most computation-intensive aspect of 3D graphics. Simple objects and scenes may take only a few seconds to render, but you'll soon be creating setups that take minutes or even hours to render. You'll doubtless agree that the resulting brilliant images are worth the wait.

CAREER OPPORTUNITIES

If you've read this far, you know that 3D graphics—in particular the trueSpace2 program used in conjunction with this book—can lead to a lot of fun. By taking advantage of your computer's processing power, you can create striking images and show them off to family and friends. But this can lead to much more.

With the explosion of 3D graphics in the mass media, many job opportunities are opening up for specialists, including modelers, texture-mapping experts, animators, and lighting experts. Following are some of the areas you might consider for a career in 3D graphics.

Illustration and Graphic Arts

Although the Internet is going a long way toward replacing printed media for many, there is as yet no shortage of traditional magazines, newspapers, and books. Competition in the publishing business is booming, and one way to get people to buy your product is by including compelling images. Art directors still use a lot of hand-drawn and photographed illustrations, but they are turning to 3D artists more and more to create arresting pictorial content. Thanks to trueSpace2's ability to render at high resolutions, it's well suited for creating images to distinguish magazine and book covers, as well as for inside illustrations and advertisements.

Architecture and Set Design

When creating plans for a building or similar structure, an architect uses various tools to visualize the design. Blueprints, drawings, and physical models are the traditional media for this field, but there's a lot to be said for the realism that only 3D software is capable of. Even though trueSpace2 lacks many features of today's advanced computer-aided design (CAD) software, such as a layering function that enables the logical grouping of similar elements such as furniture or walls, the Caligari program is suitable for rough architectural mockups. It can use any measuring system—even different measuring systems for different objects in the same scene. It also has numeric input capability and a tape-measure function for accurately and dynamically measuring distances.

Similarly, set designers working in theater, television, and movies can use trueSpace2 to create mockups of production sets for approval by the director.

Industrial and Commercial Design

Industrial engineers design machines used in factories and other businesses. Commercial designers develop objects we use in everyday life, from kitchenware to electronic gear. As in architecture, these professionals normally employ special high-powered (and high-priced) software tailored to meet their specific needs. For students who are pursuing these careers but can't afford or don't have full-time access to such programs, trueSpace2 is a more than adequate substitute. This program, with its accurate measuring and input tools, enables budding designers to practice their craft at their leisure—without the need for access to advanced programs and equipment.

Game Design

If you're looking at a career in interactive multimedia, you'll find there's no market segment more exciting and potentially lucrative than electronic entertainment. This is a rather broad area, covering more than just computer and video games. There's infotainment—reference works such as health guides that are fun as well as informative. Edutainment has the important goal of entertaining children while teaching them such fundamental topics as reading and arithmetic. Virtual reality, which is an entire field in itself, has a multitude of applications.

Background creation, character animation, and three-dimensional text are just a few of the ways 3D graphics can be used in any of the above fields. You can incorporate rendered output into the final product, but more important, you can export your 3D models into a program that runs on a platform capable of real-time 3D rendering, using your models as realistic objects and environments within the game. The Sony PlayStation is one of these. As a matter of fact, trueSpace2 is part of the official toolkit that Sony provides for its PlayStation developers.

Tom Marlin, a game designer and 3D artist, uses trueSpace2 in many of his products. You can read a short essay by Tom about his working methods in Appendix C, Using trueSpace2 with Other Programs.

Animation and Video

Of course, entertainment that incorporates 3D graphics doesn't have to be interactive to be fun and effective. Examples of recent popular titles that use 100 percent computer graphics imagery include the movie *Toy Story* and the Saturday morning TV series *Reboot*. Admittedly, both of these are done on high-end state-of-the-art equipment that costs more than most people's homes. But what you might not know is that many of the special effects and outerspace scenes in *Babylon 5*, to name but one show, are created with relatively affordable, off-the-shelf systems. I'm not aware of the use of trueSpace2 in any commercial productions, but there's no reason why someone like you couldn't pioneer such an effort!

Another good source of steady income is creating instructional and promotional videos for commercial clients. Very often, scenes that would be difficult, costly, or even impossible to photograph—such as demonstrations of technology still in the early development stages—are suitable for re-creating in 3D graphics. If you're not set up for full-scale video production, you might consider establishing a consulting business for video producers in your area.

Web Design

As more and more businesses learn of the World Wide Web's extraordinary potential to enhance profits and market share, there's a mounting frenzy to go online that seems unlikely to abate. Many business owners and executives, lacking any experience designing for the Web, hire outside consultants to create online presences—usually at fairly hefty fees ($100 an hour is not unheard of). Most Web development has been done in HyperText Markup Language (HTML) with 2D graphics plus text. But Web sites are beginning to incorporate 3D worlds in the form of Virtual Reality Modeling Language

(VRML). Thanks to Caligari's Pioneer, a version of trueSpace2 that incorporates special VRML features, you can get a head start on this trend and be ready to earn big bucks creating 3D Web sites for eager corporate types. The CD-ROM that comes with this book includes a demo version of Pioneer, which is also discussed in Chapter 13, VRML Authoring with Pioneer.

YOUR PORTFOLIO

It's not within the scope of this book to go into great depth about how to get started as a 3D graphics professional. However, I can encourage you to become skilled at creating 3D graphics and then show off your work.

If you intend to specialize in still-image or modeling work, submit your best-looking work to computer graphics magazines (see the list in Appendix A, Additional Resources). When your work is published, clip it out of the magazine and keep it in clear plastic sleeves in a scrapbook. You might also want to hire a service bureau in your area to create high-quality printed output of your hottest images.

If animation is your forte, it's imperative to create what's known in the trade as a *demo reel*. This is a collection of your top-notch, commercial-quality animations *on videotape*. It's not good enough to have them on floppy disks, a recordable CD-ROM, or even on a laptop's hard disk. They must be easy and convenient to view in any environment, and only videotape fulfills this requirement. There are a number of ways to tape your animations, but unless you need the service frequently, it's probably better to have someone do the work for you than to buy special equipment. You can find out more about taping your work from the information resources in Appendix A.

Finally, if you want to get into the Web page design business, research your competition by visiting sites. Use a Web search engine such as Yahoo! and look up the keyword 3D. If you don't have a home page, ask your Internet service provider about setting one up and put your best foot forward in cyberspace.

WHAT NOW?

At this point, I could get into a long-winded discussion of the hows and wherefores of 3D graphics, but that would be boring. The best way to learn is by doing, and that's the whole idea behind this book. In the next chapter, we'll examine some of trueSpace2's interface elements, after which you'll roll up your sleeves and start working with the program.

2

INTRODUCING THE TRUESPACE2 INTERFACE

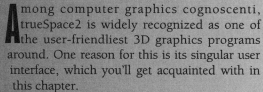

2

Among computer graphics cognoscenti,
trueSpace2 is widely recognized as one of
the user-friendliest 3D graphics programs
around. One reason for this is its singular user
interface, which you'll get acquainted with in
this chapter.

The trueSpace2 interface is unique
among Windows applications for several
reasons. For example, although the program
uses regular Windows menus for operations
such as saving and loading files, the Menu
bar appears at the bottom of the screen
rather than the top, as in most programs.
Actually, you can set the Menu bar and
tool groups (of iconic program controls)
to appear at the top of the screen if you
like, but most users go along with the
program interface as originally
designed because it seems to work
well. As you work through this book,
you'll discover other ways in which
trueSpace2 is unique—as well as why
this interface has so many fans. As
unusual as it is, you'll find it very
easy to learn and to remember what
everything does. On the other
hand, no interface is perfect;

compromises exist in every interface, and trueSpace2 is no exception. I'll try to point these out as I go along.

NOTE: One inconsistency in trueSpace2 is in naming things; often a tool is called one thing in the manual and another in the program. To avoid confusion, this book uses the names found in the program.

EXAMINING THE WORKSPACE

Let's begin by taking a look at the interface the way it appears when you start the program after first installing it. Take a look at Figure 2-1.

The largest area of the interface is the view into the workspace, which is the virtual three-dimensional space in which all direct interaction with your objects and scenes takes place. This view is a *Perspective* view, so objects that are nearby appear larger than objects that are farther away, just as in real life. This is one of trueSpace2's best features; in most other 3D graphics programs, the standard working view is *Orthogonal*, which means that all objects remain a constant size no matter where they are in relation to your point of view.

Orthogonal views can be quite helpful, as when setting up precise positional relationships between objects, and they are available in trueSpace2. You can change trueSpace2's main view to an Orthogonal view from the top, side, or front, and open additional smaller

Figure 2-1 The trueSpace2 interface when it is first installed

windows with Perspective and Orthogonal views; I'll go into more detail about that later in this chapter.

Note the *reference grid* or ground plane that helps illustrate the perspective. This is a fixed aspect of trueSpace2; it cannot be moved, rotated, scaled, or turned off. The reference grid does not appear in rendered scenes.

When you use the default Perspective view, you're looking into the workspace with an invisible "eye"—a default camera, although it doesn't manifest itself as an actual object, the way a camera object (a special type of object, which resembles a wireframe view camera, and can be used for alternative views into the workspace) does—that can be positioned anywhere in the workspace, rotated, and zoomed in and out. You can also set up any number of camera objects in the workspace and open Perspective views from them. As a matter of fact, in trueSpace2, any object can be a camera, which means that a window can be set to show what it's "looking" at! But that can become confusing, so in general it's best to stick to using camera objects. By the way, cameras don't appear when you render your scenes.

USING THE TOOLS

Below the workspace are your working tools, which appear as rectangular buttons with icons on them. If you're ever uncertain as to what a tool does, simply position the mouse cursor over it and a description appears in the Help bar, which is the gray horizontal strip between the tools and the Menu bar.

Tools are grouped more or less according to function (see Figure 2-2), as described in the following paragraphs. You can enable and disable display of each of the above tool groups with the Groups menu in the Menu bar.

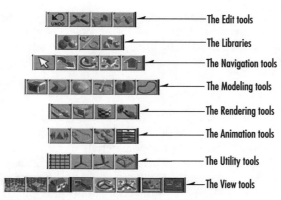

Figure 2–2 The trueSpace2 tool groups

Edit Tools

The Edit tools are used to undo and redo operations, delete and copy objects, and create and modify *object hierarchies*, or parent/child/sibling relationships between objects. These tools are covered in Chapter 7, Utility and Edit Tools, along with the Utility tools.

Libraries

Libraries are real work savers. When you've spent a lot of time creating a certain type of entity, you can save it in a library and reuse it whenever you want—without having to go through file operations. There are three types of library: Materials, Paths, and Primitives. Materials are used in modifying objects' surface appearances, and Paths are used for animation and Sweep operations. The Primitives panel is for creating various types of basic shapes and text, adding lights and cameras, and creating deformation matrices.

Because the functions of these three different libraries are so disparate, instead of getting their own separate chapter, they're covered in relevant sections about the tools to which they're related. The Materials library is covered in Chapters 9 and 10, and the Primitives panel and Paths library are covered in Chapter 5, Basic Modeling.

Navigation Tools

You use Navigation tools for basic manipulation of objects, including movement, rotation, and scaling. There's also a tool for moving up and down in object hierarchies. These Navigation tools are covered thoroughly in Chapter 4, Navigation: Getting Around in trueSpace2.

Modeling Tools

The Model tool group contains powerful tools for manipulating sections of objects, making 3D objects from 2D outlines, deforming objects, sculpting object surfaces, Boolean operations in which you subtract objects from and add objects to each other, and creating polygons, both rounded and straight-edged. Find out more about the Model group tools in Chapter 5.

Rendering Tools

You can use Rendering tools to create materials, defined as a particular combination of color, texture, and attributes such as shininess. You can apply materials to an object's entire surface, a polygon at a time, to vertices only, or only where another material already exists. You can also apply a material to a rectangle that you place on the object's surface arbitrarily. Last but not least, you can use Adobe Photoshop–compatible plug-ins to modify the appearance of objects and scenes. See Chapter 12, Rendering, for a detailed discussion of these tools.

Animation Tools

Animation brings your scenes to life; you'll find tools here to let you set up and modify animations with a great deal of ease and power. For more on the Animation tools, see Chapter 11, Animation.

Utility

The Utility tools aren't used all that often, but when you need them, they're great to have around. The trueSpace2 utilities include Grid functions, modifying object axes, and subdividing surfaces. Chapter 7 covers all the utilities.

The View Tools

A View tool group is permanently attached to each window; you can see the main window's View group in its lower-right corner.

The View tools let you move, rotate, and zoom the view; switch the view to different vantage points; open new view windows; and switch between Wireframe and Solid display modes (more on those shortly). Several other utility functions are included in this group as well.

Using Tool Variants

Many tools have variants, as indicated by a small black triangle in the icon's upper-left corner. In most cases, a tool's variant version performs a slightly different function. For example, the Lathe tool is a variant of the Sweep (or extrude) tool; both are used to turn flat shapes into 3D objects. In some cases, variants may not seem to have much in common with the tool to which they're attached; for example, the Dimensioning tool, which helps you measure objects, is attached to the Smooth Quad Divide tool, which subdivides polygons for greater surface resolution.

Access tool variants by clicking and holding the left mouse button on the tool and then either dragging the mouse a short distance or waiting a moment. The variants then pop up in a vertical strip or *pop-up*. Drag the mouse up to the desired tool and then release the button. In many cases (but not all), the variant then replaces the previous tool in the tool group for easier subsequent access.

Property Panels

Another important aspect of tools is that many have associated property panels that open when the tool is invoked; tools that have these panels have a small red triangle in the upper-right corner. Property panels let you change the way the tool works—either before or during use of the tool. For example, the Poly Modes panel, associated with the Polygon and Regular Polygon tools, gives you iconic controls for determining how multiple polygons interact (for example, a second polygon can be subtracted from or added to another polygon). Other property panels give you numeric settings, such as the depth of Sweep operations. As we examine the various tools in subsequent chapters, we'll discuss all of the property panel settings for each.

NOTE: If you have closed the property panel for the currently active tool and want to reopen it, simply right-click on the tool icon.

HELP BAR

The Help bar is the horizontal strip between the tool groups and the Menu bar. In most cases, when you position the mouse cursor over a tool or panel item, a short descriptive message shows up in the center section of the Help bar. If there's a keyboard equivalent for the tool in question, it's displayed at the left end of the Help bar. Once you start using the tool, the Help bar often displays messages about what to do next. At the right end of the bar is a set of controls equivalent to the Coordinates property panel, which is described in Chapter 5.

USING TRUESPACE2 MENUS

Most program functions are accessed through the tool icons, discussed above. In addition, however, there are four standard Windows menus.

The File Menu

This menu lets you load and save disk files. From this menu, trueSpace2 uses two types of files: *objects* and *scenes* (there are also material, path, and image files, which are handled from other parts of the program). Here we have one of trueSpace2's inconsistencies: Though scene-related functions have their own submenu, object-related file functions are each listed separately in the File menu. Oh well; as the poet Ralph Waldo Emerson said: "A foolish consistency is the hobgoblin of little minds...." File menu entries include the Scene submenu and other entries described in the following sections.

Scene

In trueSpace2, a scene is defined as the entire contents of the current workspace, including all objects, lights, cameras, and animation. Scene files use the .SCN format, which is exclusive to trueSpace2 and other Caligari programs. The File menu's Scene submenu includes these commands:

New

Erases the current scene from memory, letting you start fresh. If you use this command without having saved changes to the current scene, you're warned that changes will be lost.

Load

Loads a scene from disk, erasing the current scene.

Save

Saves the current scene to the same disk file from which it was loaded, or under which it was last saved during the current session. If using Save for the first time with a new scene, you're prompted for file information.

Save As

Use this command to save the current scene under a new file name, or to a different disk drive or partition.

Load Object

This command loads an object from a disk file, including any materials and/or animation associated with the object.

One of trueSpace2's truly versatile aspects is that it can load objects in any of the following formats:

trueSpace2 .COB

Amiga Caligari .SOB (trueSpace2 in previous versions on the Amiga computer was called Caligari)

Autodesk 3D Studio binary .3DS

3D Studio ASCII .ASC

3D Studio project .PRJ

Autodesk AutoCAD .DXF

Imagine .IOB (a 3D graphics application for Amiga computers and DOS PCs from Impulse, Inc.)

NewTek LightWave .LWB

PostScript .PS and Encapsulated PostScript .EPS

VideoScape .GEO (an old Amiga 3D application, the predecessor to LightWave)

Wavefront .OBJ

For information on how trueSpace2 handles these various formats, see the trueSpace2 Help section File Formats/3D Import Formats.

Save Object

This command saves the currently selected object, including materials and any animation, to the same disk file from which it was loaded, or under which it was last saved during the current session. When you use Save Object for the first time with a new object, the function works the same as Save Object As (see below).

Save Object As

This command saves the currently selected object under a new file name, or to a different disk drive or partition. After invoking the command, you're prompted for file information. The trueSpace2 program can save objects in any of these formats:

trueSpace2 .COB (The ASCII switch in the Save Object dialog applies to this format. When ASCII is enabled, trueSpace2 saves the object file in a text format that is larger than the standard binary format, but which can be more easily used by other programs.)

3D Studio ASCII .ASC

Autodesk AutoCAD .DXF

Animation only .CAN (As trueSpace2 cannot reload this format, its value is questionable.)

For information on how trueSpace2 handles these various formats, see the trueSpace2 Help section File Formats/3D Export Formats.

Preferences

Selecting the File menu's Preferences item opens the panel shown in Figure 2-3, used for setting various global program defaults.

The panel contains the following items (for more details, check the Help file under Program Operation/Preference Settings):

Dynapick: When this option is enabled, you merely need to click and drag to manipulate a nonselected object. If Dynapick is disabled, trueSpace2 requires an initial click-and-release to select an object before letting you manipulate it.

OrthoNav: Affects vertical motion in the Orthographic views. In the Front and Left Orthographic views, when OrthoNav is enabled (the default setting), you use the left mouse button to control horizontal *and* vertical movement. In the Perspective view, however, you use the *right* mouse button to move objects vertically. To be more consistent with Perspective view operation, you can disable OrthoNav, necessitating use of the right mouse button for vertical movement in the Front and Left Orthographic views.

LoadScene: When this option is enabled, the scene file last saved during the previous session, if any, is automatically loaded upon restarting trueSpace2.

TopMenu: When this option is enabled, the Menu bar, tool groups, and property panels automatically appear at the top of the screen.

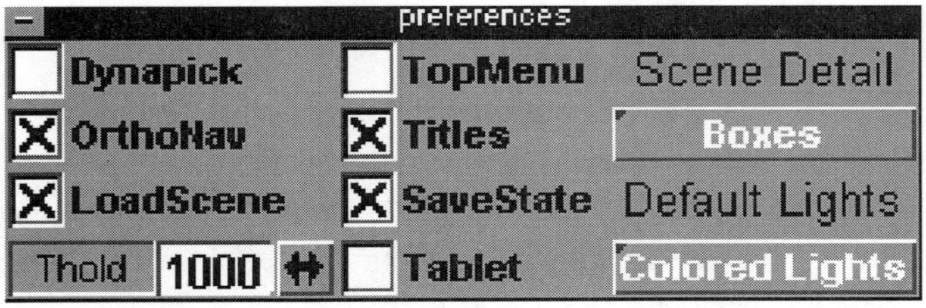

Figure 2-3 Preferences panel

🛰 Titles: When this option is enabled (the default setting), standard Windows title bars appear above property panels. Turn this off to conserve a slight amount of screen real estate.

🛰 SaveState: When this option is enabled, trueSpace2 automatically saves the entire workspace contents and all program settings upon quitting the program and automatically loads everything the next time the program is run.

🛰 Tablet: Enables use of a graphics or digitizing tablet with trueSpace2.

🛰 Thold (Threshold): This is a relative setting that determines the maximum time required to redraw objects before trueSpace2 resorts to using a bounding box. The higher the setting, the more likely that complex objects will remain as wireframes (or solid objects in Solid Mode) when manipulated.

🛰 Scene detail: The various settings available from this pop-up menu determine how the scene is redrawn. With complex scenes, you'll get faster feedback by using settings near the top of this menu.

🛰 Default lights: Determines how trueSpace2 automatically sets up lighting when you use the Scene/New command. The default setting is Colored Lights, which works well for scene setup in Solid mode.

Exit

Quits the program. Alternative exit methods are double-clicking on the Windows control box (at the left end of the Menu bar), clicking on the Windows control box and selecting Close, pressing [ALT]-[F4], and, in Windows 95, clicking on the Close box, which contains an X and appears near the left end of the Menu bar.

The Edit Menu

This menu contains the same functions as the first three tools in the Edit group. These are covered in Chapter 7. Also found here is the Image Utilities command, which is covered in Chapter 10, Advanced Surface Attributes.

The Groups Menu

Use this menu to enable and disable display of the various tool groups except View, which is permanently attached to the program window(s). If a check mark appears next to an item, the corresponding group is currently being displayed. Tool groups cannot be moved; they can only be turned on and off. If you disable display of a group, the remaining groups automatically "close ranks" and fill the remaining gap. When you enable display of a group, it is automatically placed at the right end of the row of currently displayed groups. If there is no room there, a second row above (or below) the first is started.

The Help Menu

The Help menu contains the following items.

Help Bar

Use this to toggle display of the Help bar. Turn off the Help bar to recover a small amount of screen real estate.

About

Displays the About box with basic program information, including the current PixMap mode, the registered owner, serial number, and program credits. The PixMap setting determines how the program display is configured. You can access the PixMap dialog by holding down the CTRL key as you launch trueSpace2. A Configure trueSpace dialog appears with a Help selection that explains the choices.

Contents

Displays the standard Windows help system for trueSpace2.

THE GREAT CONUNDRUM: WORKING IN 3D BUT SEEING 2D

With any good 3D graphics program, one of the most important functions of the interface is to help you out as much as possible in an unnatural situation; that is, the contradiction of working with three-dimensional objects and scenes in a two-dimensional display. One day soon, you'll be able to work with stereoscopic 3D displays that avoid eyestrain, using motion-tracking equipment that lets you sculpt great-looking objects merely by gesturing. But until then, you're stuck with multiple compromises, the greatest of which is that no matter how well designed the interface, a flat screen doesn't accurately show what's happening in your virtual 3D space.

This situation is exacerbated by the standard wireframe display mode used in most 3D graphics programs, including trueSpace2. In trueSpace2's Wireframe Display, objects are represented by drawing only the edges of the polygons that make up their structure. This generally gives you a good idea of how the object is shaped. However, because you can see "through" the object, all faces are visible—even those facing away from you. With most objects beyond very simple shapes, this fosters confusion, because you can't tell which polygons are in the front part of the object and which are in the back. Some 3D applications have a "hidden line" mode in which only polygons facing you are visible, giving a more solid appearance, but alas, trueSpace2 isn't one of them.

The trueSpace2 interface has several ways of helping you through this dilemma. As mentioned earlier in this chapter, the default perspective display is an advantage. But when objects are displayed as wireframes, there's always some ambiguity with the single view. For example, say you've just walked up to a machine on which trueSpace2 is running and you see a cube and a sphere, slightly overlapping, as in Figure 2-4. The sphere appears smaller than the cube. Does that mean it's farther from the point of view than the cube, or just smaller?

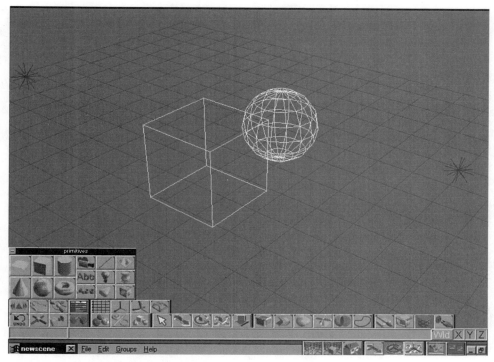

Figure 2–4 Wireframe view of cube and sphere

Solid Mode Saves the Day

Well, trueSpace2 has a solution for this. It's called Solid Render Display (sometimes shortened to Solid Display), which means that objects are always shaded, making it easy to tell when objects are in front of and behind each other. In some 3D graphics programs, when you're working with objects, they always appear as wireframes; you have to render them to see them as solids, which takes time and interferes with the creative process.

Turn on Solid Render Display by accessing the Wireframe Display pop-up at the left end of the View group and selecting the 3DR icon. Figure 2-5 shows how the above scene looks in Solid Display. As you can see, it's easy to tell that the cube is closer than the sphere.

What's great about Solid Display is that you can use it while performing any program function, from simple object manipulation to complex operations such as deformation and Boolean functions. In most cases, you'll find that working in Solid Display gives you a much better idea of what's going on, especially with lighting setup. Nevertheless, sometimes it's advantageous to use Wireframe mode, for example, when working with very complex objects.

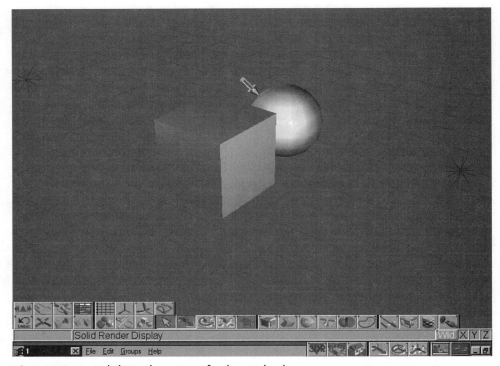

Figure 2–5 Solid Display view of cube and sphere

Which brings me to another, less pleasant aspect of Solid Display mode: It requires a good deal more computer power than Wireframe Display. If you're using a fast Pentium computer and/or working with relatively simple objects, there's no problem. But if your virtual reach exceeds your computer's grasp, waiting for Solid Display redraws can be a real drag. Some of the Preferences panel settings give you more control over how redraws work; these are explored later in this chapter.

NOTE: Although trueSpace2 is a 32-bit application, its interface uses 16-bit program code. The program will run in Windows NT, which is a full 32-bit operating system, but it doesn't run very well. Therefore, it doesn't take advantage of the full power of Intel's 32-bit Pentium Pro processor. Caligari Corporation has announced that future versions of trueSpace will use 100% 32-bit code, at which time the program will work very fast on Pentium Pro–based PCs with 32-bit operating systems.

Solid mode takes advantage of Intel's real-time rendering technology and trueSpace2 comes with 3DR drivers that support Solid Display for most popular display cards. If you use the Matrox Millennium accelerator card in Windows 3.1 or 3.11, you can take advantage of the Millennium's hardware 3D acceleration using its special 3DR drivers. Matrox is reportedly working on 3DR drivers for Windows 95, which may be available by the time you read this. Contact Matrox for further information.

NOTE: In most of the exercises in this book, feel free to use whichever display mode you feel most comfortable with. I'll let you know whenever it's important to use a particular mode.

WINDOWS AND THEIR VIEWS

In many cases, especially when setting up complex scenes, there's no substitute for being able to look at the workspace from different points of view, whether consecutively or simultaneously. In trueSpace2, you can do either or both by changing the window view and/or opening new windows.

Changing the Window View

The View Select tools (see Figure 2-6) are found in the pop-up attached to the Perspective View tool (an angled view of a house), third from the left in any window's View group. These tools are used to change the view in the current window. Each window has a View Select pop-up from which its view can be changed at any time.

From bottom to top, the View Select tools follow.

Perspective View

Use this tool to change the window to the default Perspective view. If you alter the Perspective view, then change the window to some other view and then return to Perspective; the changed settings are restored. To restore the default Perspective view (main window only), use the Reset View tool (discussed below, under Using View Utilities).

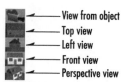
— View from object
— Top view
— Left view
— Front view
— Perspective view

Figure 2–6 The View Select pop-up menu

Front View

Use this tool to change the window to an Orthographic view from the front—that is, positioned at the positive end of the y axis, looking down the axis in a negative direction.

Left View

Use this tool to change the window to an Orthographic view from the left side—that is, positioned at the positive end of the x axis, looking down the axis in a negative direction.

Top View

Use this tool to change the window to an Orthographic view from the top—that is, positioned at the positive end of the z axis, looking down the axis in a negative direction.

NOTE: Orthographic views can be moved and scaled, but they cannot be rotated.

NOTE: The x axis, y axis, and z axis are used in 3D graphics to describe various attributes of both objects and views. Chapter 4, Navigation: Getting Around in trueSpace2, discusses these in depth. For the moment, think of them as breadth, depth, and height.

View from Object

This tool is called Camera View in the trueSpace2 reference manual, but the in-program name (displayed in the Help bar when you point at the icon) is View from Object. I think this name is more accurate, because any object can act as a camera in trueSpace2. To view the scene from an object's point of view, select the object, then select this tool.

Any object used as a camera looks at the scene along its z axis. When you add an actual "camera" object from the Primitives panel (discussed in the next couple of chapters), its z axis is parallel to the "ground" or reference grid. However, all other objects, by default, have their z axes pointing straight up, so you may get unexpected results when switching the view to an object that you haven't first adjusted so its z axis is properly oriented. Chapter 7 covers the use of object axes more thoroughly.

The New View Tools

In the main window's New View tool group, notice the seventh tool from the left, which defaults to the New Perspective View tool (an angled view of a house, with a white bar underneath). If you click and hold on this icon, a pop-up menu appears with tools for opening new windows with Perspective and Orthographic views. The icons resemble those of the View Select tools; the difference is that the New View tools have a small gray bar at the bottom of the icon button and the icon image is slightly ghosted.

The windows opened via these tools have several attributes and characteristics in common:

🦗 They are about one-sixth the size of the full-screen main window.

🦗 They can be reduced in size by positioning the mouse cursor at the lower-right corner and clicking and dragging upward and/or leftward, but they cannot be made larger than the size at which they first appear.

🦗 They can be repositioned by clicking on the name area in the lower-left corner and dragging.

🦗 Windows are not coordinated; that is, they don't necessarily show different views of the same part of the workspace. If you have a Top view zoomed in on an object in a remote part of the workspace, then open a new Front view, you'll need to use the Eye Move and Zoom tools to adjust the view to see the object in question. The introductory tutorial in the next chapter covers these functions.

🦗 These windows contain the same tools as the main window's View tool group, except for New View and Close All Panels (etc.) items.

🦗 No more than three views in addition to the main window can be opened.

NOTE: Only one window is active at a time, as indicated by the dark color in its Title bar in the lower-left corner. However, the main window's Title bar is always dark, so if other windows are open, the only way to tell if the main window is active is to check that no others are active. To activate a window, click on it.

The following functions are available from the New View pop-up (see Figure 2-7), from bottom to top.

New Perspective View

Use this tool to open a new window showing the default Perspective view, which is the one shown when you first start trueSpace2. It has the "eye" positioned above one corner of the ground plane, or reference grid, and pointing toward the center of the workspace.

—— New top view
—— New side view
—— New front view
—— New perspective view

Figure 2-7 The New View pop-up menu

27

New Front View

Use this tool to open a new window showing the view from the front—that is, positioned at the positive end of the y axis, looking down the axis in a negative direction.

New Left View

Use this tool to open a new window showing the view from the left side—that is, positioned at the positive end of the x axis, looking down the axis in a negative direction.

New Top View

Use this tool to open a new window showing the view from the top—that is, positioned at the positive end of the z axis, looking down the axis in a negative direction.

Using the View Utilities

At the right end of the main window's View tool group is a pop-up menu, shown in Figure 2-8, containing four tools, two of which are related to panels and two of which are related to the main window view. From bottom to top, these tools follows.

Close All Panels

Panels such as Preferences and Primitives can be closed individually by clicking on the small box in the upper-left corner. Sometimes the screen is cluttered with panels and you want to get rid of all of them at once. That's what this tool is for. Select it to close all currently open panels. It does not affect windows or tool groups.

NOTE: If you have used Preferences to disable panel Title bars, you can close a panel by positioning the mouse pointer over the panel, then clicking and holding the right mouse button and dragging the mouse off the panel. A large X appears on the panel, at which point releasing the mouse button closes the panel.

Dock All Panels

Normally, panels open beside or above tool groups, but they can be moved by dragging their Title bars. If you have panels scattered all over the display and want to clear some screen space, use this tool to line up all open panels above (or below, if Preferences/TopMenu is enabled) currently open tool groups.

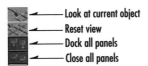

Look at current object
Reset view
Dock all panels
Close all panels

Figure 2–8 The View Utilities pop-up menu

Reset View

This function affects the active window. It restores the Perspective, Front, Left, and Top views to the default mode, as described earlier. If the window is set to View from Object, this command has no effect.

Look at Current Object

This function affects the active window. In Perspective view, it rotates the "eye" to point toward the currently selected object, if any. In Front, Left, or Top view mode, it moves the point of view to point at the current object. If the window is set to View from Object, this command has no effect.

SETTING KEYBOARD SHORTCUTS

Many tools in trueSpace2 have keyboard equivalents, which appear at the left end of the Help bar when you point at the icon. As you become familiar with trueSpace2, you'll find it much more efficient to work with both mouse and keyboard, using the mouse to manipulate onscreen entities and the keyboard to select tools.

You can assign your own choices of keyboard shortcuts, too, consisting of any letter or number key, or any combination of ALT, CTRL, and SHIFT in conjunction with a letter or number key. Keyboard shortcuts can be assigned to almost any tool. As a matter of fact, you can assign up to three different key shortcuts to each tool; talk about convenience!

To set or change a tool's keyboard equivalent, position the cursor over its icon and press CTRL-F1 (curiously, this does not work for the Display Photoshop Plug-in Interface tool). The dialog in Figure 2-9 appears.

Done

Click this button or press ESC to quit the dialog.

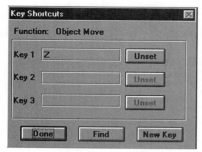

Figure 2-9 The Key Shortcuts dialog

Find

If you're not sure whether a key shortcut you want to use is already assigned to another command, click Find and then press the key shortcut in question. If it's in use, the dialog displays the name of the tool to which it's assigned, as well as any other shortcuts assigned to that tool.

New Key

When you're ready to assign a new key shortcut to a tool, click this button and then press the keyboard equivalent. The new key assignment then appears in the first empty slot in the dialog. Also, when you subsequently move the cursor over the tool, the key shortcut in the Key 1 slot appears at the left end of the Help bar.

WARNING: If you assign an existing key shortcut to another tool, the program simply changes the assignment without warning you and removes it from the previous tool. Make liberal use of the Find function to avoid unexpected alterations of key shortcut assignments, especially because the Key Shortcuts dialog does not have a Cancel function.

TIP: When you add or change key shortcuts, trueSpace2 automatically remembers them when you exit the program normally and restores them in subsequent work sessions. The Preferences/SaveState switch need not be enabled.

Unset

Use the Unset button to remove an existing key shortcut. Any other keyboard equivalents in higher-numbered slots move up to fill the gap left by the deleted assignment.

WHAT NOW?

Most of the concepts introduced in this chapter are explained more fully later in the book. You may want to reread this chapter once you've become more familiar with the program. For now, proceed to Chapter 3, Quick Start Tutorial: A Guided Tour of Major Features, where you'll take an exciting whirlwind tour of trueSpace2!

3
QUICK START TUTORIAL: A GUIDED TOUR OF MAJOR FEATURES

3

As you can see by the size of this book, there's quite a bit to trueSpace2. The best way to learn the program, and thus learn about 3D graphics, is to read *all* the chapters and follow *all* the examples. But you're probably champing at the bit by now, eager to get your hands on this software and start creating animations. Who could blame you? Think of this chapter, then, as a little reward for having come this far. But it won't be much of a reward if you haven't at least read Chapter 2, Introducing the trueSpace2 Interface, so be sure you've digested that first. To get the most out of this guided tour, you'll need to be acquainted with some of the interface aspects mentioned there.

The following "overview" tutorial covers some of the program's principal functions and shows how easy they are to use. Then, when you want to use the program for a unique new project, you'll know enough about trueSpace2 so you'll be able to work with it and know where to turn as you encounter the challenges of your work.

In this chapter, you'll get a quick introduction to

🛰 Moving around in the trueSpace2 workspace

🛰 Changing the point of view

🛰 Selecting and moving objects

🛰 Creating materials and applying them to objects

🛰 Rendering objects, and

🛰 Creating animation

So roll up your sleeves, fire up the computer, and let's get started!

LESSON 1: NAVIGATING IN THE INTERFACE

The first thing you'll look at is how to get around in trueSpace2. In the program's parlance, *navigation* is the process of manipulating the point of view as well as objects in the workspace.

NOTE: For the fastest feedback, I recommend you stay in Wireframe Display for most of this tutorial.

1. Start trueSpace2. You'll probably see an (almost) empty scene, as in Figure 3-1. The star-shaped objects are light sources that automatically appear in new scenes. You can change this arrangement with the Default Lights menu in the Preferences panel, as explained in Chapter 8, The Importance of Lighting. If any wireframe objects appear, use the File/Scene/New menu command to clear the workspace.

2. Start by adding a spherical object as a point of reference. At the right end of the Library tool group, find the Primitives Panel icon, which looks like a small group of objects: a cone, a cube, and a sphere. It's normally eighth from the left in the bottom row of icons. Click it to open the Primitives panel (see Figure 3-2).

3. Click on the Add Sphere icon near the bottom-left corner of the panel. This places a sphere object in the center of the workspace.

Moving the Point of View

Right now you're viewing the scene from the default Perspective view, which is an invisible "eye" looking down at the center of the workspace. In the next few steps, you'll learn how to position the eye, or viewpoint; change the view orientation; and zoom in and out.

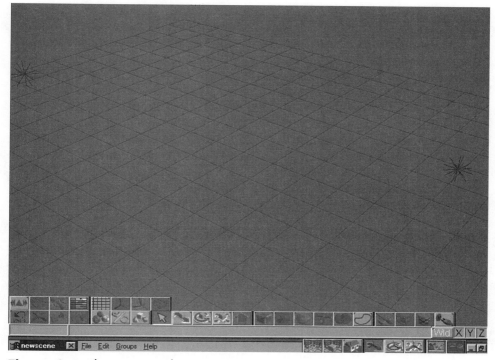

Figure 3–1 The empty workspace

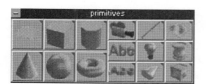

Figure 3–2 The Primitives panel

1. When you first start trueSpace2, the Eye Move tool is active. Check the View group at the bottom-right side of the main window to ensure this icon is selected (appears pushed in and is slightly darker than its neighbors). If it isn't, click on it to select it.

2. Move the mouse cursor to any position in the workspace. Press and hold the left mouse button. Notice that the mouse cursor disappears temporarily. That's okay; it'll reappear as soon as you release the button. Still holding the button down, drag the mouse to the left, then back to the right. The scene appears to shift in the direction *opposite* that of the mouse movement. Actually, the scene is staying the same, but you're shifting the point of view.

3. Now move the mouse forward (i.e., away from you or toward the far edge of the mouse pad) and then back toward you. The "eye" is now flying over the scene toward and then away from the back corner. Try to end up about where you started, with the sphere positioned near the center of the screen. This motion lets you start to see the benefit of the realism of trueSpace2's default Perspective view. The sphere becomes larger as your point of view approaches it and vice versa. It means you always have a pretty good idea of where you are "standing" and how objects are laid out.

4. In the two previous steps, you were moving the point of view parallel to the "ground," or the reference grid. Let's try something different. Release the left mouse button and press and hold the right button. Repeat Step 3, dragging the mouse away from you and then back toward you. Again, try to end up about where you started, with the sphere positioned near the center of the screen. Now you're moving your point of view vertically in the workspace; first up, then down.

This is a standard, consistent aspect of trueSpace2's user interface: The left mouse button manipulates things on the x and y axes (left/right and in/out), and the right mouse button affects the z axis (up/down). You'll get better acquainted with these axes in Chapter 4, Navigation: Getting Around in trueSpace2.

Rotating the Point of View

Next, try rotating the view. First return the eye to its default position.

1. Click and hold the left mouse button on the View group's rightmost icon, the Close All Panels tool, until the pop-up icon menu appears, then drag up until the cursor is over the Reset View tool. If you're not sure about which one it is, keep your eye on the Help bar and you'll see the tool names change as the cursor passes over them. When Reset View appears in the Help bar, release the mouse button and the view will change back to the original setting.

 TIP: The Reset View tool now appears in the View group instead of Close All Panels, so you can use the tool whenever you want without having to access the pop-up menu. By the way, this change remains in effect during the current work session only; the next time you use trueSpace2, Close All Panels is again the default tool.

2. In the View group, click the Eye Rotate tool. Move the mouse cursor into the workspace and drag in various directions. Try using both mouse buttons, one at a time. Use the Reset View tool when you're finished experimenting with Eye Rotate.

In Chapter 12, Rendering, you'll learn how to use the Look At function to adjust orientation automatically continually during motion to stay pointed at an object.

If you've ever used a camera or camcorder with a zoom lens, you probably have a pretty good idea of how trueSpace2's Zoom function works. Like a zoom lens, instead of actually moving the eye closer to or farther away from the object, it simply changes the magnification or focal length, thus maintaining the same perspective.

3. Select the Zoom tool from the View group now. In the workspace, drag to the upper right; this zooms in on the sphere. Drag short distances using first the left mouse button, then the right, and then both together. Note that there's no difference: You cannot scale (change the focal length of) the view on a single axis. Using any mouse button, keep dragging to the upper right until there's no effect. This demonstrates that, as with a camera's zoom lens, there's an upper limit to the magnification. Try zooming back out by dragging to the lower left and see if you can find the limit here as well. Use the Reset View tool when you're finished zooming around.

4. Now, instead of manipulating the eye, try moving the sphere object. In the tool groups, just above the Help bar, find the Object Move tool (it's immediately to the right of the Object tool, whose icon is a white arrow pointing toward the upper left) and click it.

5. Move the mouse cursor back into the workspace somewhere. Press and hold the left mouse button and drag the mouse left and right, then in and out. Again, you're producing motion on the horizontal (x-y) plane, but this time you're moving the sphere instead of the point of view. Note that the sphere follows your hand motion fairly closely.

6. Again holding down the left mouse button, try dragging the mouse diagonally on the pad and see if you can get it to follow the reference grid lines. Not too easy, is it? In Chapter 4, you'll learn how to use the axis button's trueSpace2 Coordinates panel to enable movement along a single axis.

7. Try using the right mouse button to move the sphere perpendicular to the reference grid.

Selecting Objects

Let's try an experiment in selection.

1. The Primitives panel should still be open. If it isn't, open it as you did earlier.

2. Click on the Add Cube tool, and a new wireframe cube object appears at the center of the workspace. Note that it is selected, or highlighted, as indicated by the wireframe appearing in white. The sphere becomes deselected, with the wireframe redrawn in dark blue.

NOTE: Only one object can be selected at a time in trueSpace2, although you can group objects for simultaneous manipulation; Chapter 7, Utilities and Edit Tools, explores that.

3. The cube and the sphere should be superimposed, as shown in Figure 3-3; if not, drag the cube over the sphere.

NOTE: You can click and drag anywhere in the workspace to manipulate the current object, even with more than one object in the workspace; you needn't click directly on the object.

4. Now click and release on a spot anywhere the two objects overlap. The sphere becomes selected and the cube is deselected. Click again in the same spot. The highlighting switches again, and the cube is again selected.

TIP: In complex scenes, where it's difficult to see overlapping objects' boundaries, this facility is helpful for selecting particular objects. It even works in Solid Render Display. (Unfortunately, the scheme breaks down when three or more objects are superimposed; subsequent clicks alternate between only two of the objects.)

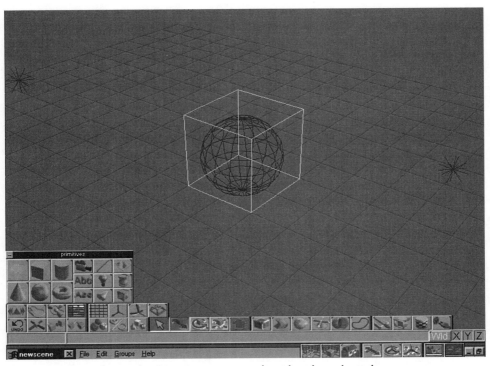

Figure 3-3 Cube and sphere superimposed, with cube selected

5. Press the ⬅ key on the keyboard. Note that the sphere is now selected. Press the ➡ key to reselect the cube. This is another handy method of selecting objects: The ➡ key selects them in the order that they were created, and the ⬅ key selects them in the reverse of that order. Press both keys a few times. You can also select light sources in the same way. Keep pressing until the sphere is selected.

6. While you're at it, try a quick experiment. The Object Move tool should still be active. Click on the selected object and drag in any direction to move it. Then return it to the original position. Try it again. The same object moves; you're no longer alternating the selection with successive clicks. That's because, by moving the mouse *before* releasing the button, you're telling the program that you're initiating a manipulation action rather than a selection. Thus, you can see that you must first select an object in an independent operation (by clicking and releasing on it or using an arrow key) before you can manipulate it.

7. Here's how you can save a step. From the File menu, select Preferences. In the Preferences panel, click the DynaPick check box, so an X appears in it. Now repeat the click-and-drag operations from Step 6. You can see that with DynaPick on, you're combining the selection and manipulation steps into a single action. Of course, this can lead to other problems, such as moving the wrong object or not being able to pick an object with the mouse—especially when more than two are superimposed. Generally, leaving DynaPick turned off is preferable (that's why it's the default). Turn it back off now, and then close the Preferences panel by clicking on the Close box in its upper-left corner.

8. Select the cube using any of the methods you've just learned. Then press the (DELETE) key on your keyboard. The cube is erased from the workspace.

9. Press the ⬅ or ➡ key to select the next object. Nothing happens! That's because nothing is selected, so the program doesn't know which is the "next" object. Be aware that when you delete an object in trueSpace2, another object does not automatically become selected. You might expect that the program would automatically select the next object in the lineup, but that's not what happens. This is useful to know about for those rare occasions when you need to have no objects selected. There's no way to "deselect" an object, so just add a new object and then delete it.

LESSON 2: RENDERING AND PAINTING OBJECTS

In this section, you'll learn how to turn wireframe objects into solids and how to modify their appearances by creating materials—sets of surface attributes—and applying them to object surfaces. Let's start by seeing how the sphere looks as a rendered solid in its "natural state."

1. Select the sphere by clicking on it. In the View group, click the Render Current Object tool (second from the left). The sphere quickly becomes solid in appearance, and you can see a certain variegated coloration on its surface. This is due to the default Colored Lights setup in Preferences, in which the right front light is white, the one in the left front is a shade of orange, and the backlight, at the rear of the scene, is blue.

2. To see how the sphere is actually colored, the lighting should be white. There are several ways to accomplish this, but the easiest is via Preferences. From the File menu, select Preferences. In the lower-right corner of the Preferences panel, click and hold on the box under Default Lights. In the pop-up menu that appears, drag the mouse to White Lights and release the button. You are asked to confirm the change; click the Yes button or press ENTER. Close Preferences.

3. The sphere returns to wireframe, and star-shaped colored Local lights are replaced by a cluster of arrow-like Infinite lights at the center of the workspace. (Chapter 8 discusses trueSpace2's various light sources.) Select Render Current Object again to see the effect of the new lighting setup. Now the object is all white, showing the default material as it naturally appears.

NOTE: Remember, *material* refers to basic attributes such as color and shininess, plus optional textures such as wood or marble.

4. Try changing the material. Find the Paint Face tool, leftmost in the Render group (it resembles a purple paintbrush over an orange-and-white rectangle) and select it. You're not actually going to paint faces—this is the default Paint tool, and it's the easiest way to open the four Materials panels. They should now be visible, as in Figure 3-4.

When you open the Materials panels with an object selected, their settings show the most recently used material, which is not necessarily the same as the current object's overall material. (An object can have more than one material applied, as you'll see in Chapter 9, Materials Part 1: Basic Surface Attributes.) But in this case, because you haven't changed any material settings, the panels correspond with the object's material.

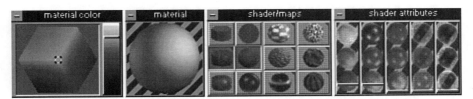

Figure 3–4 The Materials panels are easy to open with the Paint Face tool

5. Try changing the object's color. In the Material Color panel, which contains a rainbow hexagon, click on the rightmost corner of the hexagon, where the red color is deepest. The sample sphere in the panel labeled Material is immediately repainted to reflect the change.

6. To apply this new color to your sphere, use a different tool from the Paint tool pop-up. While you're at it, you'll learn a new way of accessing the menu. Last time, to access an icon pop-up, you clicked and held on the icon. This time, click and hold on the Paint Face tool and immediately drag a small distance. This brings the menu up a bit more quickly than the previous method, but requires a slightly greater amount of work on your part. You might say it reflects the American work ethic (work harder for faster results); at any rate, it's nice to have a choice!

7. With the mouse button still held down, drag upward until the pointer is over the topmost tool, Paint Object (a purple funnel), then release the button. The altered material is applied to the sphere, and the object is rendered so you can admire its new paint job.

 TIP: You can always halt the rendering process by pressing the ⟨ESC⟩ key. If you do, select the Wireframe Display tool from the View group to get back to wireframe display.

Note that, unlike the previous time when you chose a variant tool from an icon pop-up, the Paint Object tool doesn't replace the Paint Face tool in the Render group. This is because Paint Face (unlike the other Paint tool variants) takes effect immediately; so to avoid accidents, trueSpace2 never makes it the default variant. (Well, almost never. Actually, sometimes it does become the default—an unpredictable inconsistency.)

8. Try adding a bit of visual interest to the sphere. Create a new material using a gradient texture map from the CD-ROM supplied with this book. In the third Materials panel—Shader/Maps—click on the Use Texture Map icon (a checkered sphere in the top row, second from the right). The sample sphere changes to show the default checkered texture map, with built-in transparency (you'll see how that works in Chapter 11, Animation).

9. Right-click on the same icon to open the Texture Map property panel, as shown in Figure 3-5. Click once on the rectangle to the right of the checkered ball image in the top row (currently labeled checker) to open the Get Texture Map file dialog.

10. If the disc included with this book isn't in your CD-ROM drive, insert it now, then use the file dialog's controls to go to the CD-ROM drive and open the TUTORIAL\CH3 directory. From that directory, click on the file named CH3-GRD.BMP and then click OK. You'll see the sample sphere rerendered with the gradient texture map. Congratulations: You've just created a new texture-mapped material! To apply the new material to the sphere, use the Paint Object tool as before.

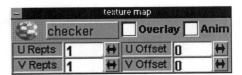

Figure 3-5 Texture Map panel

NOTE: If you have any images of your own you'd like to use instead of the one supplied here, feel free. Image file formats supported in trueSpace2 include Targa, Windows Bitmap (BMP), JPEG, and others discussed in Chapter 10, Materials Part 2: Advanced Surface Attributes. You can even apply AVI-format animations and videos to objects. You'll learn how in Chapter 10.

11. Because you've gone to all the trouble of creating a new material, save it in a Material library. That way you can apply it to other objects in the future without having to re-create the setup. Click on the Material Library tool (leftmost in the Libraries tool group) to open the Material Library panel (see Figure 3-6).

12. You can see that there are a number of interesting materials here; in fact, trueSpace2 ships with many more, organized into eight different libraries. To add your material to the library, click on the Add Material to Library button, which is the arrow in the panel's lower-left corner that looks like it's pointing toward the library. A sample sphere with your material on it appears in the panel, probably in the second slot. (Materials added to the library appear to the right of the current material, which, by default, is the first. Look for a red line under the material's representation.)

13. Name your material. If it's not selected in the panel, click on it now. Then click in the white rectangle in the panel's lower-right corner. Type in the name My Material or any other name you like.

WARNING: Press ENTER after typing the new material name. If you don't and then you move on to another operation, the new name doesn't "take" and remains the default, Untitled. This is true of all keyboard entry fields in trueSpace2 except for file dialogs, where pressing ENTER is the equivalent of clicking OK.

Figure 3-6 Material Library panel

14. There's one more thing to do if you want to use the new material in future sessions. Click on the gray rectangle to the left of the scroll bar, which currently displays Simple. On the Material Library file menu that appears, click on Save. The default Material library, Simple, is saved with your new material. (If you like, get the Material Library file menu back again and click on Load to see the other Material libraries that come with trueSpace2. Try loading a few to see some of the cool textures.)

WARNING: Neither the material nor the library that contains it actually incorporates your texture map; it only points to the image file. If you delete, move, or rename an image file used in a material (or, in this case, remove the CD from the drive), trueSpace2 won't be able to find it, and you'll need to change the material definition, or reinstate the file or disc, to be able to use it again.

Try This for Fun

Here's an optional exercise: Once you've applied a material to an object, and if you have a reasonably fast computer, it's fun to use 3DR to see how it looks from various angles.

1. From the Wireframe Display pop-up at the left end of the View group, select Solid Render Display (the 3DR icon). After a few seconds, the sphere renders as a solid object. But where's the material?

2. By default, materials are turned off in Solid Render Display for faster feedback, but you can turn them on. Right-click on the Solid Render Display button to open the Render Quality panel (see Figure 3-7). Position the mouse cursor over the checkered ball icon and look at the Help bar. You can see that this button is for toggling the use of textures with Solid Render Display active. Click the button now, and you'll see the texture map appear on the sphere's surface.

3. In the Navigation group, select the Object Rotate tool and make sure the Object tool is also selected. Move the mouse pointer into the workspace and click and drag in various directions. You'll see the sphere rotate in real time (or at least as near to it as your computer can handle), showing the texture mapping from different angles. Neat stuff!

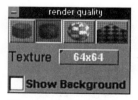

Figure 3-7 Render Quality panel

4. When you're ready, use the leftmost View group pop-up to return to Wireframe Display. You're about to go into animation, and you'll need all the speed you can get.

LESSON 3: SETTING UP ANIMATION

After setting up your objects and adding materials to determine how they look, you can use trueSpace2's animation functions to make them move. But don't be intimidated: As you'll see shortly, hardly anything could be easier. The Animation panel acts as your "command center," giving you full control over when things happen.

1. There are probably several panels open at this point, so start by clearing some working room. From the rightmost pop-up in the View group, which currently displays the Reset View tool, select the Close All Panels tool. Now your screen displays only the tool groups and your wireframe sphere.

2. Select the Animation tool, which opens the Animation panel (see Figure 3-8).

TIP: Notice that the start frame is number 0. That's how trueSpace2 starts counting animation frames. If, for example, you want to make a 30-frame animation, you would make the last frame frame number 29. If you find this numbering scheme confusing, go ahead and use frame numbers such as 30 and 60 as keys when you need a specific number of frames in your animation. These numbers are easier to calculate with because they're integer multiples of the number of frames per second in playback, which is usually 15 or 30. Then just don't render frame 0.

3. Use the Object Move tool to position the sphere on the left side of the screen, as shown in Figure 3-9. This gives you a starting point for the sphere.

In general, you set up animations in trueSpace2 using the *keyframe method*: You go to the frame in which a motion is to start or change (called the *keyframe*). Then you use

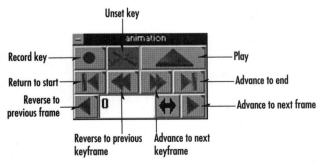

Figure 3-8 The Animation panel first opens at the start frame

Figure 3–9 Setting up the first keyframe for the animation

standard tools to manipulate the animated object and continue in that fashion. Every time you change an object in a keyframe, the program remembers your actions, sets a *key*, and creates motion by interpolating changes between keys in intervening frames.

4. Next go to frame 20. There are several ways to do this. I'll tell you about two and let you decide which you prefer.

Click in the Current Frame Number box in the Animation panel and type in 20. (Using this method, it's fastest to double-click on the existing frame number, highlight it, and then type in the new number. The first keystroke replaces the highlighted entry.) Then press (ENTER).

The alternative method of changing the frame number is to use the two-headed arrow to the right of the Current Frame Number box. Click and hold on the arrow, then drag to the right to increase the frame number or to the left to decrease the frame number. For small frame number changes, this method is usually easier and quicker than keyboard entry.

5. Now that you're at frame 20, again use Object Move to position the sphere near the rear center of the workspace, as in Figure 3-10.

6. For the third and final key, go to frame 40 and position the sphere on the right side of the screen, opposite its original position, as in Figure 3-11.

7. You're ready to go! In the Animation panel, click on the Play button (a red triangle) to play back the animation frames in succession one time. Chapter 11 shows you how to set up looped playback so you can play back the animation more than once.

8. Let's try one more thing, and then I'll wrap up this tutorial by showing you how to render the animation to an AVI file. You need to return to frame 20. You already know two ways to do this, but now that there's a key for the current object at that frame, I'll show you a third, easier method. In the Animation panel, click on the Reverse to Previous Keyframe button (two triangles pointing leftward). Voilà! You're at frame 20.

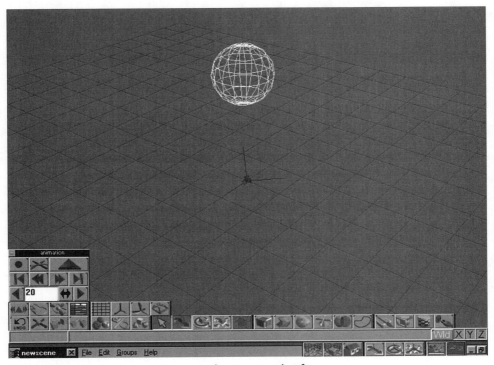

Figure 3-10 Setting up the second animation keyframe

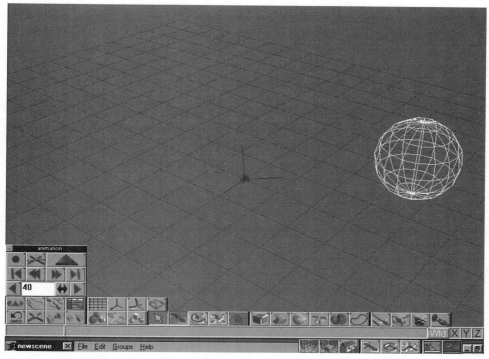

Figure 3-11 Setting up the third animation keyframe

9. Select the Object Rotate tool (to the right of Object Move) and rotate the object back about a quarter turn, so the top is now pointing away from you. This is just an exercise, so don't worry about accuracy. In fact, it's not even important which way you rotate it, as long as you rotate it.

10. Play back the animation again. You can see that the object rotates between the first two keys, but doesn't rotate back between the second and third keys. That's because when you set the original key at frame 40, you were in Object Move mode, so trueSpace2 saved only the positional information for that key, not the rotational information. This is easy to fix.

11. As is usual when you play back an animation, you're now at the last frame. Simply rotate the object back to its original orientation (use the opposite motion of what you used at frame 20), and it's done! Play back the animation again to demonstrate that the object now rotates away from you between frames 0 and 20 and back toward you between 20 and 40.

TIP: If your computer is very fast, the animation may play back too quickly for you to see easily what's going on. Not to worry; once you start working with more complex models, that won't be a problem! For now, though, there are several ways to get around this. You can rewind to the first frame by clicking on the Return to Start button (triangle pointing left at vertical line, left end of center row) in the Animation panel. Then click repeatedly on the Animation panel's Advance to Next Frame button (triangle pointing right, bottom-right corner) to view the animation a frame at a time. You can turn on Solid Render Display, which will give you a much better idea of how the animation will look when rendered. Or you can simply slow down the computer by disabling the Turbo button! (If your computer has one, it's probably on the front panel. Don't forget to turn it back on when you're done.)

LESSON 4: RENDERING YOUR ANIMATION

I'll close this chapter by immortalizing your animation, creating a disk file that you can play back any time with Media Player or any other program that can display Windows video files.

1. In the View group, click and hold (or drag) on the Render Current Object tool. From the top of the pop-up that appears, select the Render Scene to File tool to display the Render to File dialog (see Figure 3-12). You'll need to set several items.

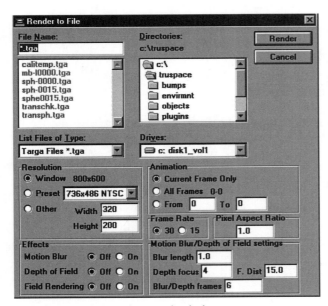

Figure 3–12 Render to File dialog

2. Tell trueSpace2 that you want to render an AVI file, which is the standard video format for Windows. Do this simply by giving the file name the proper extension. Note that the contents of the File Name box are highlighted, so you can simply enter a new name. Type sph-ani.avi. But don't press (ENTER) yet, because that would start the rendering, and you haven't finished setting up.

 WARNING: Even though you may be running trueSpace2 under Windows 95, the program doesn't recognize long file names, so you'll need to stick to the DOS/Windows 3.1 8.3 file name convention.

3. Note that you're in the TRUSPACE main directory, which is where the program places output files by default. You'll want to remember that for finding the file later. Next, tell trueSpace2 what image size to render. In the Resolution section beneath the File Name list box, click Other, which is set to 320 Width x 200 Height. This is a good resolution to use for a fast test render.

4. Take a look at the Animation settings. Right now the rendering is set to Current Frame Only. But you want to render all the frames, so click the All Frames 0-40 option. Press (ENTER) or click OK to continue.

5. Next, the AVI Compression dialog appears, asking for the Compression method, Quality, and so on (see Figure 3-13). Whichever default it's set to (depending on the video codecs installed on your system) should work fine for this simple animation. Click on OK to start rendering.

6. You're now returned to the trueSpace2 main interface, where you see the animation being rendered frame by frame in the center of the screen. The number of the frame currently being rendered appears in the lower-left corner, and some rendering statistics appear in the Help bar. After the last frame is rendered, all this goes away and the display returns to its previous state.

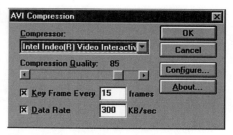

Figure 3-13 The AVI Compression dialog lets you determine the compression method

7. Because trueSpace2 doesn't have an AVI playback facility, you'll have to go to a different application to see the animation. Minimize the trueSpace2 interface and run the Media Player program from Windows Accessories. If you're using Windows 95, go to the Start menu and choose Programs/Accessories/Multimedia/Media Player. From Media Player, select File/Open, go to the TRUSPACE directory, select the SPH-ANI.AVI file, and click OK. After the file loads, click the Play button to view the animation. Not bad for your first effort!

8. You won't be using this scene again, but if you like, you can save it for your own purposes. Maximize trueSpace2 and go to the File menu and select Scene/Save or Scene/Save As. Enter the SCENES directory, type in a file name (you needn't type the .SCN extension; trueSpace2 provides it for you automatically), and press ENTER or click OK.

WHAT NOW?

This chapter has provided you with a brief but enticing look at some of trueSpace2's most important tools and techniques. I've only touched on a tiny percentage of the program's capabilities. Follow along with the rest of the tutorials in this book to learn what an amazingly powerful but easy-to-use program trueSpace2 is.

4

NAVIGATION: GETTING AROUND IN TRUESPACE2

ere's where you start really digging into trueSpace2's nuts-and-bolts functionality. The material in this chapter builds on the concepts discussed in the first part of the Quick Start tutorial in Chapter 3, Quick Start Tutorial: A Guided Tour of Major Features. If you haven't completed the Chapter 3 tutorial, you should do so before continuing.

NAVIGATION PRINCIPLES

As mentioned in Chapter 3, trueSpace2 uses the term *navigation* to refer to the operations of changing your viewpoint in the workspace and of manipulating objects. This chapter deals primarily with the tools found in the Navigation tool group, which provide, among others, three basic functions: movement, rotation, and scaling of objects.

Object movement, known in traditional computer graphics lingo as *translation*, refers to changing an object's location in space.

Object rotation means staying in one place, but changing orientation—that is, the direction the object is pointing.

Object scaling involves making an object bigger or smaller on one, two, or three axes.

NOTE: Navigation with the viewpoint or eye uses analogous controls found in the View tool group, which were covered in Chapter 3.

Understanding Axes

Using navigational controls in trueSpace2 is so intuitive that you don't usually have to think about the underlying system. But it is helpful to understand how it works, especially when you need exact results.

If you studied graphing in high school, you'll recall that the horizontal axis is called x and the vertical axis is called y. This is called the *Cartesian coordinate system*, and it lets you specify any point in a plane, called the x-y plane, with two numbers. There's a very similar system at work in 3D graphics, also called the Cartesian coordinate system, but with a couple of significant differences.

First, in trueSpace2, the vertical axis is called z. This is true of many 3D programs, but not all. Second, and far more important, there's now a third axis, labeled (naturally) y. The y axis is perpendicular to the plane created by the x and z axes. This defines an "in-out" direction in addition to the x axis's "left-right" and the z axis's "up-down." Of course, this is all relative and depends on your viewpoint. By adding this third (z) axis, you can specify the location of a point anywhere on the x-z plane, as well as a y distance in front of or behind the plane, thus creating three-dimensional data. Another way of looking at it is that the "horizontal" reference grid or ground plane you've already seen in trueSpace2 represents the x-y plane and the z axis defines a distance above or below it.

LESSON 1: LOADING THE AXES OBJECT

Enough talk! Let's take a look at an object created especially for this book that you can use to easily visualize how the axis system works in trueSpace2. You'll need to load a scene file from the *3D Construction Kit* companion CD-ROM.

1. Run trueSpace2 now, if it isn't already running, and access the File/Scene/Load command.

2. If the disc included with this book isn't already in your CD-ROM drive, insert it now. Then use the file requester to go to the disc and open the TUTORIAL\CH4 directory. From that directory, click on the file named AXES.SCN and then click the OK button.

3. Make sure you're in Wireframe Display. You should be seeing the display shown in Figure 4-1.

4. The Axes object is located at the center of trueSpace2's workspace, at the 0 location on the x, y, and z axes. Let's verify this. Right-click on the Object tool to open the Object Info panel for the Axes object (see Figure 4-2). You can see in the panel's Location fields that the x, y, and z values are all 0.

Take a look at the Axes object, which shows the directions of the x, y, and z axes not only for the trueSpace2 world, but for newly created objects as well. (This is an important distinction, which I'll explore further in this chapter and briefly in Chapter 7, Utilities and Edit Tools, where you'll learn how to see and manipulate an object's axes.) A newly created object's axes are aligned with the world axes, but once the object is rotated, this is no longer necessarily the case. As you'll see shortly, you can manipulate the object along or about its own variable axes or the world's constant axes. Notice that the positive x direction is to the lower left and the negative x direction is to the upper right. Likewise, the positive and negative y directions are to the lower right and upper left, respectively. And as you might expect, the positive and negative z directions are straight up and down, respectively.

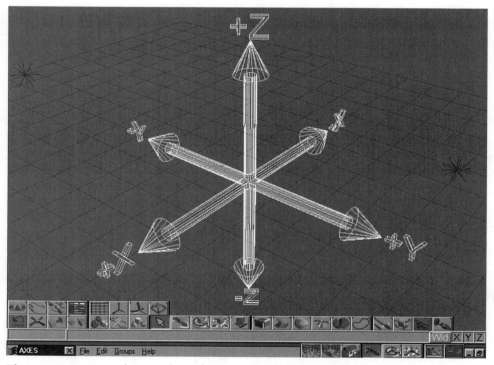

Figure 4-1 Special Axes object from CD-ROM file TUTORIAL\CH5\AXES.SCN

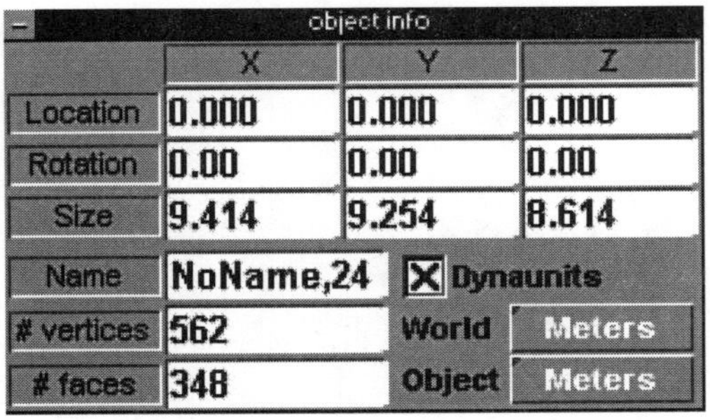

object info	X	Y	Z
Location	0.000	0.000	0.000
Rotation	0.00	0.00	0.00
Size	9.414	9.254	8.614
Name	NoName,24	☒ Dynaunits	
# vertices	562	World	Meters
# faces	348	Object	Meters

Figure 4–2 Object Info panel

LESSON 2: MOVING OBJECTS

To improve your understanding of axis directions, let's move the Axes object around in the workspace.

1. Select the Object Move tool and move the mouse pointer into the workspace. Click and hold the left mouse and drag in various directions. Keep the mouse button down and note how the object follows your movement fairly closely, moving only in the horizontal plane.

2. Release the mouse button. Then select the Undo tool (the very first icon, a blue curved arrow) or press CTRL-Z. The object returns to its starting 0,0,0 location. If it doesn't, it may mean that you dragged the object a few times. Not to worry! Select Undo again; each time you do so, you undo the previous operation. Multiple Undo is another one of trueSpace2's nifty features! Keep clicking on Undo until the Axes object returns to its original position.

3. Now, holding the left mouse button again, move the object along the x axis by dragging down and to the left on your mousepad. As you drag, observe the X, Y, and Z fields of the Location line in the Object Info panel. These values are dynamically updated as you move the mouse. You'll see the X value increasing. You may also see the Y value change, because it's tough to drag in exactly the right direction. You're about to see how trueSpace2 helps you handle that.

Locking Axes and Switching Coordinate Systems

Take a look at the right end of the Help bar, where you'll see the group of controls shown in Figure 4-3. If you don't see it, access the Help menu and select the Help Bar item. This is the Coordinates panel, which you use to lock movement to specific axes. These controls are also used to select the coordinate system—World, Object, or Screen—used for navigation. (We'll look at this shortly.)

The reason it's difficult to constrain movement of the Axes object to only the x axis is because, normally, dragging objects with the left mouse button enables movement on

Figure 4-3 Coordinates panel

both the x and y axes. If you want to move an object freely in the horizontal plane, this works well, but if you want to move it along a specific axis, it helps to be able to turn off movement on the other axis. Let's see how this works.

4. Click on the Y button in the Coordinates panel, so it appears to have "popped out." You have just "turned off" the y axis, so that dragging with the left button causes movement only on the x axis.

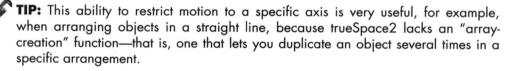 **NOTE:** In the trueSpace2 graphical interface, when an icon or button appears pushed in, it's active, or selected; when it is popped out, the associated control is disabled, or deselected.

5. Move the mouse pointer back into the workspace. Click and hold the left mouse button and drag in various directions. You'll see that dragging up or to the right now causes the object to move in the negative x direction, and dragging down or to the left causes positive x motion. It's as if the object is moving along a rail.

TIP: This ability to restrict motion to a specific axis is very useful, for example, when arranging objects in a straight line, because trueSpace2 lacks an "array-creation" function—that is, one that lets you duplicate an object several times in a specific arrangement.

You will also want to know about the alternative Coordinates property panel attached to each navigation tool, although these are somewhat less convenient to use than the buttons on the Help bar. Right-clicking on any navigation tool brings up the related Coordinates control panel. Try right-clicking on the Object Move tool now. You'll see the alternative Coordinates property panel pop up above the tool, as depicted in Figure 4-4.

The alternative Coordinates panel has icons for the three different coordinate systems, and its y-axis button is still disabled. Move your mouse over the three top icons and watch the Help bar to see what they represent. The same three coordinate systems are available in the Help bar Coordinates panel, from a pop-up to the left of the X, Y, and Z buttons (currently labeled Wld). You'll learn more about the coordinate systems in the next section, on object rotation.

Figure 4–4 Alternative Coordinates property panel with y axis disabled

6. One convenient aspect of trueSpace2's navigation system is that the program remembers each navigation tool's setup individually. To see how this works, select the Eye Move tool from the main window's View group. Note that the alternative Coordinates property panel goes away, and the one on the Help bar returns to its default state, with all three axis buttons selected. Click the X button to disable x-axis movement of the point of view. Drag in the workspace, and notice that the viewpoint moves parallel to the y axis.

7. Select the Object Move tool again. The Coordinates panel reverts to its previous state, with the X button selected and the Y button deselected.

8. Let's briefly look at vertical movement. Position the mouse cursor anywhere in the workspace. Then press and hold the right mouse button and drag vertically across the mousepad. Do not release the mouse button. As you learned in Chapter 3, using the right mouse button causes movement only along the vertical axis. Still holding the right button, press and hold the left button and drag the mouse in various directions. Using this technique, you can move the object to any location in the plane defined by the x and z axes.

As you probably have experienced, this method of positioning an object is somewhat awkward. In general, it's best to move the object first on one axis, then the other.

LESSON 3: OBJECT ROTATION

Just as moving objects is useful for positioning things where you want them, object rotation is useful for turning objects so they're oriented correctly. For example, in a dining room setup, you'd want each chair to be turned so its seat is under the table.

I've been referring, somewhat vaguely, to the different Coordinates systems available in trueSpace2. You're about to find out exactly how they work, in conjunction with learning about rotating objects.

1. Select the Object Rotate tool and note that the Coordinates button on the Help bar property panel changes from World (Wld) to Object (Obj).

2. Move the mouse pointer into the workspace and, while holding the left button down, drag left and right, then up and down. You can see how natural this movement is; it's almost as if you're actually reaching into the workspace and turning the object with your hand.

3. Compare this to rotating in the World coordinate system. Click and hold on the Obj button at the right end of the Help bar, and when the pop-up appears, drag to Wld and release. The Wld label should now appear in the place of the Obj label.

4. Return to the workspace and repeat Step 2. There shouldn't be any difference. So why are there different coordinate systems?

About Coordinate Systems

There are actually three coordinate systems that you can use for navigation in trueSpace2: World, Object, and Screen. In the World system, the axes are always as represented by the Axes object when it's first loaded. In the Object system, the axes are built into the object and their orientation changes with that of the object (although you can manipulate an object's axes independently, as you'll see in Chapter 7). In the Screen coordinate system, the axes are as follows: x is horizontally on the screen, y is vertically on the screen, and z is perpendicular to the screen.

Use of the various coordinate systems applies mainly to manipulating objects (or the view) *on a single axis*. The easiest way to see this is to use the right button to rotate the Axes object on the z axis. You'll try that in a moment, but let's first return the object to its original orientation. You may remember from the previous section that you could achieve this by using the Undo function repeatedly. However, this time you'll use the direct approach.

1. The Object Info panel should still be open. Take a look at it now. You should see nonzero numbers in all three Rotation slots.

2. Double-click in the X Rotation box so it highlights, then press ⓪ (zero) on the keyboard and press the TAB key. This has the dual function of changing the object's orientation from the previous value to the new one, as well as highlighting the next field.

3. Once more, press ⓪ and then the TAB key.

4. Finally, press ⓪ and then the ENTER key. The Axes object is now back to its original orientation.

TIP: Here's something interesting, which is actually a minor bug in the program. Click the Undo tool three times and note that the axis orientations are restored in the *reverse* order that you changed them. Then click and hold on the Undo tool. In a moment, a pop-up appears containing the Redo tool. Select Redo three times,

continued on next page

continued from previous page

and watch the object return to its original orientation—but the Rotation row values in the Object Info panel haven't changed! Although the Rotation values have in fact been returned to 0, the panel does not reflect it. Verify that they are actually all at 0 by using Object Move to drag the object a slight distance, whereupon the panel is updated correctly. You needn't return the object to its original location, although you can if you like. If you do move the object, select the Object Rotate tool again when you're finished and note that its coordinate system is still World; it hasn't returned to the default Object system. Very considerate!

Now you're ready to practice rotating on the z axis.

5. Rotate the Axes object on the World z axis by dragging with the right mouse button. What happens is pretty much what you might expect: The object rotates on its vertical axis.

6. Next, use the left mouse button to change the orientation of all three axes. Then go back to the right button and rotate again. You can see that the object is still rotating on the (invisible) World vertical axis, which is always perpendicular to the ground plane.

7. Return to the Object coordinate system using the Help bar pop-up. Again, use the right mouse button to rotate the object on the z axis. This time, you can see that the rotation occurs about the object's own z axis, no matter how the object is oriented.

8. If you like, try using the left mouse button to change the z axis orientation. Then repeat the previous two z-axis rotations (World, then Object). You'll see the results are the same as before.

9. Also, try rotating the object on the x axis only, in the World and Object coordinate systems. You'll see the following principles in action: Rotating on the World x axis always rotates on the southwest-to-northeast axis. Rotating on the Object x axis turns the object around its own x axis, no matter which way it's pointing. And if you like, try the y axis as well; you'll get similar results.

While you're at it, take a look at the third coordinate system—Screen, which is labeled Scr on the Help bar pop-up.

10. Select the Object Move tool and then choose Scr from the Help bar pop-up. Disable y-axis movement and enable x axis movement.

11. Holding the left button, drag the mouse in various directions in the workspace.

12. Next, disable x-axis movement, enable the y axis, and repeat the motions of Step 11. You can see that the Screen x axis is always left/right and the y axis is always up/down in relation to the screen.

13. To verify this, try using Eye Rotate to change the view orientation. Then select Object Move again and repeat the object movement on the isolated x and y axes.

14. But what about the screen z axis? As you might suspect, it's perpendicular to the screen plane, so z-axis movement is always in and out with respect to your point of view. To confirm this, simply move the mouse pointer into the workspace and hold down the right mouse button. Drag toward the lower left to bring the object closer and to the upper right to move it farther away.

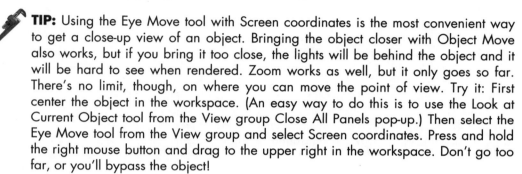 **TIP:** Using the Eye Move tool with Screen coordinates is the most convenient way to get a close-up view of an object. Bringing the object closer with Object Move also works, but if you bring it too close, the lights will be behind the object and it will be hard to see when rendered. Zoom works as well, but it only goes so far. There's no limit, though, on where you can move the point of view. Try it: First center the object in the workspace. (An easy way to do this is to use the Look at Current Object tool from the View group Close All Panels pop-up.) Then select the Eye Move tool from the View group and select Screen coordinates. Press and hold the right mouse button and drag to the upper right in the workspace. Don't go too far, or you'll bypass the object!

Do you remember how to reset the view, as discussed in Chapter 3? Here's a brief reminder; use it now, to prepare for the next exercise. Click and hold the left mouse button on the View group's rightmost icon (it will be either Close All Panels or Look at Current Object) until the pop-up icon menu appears. Then drag up until the cursor is over the Reset View tool and release the button.

LESSON 4: OBJECT SCALING

Before I close this chapter, let's take a look at how object scaling works. Scaling, or resizing, lets you fine-tune object size relationships. For example, if a scene is to depict a child with a typical tricycle, the tricycle shouldn't be much bigger or smaller than the child. If several people are working on a scene, unless it has been carefully planned, one modeler might create objects to a different scale than another. Thus, it's useful to be able to resize objects so they're all at the proper scale.

1. First, use the File/Scene/New command to clear the workspace. When the program asks you if you want to save the scene, click the No button.

2. Next, open the Primitives panel.

3. Select the Add Sphere icon near the bottom-left corner of the panel to create a sphere object in the center of the workspace.

4. Select the Object Scale tool, which will set the Coordinates panel to the default for this tool: Object coordinates with all axes enabled.

5. Move the mouse pointer into the workspace. Press and hold the left button, and drag in various directions to scale the sphere along its x and/or y axes (see Figure 4-5). If you drag between northwest and southeast on the mousepad, you're scaling on the y axis, and between northeast and southwest, you're scaling on the x axis. If you drag due east, you make the sphere bigger on the x and y axes simultaneously, creating a wide, flat, cushionlike object. Conversely, dragging due west makes a skinny ovoid. If only dieting were this easy!

6. Try turning off the x axis to scale only on the y axis, and vice versa. Also try scaling on the z axis only.

7. For bonus points, rotate the sphere and then compare scaling it on individual axes in the World and Object coordinate systems.

As you experiment, you may want to return to the original shape from time to time. Of course, you can do this with Undo, but it is often easier simply to press the DELETE key to get rid of the sphere and then add a new one. Sometimes, for efficiency's sake, you have to be ruthless! Also, if you're having trouble seeing the changes, you might want to try loading the Axes object and scaling it. I started with the sphere because it's more similar to an object you might normally use in trueSpace2.

TIP: To scale an object while keeping its proportions intact, drag with both mouse buttons pressed and all axis buttons enabled. Try it now. Make sure the Coordinates property panel is set to the defaults, then drag in the workspace with both mouse buttons pressed. Drag to the lower left to shrink the sphere or to the upper right to expand it. Note that the sphere, no matter what its shape when you started, maintains its proportions exactly.

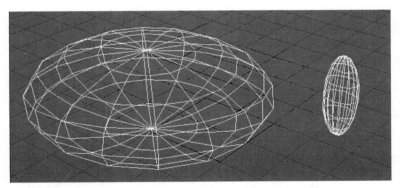

Figure 4-5 Sphere scaled up and down on x and y axes

WHAT NOW?

Spend as much time as you can afford experimenting with the different object and viewpoint navigation functions in conjunction with the various combinations available from the Coordinates property panel. The more familiar you become with trueSpace2's navigational controls, the more efficiently you'll be able to use the program in the long run. And remember, for efficient switching between moving, rotating, and scaling objects, use the keyboard shortcuts: Ⓩ, Ⓧ, and Ⓒ, respectively.

5
BASIC MODELING

5

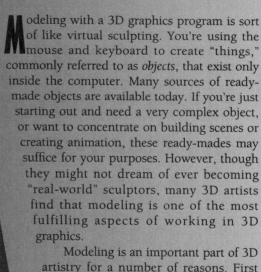

odeling with a 3D graphics program is sort
of like virtual sculpting. You're using the
mouse and keyboard to create "things,"
commonly referred to as *objects*, that exist only
inside the computer. Many sources of ready-
made objects are available today. If you're just
starting out and need a very complex object,
or want to concentrate on building scenes or
creating animation, these ready-mades may
suffice for your purposes. However, though
they might not dream of ever becoming
"real-world" sculptors, many 3D artists
find that modeling is one of the most
fulfilling aspects of working in 3D
graphics.

Modeling is an important part of 3D
artistry for a number of reasons. First
and foremost, there's no better way to
individualize your work than by popu-
lating it with objects that could only
have emerged from your unique
imagination. There's also the consid-
eration that, no matter how full your
library of standard objects is, a
client will always want something
you don't have—such as a model
of someone's dog or aunt, or a

machine made only by a particular company. And remember, you'll be much prouder of a finished image or animation that contains only your own hand-crafted objects, rather than a bunch of generic objects loaded from a $50 or $500 CD-ROM. But if you do resort to using ready-mades, your modeling skills will allow you to customize them in any number of ways.

INTRODUCTION TO 3D MODELING

The trueSpace2 program gives you a full complement of tools for creating objects. This chapter covers the following.

First, the program supplies a small library of primitives, which are simple built-in 2D and 3D shapes such as a plane, a cube, and a sphere. You can use these as building blocks, combining them in various ways to make more complex objects.

Next, you'll study several tools for making polygons—flat shapes that can be turned into 3D shapes by using functions such as Sweep and Lathe.

Finally, the chapter covers some modeling tools—in addition to Sweep and Lathe, their cousins Macro/Sweep, Tip, and Bevel.

WORKING WITH PRIMITIVES

If you're just starting out with trueSpace2, or you want a basic object to try out some ideas, the Primitives panel (see Figure 5-1) is one of your best friends. Try opening it now by selecting the selecting the Primitives Panel tool (it's the rightmost tool in the Libraries tool group).

There are 15 buttons on the Primitives panel; right now you're interested in the six on the left side. Each of these buttons depicts the type of object it creates. In increasing order of complexity, these objects are

 Plane

Cube

Cylinder

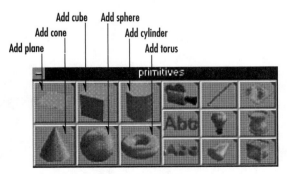

Figure 5-1 The Primitives panel

Cone

Sphere

Torus

As with most tools in trueSpace2, you can get a Help bar description of each button by positioning the mouse pointer over the tool.

LESSON 1: ADDING A PLANE PRIMITIVE

Let's start with the simplest primitive object: the plane.

1. First, clear the workspace of any existing objects by selecting File/Scene/New.

2. Select the Add Plane button (see Figure 5-1). A primitive plane—by default, a single four-sided square polygon of 2 x 2 units in size—is added to the center of the workspace.

If you're working in Wireframe Display, you'll see something like Figure 5-2. But if you're working in 3DR (Solid Render Display) mode with the shaded grid turned on, all you'll see is a three-dimensional arrow called the Active Object Indicator, as in Figure 5-3, pointing, seemingly, at nothing. (If you've moved the viewpoint closer than the default position, you may see "slivers" of the plane object.) What's going on here?

The fact is, a new plane object exists, but you may not be able to see it because it's lying in the exact same plane as the shaded grid. When that happens, trueSpace2 doesn't know how to display the smaller object, so it hides all or random parts of it.

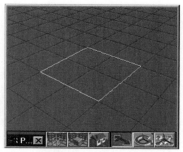

Figure 5–2 Wireframe view of newly added plane object

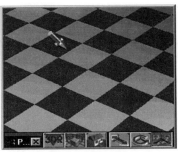

Figure 5-3 Solid Render
view of newly added plane
object

3. You can verify that the two objects occupy the same plane by selecting the New Front View tool from the New View pop-up (seventh from the left in the main window View group). Even though the main display is in Solid Render Display mode, the new view opens in Wireframe Display mode. And you can see in this edge-on view (see Figure 5-4) that the short white line of the plane is perfectly coincident with the long black line of the reference grid.

4. Close the Front View window before proceeding.

5. To make the plane visible, you need to raise it only a slight distance above the shaded grid surface. Select the Object Move tool and position the mouse cursor in the workspace. Holding down the right mouse button, drag a short distance toward the upper edge of the mouse pad until you see the plane.

Okay, so now that you have a plane in the workspace, what can you do with it? What's it good for?

You can do pretty much the same things with the plane that you can do with any object in trueSpace2: move, rotate, and scale; extrude; or lathe it. You can also use it as a structural element in a larger composite object.

Figure 5-4 Edge-on view
of newly added plane object

TIP: One thing a plane is particularly useful for is creating a landscape (that is, a surface with hills and valleys) using the Deform functions, which Chapter 6, Advanced Modeling, covers. Also, by applying a material rectangle to a plane object, you can use it as a business card, poster, painting, or photograph. Chapter 10, Materials Part 2: Advanced Surface Attributes, discusses material rectangles.

Let's take a quick look at the one property panel option that is available with the plane primitive.

6. First, make sure you're in Wireframe mode so you can see the object's structure. Note that the plane object is composed of a single polygon.

7. Delete the object by pressing (DELETE) or selecting the Erase tool.

8. Now right-click on the Add Plane button in the Primitives panel to display its property panel.

9. The single available property lets you set the resolution (number of subdivisions) in the plane. The default value is 1. Change the value to 4 by clicking on the two-headed arrow and dragging the mouse a short distance to the right. Or you can click on the number 1 and enter the new value from the keyboard. As with all such value fields in trueSpace2, if you use the keyboard, you must press (ENTER) for the change to be recognized.

10. Now click the Add Plane button again. Note that the new plane is subdivided into four polygons per side, resulting in 16 polygons total in the surface (see Figure 5-5). This plane is more suitable for applying Deform operations than the single-polygon plane.

NOTE: You can also create the same subdivision with two clicks on the Quad Divide tool, which is covered in Chapter 7, Utilities and Edit Tools. Every time you select Quad Divide, it subdivides each polygon into four parts, giving you the equivalent of any resolution that's a power of the number 2 (2, 4, 8, 16, and so forth).

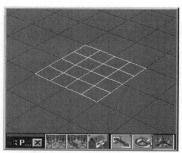

Figure 5-5 Plane object with resolution of 4

71

LESSON 2: ADDING A CUBE PRIMITIVE

The next shape in the pantheon of primitives is the cube. Let's take a look.

1. Clear the workspace of any existing objects by selecting File/Scene/New. Set your preferred display mode, Solid Render or Wireframe.

2. In the Primitives panel, click the Add Cube button (see Figure 5-1). A new cube object appears in the center of the workspace. You can also create a cube by extruding a plane with the Sweep tool, but this is much easier. As with all the primitive objects except plane, you'll have no trouble seeing it if you're in Solid Render mode (see Figure 5-6). Actually, the cube's bottom surface is coincident with the reference grid, but that's normally not a problem.

The cube is generally considered to be a more useful building block than the plane for constructing solid objects. By scaling cubes on individual axes and combining them in various ways, you can build all kinds of furniture and appliances, architectural objects such as houses and cityscapes, and much more. Thanks to trueSpace2's powerful 3D Boolean operations, which Chapter 6 explores, you can add and subtract other 3D shapes for added versatility. For example, to make an empty open-top box, you could add two cubes, scale one of them down a bit, and then subtract it from the larger one. (The trueSpace2 program also has 2D Boolean functions, which are covered in this chapter.)

3. Like the plane object, the cube has only one manipulable property: resolution. Switch to Wireframe Display mode if you're not already in it. Erase the cube you just added; then right-click the Add Cube button to display the Cube Resolution panel. Change the resolution to 5.

4. Add another cube. Note that each edge of the new cube is divided into five polygons, giving each face 25 subdivisions (see Figure 5-7).

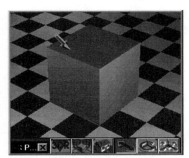

Figure 5-6 Solid Render view of newly added cube object

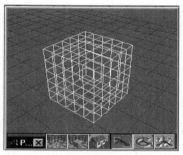

Figure 5-7 Cube object with resolution of 5

Because five is not a power of two, this resolution is not achievable by using the Quad Divide function. As with the Plane object, subdividing a cube lets you apply interesting deformations, such as convex or concave sides.

5. Save the cube as an object to disk. Select the File/Save Object menu command. When the Save Object dialog appears, enter a name such as MYCUBE under File Name: and click OK or press ENTER. The program saves the object in the native trueSpace2 format, automatically adding the .COB file name extension.

You can now load this cube into a scene with the File/Load Object command.

LESSON 3: ADDING A CYLINDER PRIMITIVE

A cylinder is essentially an extruded disk. The cylinder object is useful for modeling a number of different items, including axles, columns, and cans.

1. Clear the workspace of any existing objects by selecting File/Scene/New. Set your preferred display mode, Solid Render or Wireframe.

2. Click on the Add Cylinder button (see Figure 5-8) to place a new cylinder in the workspace. Pretty straightforward, right? As with all the primitives, the flat bottom surface is coincident with the reference plane, but that doesn't prevent you from seeing the cylinder in either viewing mode.

3. Let's examine the cylinder's adjustable properties. Right-click on the Add Cylinder button to display the Cylinder property panel (see Figure 5-9).

Now things start to get a little more interesting! Here you have three parameters to play with: Latitude, Longitude, and Top Radius.

73

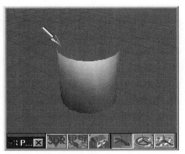

Figure 5-8 New cylinder in Solid Render mode

Cylinder		
Latitude	2	↔
Longitude	16	↔
Top Radius	1	↔

Figure 5-9 Cylinder property panel

Latitude

The Latitude property determines the number of evenly spaced "floors" or cross sections along the cylinder's length. By default, there are two: the top and the bottom. As it happens, two is also the minimum Latitude value; with one, you only have a disk. And 1,000 is the maximum value, but it's unlikely you'll ever need to use a value greater than 100 or so.

4. Go to Wireframe Display mode (if necessary). Then try changing this value and adding new cylinders. Remember to press ⌈ENTER⌉ if you use the keyboard.

5. When you're done experimenting, delete all cylinders and return the Latitude setting to its default value of 2.

In Figure 5-10, you can see cylinders with Latitude settings of 3, 5, and 10.

 TIP: Cylinders with higher resolution along the length are more malleable, thus better suited for bending into snakes, pipes, and other similar shapes.

Longitude

Longitude, as you might guess, controls the number of subdivisions around the cylinder's diameter. The default value is 16, which produces a reasonably circular cross section. Minimum value is 3, which gives a triangular cross section. Maximum value is 10,000, although what that could be useful for, I have no idea.

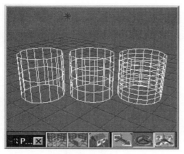

Figure 5-10 Cylinders with varying Latitude settings

6. Try adding cylinders with different Longitude values.

7. When you're done experimenting, delete all cylinders and return the Longitude setting to its default value of 16.

In Figure 5-11, you can see cylinders with Longitudes of 3, 4, 8, and 36.

Top Radius

The Top Radius parameter lets you create conical cylinders. The maximum value is the default of 1; the minimum is 0.01, which yields a cylinder that looks very much like a true cone. If you examine it closely, however, you can see that the top is actually a disk rather than a point.

TIP: You can't create a cylinder whose top is larger than its base; however, if you need one that flares outward, you can simply create a conical cylinder and flip it over. Or you can use the Point Edit tools, covered in Chapter 6, Advanced Modeling, to pick the top face and make it larger.

Figure 5-12 shows cylinders with Top Radius settings of 1.0, 0.5, and 0.01.

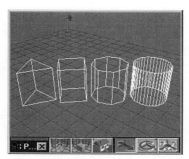

Figure 5-11 Cylinders with varying Longitude settings

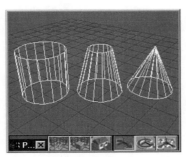

Figure 5-12 Cylinders with varying Top Radius settings

LESSON 4: ADDING A CONE PRIMITIVE

A cone is a disk extruded to a point. You can also make a cone by adding a regular polygon and then using the Tip tool (both are covered later in this chapter). Of course, the Add Cone tool is easier. You can use cones to model various conical objects, including traffic pylons, dunce caps, and ice cream cones (of course!).

1. Clear the workspace with File/Scene/New.

2. In the Primitives panel, click the Add Cone button to create a cone in the center of the workspace, as shown in Figure 5-13.

3. Right-click on the Add Cone button to see the Cone property panel.

You're back to two adjustable settings—Latitude and Longitude—just as in the Cylinder property panel, and the two settings work the same here.

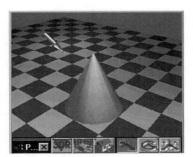

Figure 5-13 New cone in Solid Render mode

LESSON 5: ADDING A SPHERE PRIMITIVE

If you've seen more than a few 3D-rendered images, you've probably seen the ubiquitous mirror sphere hovering over a checkerboard floor. You should probably try creating one of your own at some point, if only to get it out of your system. At any rate, there's a good reason why spheres are so popular with 3D artists: No other shape so strongly suggests depth. Spheres can be used to model planets and other heavenly bodies, balls used in various athletic endeavors, and as the starting point for a head.

1. Clear the workspace. If you're in Wireframe Display mode, go to Solid Render mode.

2. Click on the Primitives panel's Add Sphere button to create your very own sphere, as shown in Figure 5-14. Although your new sphere looks spherical enough, look closely. You can see the individual flat polygons that make up the surface. Also, examine the edges for further evidence of the sphere's polygonal origins.

3. Let's see how to make a rounder sphere. Go to Wireframe Display mode to see the object structure better.

4. Right-click on the Add Sphere button to open the Sphere property panel. Once again, you have settings for Latitude and Longitude. Set them both to 36, remembering to press TAB for the first and ENTER for the second if you use the keyboard.

5. Add another sphere. It's placed directly on top of the first sphere, so select Object Move and drag the new sphere to one side of the first. Compare the structures of the two—the difference is obvious! Then return to Solid Render Display mode (see Figure 5-15).

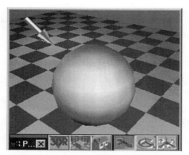

Figure 5–14 New sphere in Solid Render mode

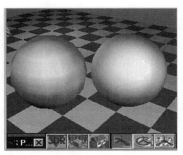

Figure 5–15 Default and high-resolution spheres in Solid Render mode

6. Of course, the usual trade-off holds here: The more complex object looks better, but it consumes considerably more memory, disk space, and rendering time. Let's take a look at the two spheres' statistics to confirm this. Select the first sphere; then right-click the Object tool to open the Object Info panel. Look at the panel's bottom-left box and note that the value next to # faces is 128. Now select the other sphere. It has more than 10 times as many faces! Now, this doesn't mean it takes 10 times longer to render; it's actually more like twice as long. But that's still a pretty significant increase in rendering times, and when you're dealing with interesting-looking (that is, complex) scenes, rendering times can become dauntingly slow—even with a fast Pentium-based computer.

7. Before leaving the Sphere object, you'll briefly explore its parameters some more in the next section. Return to Wireframe Display mode and delete both spheres. (Note that deleting the selected sphere leaves the other unselected, so you must click on it to select it before erasing it.)

Latitude and Longitude

As with the previous rounded objects, a sphere's Latitude setting determines resolution parallel to the "equator," whereas Longitude refers to the number of pole-to-pole divisions (like orange sections). You can obtain some interesting objects by varying these settings.

8. Set Latitude to its minimum value. An easy way to do this is to double-click on the existing number, press Backspace to delete it, and press ENTER. The program automatically enters the minimum value in the box (in this case, 2).

9. Now add a new sphere.

Note in Figure 5-16 that the sphere resembles two cones placed with their bases together so their tips point in opposite directions. The *trueSpace2 Reference Manual* states that the sphere object's Latitude value determines the number of horizontal circles that make up the sphere, but doesn't it seem that the number of horizontal circles is actually the Latitude value minus 1? Let's test this theory.

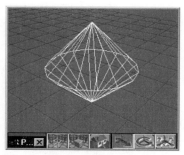

Figure 5–16 Sphere of Latitude 2

10. Delete the "sphere." Change the Latitude setting to 4 and add another sphere. Count the horizontal rings. If you counted three, you're right! It seems the theory holds. (Actually, the manual is probably referring to rings of polygons.) If you like, set the Latitude to some other values and count the horizontal rings. The Sphere object's maximum Latitude value is 1,000.

11. Delete any remaining spheres and set Latitude back to its original value of 8.

12. Set Longitude to its minimum value of 3. As with the cylinder and cone objects, the sphere object's maximum Longitude value is 10,000.

13. Click Add Sphere. The new sphere is made up of three vertical circles, giving it a triangular outline as viewed from the top (see Figure 5-17).

14. Verify this by selecting the Top View tool from the Perspective view's pop-up, third from the left in the Window group at screen bottom right. Return to perspective view by selecting Perspective view from the same pop-up.

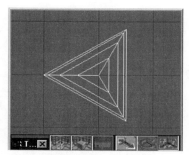

Figure 5–17 Sphere of Longitude 3, viewed from above

Here's another simple exercise: What Longitude setting would give you a square cross section as viewed from the top? Try it and see.

LESSON 6: ADDING A TORUS PRIMITIVE

The final 3D trueSpace2 shape this chapter covers is the torus, which you'll recognize if you've ever seen a doughnut or bagel. It's a mathematically complex shape, but easy to make in trueSpace2: Just click the button and it's there!

1. Clear the workspace, choose your display mode, and click the Add Torus button to create a fresh, calorie-free virtual doughnut (see Figure 5-18). You might not use the torus object every day, but it's nice to know it's there.

2. Let's take a brief look at the torus's adjustable parameters. Switch to Wireframe Display mode (if necessary). Then right-click on the Add Torus button to display its property panel. There are your familiar friends, Latitude and Longitude, accompanied by a new acquaintance, Inner Radius. The latter is used to set the torus's "fatness." For a bagel-like ring, you'd set it to a low value. Because this shape is somewhat different from the rest, let's briefly explore all three properties.

3. Press the [DELETE] key to erase the first torus. Then change Latitude to 3, the minimum value.

4. Add a new torus. As with the cylinder, you can see that Latitude determines the resolution of the torus's cross section. (See Figure 5-19.)

5. Delete the torus. Then set Latitude back to 16 and change Longitude to its minimum value, which is also 3.

6. Click Add Torus. Note that, similar to the sphere object, Longitude determines the number of vertical circles that make up the shape. (See Figure 5-20.)

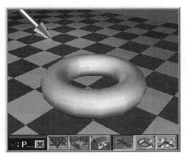

Figure 5-18 New torus in Solid Render mode

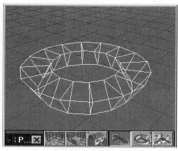

Figure 5-19 Torus of
Latitude 3

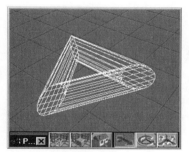

Figure 5-20 Torus of
Longitude 3

7. Delete the torus. Reset Longitude to 16 and change the Inner Radius setting to its minimum value of 0.001. Pretty bagel-like, isn't it?

8. Let's see what the torus object's maximum Inner Radius setting does. One way to determine a setting's maximum value is to double-click on the number, then enter a very large number from the keyboard. Double-click on the Inner Radius setting now, type 100, and press (ENTER). Notice that trueSpace2 resets the value to 0.999.

9. Click Add Torus and note that the new torus is about as skinny as can be, resembling a circle (see Figure 5-21).

From this you can see that the Inner Radius setting is not an absolute value, but more like a ratio. The minimum value of 0.001 gives an inner radius that's a small fraction of the outer radius, and the maximum of 0.999 yields an inner radius that's only a tiny bit smaller than the outer radius. Now you understand why the maximum Inner Radius setting is 0.999—if it were 1, the inner and outer radii would be exactly the same, and there would be no torus at all!

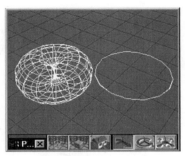

Figure 5–21 Torus with inner radius of 0.001 and torus with inner radius of 0.999

CREATING POLYGONS

All objects in trueSpace2, as well as most other 3D programs, are made up of *interconnected polygons*. What is a polygon? Actually, before I define a polygon, I have to define the *vertex*, which is simply a point in space. Take three or more vertices in different locations, connect them with a surface, and you've got a two-dimensional polygon. Some programs let you create 3D objects vertex by vertex, but trueSpace2 isn't one of them; you have to start with at least a polygon.

NOTE: Although trueSpace2 does let you construct one type of polygon point by point, this is done on a plane. In fact, you can then point edit the polygon, moving points up and down to create a 3D object. However, this isn't a good idea, because nonplanar polygons can pose rendering problems, such as errors in shading.

Once you've created a polygon, you can use the other tools discussed in this chapter and the next to make the polygon into a 3D object. As is, however, you can use the flat polygon for a sign, a sheet of paper, and the like.

In many 3D programs, all polygons must be triangular, but that isn't the case in trueSpace2. Most actually turn out to have four sides, and you can use the Polygon tool variants to make polygons with as many as 100 sides.

You'll find the Polygon tool pop-up at the right end of the Model tool group. When you first start trueSpace2, the default Polygon tool variant is Spline polygon, which looks like a liver-shaped outline.

LESSON 7: ADDING A REGULAR POLYGON

Start by resetting the program (File/Scene/New) and use Reset View if you've changed it. If you're in Solid Render Display mode, switch to Wireframe Display.

There are three types of polygons in trueSpace2: regular, irregular, and spline. I'll begin the exploration with the simplest type, which is a regular polygon, so-called because every side is the same length. With point editing, you can change the polygon's shape after adding it. Chapter 6 covers that.

1. First, position the mouse pointer over the Polygon tool (currently Spline Polygon, it's the rightmost icon in the Model tool group) and click and hold the left mouse button. When the pop-up icon menu appears, select the Regular Polygon tool (its icon is a hexagon). The Poly Modes panel appears (see Figure 5-22).

NOTE: "Poly" is short for "polygon"—the two terms are used interchangeably.

This panel contains icons for setting 2D Boolean operations, which I'll explore shortly, as well as the control you're interested in at the moment: the numeric setting for the number of sides in newly created regular polygons. By default, it's set to 6, which you'll use at the outset.

2. Position the mouse cursor near the center of the workspace. Press and hold the left mouse button and drag slowly in any direction. You'll see a hexagonal polygon appear and gradually increase in size. Note that you're setting the polygon's radius, drawing from the center to the edge, rather than its diameter, drawing from edge to edge. Try dragging the mouse in a circle and note that you can rotate the polygon as you create it.

3. Try changing the number of sides, via the Poly Modes panel, to other settings such as 3, 4, 8, and 12. Then add new polygons with each setting to see what they look like (see Figure 5-23). Once you get past 16, they start to look pretty circular.

LESSON 8: ADDING A POLYGON

Next, I'll look at what you might regard as an "irregular" polygon, which trueSpace2 just calls a polygon. This is the tool mentioned earlier, which lets you construct the polygon point by point.

Figure 5–22 The Poly Modes panel

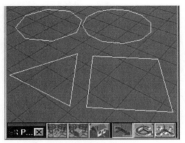

Figure 5-23 Regular polygons with 3, 4, 8, and 12 sides

1. Clear the workspace (File/Scene/New) and set the display mode to Wireframe, if necessary. Then select the Polygon tool from the pop-up icon menu.

2. Position the mouse cursor near the center of the workspace and click and release the left mouse button. This sets the polygon's first vertex; unfortunately, there's no visual indication of it. Move the pointer about an inch away in any direction, then click and release again. Note that you now have a line connecting the two points, which you created by setting the endpoint of the first side of the polygon. Click again at any other location to set a second endpoint, and you now have two sides of a triangle. To close the polygon, click the right mouse button. (This instruction appears in the Help bar during polygon creation.) This automatically draws a final line segment between the most recent endpoint and the starting point.

3. The Polygon tool is still active. Let's try a slightly different method of starting a polygon. Position the mouse cursor at the first point, press and hold the left mouse button, then drag in any direction. Notice that you're creating the first side of the polygon in a single click-and-drag operation, rather than with two clicks, as before. Position the cursor a little below and to the right of the first point and release the button.

4. Move the cursor up and to the right and click once to make a V. Now click again opposite the second point, as if you're going to make a W (see Figure 5-24).

5. Try closing this polygon by right-clicking. The computer beeps, but nothing else happens. What's going on? trueSpace2 does not let you create a polygon whose sides cross over each other, as would happen if this polygon were closed now. (Interestingly enough, you can make sides intersect via point editing, although it's neither useful nor a good idea. For example, you cannot extrude a polygon with intersecting edges.)

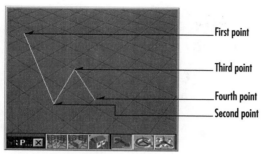

First point

Third point

Fourth point

Second point

Figure 5-24 Starting a
W-shaped polygon

6. At this point, you have several options. You could simply give trueSpace2 another
vertex from which it could close the polygon without intersecting itself. Or you
could use Undo to erase the last side. You could also choose another tool, such as
Object, to abort the operation entirely. Let's try the first option, with a slight variation. Position the mouse cursor anywhere in the workspace, press and hold the left
mouse button, and drag the mouse. You can see that, as with setting the current
polygon's first side, you can position new endpoints as you create them.

Spend a little time experimenting with the Polygon tool. You might find you get a
better idea of exactly what you're drawing from an overhead view, which you can get by
using the Top View tool from the View group in the main window. Also, once you have a
few polygons in the workspace, take a look from the Front view or Side view. Note that all
the objects are coincident with the reference plane, even though you may have drawn
them from the Perspective view. Of course, you can use the object navigation tools to
translate and rotate them to any position.

LESSON 9: ADDING A SPLINE POLYGON

The third polygon tool, Spline Polygon, is quite a bit different from the first two, although
the basic concept is similar to that of the Polygon tool. As with the latter, you select the
tool, then place points, called *nodes*, by clicking and optionally dragging. In this tutorial,
you'll learn about drawing spline polygons, plus the various adjustments available, such as
spline handles and number of segments.

1. After clearing the workspace and setting the display mode to Wireframe, select the
Spline Polygon tool from the Polygon tool pop-up (rightmost in the Model tool
group). It's the default tool in its slot, so if you're just starting the program, you
don't need to access the pop-up.

2. Place four or more points around the workspace. Try a roughly rectangular shape.
Right away you'll see several differences. First, after you place the third point
(assuming it's not colinear with the first two), you're creating a continuous curve,

not a series of straight line segments with sharp corners. Second, notice the blue dots, or *segments*, along the curves. Third, there's a short green line emanating from each new (green) point, or node, that you place.

3. Close the polygon by right-clicking.

Note that the polygon remains "active." It now has a double green line tangent to the last/first node. This is called a handle, and its function is to let you change the shape of the curves on either side of the node to which it's attached. The Help bar is telling you to Move point, or drag end point of handle (left button: both handles, right: change angle) What is the meaning of this cryptic message?

Handles and Nodes

Let's start with the first part of the message, about moving the point.

4. Position the mouse cursor anywhere in the workspace (except on the handle ends). Press and hold the left mouse button and drag in any direction. By doing so, you're moving the currently selected node, as indicated by the attached handles. You can see that this affects not only the two curves attached to the node but the curves attached to *them* as well. So, assuming there are at least four nodes in the polygon, you're controlling four curves by moving one node. That's power!

5. Next, click on one of the dots at either end of the green line and drag toward the center of the line, shortening the handle. Note that the curves on either side of the node straighten out, losing their curvature. Now drag away from the center, causing the handle to become longer. The curves become exaggerated (see Figure 5-25). The term for the property you're adjusting is *tension*.

6. Try dragging in other directions; you'll find that you can influence the curves' shapes in various ways, even creating a loop, although that's not a good idea. Release the mouse button when you're done. By changing the tangent angle between the handles and the spline curve, you're adjusting the *bias*.

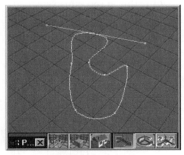

Figure 5-25 Exaggerating the curves by extending the handle

TIP: You can restrict manipulation to tension only by holding down the (SHIFT) key before clicking on the handle, and you can restrict manipulation to bias only by holding down the (CTRL) key before clicking on the handle.

7. Now try clicking and dragging in an empty part of the workspace. Instead of moving the node, as before, you're still moving the handle. If you want to go back to moving the node, this time you must specify that explicitly, by clicking on the node and then dragging.

8. Release the mouse button; then right-click and drag on one of the handle endpoints. If you drag parallel to the handle, there's no difference from using the left button— you're adjusting the tension. But if you drag in any other direction, you can see that you're changing the angle between the handle's left and right sides, altering the curves on either side accordingly (see Figure 5-26). In this way, you're adjusting the continuity. If you drag the handle toward the polygon, you can make a sharp corner, and if you drag it away, you make a sharp dip.

 TIP: To restrict right-mouse-button manipulation to continuity only, hold down the (CTRL) key before clicking on the handle.

9. Now click on any of the other green vertices in your shape. This selects the node, with which you can perform the same reshaping operations as with the previous points.

Spline Segments

What about the blue dots? Take a look at the Draw Path panel (see Figure 5-27) that appeared when you selected the Spline Polygon tool back in Step 1 of this lesson. Notice the bottom value box for Segments. Currently, it's set to the default, which is 10. That means each section of the curve, between nodes you place, is broken up into 10

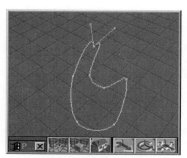

Figure 5–26 Making a point with the right mouse button

straight-line segments. This is something you can alter only *before* placing or adding nodes. That is, each time you go to place a new node, if you first change the Segments setting, you can determine the resolution of the curvature of the line between the new node and the previous one. Let's see how this works.

10. To start a new polygon, in the Draw Path panel, select the Start New Spline button (the third button from the left in the top row, a red dot with an arrow emanating from it, pointing to the upper right). When you do so, the previous polygon is deselected.

11. Place two nodes a few inches away from each other in the workspace. So far, so good; you're getting the same results as when you started the previous spline poly.

12. Before you place the next node, position the mouse cursor over the double arrow in the panel's lower-right corner. Press the left button and drag leftward until the setting is 1, which is the lowest it can be. Place another node at right angles to the first two. You can see that the first part becomes curved, but the second part is a straight line. That is because, with only one segment, there's no room for curvature.

13. Change the Segments setting to 2 and place another node at the fourth corner of a rectangle. You can see that this third section has a single blue vertex in its center, giving it an angled "curvature" (see Figure 5-28).

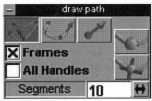

Figure 5-27 The Draw Path panel

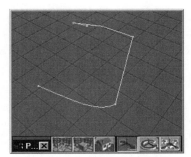

Figure 5-28 Spline polygon with 10, 1, and 2 segments in counterclockwise order from bottom

14. Now I'll show you how you can edit the polygon as you draw it. In the Draw Path panel, the top row's second icon, Draw new spline point, is highlighted. Click on the first icon, Point move, in the upper-left corner.

15. Click and drag on the last mode you placed to demonstrate that you can position it anywhere. Next, click and drag on its handle's endpoint, noting that you can move it only in line with the handle. Finally, click on the second and third nodes and practice moving them and their handles. As you're working with one of the handles, while you're dragging with the left mouse button, click and hold the right button too. Drag to change the handle angle, then release the right mouse button to return to manipulating the entire handle.

Other Controls

Before moving on, let's look at the other Draw Path panel settings. The Frames and All Handles settings let you toggle display of the blue dots and all handles.

16. Click in the box next to Frames to turn off display of the blue dots. These are called *frames* because spline paths are also used in animation, and the number of frames determines how quickly an object moves from one keyframe to the next. Chapter 11, Animation, explores this further. Turn Frames back on.

17. Click in the box next to All Handles. You can see that all the current spline poly's handles are now displayed. However, now there's no way to tell which node is selected, so it's best to leave this toggle turned off. Click again in the box to disable display of all the handles.

18. Let's look at the two controls on the right-hand side of the Draw Path panel. Click on the upper one, Add new spline point. Then click in the center of either segment in the two-segment side (the last one you placed). In Figure 5-28, that could be the upper-right segment, at about 2 o'clock in the poly. When you do this, two things happen: The Add new spline point button turns itself off and a new node is placed in the center of the section, with new frames on either side. Try changing the number of segments and adding nodes in different places on the poly. (You'll need to reselect the Add new spline point button each time.)

NOTE: You won't be able to add a node on the one-segment section. Apparently you need at least one frame in a spline poly section before you can subdivide it.

19. Finally, under Add new spline point, you have the Delete spline point button. Click on it now and note that it has the immediate effect of deleting the current node. Fortunately, this is undoable. Try combining multiple spline-point deletions with multiple clicks of the Undo tool. There's quite a bit of flexibility and power here.

20. Before leaving spline polygons, one last point. Draw a new spline polygon, close it, and then select the Object tool. The spline becomes a white plane. It's now a simple polygon, and there's no way to use the spline editing tools to modify it further. You can, however, use the Point Edit and Deform Object tools to change its shape. Chapter 6 looks at those.

NOTE: By right-clicking on the Spline Polygon tool, you access the Spline property panel, which gives you presets for sharp, smooth, and very smooth corners. You can open a numeric setting panel for tension, continuity, and bias by right-clicking on any of the presets. Chapter 11 covers the Spline Property panel in greater depth, and you can find additional information in the Help file.

LESSON 10: BOOLEAN OPERATIONS WITH POLYGONS

Let's take a look at *Boolean operations* on polygons. They're named after George Boole, a 19th-century British mathematician and logician who developed a calculus of symbolic logic. In computer graphics, you can create new shapes by adding, subtracting, and finding the intersection of existing regular and irregular polygons using techniques based on Boole's findings.

1. Clear the workspace.

2. Select the Regular Polygon tool. When you do so, the Poly Modes panel appears (see Figure 5-22). All its iconic tools except the top left one, Draw new polygon (which you're currently using), are grayed out and inaccessible.

3. Draw a new polygon of any size and any number of sides. As soon as you release the mouse button to finish adding the polygon, the second, third, and fourth Poly Modes panel buttons "light up" and become accessible (see Figure 5-29). When you select one of these *before* drawing another polygon, the second interacts with the first according to Boolean mathematics.

Adding Polygons

Using the Boolean *union* operation, you can automatically and seamlessly combine newly drawn polygons with existing ones.

4. Select the top right button, Union new polygon with selected polygon. Change the number of sides if you like.

5. Then, starting with the mouse cursor on a corner or an edge of the first polygon, draw a second object of any size (but don't let it entirely cover the first). Release the mouse button and the program "ANDs" the two together, creating a single polygon consisting of the combined shapes of both (see Figure 5-30).

Figure 5–29 The Poly Modes panel after drawing a polygon

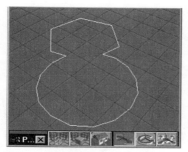

Figure 5–30 Union of a six-sided polygon with a 16-sided polygon

6. Try drawing some more polygons, changing the shape and size as you like. Also try switching between drawing regular and "irregular" polygons. As shown in Figure 5-31, you'll find you can create very complex shapes with relative ease using this technique.

By the way, polygons don't have to intersect to be ANDed. If you draw nonintersecting polys using the Union option, you're creating a single polygon with noncontiguous segments.

Subtracting Polygons

The Boolean *subtract* operation lets you cut new shapes out of existing ones.

7. Press the DELETE key to remove your wacky multipolygon from the workspace and note that this automatically selects the Object tool. Again, select the Regular Polygon tool and draw a polygon.

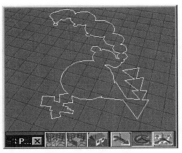

Figure 5–31 Complex polygon created by ANDing many regular polys

8. This time, before starting another shape, select the third Poly Modes panel tool, Subtract new polygon from selected polygon. Again, draw a polygon starting at the edge or corner of the first. Don't make it larger than the first. When you release the mouse button, you'll see that the second polygon has indeed been subtracted from the first, and you're left with the portion of the original one not covered by the second.

9. Now try drawing a third, smaller polygon entirely enclosed by the existing one. In Wireframe mode, it's hard to tell, but you've actually created a hole in the first one. Switch temporarily to Solid Render mode, or use the Render Object tool, to see the "holey" shape, as in Figure 5-32.

10. Switch back to Wireframe Display mode and try drawing another polygon entirely outside the first. Nothing happens! That's because, when you subtract a shape from empty space, you're left with empty space (there's no such thing as "negative space").

11. Once again, try alternating between subtracting regular and "irregular" polygons from the first shape. When you want to start a new shape, simply select Draw new polygon in the Poly Modes panel's upper-left corner.

Intersecting Polygons

Let's look at the third Boolean option, Intersect new polygon with selected polygon. The intersection of two polygons is defined as the space occupied by both. You can illustrate this graphically by drawing a new polygon, selecting the Intersect icon from the Poly Modes panel, and then drawing another polygon that overlaps the first. The result is a polygon consisting of only the overlap area. You can use this, for example, to trim the sides of a circle with a square, leaving straight sides and rounded corners, as in Figure 5-33.

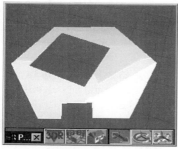

Figure 5–32 Hexagon with squares subtracted from edge and interior

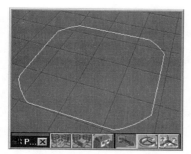

Figure 5–33 Intersection of square and circular polygons

Experiment with intersecting various types of polygons to see all the different combinations you can come up with.

Other Important Points About Booleans

To close this lesson, here are a few important items you should know about performing Boolean operations on polygons:

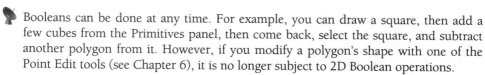 Booleans can be done at any time. For example, you can draw a square, then add a few cubes from the Primitives panel, then come back, select the square, and subtract another polygon from it. However, if you modify a polygon's shape with one of the Point Edit tools (see Chapter 6), it is no longer subject to 2D Boolean operations.

You can perform Boolean operations between existing 2D polygons, and between 3D objects and 2D polygons, but you'll need to use the 3D Boolean functions. You'll learn about those in Chapter 6.

You can perform 2D Boolean operations on "frozen" spline polygons, but not with them. For example, you can subtract an irregular polygon from a spline poly, but not vice versa.

If you change the setup in the Poly Modes panel, all settings stay that way until you quit the program or change them again. That is, if you're subtracting polygons, go away to use a different program function, and then return after selecting a polygon, you'll still be in subtract mode.

LESSON 11: ADDING TEXT

Before you move on to examining tools for converting polygons to solid objects, let's take a look at a specialized but very handy polygon-creation tool; it's used for adding text. Actually, there are two variants of this tool: Add Vertical Text and Add Horizontal Text. You'll find them both in the middle of the Primitives panel, under the Camera icon.

1. Clear the workspace, then open the Primitives panel, if it isn't already open. Select the Add Vertical Text tool—it's the upper ABC button in the Primitives panel.

2. Note that a white line now appears in the center of the workspace. This is your text cursor. You can reposition it by clicking the mouse anywhere you like.

3. Simply enter your text from the keyboard (*don't* press ⟨ENTER⟩). To enter another text phrase, click in a different part of the workspace.

4. To finish entering text, simply select another tool.

Note that this text is vertical, that is, perpendicular to the reference plane (see Figure 5-34). To create text that lies flat on the reference plane, use the Add Horizontal Text tool, immediately below Add Vertical Text in the Primitives panel.

Figure 5–34 Vertical text in various fonts

Changing the Font

The trueSpace2 Add Text tools can use almost any TrueType font installed in your system. To change the font before or during text entry, right-click on either Add Text tool. This opens the Font requester (see Figure 5-35). It works just like a font requester in many other programs. You can choose the font, style, and point size from scrolling lists, and you see a sample of the current choice. There's also a Script pop-up list, which shows the available language scripts for the specified font. Choose the one that corresponds to the language for which your operating system is set up.

 TIP: Not all TrueType fonts work with trueSpace2's Add Text tools. If you start typing and the cursor moves but no characters appear, try a different font.

WORKING WITH SWEEP, LATHE, AND OTHER MODELING TOOLS

Once you've created a polygon, you can use these tools to turn it into a 3D object. For example, you can create solid-looking logos from 2D text with the Sweep tool, or a bicycle tire from a U-shaped poly with the Lathe tool.

LESSON 12: SWEEPING POLYGONS

The Sweep tool is used for *extruding* 2D polygons into 3D shapes. The process of extrusion is commonly compared to pushing Play-Doh™ through a cut-out opening. Extrusion is also used frequently in manufacturing. It's among the most important functions in trueSpace2 modeling, and one for which you'll doubtless find many uses.

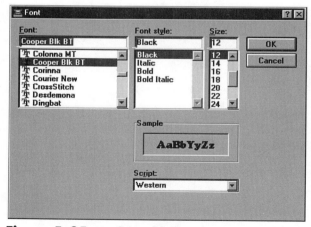

Figure 5-35 trueSpace2's Font requester

1. Start by clearing the workspace and setting the display mode to Wireframe. Add a polygon using any of the techniques you've learned so far in this chapter. For simplicity's sake, I'll use the default hexagonal regular polygon as an example here.

2. Next, click on the Sweep tool, which is the default variant in its pop-up, found second from the left in the Model group. This has an immediate dual effect: First, the polygon is extruded upward into a three-dimensional shape. Second, the Point Navigation panel appears (see Figure 5-36).

Notice that the new upper layer of the extruded polygon is outlined in green and the lower original layer is outlined in aqua. This visual code denotes that you now have two "floors" available for manipulation with the Point Navigation controls, and that the upper green one is "live" and ready to manipulate.

Editing Swept Polygons

Are you ready? Let's do the manipulation!

NOTE: Look in the Point Navigation panel, and see that the upper-left icon, Point Move, is highlighted. This is somewhat misleading, because you're actually manipulating a polygon, but trueSpace2 uses "Point Navigation" to refer to any manipulation of part of an object, so you'll have to get used to it.

3. Move the mouse cursor into an empty part of the workspace. Press and hold the left button and drag in various directions to move the upper polygon parallel to the reference grid (see Figure 5-37). Release the left button.

4. Now press and hold the right button and again drag in different directions to move the polygon vertically.

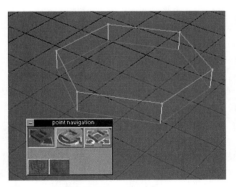

Figure 5–36 Extruded hexagon with Point Navigation panel

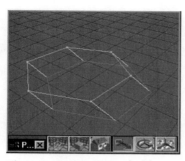

Figure 5-37 Extruded hexagon
with top floor moved

This works very much the same as the Object Move function, except this time you're just moving part of an object, so you're actually reshaping the entire object while doing so. When you move the polygon sideways, you're inducing skew by slanting the sides, and when you move it vertically, you're changing the object's height.

5. While you're at it, click on the bottom floor (outlined in aqua), causing it to become green, or "live." The upper floor turns aqua. Now you can manipulate the bottom floor just as you did the upper floor. When you're done, select the upper floor again.

6. You can also rotate and scale the floors. Use the standard object navigation techniques you learned in Chapter 4, Navigation: Getting Around in trueSpace2, with the Point Navigation panel's Point Rotate and Point Scale tools. Try rotating the upper floor slightly, first with the left button and then with the right, to give the object a small twist. Then scale it down a little.

7. Now click a few more times on the Sweep tool. Surprise! Your manipulations are preserved and extended in subsequent operations, so instead of extruding straight up, you get something like object in Figure 5-38.

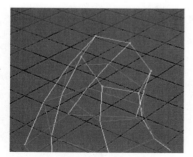

Figure 5-38 Swept hexagon
with top floor manipulated,
then swept twice more

Now you have several floors, with the top one selected. Try manipulating any or all of them in various ways, just for a little hands-on experience.

 TIP: When sweeping, you can subdivide floors by first right-clicking on the Sweep tool, which causes the Sweep/Tip panel to appear. Increase the Segments setting to create any number of subdivisions. This gives smoother curves to edges between floors when manipulated. You can also use this panel to preset the Sweep offset on the x , y, and z axes.

Using Sweep Paths

You probably haven't realized it, but during this process you've been creating a *path*, or *macro*, that you can use to apply the same sequence of operations to other polygons. Here's how:

1. From the Sweep tool pop-up, select the Macro/Sweep tool (fourth from the top, looks like an oval aqua outline). A segmented line now extends from your object's top floor tool (see Figure 5-39).

NOTE: This is a somewhat abstracted visual representation of the steps you used to create the current object. As a one-dimensional line, it can't show scaling or z-axis rotation, but it can show rotation on the x and/or y axes and z-axis translation.

2. The act of invoking the Macro/Sweep tool places a copy of the path in memory, from which it can now be recalled to sweep another polygon in exactly the same way. To do this, simply draw or select another polygon. Then click the Macro/Sweep tool twice: once to recall the macro to the object and again to perform the sweep according to the macro (see Figure 5-40). Note that, after you click the

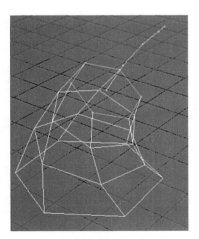

Figure 5-39 Macro/Sweep path extending from object

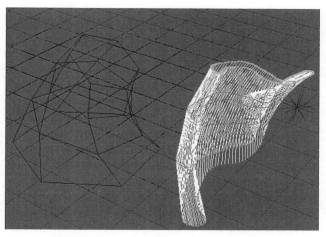

Figure 5–40 Spline poly swept with hexagon's macro

first time, the Help bar tells you that you can Drag line to rotate macro.... You can use either mouse button to rotate the macro on its z axis only. Try it out on another poly.

Multiple Simultaneous Sweeping

Now here's where things start to get really interesting. One of trueSpace2's truly unique features is the ability to extrude simultaneously any number of polygons belonging to the same object.

3. To demonstrate this, delete any existing objects. Then add a sphere from the Primitives panel.

4. Select the Point Edit: Context tool, which is the first icon in the Model Group. (Chapter 6 takes a closer look at this tool and its variants.)

5. Click in the middle of one of the sphere's faces. Be careful not to click on an edge or vertex. You'll see the rectangular face outlined in green.

6. Press and hold the (CTRL) key and select any other face not adjacent to the first. In this case, you could also use the (SHIFT) key.

7. Select the Macro/Sweep tool twice. With the first click, you'll see your macro extending from the first polygon. With the second, both faces are extruded according to the path (see Figure 5-41). Pretty nifty, eh?

Of course, you can sweep multiple object faces simultaneously with the regular Sweep tool as well.

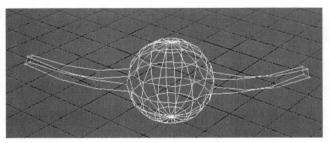

Figure 5–41 Sphere's faces swept with macro

LESSON 13: USING THE PATH LIBRARY

What if you've created a path you really like and want to use it in future sessions? Or what if you want to sweep a polygon according to a spline poly's outline? That's where trueSpace2's *Path library* comes in! Later, you'll see that you can even sweep polygons with an animation path, and vice versa.

1. Using the Path library is very easy. You already have a path from Lesson 12, so call it up. Select or create a polygon, and then select the Macro/Sweep tool, causing the path to appear.

2. Next, from the Libraries tool group, select the Path Library tool (in the center of the group). This brings up the Path Library panel, shown in Figure 5-42. Scroll through the list of existing macros to see what's available.

3. To add your currently active path, simply click the Add Path to Library button in the lower-left corner. This works just like the Material library's comparable function, which you may recall from the Quick Start tutorial in Chapter 3, Quick Start Tutorial: A Guided Tour of Major Features. There is a new addition at the bottom of the list, named Macro,1 (you may have to scroll the list down to see it). It's highlighted in magenta to show it's currently active.

4. Rename the path. Click on its name in the list to place it in the box in the panel's upper-left corner. Position the mouse cursor over the box; it turns into a text cursor, and the Help bar tells you how to rename the path. The easiest way is to double-click in the box, then simply type a new name, such as "my path." Don't forget to

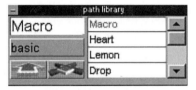

Figure 5–42 Path Library panel

press the ENTER key, or it won't "take." To make the addition permanent, save the library using the Load/Save Path Library button, which displays the name of the current library (basic, by default).

5. To sweep another polygon with the same path, add or select a polygon, select the Macro/Sweep tool, select your path in the Path Library list, and then click the Macro/Sweep tool again.

Sweeping with Spline Polys

You can also use an open or closed spline poly as a sweep path via the Path library.

1. Clear the workspace, then add a small three- or four-point spline polygon, but don't close it.

2. Click the Path Library panel's Add Path to Library button and note that a new entry named Path has been added to the library. Rename it if you like.

3. Add a polygon, say, a four-sided regular poly. Make it small, so you can easily see the results of the sweep. You can see that the spline poly is automatically closed when you select the Regular Polygon tool.

4. Select Macro/Sweep and click on your path's name in the Path library. It gets attached to the polygon.

5. Rotate it if you like, then click Macro/Sweep again to perform the path extrusion. The left-hand object in Figure 5-43 illustrates the result; I've added a polygon from the Path library to show you the sweep path's shape (see the last paragraph in this lesson for an explanation). All floors in the swept object are parallel to the original polygon, resulting in a squashed appearance at the top of the object.

6. Let's try a variation on the Macro/Sweep function. Add another small poly and reselect the Macro/Sweep tool to add the same path.

7. Right-click on the Macro/Sweep tool. The Macro panel appears with a Rotate numeric setting and a Bend button. In the panel, click on the Bend button.

8. Select the Macro/Sweep tool again. This time, each floor in the swept object is created perpendicular to the Sweep path, giving a more natural appearance at the top of the object (see the right-hand object in Figure 5-43).

NOTE: Unfortunately, there doesn't seem to be any way to turn Bend off, other than by using a different Sweep tool variant first. Also, the Angle setting in the Macro panel, which is supposed to let you adjust the angle of the path to the extruded object, seems to be broken. Of course, you can adjust the angle interactively by left-button dragging in the workspace.

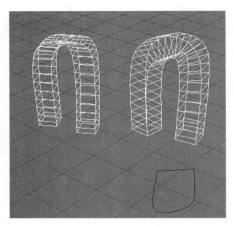

Figure 5–43 Square poly swept along spline poly outline, without and with Bend

9. While you're here, let's see what sort of paths already exist in the library. Click Undo or press CTRL-Z and then click on the various Path library entries. Path names such as Lemon and Heart are pretty self-evident, but what about Glass, which is a straight line? Try it on a round polygon and see—it's martini time!

You can also use the objects stored in the Path library as polygons. Clear the workspace, then select some of the Path library entries to add them as polygons. Most versatile, that Path library!

NOTE: Of course, trueSpace2 doesn't support one-dimensional polygons, so the Glass and Macro,1 paths don't work for adding polygons.

LESSON 14: USING THE LATHE TOOL

The Lathe tool is analogous to the Sweep tool, except Lathe is used to sweep polys along circular or spiral paths. Let's take a look.

1. Clear the workspace, then add a polygon. For the heck of it, use the Lemon preset from the Path library, but you're welcome to use any of the methods you've learned so far.

2. From the Sweep tool pop-up, select the Lathe tool variant (third from the top). This adds the default lathe path to the polygon, as shown in Figure 5-44.

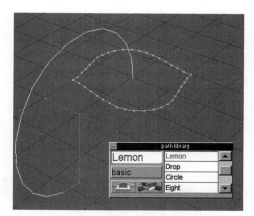

Figure 5–44 Poly with default lathe path

3. While you're at it, let's take a look at the Lathe property panel. Right-click on the Lathe tool to open the panel (see Figure 5-45). You can see that the _-circle (Angle=270°) lathe path extends from the center of the polygon for two grid units (Radius=2) along the x axis (Rotation=0), and that it consists of 16 segments (marked by the blue dots).

4. You can adjust all these settings and more, but for now, let's see what the defaults do. Select the Lathe tool again and check out the result (see Figure 5-46, in which the object has been rotated to give you a better idea of the shape). This is a fairly complex object, so you might want to switch temporarily to Solid Render mode to get a better look.

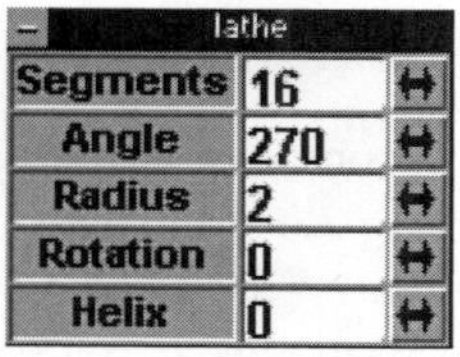

lathe		
Segments	16	
Angle	270	
Radius	2	
Rotation	0	
Helix	0	

Figure 5–45 Lathe property panel with default settings

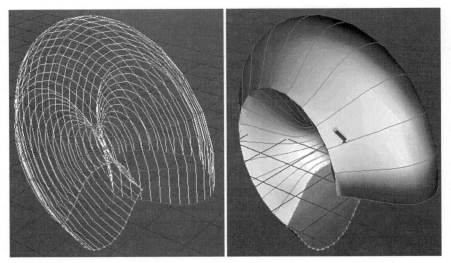

Figure 5–46 Lathed lemon-shaped polygon, Wireframe and Solid views

Note that, as with a polygon that's been swept several times, there are a number of floors, outlined in aqua. In fact, the Point Navigation panel has shown up again, so you can manipulate any of the floors. Try it now. The Move and Scale operations are particularly impressive, because they affect the shape of the entire object.

Adjusting Lathe Settings

Okay, let's go back and look at the Lathe parameters.

5. Click the Undo tool or press CTRL-Z repeatedly until you're returned to the polygon in its unlathed state. Also, reopen the Lathe property panel, which closed when you performed the lathe.

NOTE: You may notice that the path has been rotated 180° around the vertical axis from its original position, although the panel's Rotation setting doesn't reflect this. This isn't exactly a bug, but more like an "undocumented feature." Depending on whether the lathed shape is symmetrical or not, this can cause problems.

6. Set the path back to where it was. Position the mouse cursor over the either end of the horizontal "cross bar" at the center of the lathe path (see Figure 5-47), click and hold the left button, then drag the mouse in a clockwise or counterclockwise half-circle.

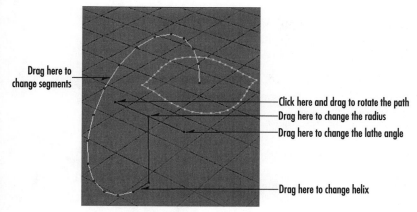

Drag here to change segments

Click here and drag to rotate the path
Drag here to change the radius
Drag here to change the lathe angle

Drag here to change helix

Figure 5–47 Lathe path with descriptions of interactive functions

As you drag, you'll see the path rotate. Try to end up with the lathe path at the same size and position as at the start. Not too easy, is it? In many cases, eyeballing the settings works well, but when you need exact results, it's nice to have the numeric alternative. In the Property panel, set Rotation to 180.

7. You can change the Rotation and Radius settings at the same time interactively by dragging on the cross bar anywhere between the ends and the center, and you can change the Radius setting interactively by dragging on the bar's center point. Try both now.

8. The interactive Radius setting has a "snap" feature that lets you lathe around a specific edge of the polygon being lathed. Drag the horizontal cross bar *slowly* toward the polygon and when it gets very close, notice how it jumps to the edge, and that you have to drag a short distance before it starts moving again. If you don't get the snap, you may have to rotate the polygon a bit first. This is easier to see on a polygon with a fairly large edge, such as a triangle or a square.

9. To change the lathe angle, click and drag on the vertical blue line that extends in a perpendicular direction from the center of the cross bar (it connects the cross bar to the path). If you drag it toward the polygon, it stops when the two ends of the lathe path meet, which is 360°, or a full circle.

10. To change the number of segments, and thus the smoothness of the lathe path, click and hold on the path and drag leftward to decrease the number of segments and rightward to increase the number. The minimum number of segments is three, yielding a triangular path. The maximum is 10,000, although it's unlikely you'll ever need a lathe path of anywhere near that resolution.

Lathing Helically

What if you want a helical lathe path? This can be useful, for example, when creating screw threads, party streamers, and other similar shapes. That's where the Helix control comes in.

11. You can adjust this interactively by clicking and dragging on the blue segment at the end of the lathe path. Try it now, dragging left and right, and notice that there's a snap point at the center.

12. Set Helix to 1 or so, then grab the lathe angle control again and drag to the right. Notice that the angle setting no longer maxes out at 360, but can go as far as you like. However, the Segments setting stays the same, so the longer the path, the more angular it becomes. Of course, in such a case, it's best to increase the number of segments as well. See Figure 5-48 for an example of the type of object you can create using these techniques.

Try creating helical lathes with various settings and polygons. This is a powerful and useful tool.

Closing Comments About Lathing

Here are some other things to know about lathing:

You can reposition the polygon while adjusting the lathe path by simply dragging it, or even clicking on an empty part of the workspace and dragging.

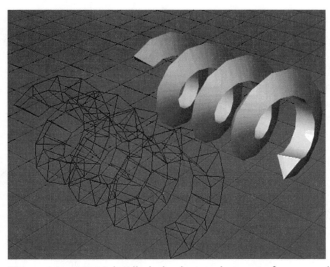

Figure 5–48 Helically lathed triangle in wireframe and solid

Thanks to trueSpace2's relatively nonmodal design, you can use any of the Object Navigation and Eye Navigation tools at any time during adjustment of the lathe path. To return to adjusting the path, click and drag directly on its control elements.

To make a spiral object, simply scale one end of the lathed object using Point Scale.

As with the Spline Polygon and Sweep tools, once you select another tool, the object is "set" and you can no longer go back and use the spline editing functions.

LESSON 15: USING THE TIP TOOL

This one's a no-brainer. The Tip tool simply sweeps polygons to a point—not particularly useful, but if you want to create a spiked mace ball for a medieval knight, it does the trick. If you're planning to texture-map the object, though, the Tip tool can cause mapping problems. In that case, it's better to use the standard Sweep tool, then scale the new floor down until it's very small.

To use the Tip tool, add or select a polygon or polygons. Then select the Tip tool from the Sweep pop-up (second from the top).

As with the Sweep and Lathe tools, using Tip brings up the Point Navigation panel, letting you manipulate the tip. However, because the new floor is a single point, you can only move it, not rotate or scale it.

To bring up the Tip property panel, right-click on the Tip tool. This offers numeric settings for the number of segments, as well as the tip's X, Y, and Z location.

WARNING: The panel doesn't seem to have been quite finished, programming-wise, because changing the X, Y, and Z settings doesn't have any effect. However, the settings do show the result of moving the tip interactively with Point Move. The panel's Segments setting affects subsequent Tip operations, determining the number of subdivisions between the polygon and its pointy little head (see Figure 5-49).

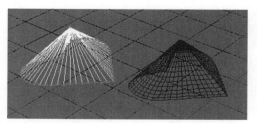

Figure 5–49 Heart-shaped polygon tipped with 1 and 15 segments

LESSON 16: USING THE BEVEL TOOL

The Bevel tool works on any polygon, but is particularly useful for adding a professional look to extruded text, particularly in plain fonts. Let's try it now.

1. Clear the workspace, then add some text and use Sweep to extrude it. Then select the Bevel tool from the Sweep pop-up (fifth from the top). This performs the beveling operation (see Figure 5-50).

2. Right-click on the Bevel tool to open the Bevel property panel. Note that the Point navigation panel does *not* appear. Beveled surfaces may appear to be simply swept and scaled-down polygons, but they're actually a special case.

3. Try dragging the mouse slowly in an empty portion of the workspace, using either button. Dragging to the left pushes the beveled surface back in toward the text and enlarges it, ending up flush with and the same size as the text's front surface, whereas dragging to the right extends the bevel and reduces its size. Once you get past a certain point, the bevel edges actually cross over themselves and start to grow larger again. This is not a good thing, so try to avoid it.

4. While adjusting the bevel interactively, notice that the Angle setting in the Bevel property panel doesn't change. This determines the angle between the bevel edge and the normal-to-the-beveled surface (that is, the sides of the extruded text). To adjust it, click and drag on the double-headed arrow to the right of the setting. You

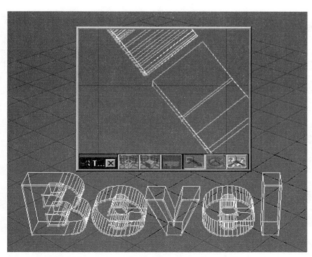

Figure 5–50 Swept and beveled text from Perspective and Top views

can see this more easily by viewing it from the top or side. Setting Angle to 0 makes the bevel go straight out, and setting it to less than 0 makes the bevel front surface larger than the original surface, which isn't particularly useful. If you set Angle to an amount greater than 45, creating a shallow bevel, again be careful that the bevel edges don't cross over themselves; you may have to reduce the Bevel setting to compensate for this.

TIP: Creating text with a rounded bevel in trueSpace2 isn't very easy, but it's possible. First, extrude the text and bevel it a very short distance using a low Angle setting (15 or so). Select any Point Edit: Faces tool; then use Bevel again at the same distance with a slightly higher Angle setting (say, 25). Continue this routine until you achieve the desired bevel roundedness (see Figure 5-51).

WHAT NOW?

You can see from this preliminary view that trueSpace2 offers a truly impressive amount of modeling power. That's only the tip of the iceberg, though. If you're impressed now, you'll be blown away by what's in Chapter 6! Meanwhile, spend as much time as possible practicing with the tools you've learned so far, and you'll be that much better prepared for what's to come.

Figure 5–51 Text with rounded bevel

ADVANCED MODELING

This chapter is not a course in building specific complex objects—like the Taj Mahal or (even more complex) the human body. Much like the rest of this book, here in Chapter 6 you'll find a thorough introduction to trueSpace2's advanced modeling tools, with as much arcane knowledge as I can think of. You take it from there.

USING TRUESPACE2'S HEAVY CONSTRUCTION EQUIPMENT

This chapter covers the following tools for advanced modeling:

- Detailed Object Editing: Using the Point Edit tools for manipulating parts of objects

- Object Deformation and Sculpt Surface: Two powerful sets of tools for manipulating objects as if they were made of clay

- 3D Boolean operations: Combining three-dimensional shapes for unprecedented modeling power

NOTE: If you're interested in learning how to use these tools to create truly complex and intricate objects, you should subscribe to Caligari's excellent trueSpace Internet mailing list; you can find out how in Appendix A, Additional Resources, of this book.

This is a heavy construction zone, so don your hard hat, roll up your sleeves, and let's get busy!

WHAT IS POINT EDITING?

Point editing is the generic term that trueSpace2 uses to refer to direct manipulation of an object's vertices, edges, and faces (collectively known as *entities*). Remember, a *vertex* is a point in space; a collection of vertices, connected by straight-line *edges*, is used to define an object's structure; and the *face,* or *polygon*, is a flat area outlined by edges, used to give objects apparent solidity. Point editing is about the closest to real-world sculpting that you can get with computer software. Point editing also comprises some unique operations called Slice, Separate, and dimensional promotion. I'll cover all these in the lessons of this chapter.

LESSON 1: MANIPULATING VERTICES

In Chapter 5, Basic Modeling, Lesson 12, you used the Point Edit: Context tool to select two faces (or polygons) in a sphere. Let's take a closer look at it now, along with its cousins: Point Edit: Vertices, Point Edit: Edges, and Point Edit: Faces (see Figure 6-1). As you can probably guess, these three tools let you work with an object's vertices, edges, and faces, respectively. Point Edit: Context lets you work with all three or any combination thereof. Let's start with vertices and work our way up to context.

1. Start trueSpace2 or, if it's already running, clear the workspace of any objects. Make sure you're in Wireframe Display mode.

2. Use the Primitives panel to add a cube.

Figure 6-1 The Point Edit: Context, Point Edit: Vertices, Point Edit: Edges, and Point Edit: Faces tools

3. Position the mouse cursor over the Point Edit: Context tool (leftmost in the Model tool group). Press and hold the left mouse button and, when the pop-up menu appears, select the Point Edit: Vertices tool (see Figure 6-1). Notice that the Context icon displays a brown highlighted edge (upper left), vertex (center), and face (lower right), but the Vertices tool has only a vertex highlighted.

4. When you select the Point Edit: Vertices tool, the Point Navigation panel (see Figure 6-2) opens with the Point Move tool selected. Also, the Help bar now displays the message Pick Vertex and/or Move it. That's pretty much what you're going to do here. But first, to see better what's going on, use the New View pop-up and open a New Front view. When the window appears, drag it to the upper-left or upper-right corner of the screen so it's not in the way.

5. Try clicking on the cube's various corners. The vertex at each corner turns green as you click on it to indicate it's selected. When you click on a different one, the previous vertex's highlighting is turned off. Finish by selecting the vertex closest to your point of view, as shown in Figure 6-3. Later you'll learn how to select multiple vertices for simultaneous manipulation.

Using the Object Coordinate System with Vertices

There are a few surprises in store with trueSpace2's point-editing system. This section looks at some of them and offers explanations of the underlying principles.

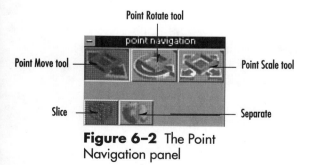

Figure 6-2 The Point Navigation panel

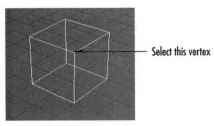

Select this vertex

Figure 6–3 Select the vertex
closest to your point of view

1. Move the mouse cursor into an empty part of the workspace and press and hold the left button. Drag the mouse left and right and watch the vertex follow the mouse movement, just as with moving an object.

2. Now drag the mouse forward and back, and note in the Front view that the vertex is actually moving vertically. Wait a second; what's going on here? Aren't you supposed to need the right mouse button for vertical movement?

3. Well, let's try that. Release the left button, click and hold the right button, and drag the mouse forward and back. You are still getting vertical movement, but now it's at right angles to the previous movement.

4. Let's confirm that y-axis movement is at a 45-degree angle to what you may have thought it was supposed to be. At the right end of the Help bar, click on the X button to disable x-axis motion. Then left-button drag the mouse vertically in the workspace. You're getting pretty much the same movement as in Step 2.

5. Now reenable x-axis motion. Look again at the Help bar. There's a clue there to what's going on. See the Obj button? It means the Object coordinate system is in effect; that's the default for point navigation.

Actually, each vertex has its own set of x, y, and z axes, in which the z axis runs from the object's center to the vertex and the x and y axes are tangent to the vertex. For an idea of how this looks in 3D, hold up your right hand with the palm facing leftward, make a loose fist, then stick the middle finger out to the left (that's the x axis), the index finger straight up (that's the z axis), and the thumb pointing straight at you (that's the y axis). Now tilt the hand away from you so the index finger is pointing diagonally at a spot on the floor in front of you. That's what the vertex's axis looks like. Unfortunately, I can't display it in trueSpace2, but I've faked it in Figure 6-4 so you can get a better idea.

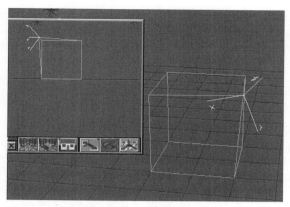

Figure 6–4 The front vertex's axis

NOTE: You may notice that your thumb and index finger are pointing in the opposite directions of the y axis and z axis, respectively, in Figure 6-4. I did it this way to avoid having you twist your hand too much. The axes in the illustration are pointing in their respective positive directions. You can find this object on the companion CD-ROM in a file named VERTAXES.COB in the TUTORIAL/CH6 directory. You'll have to select the Axes tool (second from the left in the Utilities group) to see the axes. Once you've done that, use the Eye Rotate tool to see the object from different angles.

This usage of a "local" set of object axes also applies to edges and faces. In Chapter 5, when you swept the sphere's two faces, each extrusion "went its own way." That's because each face was swept according to its individual axis.

If you still have trouble conceptualizing this, find a small box and a piece of thin cardboard. Position the box so one of the top corners is pointing toward you. Then place the cardboard so the center is touching the box corner and the cardboard surface is at approximately the same angle to the three adjacent sides (at about a 45-degree angle from the perpendicular or ground). The vertex's x and y axes reside in the plane of the piece of cardboard, and the z axis is perpendicular to the surface.

The fact that each entity in an object has its own set of axes has some interesting consequences. Let's take a look at a few of these.

6. Move the vertex back to its original position, either manually or with Undo. Now, press and hold the CTRL key and click the far top corner, opposite the first one you selected.

You've just learned a new technique: Namely, to select multiple *nonadjacent* object entities during point editing and hold the CTRL key while doing so. (Vertices are always nonadjacent; selecting adjacent edges and faces is covered shortly.) This is easy to remember, as it's standard procedure for selecting multiple items in list-type programs such as database managers. However, as mentioned in Chapter 3, Quick Start Tutorial: A Guided Tour of Major Features, in the Selecting Objects section, this technique doesn't work for selecting multiple objects. That's what the Glue tools are for—grouping objects—which you'll study in Chapter 7, Utilities and Edit Tools.

NOTE: Unfortunately—and this, in my opinion, is something of a design flaw—you can't deselect a selected entity by CTRL-clicking it again. However, you *can* deselect entities in the reverse order of the original selection by repeatedly using the Undo function. Otherwise, all you can do is release the CTRL key and select an entity, thus deselecting *all* other entities, and then reselect any other entities you want using the CTRL key again. Also, there's no drag-box provision for selecting multiple entities.

7. Now try left-button dragging the two selected vertices. Interesting, isn't it? They're moving in opposite directions! Again, that's because each vertex has its own set of axes and the two are horizontally (left to right) mirrored. Return them near to their original positions and then right-button drag vertically. From the Perspective (main) view, it looks like the farther vertex is moving a greater distance than the nearer one; but if you look at the Front view, you can see they're moving equal distances, at right angles to each other.

8. Okay, if you have mirror symmetry from front to back, what about in the vertical dimension? Without holding down the CTRL key, select the first point again, deselecting the second point. Then CTRL-click the bottom-front vertex, immediately below the first. Try left-button dragging them both horizontally and note that they move in the same direction. Then try right-button dragging vertically. Once again, you get opposite movement because of the individual axes.

Rotating a Face by Moving Points

A few more experiments, and then you'll move on.

1. Press the DELETE key or select the Erase tool. This doesn't actually delete anything, but simply takes you out of Point Edit mode. You are left in a sort of limbo where no function is operating, so you can't really do anything except select another function. Press DELETE or Erase again, and the cube disappears.

2. Add another cube, activate the Point Edit: Vertices tool, select one of the top corners, and then CTRL-select the other three. Again, you're automatically placed in Point Move mode. Left-button drag the mouse to the left and right. As you drag, you're rotating the top surface of the cube while simultaneously changing the size and height.

The rotation is caused by moving the vertices along their x axes (remember, each has its own set of axes). The height and size change results from y-axis movement. (Try isolating the movements with the Help bar X and Y buttons to see how this works.) You'll find, if you move the vertices far enough, that the object's vertical edges cross over one another. This isn't particularly desirable, but may be useful for special effects. That's one of the beauties of 3D graphics: You can do many things that are impossible in the real world, thus creating effects that may amaze your audience.

3. Next, change to either World or Screen coordinates. (Remember how to do this? Use the pop-up from the Obj button at the right end of the Help bar.) Try selecting individual vertices and groups and moving them on the World and Screen axes. This motion is pretty much what you'd expect, and there's not a whole lot to say about it, except that it's useful for reliably moving multiple selected entities in the same direction.

Lastly, bear in mind that you can't rotate or scale vertices—not one, not 100. Give it a try, just to see.

Manipulating Edges

You *can,* however, rotate and scale edges, as well as move them, using the Point Edit: Edges tool.

1. Delete the current cube and add a new one.

2. Select the Point Edit: Edges tool from the Point Edit pop-up menu.

3. Click on the top-left edge that's closer to you (see Figure 6-5). Try moving it along the individual x, y, and z axes, isolating first x-axis and then y-axis left-button movement with the X and Y buttons on the Help bar. Note that x-axis movement is parallel to the edge, y-axis movement is tangent to the edge, and z-axis movement is perpendicular to it. Try doing the same with any of the other horizontal edges and you'll see you get analogous motion.

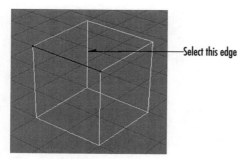
—Select this edge

Figure 6–5 Cube with front top-left edge selected

4. Now try manipulating a vertical edge the same way. Notice that the x and y axes seem to have exchanged roles. The x-axis movement is now tangent to the edge, and the y-axis movement is parallel to the edge.

You can see that, although an entity's axes may be aligned with the entity, the axes retain a relationship to the World coordinate system. For example, trueSpace2 will never make an entity's x axis perpendicular to the reference grid.

5. Let's look at edge rotation next. Delete the current cube and add a new one.

6. Select the front top-left edge again. Disable y-axis rotation and then try rotating the edge. There's no visible change because the edge is coincident with its x axis; thus, you're rotating it about its own length.

7. Enable y-axis rotation again and try rotating the edge again. It helps to open a new Top view to see this. The edge is rotating around a line tangent to itself. You could get the same effect, but not nearly as easily, by moving the edge's individual endpoints. If you rotate around the z axis, the edge is rotating about a line that goes from the center of the edge to the cube's center. When you finish experimenting, leave the edge rotated somewhat on the y and z axes.

8. Select the Object tool to deselect the edge. Then reselect the Point Edit: Edges tool and select the front top-left edge. Again, disable y-axis rotation and try left-button rotating the edge. (Hint: Move the mouse forward and back on the pad.) This time you get a baton-twirling effect. Why the change? Simple: When you exit Point Edit mode, trueSpace2 resets manipulated entities' axes to their original orientations. This fact isn't something you'll use every day, but it's important to know about.

9. Let's look briefly at edge scaling. Start with a fresh cube, select the same edge, and try scaling it on the individual axes. Because the edge is a one-dimensional entity, you'll get a visible result only from scaling on the x axis.

In some 3D applications, scaling a point or edge on an individual axis actually moves it along that axis, but not so in trueSpace2. Like edge rotation, you could get the same result by moving the two endpoints equal distances along the x axis, but this is easier. If you want to scale the edge around a point other than its center, scale the edge and then move it along the x axis.

Using the Slice Function

You may have noticed that, as soon as you select an edge, the icon in the Point Navigation panel's lower-left corner becomes available. If you position the mouse cursor over it, the Help bar displays Slice object by selected line/plane. What's up with that? Let's see.

1. If you're not continuing from the tutorial in the above section, add a cube and scale the front top-left edge slightly bigger or smaller than its original size.

2. Select the Slice tool icon in the Point Navigation panel (refer to Figure 6-2).

Now the Help bar message says Drag mouse (right button keeps previous selection). To return to picking mode, deselect the Slice tool. (If your display resolution isn't 1600 × 1200, you may not be able to read the entire message.)

3. Left-button drag the mouse to the left and right on your pad and note that a new edge has appeared and is following the mouse movement. If you drag as far as you can in one direction (you may have to use multiple drags, picking up the mouse to do so), you'll see that the "slice" edge stops at the next edge. Bring it back a short distance from the other edge and release the mouse button. The new edge is created where you stopped dragging. You've essentially subdivided one of the faces to which the original selected edge belongs.

4. Select Slice again and this time drag with the right mouse button to place the new edge. When you release this time, both the original edge and the new one remain selected, ready for simultaneous manipulation with the Point Navigation functions. If you try to slice again, the new edge is created only from the most recent one. Similarly, if you hand-select several edges and then select the Slice tool, only the last edge you selected is sliced. But all remain selected afterward.

Slice is a unique tool; I haven't seen anything quite like it in any other 3D graphics program. Its advantages include letting you subdivide part of an object in a specific way for fine-tuning its shape with point editing, as well as for vertex painting. You'll learn about the latter function in Chapter 9, Materials Part 1: Basic Surface Attributes. There are other tools for more formulaic subdivision of faces, which I'll explore in Chapter 7. Slice can be applied to faces as well as to edges; I'll look at that in the next section.

Working with Faces

Let's move on to face manipulation.

1. Clear the workspace and add a new cube.

2. Select the Point Edit: Faces tool from the Point Edit tool pop-up menu (refer to Figure 6-1).

3. Try selecting various faces on the cube. Notice that you can select only faces that are facing toward you. This is different from the Point Edit: Vertices and Point Edit: Edges tools; they allow you to select entities anywhere on the object. Thanks to trueSpace2's nonmodal interface, though, you can rotate an object while selecting multiple faces, so there's no real limitation here.

4. Turn off y-axis movement and try moving each of the three accessible faces along the x axis. The two front faces move parallel to their top and bottom edges. The top face, which is parallel to the reference grid, moves along the World x axis. It's a similar situation with the y axis. The two front faces, when moved along their y axes, move vertically, whereas the top face's y axis is aligned with the World y axis. In each case, moving a face along its z axis causes motion perpendicular to the plane of the face.

Rotating and Scaling Faces

1. Delete the old cube, add a new one, and select Point Edit: Faces again.

2. Try isolating x- and y-axis movement and rotating each of the three faces that are facing you along each axis. If you understand the principles covered so far, you won't be surprised by what you see.

3. Before you try z-axis rotation, start with a fresh cube.

4. Open the Object Info panel by right-clicking the Object tool. Now right-button rotate the top face clockwise. Notice that this motion "twists" the cube until the top face is rotated halfway around, and then "untwists" for the second half-turn. In the Object Info panel, the z-axis Rotation setting increases to 180 degrees (at the halfway point), then immediately "jumps" to -180 degrees. As you drag, it continues to increase back to 0 degrees when it's turned full circle. The same thing happens if you rotate the entire object.

NOTE: This brings up an important point that is actually more relevant to animation, which involves object manipulation. Bear in mind that trueSpace2 will never animate something beyond 180 degrees in a single action. That is, if you want to rotate an object 270 degrees in one direction, if you don't set it up properly—for example, by adding another key with an intermediate value—it'll end up rotating 90 degrees in the opposite direction. Incidentally, you can't animate object shapes via entity manipulation. However, you can do so with deformation, which I'll cover later in this chapter.

5. Try experimenting with scaling object faces on your own. No major revelations here; just keep in mind that if you want a face to retain its proportions, drag with both mouse buttons held down. And, of course, you can't scale a face along its z axis, because its size on the z axis is 0, and 0 multiplied by any factor is always 0.

Slicing with Faces

1. Finally, let's look at slicing with faces. Clear the workspace and add a sphere.

2. Select one of the frontmost faces; then select the Slice tool. Drag the mouse away from you on the pad and watch the sliced face, which starts out rectangular in shape, eventually become circular as it travels "through" the sphere (see Figure 6-6). Move it as far as you can and note that it ends up as the face diametrically opposite its origin.

3. Position the slice near the middle of the sphere. Select Slice again and drag the new slice a short distance. Repeat this operation several times. Note that you can create a whole new substructure consisting of concentric circles, which you could use for sculpting unusual objects, such as a space alien. Once a circular slice is deselected, however, the only way to reselect it is by CTRL-selecting each of the edges that composes it—at best, an arduous process.

LESSON 2: DIMENSIONAL PROMOTION

Ready for a new point-editing technique? It's called *dimensional promotion*, another feature unique to trueSpace2. You'll start by doing it the easy way, and then go into the full-blown process.

1. If you're continuing from the previous lesson, you can use the sphere you already have or start with a new one—it doesn't matter.

2. Select a face from the front, click the Slice tool, and drag the slice line about a third of the way through the sphere. Release the mouse button.

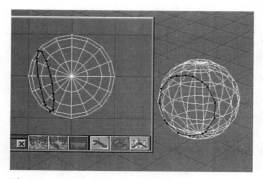

Figure 6–6 Face-sliced sphere from Top and Perspective views

3. Press and hold the SHIFT key and click on any vertex in the sphere. Try to click on one near the front center, but it's not that important. Depending on where you click, all the faces on one side or the other of the slice line will be highlighted in green (see Figure 6-7). This means the whole section is selected and ready for manipulation.

4. What's even cooler is that you can now separate the object into two new objects with a click of the Separate button—the other one on the bottom of the Point Navigation panel, which you've ignored until now (refer to Figure 6-2). Click it and note the change. The part of the sphere that was white stays white, but the other part's wireframe goes dark blue, designating that it is an unselected object. Select the "sliced-off" part and move it away from the other to confirm that they are indeed now two separate objects.

TIP: The Separate tool is great for creating explosions, with pieces of an object flying off in all directions, or for separating an imported human or animal figure into constituent parts for subsequent hierarchical reconstruction and animation. You can also use Separate for creating interesting sets of polygons for further modification, such as with the Sweep tool.

What you've just accomplished is called dimensional promotion, and it's just what it sounds like. In the above example, you went from selecting a two-dimensional ring of edges to a three-dimensional entity consisting of the ring and all faces on one side of it—with a single SHIFT click. But you don't have to start at two dimensions; you can start as low as zero dimension and work your way up from there.

NOTE: Did you know that a vertex has no dimension? You can demonstrate this (as you may have already) by selecting a vertex in a trueSpace2 object, then trying to scale it. Also, open the Object Info panel and note that its size on all three axes

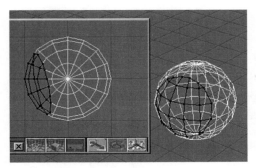

Figure 6-7 Selected area

is 0. An edge, or line, has one dimension (length), and a plane, face, or polygon has two (length and breadth). And, of course, you already know what has three: every single real-world object you've ever dealt with. Zero-, one-, and two-dimensional objects exist only in theory, but they're very useful for mathematicians and 3D artists.

5. Clear the workspace and add a sphere.

6. Select the Point Edit: Vertices tool and select a vertex near the front center of the sphere.

7. Press and hold the (SHIFT) key; then click on another vertex at the opposite corner of any of the four polygons adjacent to the first vertex. A diagonal edge appears between the two vertices, highlighted in green (see Figure 6-8). You've just promoted from zero dimension to one.

8. Actually, you didn't have to click on a vertex. Press (CTRL)-(Z) to undo the change, then (SHIFT)-click anywhere on the outer edge of the rectangle consisting of the four faces surrounding the first vertex. A new vertex is created where you click, and an edge appears between the two vertices. (As a point of interest, if you click on one of the four edges connected to the first vertex, it's simply promoted to the entire edge—you needn't do this now.)

NOTE: With no vertices selected, if you (SHIFT)-click on an object edge with the Point Edit: Vertices tool active, you create a new vertex at that point.

9. To prove a point, undo the addition of the new edge created in Step 8, then try (SHIFT)-clicking on other vertices and edges farther away from the original vertex. Note that you can promote a vertex to an edge only by clicking on two parts of the same polygon. (SHIFT)-click the original second vertex or edge to reestablish the new edge.

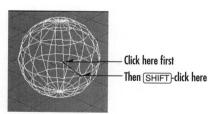
Click here first
Then (SHIFT)-click here

Figure 6–8
Promoting a point to a line

10. Ready for the next dimension? (SHIFT)-click on another edge or vertex anywhere else on the sphere, except on the face that's bisected by the new edge. Voilà! As shown in Figure 6-9, a new series of edges is created, much like that created by the slice-drag process you learned in the section titled Using the Slice Function, earlier in this chapter.

11. You already know how to achieve the final promotion: Just (SHIFT)-click on any point in either part of the bisected sphere.

Here's a review of the dimensional promotion procedure:

🦆 Select (or add) a zero-dimensional vertex.

🦆 (SHIFT)-click to create or select a one-dimensional edge.

🦆 (SHIFT)-click again to create a virtual two-dimensional plane bisecting the object.

🦆 (SHIFT)-click once more to select either half of the bisected object.

🦆 Use the Point Navigation tools to manipulate the selected portion, or click the Separate tool to split it off from the main object.

The difference between dimensional promotion and using the Slice function is that you can bisect the object with a plane through any three points on the surface, not just parallel to a particular face.

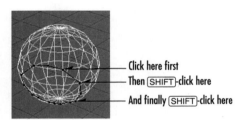

Click here first
Then (SHIFT)-click here
And finally (SHIFT)-click here

Figure 6–9
Promoting one dimension to two

LESSON 3: SELECTING ADJACENT FACES

Earlier in this chapter, you learned that holding the CTRL key lets you select only multiple *nonadjacent* entities. Try to CTRL-click to select two faces that share an edge, or even a single vertex, and the second one simply refuses to be selected. So how do you select adjacent entities? Easy: with the SHIFT key. Normally, as you've just seen, the SHIFT key is used for dimensional promotion. But it does double duty for selecting adjacent entities.

To demonstrate this, as well as get to know an interesting new use of the Separate tool, follow these steps.

1. Clear the workspace and add a sphere.

2. Set the main window to Front View, via the pop-up in the View tool group (third from the left, center icon; looks like the front of a house).

3. Select the Point Edit: Faces tool. Then click on a face on either side of the center line running vertically through the sphere.

4. Press and hold the SHIFT key, then click on all faces directly above and below the first one (see Figure 6-10).

5. Activate the Separate tool. This performs the separation, then places you back in Object Move mode.

6. Press the DELETE key to erase the sphere from the workspace, leaving the unselected "wedge" of connected faces.

7. Select the wedge object and activate the Sweep tool. Nothing happens, except that a Selection Error dialog appears telling you No face(s) selected. In general, you can't just extrude all of an object's faces without first specifying them by selecting them. Click the OK button to continue.

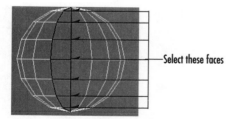

Figure 6-10 Sphere from front with selected faces

8. Select the Point Edit: Faces tool. As before, click on one face and then SHIFT-click on each of the rest. Alas, there's no easy way to select all an object's faces.

9. Return to the Perspective view. Select the Sweep tool again and admire your nifty new curvy wedge object. Render it for a better look (see Figure 6-11). Makes a neat crescent moon, doesn't it?

There are other ways to create such a model, but this is one of the easiest. Another would be to create a flat crescent-shaped polygon by subtracting one round regular polygon from another and then lathing it a short distance. However, it's sometimes difficult to get sharp corners as viewed from above with that method.

You can separate any one or more selected faces from an object; they don't have to be contiguous. If you separate a single face or several noncontiguous faces, you can then perform a sweep or lathe without having to select the faces with the Point Edit tool first. (You do have to select it as an object, of course.)

NOTE: Another important point about using the SHIFT key to select adjacent faces: If you select faces that are connected by a single vertex (corner to corner), you can manipulate them using the standard Point Navigation tools, but you can't do anything else (e.g., slice, separate, or sweep).

LESSON 4: USING THE CONTEXT TOOL

Once you've gained some experience with selecting points, edges, and faces using the dedicated tools, you'll appreciate the Point Edit: Context tool even more. It lets you select any type of entity, depending on where you click.

Clear the workspace, add a sphere, and select the Point Edit: Context tool. Then practice selecting points, edges, and faces and note that it's necessary to be fairly explicit where you click to select the desired entity. For example, if you click on a edge where it intersects a point, you'll get the point instead of the edge. To select a face, you must click on a

Figure 6-11 Column of sphere faces, separated, swept, and rendered

part of it where there are no points or edges. But in the long run, this is a much more efficient way to work, especially if you're manipulating more than one type of entity simultaneously. As with the previous tools, simply (CTRL)-click after the first selection to select multiple entities.

LESSON 5: USING THE DELETE FACE TOOL

There's one tool left on the Point Edit pop-up that you haven't used: the Delete Face tool.

You have learned that, when you select an entity and press the (DELETE) key or click the Erase tool, nothing is deleted except the selected state of whichever entities were highlighted. Actually, though, it makes sense that you would want to delete vertices or edges, because objects sometimes turn out needlessly complex, causing long rendering times.

NOTE: Converting several adjacent faces into a single contiguous face to simplify the object is called *optimization*. Unfortunately, few programs have that feature built in (it's available as a plug-in for 3D Studio, for example), and trueSpace2 certainly doesn't.

You may have noticed, if you rendered an object created with the Separate tool, that the new surface where the "split" occurs is flat, which gives the impression that trueSpace2 objects are solid. In actuality, they consist of polygon shells around empty space. You can easily demonstrate this by positioning a camera inside an object (point it at a curved surface or a corner) and rendering the object from the camera's viewpoint. (Don't use 3DR, because as implemented in trueSpace2, it doesn't seem to like rendering an object's inside surface.)

To remove part of an object's shell so you can see inside it from the outside, the Delete Face tool is the one to use. It's pretty straightforward: Select the object, select the tool, and then select the face. The only tricky part is that, in Wireframe Display mode, you can't see any change when the polygon is deleted.

1. Try it now. Clear the workspace and then add a cylinder primitive.

2. Choose the Delete Face tool from the Point Edit pop-up, then click on the cylinder's circular top polygon. Looks the same, doesn't it?

3. To see the change, simply select the Render Current Object tool (second from the left in the main window's View group). You can now see the cylinder's inside and outside surfaces (see the rightmost object in Figure 6-12).

For curiosity's sake, go to Solid Render mode by selecting the 3DR icon from the leftmost pop-up in the main window's View group. All you'll see is the front part of the surface (see the leftmost object in Figure 6-12).

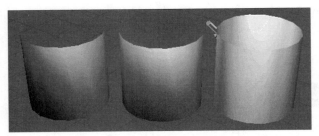

Figure 6–12 Left to right: Open-top cylinder rendered in 3DR, standard cylinder, open-top cylinder rendered with Render Current Object tool

NOTE: Rumor has it that Intel has given up on 3DR and is letting the technology die; at this writing, Microsoft is working hard on its Direct3D system, which Caligari will probably incorporate in the next version of trueSpace.

LESSON 6: USING THE POINT EDIT PROPERTY PANEL

There are a couple of important issues regarding point editing that I haven't touched on so far. The first is about slow redraws during editing of complex objects, and the other has to do with point editing's deleterious effects on polygon planarity. Both of these problems can be handled with the Point Edit property panel.

Improving Performance by Changing the Draw Mode

When you're dragging around vertices, edges, and faces, by default trueSpace2 constantly redraws the entire object in all windows in which it appears, so you can have a good idea of how you're changing it. With simple objects, this isn't a problem—however, most attractive objects are not simple. In fact, as you gain experience working in 3D graphics, you'll doubtless spend inordinate amounts of time trying to keep your objects' face counts to a minimum. In all likelihood, you'll probably also devote much time to point editing, especially if you work with organic objects.

Here's a preview of the sort of redraw times you can expect with complex objects.

1. Clear the workspace, open the Primitives panel, and right-click on the Add Sphere tool. In the Add Sphere property panel, change both the Latitude and the Longitude settings to 64 and left-click Add Sphere. The sphere you've just created contains 4,096 polygons, and thus represents a moderately complex object. (By way of comparison, the Monster Truck model, MONSTRUK.COB, that comes with trueSpace2, contains 11,696 faces.)

2. If your computer isn't very fast (486/50 or below), you can skip this step. To simulate a real-world modeling situation more closely, open new Front and Top views using the New View pop-up in the main window's View tool group. Move the views into the upper corners of the screen. If you like, use their Eye Move or Zoom tools to fill the view with the sphere.

3. Activate the Point Edit: Faces tool and select about 10 faces at various points on the front of the sphere. Try not to pick faces that are connected by an edge or corner. (Remember: Hold down the CTRL key after selecting the first one.)

4. Move the mouse cursor away from the sphere, press and hold the right mouse button, and drag the mouse toward you to move the selected faces away from the sphere's surface. Then left-button drag to the left and right to move the faces around. Watch the screens of all three views get updated—in as close to real time as your computer can manage. However, unless your computer is extremely fast, you'll probably note, as well, that you're suffering from diminished feedback. In other words, the onscreen motion of the manipulated entities lags behind your mouse movement by a significant amount of time.

5. This can be remedied to a large extent, though you'll sacrifice a certain amount of feedback, via the Point Edit property panel. Release the mouse button and right-click on the Point Edit: Faces tool to open this new panel of controls (see Figure 6-13).

6. Beside Draw, click and hold on the Object box to open a pop-up text menu. Drag the mouse cursor to the word Edited, and release.

7. Move the mouse cursor back into the workspace and drag the faces around again.

This time, as soon as you start to move the mouse, only the selected faces and their nearest neighbors are redrawn in all three views (see Figure 6-14). You see the entire object again only when you release the mouse button. Because the program doesn't have nearly as much work to do in redrawing the manipulated entities, you get much faster feedback. Actually, there's not much of a drawback here; you're still seeing, in real time, everything that's changing. You're just not seeing it in the context of the entire object. If you want, try loading some of the objects that come with trueSpace2 to see how this facility can be of advantage with more realistic models.

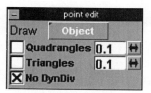

Figure 6-13 Point Edit property panel

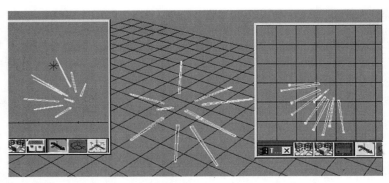

Figure 6-14 Editing sphere faces with Draw: Edited option

NOTE: Unfortunately, this Draw: Edited option does not work with views that are set to 3DR (Solid Render Display mode). In that case, the entire object is constantly redrawn during point manipulation, whether Draw is set to Object or Edited. Only in Wireframe views does the Edited option have any effect.

Using Dynamic Division

A model containing nonplanar polygons may render improperly, causing shading anomalies. Some 3D modeling programs permit triangular polygons only, with the advantage that planar triangles don't cause rendering accuracy problems. The drawback, however, is that planar surfaces with more than three vertices must be composed of multiple polygons, leading to unwanted object complexity and thus longer rendering times.

Other programs, including trueSpace2, allow polygons of any number of vertices. Polygons you create with functions such as the Polygon and Add Text tools have as many vertices as required, and polygons trueSpace2 creates by sweeping and the like are usually quadrilateral. All such polygons, when first created, are planar. If even one vertex of a polygon with four or more vertices is moved out of the plane, however, the polygon becomes nonplanar. In trueSpace2, the Dynamic Division facility accommodates for this by automatically subdividing nonplanar polygons during editing. Dynamic Division is an option with the Deformation and Sculpt Surface tools as well, and you'll see how that works in Lessons 7 and 8. For now, let's take a look at how Dynamic Division works with point editing.

1. Clear the workspace and add a cube.

2. Select the Point Edit: Vertices tool and click on the top-left corner of the cube. Then CTRL-click on the top-right corner, diagonally opposite the first (see Figure 6-15).

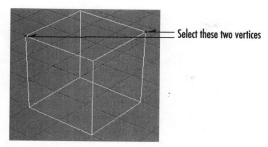

Select these two vertices

Figure 6–15 Cube with top-left and -right vertices selected

3. With the right mouse button pressed, drag vertically a few inches to lift the corners up and out from their original positions (see Figure 6-16). With a single edit, you've created a shape with not one but *five* nonplanar polygons (all but the bottom one).

4. Now render the cube by selecting the Render Current Object tool in the main window's View group (see Figure 6-17).

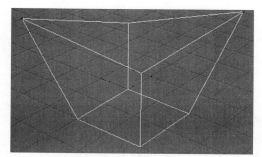

Figure 6–16 Cube with vertices moved

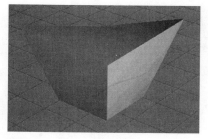

Figure 6–17 Rendered shape with nonplanar faces

The two front faces look fine, because their degree of nonplanarity is not severe, but you can see a rendering artifact already in the top face. It's the horizontal line near the rear of the face. (In Figure 6-17, I've increased the contrast to make the artifact more visible.) When rendering an ambiguous surface like the altered cube's top, the program has to make a best guess about how to divide it up into polygons, and sometimes the guess is not accurate. The resulting artifact is not all that noticeable, and the top polygon has a nicely smoothed curved surface. However, if you were to render an animation of this object rotating about its vertical axis, the rendering errors would become more obvious, with artifacts not appearing in some frames and shifting about in others.

5. Let's see what you can do to remedy this situation. Right-click the Point Edit: Vertices tool to reopen the Point Edit property panel. Take a look at the trio of check boxes arrayed along the panel's left side. Currently, the one labeled No DynDiv is selected. This means that trueSpace2 will not subdivide edited polygons, no matter how nonplanar.

6. Click the center box, labeled Triangles. Instantly the rendered object reverts to wireframe, and all five nonplanar quadrilateral polygons are divided into triangular polygons. Each of the side polys is divided from its respective moved vertex to the opposite corner, and the top poly is divided by an edge drawn in a straight line between the two moved vertices (see Figure 6-18, left side).

7. Render this object to see how it looks (see Figure 6-18, right side). I've rotated it slightly to give you a better idea of the new shape. Unfortunately, because trueSpace2 took the shortest possible route in reestablishing the polygons' planarity, you've lost that nice smooth curve on the object's top surface. How can you get it back?

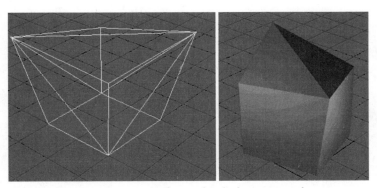

Figure 6-18 Shape with faces divided into triangles, wireframe and rendered

8. That's what the other Dynamic Division option, Quadrangles, is for. In the Point Edit property panel, click in the box next to Quadrangles. The five original polygons have been subdivided into quadrangles of various sizes, retaining as closely as possible the original, undivided shape (see Figure 6-19). Kind of magical, isn't it? You can see that the degree of subdivision is greater near the front and rear bottom corners, because that's where the highest degree of curvature exists. It's not readily apparent here, but it would be more so in an animation, especially in an object with a reflective surface.

9. Render this shape to confirm how much more closely it resembles the original object (see Figure 6-20).

10. Next you'll explore the Dynamic Division numeric settings opposite the Quadrangles and Triangles options in the Point Edit panel. These let you control the overall degree of subdivision. Set the Quadrangles amount to .2 (double that of

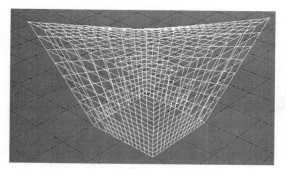

Figure 6–19 Object subdivided into quadrangles

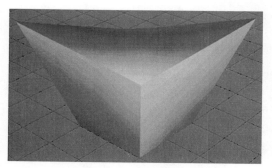

Figure 6–20 Rendered subdivided object

the default .1). Click Quadrangles again. Note that this time all the subdivided surfaces are given the same resolution as the lower corners had before. (This is probably unnecessary—the default setting works well in most cases. But it's good to have a little flexibility.) Try different values for Quadrangles and move the two vertices in various directions to see how the subdivision is affected.

I'm not sure about the effect of the Triangles setting, if any. I tried a variety of polygon types, and the results were the same—with one exception. If you set Triangles to .001, there's no subdivision. It makes sense, because as soon as you've divided all affected polygons into triangles once, no further subdivision is necessary.

NOTE: There's one important fact you should know about the Dynamic Division feature: It performs subdivision only after the fact. To observe this, add a cube and select the top surface. With Dynamic Division and Quadrangles on and the latter set to the default .1, rotate the cube top 90 degrees about the vertical axis (using the right button). You'll get a nice twisted effect (see Figure 6-21), but the vertical edges remain straight as rails.

To get a more natural-looking curve on the edges, you have to subdivide the object first and then use the Deform Object tool. You'll study that tool in the next lesson.

DEFORMING AND SCULPTING OBJECTS

In the beginning of this chapter, I promised you some superpower tools for manipulating objects as though they were made of clay. The next two lessons cover those tools: Deform Object and Sculpt Surface.

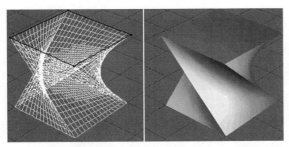

Figure 6-21 Cube top rotated with Dynamic Division, wireframe and rendered

LESSON 7: USING THE DEFORM OBJECT TOOL

Because I've whetted your appetite with the twisted cube, let's quickly see how to do it right, after which I'll go back and explore deformation in a more methodical way. Here's a quick introductory tutorial on deforming objects.

1. It's amazingly easy. Clear the workspace, open the Primitives panel, and right-click on the Add Cube tool.

2. In the Add Cube property panel, set Resolution to 8. Remember to press the [ENTER] key if you do it from the keyboard. Then add the cube.

3. Select the Deform Object tool (see Figure 6-22) from the Model tool group. It's just to the right of the Sweep tool. This causes the cube's white wireframe to turn orange and sets up a green deformation lattice around the cube.

4. Note that, by default, each of the cube's sides is divided in half vertically and horizontally by the lattice grid. When you manipulate the lattice, you want it to affect the cube's full height, not just the top half, so you must reduce the lattice resolution in the vertical dimension. To do this, right-button drag downward in the workspace. Watch the center "equatorial" green line around the cube carefully; after dragging a couple of inches, you'll see it disappear (see Figure 6-23).

Figure 6-22
Deform object tool

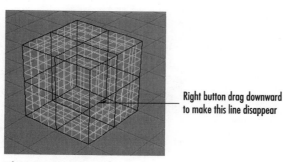

Right button drag downward
to make this line disappear

Figure 6-23 Cube with
default deform lattice

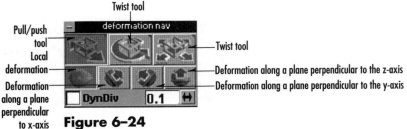

Twist tool

Pull/push tool

Local deformation

Deformation along a plane perpendicular to x-axis

Twist tool

Deformation along a plane perpendicular to the z-axis

Deformation along a plane perpendicular to the y-axis

Figure 6–24
The Deformation Navigation panel

5. Next, take a look at the Deformation Navigation panel (see Figure 6-24). In the second row of icons, select the rightmost tool, for deformation along a plane perpendicular to the z axis (as displayed in the Help bar). Only the horizontal components of the deformation lattice will remain. (By the way, I could have reversed the order of Steps 4 and 5. It doesn't make any difference which order you do them in.)

6. Click on the uppermost grid line, which turns white.

7. Back in the Deformation Navigation panel, select the center Rotation icon in the top row.

8. Right-button drag the mouse in the workspace to the left or right until the top of the cube has rotated a quarter turn. Or, if you want to be exact about it, right-click on the Object tool to open the Object Info panel and enter 90 (or -90) in the Rotation/Z slot.

That's it! You now have a beautifully twisted cube that, when rendered, looks like Figure 6-25. In Chapter 11, Animation, you'll learn how to animate this process, by which means you can create impressive effects with relatively little effort.

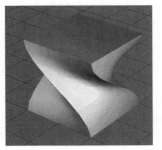

Figure 6–25 Cube twisted with Deform Object tool

TIP: By adding a subdivided cube to begin with, you've created unnecessary complexity in the top and bottom surfaces (unless you don't want to keep them flat). One alternative method would be to add an undivided cube, then select the four sides and use Quad Divide to subdivide them several times. You'll learn more about Quad Divide in Chapter 7. Even better would be to add a plane or four-sided regular polygon and then extrude it 2 meters with 16 or so segments.

Local Object Deformation

Now let's get back to the basics and learn the details about *local object deformation*. This is the default deformation mode, so called because the other mode, planar deformation, allows modifying an object's shape along an entire plane running through the object. (Planar deformation is coming up in the next section.)

1. Clear the workspace, open the Primitives panel, and right-click on the Add Plane tool. You'll use a plane primitive as a learning object because there's only one layer of polygons, so there's no ambiguity about what's going on as you change its shape.

2. Set Resolution to 8 and then left-click on the Add Plane tool to create a planar object with 64 faces.

3. Click the Deform Object tool. You'll see the plane's orange wireframe. The deformation lattice consists of a green line around the edge and two green lines bisecting the plane horizontally and vertically.

The basic procedure at this point is to click on one of the lattice intersections (in this case, one of the four corners or the center). Then manipulate it using standard navigation functions. But before doing so, you can modify the lattice resolution. The reason for doing this is to increase or decrease the deformation's area of influence. For example, in the intro tutorial for Deform Object, you decreased the lattice's vertical resolution so you could twist the cube's entire height by rotating its top surface. If you had left the center lattice line there, you would have twisted only the top half of the cube.

To change the lattice resolution on the x and y axes, left-button drag in the direction of the respective World axis. To change the vertical (z-axis) resolution, right-button drag vertically. Dragging away from you ("upward") increases the lattice resolution, and dragging toward you ("downward") decreases resolution. The illustration in Figure 6-26 should help you visualize this.

Unfortunately, in this case there is no way to disable affecting x- and/or y-axis resolution, so you may need to experiment a bit if you want to change only one or the other. To affect all three (or two, in the case of planar objects) axes equally, drag with both mouse buttons held down.

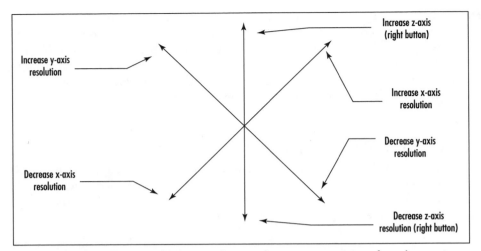

Figure 6–26 Changing lattice resolution (drag in empty part of workspace)

 WARNING: It's important to remember that, once you start deforming an object, you can no longer change the lattice resolution, so plan ahead.

4. Spend a little time playing with these controls. See if you can change resolution on one axis without affecting the other. When you're done, return to a single division on each axis. If you have trouble doing this, simply press the (DELETE) key twice, add another plane, and select the Deform Object tool again.

5. Click on the plane's center, where the two central lattice lines intersect. Note the new entity that appears: a set of four short lines emanating from the point, with yellow vertices at their endpoints and intersection. (Remember the handles from editing splines? These play a similar role in modifying object deformation, as you'll see shortly.)

6. Right-button drag upward a short distance in the workspace to raise the center point above the reference grid (see Figure 6-27). By manipulating the deformation lattice, you've modified the underlying object mesh in a dramatic way. Notice the nice smooth 3D curves between the center point and the edges.

 TIP: One way to think of the Deform Object tool is as a magnet that modifies the point you directly manipulate to the greatest degree. The "magnet" also modifies all other points between that one and the next lattice grid lines to a gradually lesser degree, the influence falling off as the distance increases.

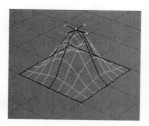

Figure 6–27 Plane center
deformed upward

7. You might also note that some of the plane's faces are now nonplanar. Fortunately, as with point editing, you have a Dynamic Division option. It's at the bottom of the Deformation Navigation property panel. Turn it on now to see the result (see Figure 6-28). It's interesting to note, in Figure 6-28's zoomed-in Top view window, that some of the polygons where the greatest curvature occurred (particularly those near the center) have been subdivided into triangles, but not in a particularly uniform way.

8. Turn off Dynamic Division for better feedback in the rest of this exercise. Then practice moving the deformation center around laterally by left-button dragging.

9. Select the Deformation Navigation panel's Rotation and Scaling tools. (Note that the Help bar refers to these as Twist and Stretch.) Practice manipulating the deformation on the various axes. As you do so, you also affect the handles sticking out from the selected lattice intersection. For example, if you scale the deformation up, the handles become longer as well.

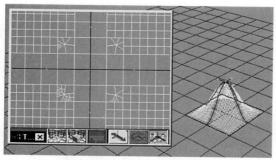

Figure 6–28 Deformed plane with
Dynamic Division

Get a Handle on Your Deformation

Let's try manipulating the handles directly.

1. To return the deformation to its original raised and centered state, as in Figure 6-27, press Undo (or CTRL-Z) repeatedly, or just start over.

2. In the Deformation panel, select the Move tool (or Push/Pull, as the Help bar calls it).

3. Left-button drag one of the handle endpoints. Notice that you're affecting only the portion of the mesh directly under the handle. Basically, you're modifying the mesh's curvature at that point. If you push the handle closer to the mesh, you reduce the curvature, creating more of a pointy deformation. If you pull it away, you increase the roundness.

The number of available handles depends on the type of object and where on the object the lattice intersection occurs. If you select one of the plane's corner lattice intersections, there are only two handles. If you select a cube's corner lattice intersection, there are three. Also, if you don't click again directly on a handle endpoint, you go back to manipulating the full lattice intersection as soon as you release the mouse button.

Try manipulating the handle endpoints with the Twist and Stretch tools active to see their effects. The amount of modeling power afforded by these tools, especially with the added convenience of multiple Undo operations, is truly impressive.

Sometimes you get a fifth handle that's perpendicular to the other four and allows for deformation around but not on the selected point. To see this, add a sphere of Latitude and Longitude 16, select the Deform Object tool, and select the sphere's top point. See the fifth handle sticking straight down? Try pulling it down to see the interesting effect shown in Figure 6-29. The handle length is several times the height of the sphere.

Figure 6–29 Sphere deformed by pulling down center handle

The Deformation Property Panel

While this sphere object is available, let's use it to examine briefly the Deformation property panel.

1. Undo the handle manipulation you just did and then right-click the Deform Object tool to open the panel (see Figure 6-30). All options in the panel are enabled and the box next to Draw says Deformed in black text, which means that it is not enabled. (The purpose of disabling any of these options would be for faster feedback, because there's less to redraw.)

2. The first check box option, RealTime, determines how the object is redrawn as you manipulate the vertex. Disable RealTime and left-button drag the selected vertex at the top of the sphere a few inches to the left or right. Note that, as you drag, the deformation has a distinctly pointy end, but when you release the mouse button, it returns to a smoothly rounded tip. Reenable the RealTime option, drag the vertex some more, and watch it retain the rounded look as you drag.

The next two options are pretty straightforward. The Handles option toggles display of the handles attached to the currently active lattice intersection. The Outlines option toggles display of the green deformation lattice. Neither of these adds much overhead to the redraw process, so it's generally best to leave them on—with one exception: If you want to be able to use the Draw Deformed option, you must turn off Outlines.

3. Disable Outlines now and notice that the Draw box text (Deformed) changes to Object (if you haven't accessed the pop-up menu) and turns white, which means it's enabled. Left-button click and hold on the box, drag to Deformed, and release. Now, as with point editing, when you manipulate the selected part of the object, only the polygons that are directly affected are redrawn.

4. Try it with the sphere and watch the bottom section disappear temporarily when you deform the top point.

If you try it with the plane, it doesn't make any difference, because you affect the entire object when you manipulate the center point.

Figure 6–30
Deformation property panel

Final Notes on Local Deformation

What if you want to manipulate a different lattice intersection? Easy—just click on it.

If you want to interrupt deforming an object to work on another part of your scene and then return to it later, no problem—trueSpace2 remembers the modified deformation lattice and keeps it with the object, even if you save and then reload it. Unfortunately, once you've started deforming an object, you can no longer change the deform lattice resolution, except as outlined in the next paragraph.

When you try to perform point editing or surface sculpting on an object you've deformed, a warning box informs you that the object has animatable deformation associated with it. You are asked if you want to delete the deformation(s) and connection(s). If you click OK, the deformation itself is not deleted; only the modified deformation grid is. If you then return to deforming the object, it's given a default deformation grid, whose resolution you can then modify as with any fresh deformation.

Spend as much time as possible using the Deform Object tool on various primitives and other objects, with and without Dynamic Division and/or 3DR turned on. The latter function, with its real-time solid-rendered feedback, is particularly helpful in this type of modeling. Keep in mind, though, that it often isn't as accurate as standard rendering, which is how your final output is created. For the best results, use the Render Current Object as often as possible during your modeling sessions.

Planar Object Deformation

The second, third, and fourth icons in the second row of the Deformation Navigation panel are for deforming objects along a plane perpendicular to the x, y, or z axis, respectively. You've already seen the latter tool in action, when you twisted the cube's top surface in the tutorial at the beginning of this section. In general, you can use these tools to manipulate an object's entire cross-section. Here are a couple of quick examples.

Deform to Your Heart's Delight

First, make a 3D Valentine's heart.

1. Add a sphere, setting Resolution to 16 for both Latitude and Longitude.

2. Open a new Left view window and zoom in on the sphere. This will be used only to observe progress; perform all manipulations in the main Perspective view.

3. Select Object Scale, turn off the y axis, and left-button drag leftward to flatten the sphere (scaling it down on the x axis).

4. Select the Deform Object tool and make sure DynDiv is turned off.

5. In the Deformation Navigation panel, choose Deformation along a plane perpendicular to the y axis, second icon from the right in the second row. This leaves a single lattice line around the object's vertical circumference.

6. Select the lattice line (it turns white), then right-button drag downward to create a (roughly) heart-shaped object (see Figure 6-31). At this point, you may want to adjust the Left view to see the entire object.

7. Not bad, but you need to sharpen up the top and bottom center vertices, which is easily done using the Local Deform tool. Select it now; it's the icon in the Deformation Navigation panel (refer to Figure 6-24) that looks just like the Deform Object tool.

8. Select the top center vertex and then the Stretch (Scale) tool in the Deform Navigation panel. In the Help bar, make sure the x axis is still turned off. Then left-button drag leftward until you get a sharp indentation.

9. Repeat the process for the bottom point. See Figure 6-32 for the final result. Pretty good for a couple minutes' work, right? Now you can make that lovey-dovey animation that will win your sweetie's eternal affection.

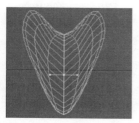

Figure 6–31 Left view of heart after pulling down center lattice plane

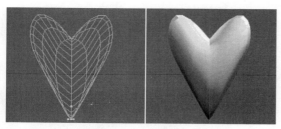

Figure 6–32 Heart after tightening up top and bottom center points, wireframe and rendered

Smash the Empire with trueSpace2

For the next trick, let's do a simple space fighter.

1. Clear the workspace and open a new Top view window. Add a cylinder primitive of Latitude and Longitude 16.

2. Select Object Scale and, in the main window, right-button drag upward to double the cylinder length, or use the Object Info panel to set the z-axis size to 4.

3. Turn off the y axis and left-button drag leftward to flatten the cylinder (see Figure 6-33).

4. Select the Deform Object tool and, in the Deformation Navigation panel, select Deformation along a plane perpendicular to the x axis. This creates an unusual deformation lattice, with two vertical lines in the front and back and a plane going through the center from left to right.

5. Select the plane, then right-button drag it upward (see Figure 6-34).

6. Next, in the Deformation Navigation panel, choose Deformation along a plane perpendicular to the z axis and Stretch (Scale), the rightmost icons in both rows. In the Help bar, make sure both the X and Y buttons are enabled and the Z button is turned off. (If not, make it so.)

7. Select the shape's top surface. With both mouse buttons held down, drag leftward to scale it down. This gives the fighter's nose a nasty pincer-like look (see Figure 6-35).

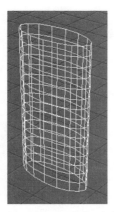

Figure 6–33 Cylinder, scaled up on z and down on x

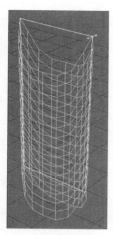

Figure 6–34 Plane perpendicular to x axis deformed upward

Figure 6–35
Top surface scaled down

8. That's it for planar deformation. Next, use the Local Deform tool with Push/Pull to pull out, and slightly back, points on the left and right sides (see Figure 6-36). The Top view is useful for the actual manipulation, after you select each point in the Perspective view.

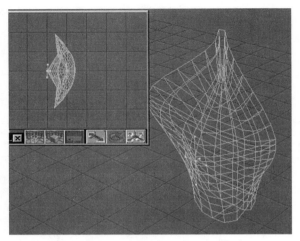

Figure 6–36 Wings and cockpit pulled out

9. Finally, pull out the center point on the flatter surface for the cockpit (see Figure 6-36). Make other modifications as you see fit. Save this object for your magnum sci-fi opus. (You'll learn how to make the cockpit transparent in Chapter 9.)

In Figure 6-37, your fighter is rotated into flying position and rendered. You can find this object as FIGHTER.COB on the companion CD-ROM in the TUTORIAL/CH6 directory.

One final note before I move on. You may have noticed two variants for the Deform Object tool in the pop-up: Start and Stop Deforming by Stand-Alone Deformation Object. These are related to the rightmost column of icons in the Primitives panel, and are usually employed in animation. You'll learn more about them in Chapter 11.

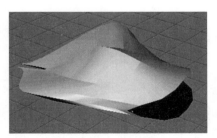

Figure 6–37 Space fighter ready for action

LESSON 8: USING THE SURFACE SCULPT TOOL

The Sculpt Surface tool is similar to the Deform Object tool, except that you're not limited to lattice lines and intersections. It has several other advantages as well, and only a few limitations: no "long-term memory," thus no animation capabilities; and only push/pull manipulation.

1. As before, you'll use the simplest possible object to explore Sculpt Surface's possibilities. Add a plane of Resolution 8, then select the Sculpt Surface tool (see Figure 6-38). When you do so, the Sculpt Surface control panel appears (see Figure 6-39). (There is no property panel for Sculpt Surface.)

Unlike Deform Object, there's no change in the object's appearance when you activate Sculpt Surface. The tool is waiting for you to click and drag a portion of the surface, as indicated by the Help bar message. Go ahead and give it a try.

2. Because you're using a plane right now, it makes the most sense to deform it vertically, so right-button click and drag anywhere on the plane. As soon as you start dragging, the mesh turns orange and a set of four short handles appears. Four handles is all you ever get with Sculpt Surface. You can manipulate these handles to modify the curvature under the selected point.

Figure 6–38
The Sculpt Surface tool

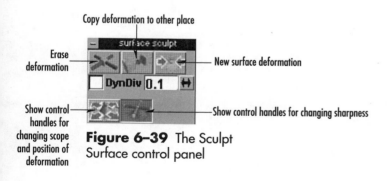

Copy deformation to other place

Erase deformation

New surface deformation

DynDiv 0.1

Show control handles for changing scope and position of deformation

Show control handles for changing sharpness

Figure 6–39 The Sculpt Surface control panel

Notice that pulling (or pushing) the surface doesn't affect the entire object, but only a small area around the selected point. You'll learn how to modify this shortly. First, let's look at the basic controls for Sculpt Surface.

3. Release the mouse button; then try clicking on a different part of the mesh. This has no effect. To sculpt a different part of the object, you first have to select the New Surface Deformation icon (refer to Figure 6-39), and then click and drag in the new area.

4. What if you've been pushing and pulling part of the surface around and decide you want to start over? You could click the Undo tool a bunch of times, but there's an easier way. Just click the Erase Deformation icon in the control panel's upper-left corner. This also returns the object mesh to white, ready for picking a new area to sculpt.

5. That leaves one other icon in the top row, the center one, which the Help bar tells us is used to Copy deformation to other place. To see how this useful tool works, add a sphere of Latitude and Longitude 24. Then select Sculpt Surface and right-button drag out a small bump anywhere on the surface. Next, click on the Copy Deformation icon, then click on another point on the sphere. Repeat several times, and you'll end up with an object like the one in Figure 6-40.

The DynDiv setting in the Sculpt Surface control panel works just like the others you've looked at, so there's no need to cover it again. That leaves the two icons at the bottom of the panel. The right-hand one is the default, which shows handles used for controlling a deformation's degree of curvature. The other icon to the left is for controlling a deformation's scope, or how much of the object it affects, as well as its location. That's right: Using this tool, you can create a deformation in one part of an object, then move it to another part.

6. Clear the workspace, then add a plane of Resolution 8. Select the Sculpt Surface tool and right-button drag a small bump anywhere on the plane. In the Sculpt Surface control panel, click the icon in the lower-left corner. Note that the deformation's handles turn blue.

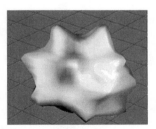

Figure 6-40 Bumpy sphere created by copying a deformation

7. Position the mouse cursor over the handle's exact center, left-click, hold, and drag. Like magic, the bump you created travels through the plane's surface wherever you drag. Try moving it to the corners and edges, then end up near the center.

8. Grab any of the handles between the center and the endpoint. Drag rightward to increase the length of the handle and the one opposite it, and leftward to decrease the length. As you drag, the bump changes size, increasing and decreasing in length along with the pair of handles. Release the mouse button when the bump extends the full length of the plane (see Figure 6-41).

9. Finally, grab the handles by an endpoint and drag the mouse to rotate the handles (you may have to zoom in to be able to click exactly on the endpoint). Watch how the bump rotates through the object surface to stay aligned with the handles (see Figure 6-42).

As powerful as the Deform Object tool is, Sculpt Surface, with its simple, intuitive interface, in some ways is a far more useful tool for customizing your meshes. This is one you'll find yourself using over and over again.

WARNING: Keep in mind that once you've finished deforming a surface with Sculpt Surface, there's no going back. Once you've exited the tool, Undo doesn't work, so always save your objects before sculpting their surfaces.

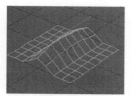

Figure 6–41 Deformation with increased scope in one dimension

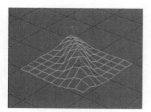

Figure 6–42
Rotated deformation

USING 3D BOOLEAN FUNCTIONS

As you near the end of this journey into trueSpace2's modeling power, it's time to explore one of the most highly valued features in 3D graphics: Boolean functions. You first met Booleans in Chapter 5, where you learned how to add, subtract, and intersect polygons. But doing the same things with 3D models is *way* cool—not to mention extremely useful. Need to cut a window or door hole out of a house wall? Need to make a round column with a square base, or a cube with rounded corners? Booleans let you easily do these and countless other tasks that would otherwise be far more arduous. You can see the three Boolean tools in Figure 6-43.

3D Booleans are tremendous fun to play with, so here are a few quick examples. Study them and then experiment on your own.

LESSON 9: BOOLEAN SUBTRACTION

Probably the sexiest 3D Boolean is Subtract, which lets you use any object as a tool to carve out parts of another. Let's take a look.

1. First, add two spheres. Move one in front of the other so they overlap by about half of one sphere's diameter (see Figure 6-44).

Figure 6–43 The Boolean tools: Object Subtraction, Object Union, and Object Intersection

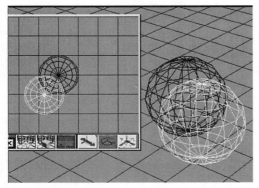

Figure 6–44 The two spheres positioned for Boolean subtraction

2. Select the Material Library tool and then choose any material. (If available, Amoeba is a good one.)

3. Select the Paint Object tool from the Paint pop-up menu. This coats the front sphere with the material.

4. Select the more distant sphere. Activate the Object Subtraction tool, which is the default 3D Boolean variant. It's immediately to the left of the Polygon tool in the Model group.

5. At this point, the mouse cursor turns into an inverted bottle and the Help bar displays the message Pick an object to be subtracted from the current object. Use the cursor to select the front object, whose wireframe is in dark blue. After a few moments, the subtraction is performed and you have a sphere with a large concave dent.

6. Render this object to see how the front sphere's material has been applied to the "scooped-out" portion (see Figure 6-45).

Okay, now that you've seen the basics of subtraction, let's look at a slightly more sophisticated application: a round column with a square base and top.

1. Before starting, clear the workspace and open new Front and Top view windows. Drag the windows into the upper corners.

2. Add a cube, activate the Object Scale tool, and right-button drag to make it as tall as you want the column to be. You'll be subtracting a modified torus from this to create the column.

3. Right-click on the Add Torus tool and change the Latitude setting to 17. Remember, the Latitude setting controls the number of rings perpendicular to the vertical axis. The ideal shape to subtract from the tall cube will have a nicely rounded top and bottom surface and a straight side. If you simply added a torus and scaled it higher,

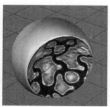

Figure 6–45 Sphere after subtraction operation

you would have rounded sides and would lose curvature on the top and bottom. You want an odd number of lines so you can raise the top part and have a single segment between it and the bottom section for the side.

4. Left-click the Add Torus tool to place a new torus in the workspace. In the Top view, you can see that the two objects are concentric.

5. For this step, as well as Steps 6 and 7, refer to Figure 6-46. In the Front view, zoom in on the torus. Activate the Point Edit: Vertices tool and select a point in the horizontal ring just above center. Check the Top view to make sure you selected a point on the outside of the torus. If you selected one on the inside, select a different point.

6. SHIFT-click on a horizontally neighboring point. Then SHIFT-click on a third point in the ring that's not next to either of the first two to select the entire ring.

7. To select the whole top part of the torus, SHIFT-click on any vertex in the top horizontal ring. All vertices and edges in and above the ring you first clicked on should now be highlighted in green.

8. Zoom out in the Front view window until you can see all of the tall cube. Activate the Object Move tool. (Do not activate the Object tool, because this would deselect the part of the torus you just selected.) In the main window, right-button drag downward until the torus is near the bottom of the cube in the Front view (see Figure 6-47).

9. In the Point Navigation panel, select the Point Move tool. In the main window, right-button drag upward until the top of the torus is the same distance from the top of the cube as the lower part is from the bottom (see Figure 6-48).

10. Now activate the Object tool (pressing the Spacebar is a handy shortcut) and then the Object Scale tool. In the Help bar, disable the Z button and enable the X and Y buttons.

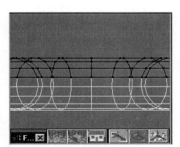

Figure 6–46 Zoomed in Front view of torus

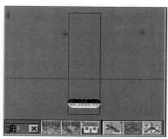

Figure 6–47 Torus with top section selected, placed near bottom of column

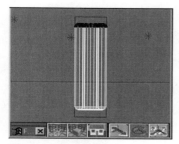

Figure 6–48 Torus with top section moved upward

11. In the Main view, press both mouse buttons and drag to the right. Increase the torus' width on both the x and y axes until the hole in the center, as viewed from the top, is near the cube outline. In Figure 6-49, I've reversed the highlighting to make the cube outline easier to see.

12. That's it for the setup. Select the cube, activate the Object Subtraction tool, and then select the torus object. Voilà—a beautiful Romanesque column (see Figure 6-50).

LESSON 10: BOOLEAN ADDITION

This one's a no-brainer. Take two objects and position them how you want (they don't have to overlap). Then use the Object Union tool to merge them forever into a single object, eliminating any overlapping geometry. Here's an example.

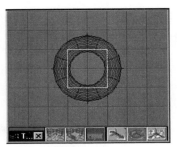

Figure 6–49 Torus
widened, from Top view

Figure 6–50
Rendered column

1. Add a cube and a sphere.

2. Scale the cube down on all three axes until it's slightly smaller than the sphere. Rotate it 45 degrees on the x and y axes. (You'll probably find it easiest to do this with the Object Info panel; right-click on the Object tool.)

3. Move the cube upward until its center is slightly below the sphere's top surface. It helps to use a Front or Left view for this.

4. Select the Object Union tool from the 3D Boolean pop-up, then select the sphere.

The result? A pointy-headed sphere, just like you've always wanted! Notice, in Figure 6-51, the smooth connections between the two objects, which you wouldn't get by merely juxtaposing them.

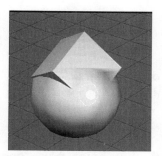

Figure 6–51 Cube
added to sphere

LESSON 11: BOOLEAN INTERSECTION

Finally, you come to Boolean Intersection, which lets you combine two objects so that only the overlapping portions remain. If you've been yearning for a doughnut with a square profile, here's how to make one.

1. Add a torus and a cube.

2. Scale the cube down until its corners are slightly inside the torus' outside edge, as seen from the top (refer to Figure 6-49—ignore the caption this time).

3. Select the Object Intersection tool and then the torus.

You end up with something like the object in Figure 6-52. Tasty-looking, isn't it?

To conclude this section on 3D Booleans, I encourage you to read the related online Help section. You'll find additional helpful information.

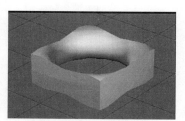

Figure 6–52 Intersection
between cube and torus

WARNING: It's important to remember that 3D Booleans are not a panacea. They don't work in every situation. For example, in this chapter's Lesson 6, you watched the editing of a sphere using Point Edit's Draw: Edited option when pulling faces out from the sphere. In creating Figure 6-14 to illustrate that process, I wasn't able to grab a screen during editing (while the mouse button was pressed), so I added another sphere in the same place as the first and tried subtracting the second from the first, leaving only the pulled-out faces. No dice. (Eventually, I ended up selecting the faces, separating them from the sphere, then sweeping them—not exactly the same, but close enough.)

WHAT NOW?

After this whirlwind tour of trueSpace2's advanced modeling tools, don't be surprised if you're a bit bewildered (or bewildered if you're surprised). There's a heap of modeling power here, so take all the time you need to digest and explore what I've covered. But don't take too long, because I'm waiting for you in Chapter 7, where you'll learn all about the trueSpace2 Utility functions.

7

UTILITIES AND EDIT TOOLS

The discussion of modeling in trueSpace2 will finish with a chapter on the program's Utility and Editing functions. You might use these tools less frequently, but that makes them no less handy, and they have a wide range of functionality.

THE UTILITY TOOLS

I'll start with the Utility group of tools, which includes the following, as shown in Figure 7-1:

- Grid Snap
- Axes
- Normalize Rotation, Location, Scale
- Center Axis
- Quad Divide, Smooth Quad Divide, and Triangulate Object
- Decompose
- Mirror
- Fix Bad Geometry (not discussed here)
- Reverse Normals
- Dimensioning

NOTE: Unless instructed otherwise, use Wireframe Display mode for all exercises in this chapter.

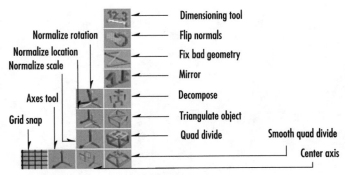

Figure 7-1 The Utility tool group

LESSON 1: NAVIGATION USING GRID SNAP

The Grid Snap tool is useful when you're interactively manipulating objects or entities in specific increments—for example, when spacing object copies regularly or rotating objects exactly a quarter turn. Of course, you can perform these functions by entering coordinates and angles in the Object Info panel, but it's usually more efficient to do it interactively, especially when performing the same transformation on a number of objects. Another, not-so-obvious, function of Grid Snap is for accurate placement of vertices when creating polygons. Let's take a look at all of these.

1. Start trueSpace2, or clear the workspace if the program is already running.

2. Use the Primitives panel to add a cube. Note that the cube sits squarely in the center of the workspace, occupying four grid squares.

3. Start by examining translation à la Grid Snap. Select the Object Move tool and then activate the Grid Snap tool, leftmost in the Utility group (see Figure 7-1).

4. Right-click on the Grid Snap tool to open the Grid Snap property panel (see Figure 7-2). The property panel's settings depend on which object manipulation tool is active. It's currently showing the default settings of 1, 1, and 1 for the x, y, and z axes, which means that the Grid Snap for object movement is 1 meter (the same as one square on the reference grid).

5. Select Object Rotate; the settings for all three axes change to 45 (degrees is implied, but not explicitly displayed).

6. Select Object Scale; the settings are now a ratio of .2.

7. Again select Object Move; then left-button drag the cube around in the workspace.

NOTE: You have to drag a certain distance to get movement with Grid Snap turned on, so if nothing happens at first, drag a bit farther. Note that the cube moves in increments of exactly one grid square.

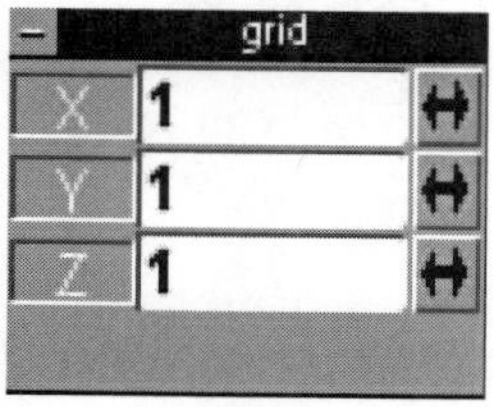

Figure 7-2 The Grid Snap property panel

8. Let's try changing one of the property panel values. Click in the box next to Y, change the setting to 2, and press <ENTER>. Then drag to the lower right or upper left to move the cube along the y axis. Now you have to drag even farther to get a response, but when the cube does move, it moves in increments of two grid squares. But if you drag diagonally in the opposite direction—along the x axis—it still moves in one-square increments.

9. You can turn off Grid Snap for any axis, using the X, Y, and Z buttons in the Grid Snap property panel. Click on X; then drag in both diagonal directions, and right-button drag for vertical movement with Grid Snap. Note that there's now no restriction on movement along the x axis, but the Grid Snap remains active for the other two axes.

10. Click on the Object Rotate tool. Note that the Grid Snap panel's X button is again selected. Then click on the Object Move tool. As with the Coordinate System controls, each manipulation tool remembers its Grid Snap settings.

11. Move the cube about one quarter of a grid square on the x axis, and then turn Grid Snap back on for the x axis. Move the object again along the x axis, and note that the specified movement increment now occurs from the new position, rather than from the original one.

Snappy Rotation

Let's look at rotation with Grid Snap on.

1. Delete the cube and add a cylinder. It will be easier to see rotation with this object.

2. Select the Object Rotate tool and change the Y setting to 90. Left-button drag to the upper right and lower left, and watch the cylinder alternate between standing up and lying on its side.

NOTE: If you continue to drag in one direction, the object actually rotates through a full circle in four increments. You can't tell this, however, unless you apply a texture map and view in Solid Render mode with textures turned on, or use some other way of making the cylinder nonsymmetrical (I'll explore this in a moment). This is useful for quick, precise adjustment of orientation, especially in animation setup.

3. With the cylinder straight up or sideways, right-button drag to rotate the cylinder in 45-degree increments around its vertical axis. Nothing happens—at least, nothing visible. The object actually is rotating, but because there are 16 divisions around the side and you're rotating it in 1/8-turn increments, the divisions always end up in exactly the same place.

4. To make the rotation visible, turn off Grid Snap for a moment by clicking on the icon. Then select any Point Edit tool variant and move a vertex, edge, or side face slightly out of position. (Incidentally, you didn't have to turn off Grid Snap, but it also affects point editing, and you want to move the entity only a short distance.)

5. Turn Grid Snap on again, select the Object tool and then Object Rotate, and then try rotating the cylinder about its z axis again. Now it looks like the displaced entity is moving through the object's surface, because the entity is seemingly the only part that changes. Rest assured; because you're in Object Rotate mode, you're actually rotating the entire object.

Scaling with Snap

Movement and rotation are fairly straightforward, but scaling with Grid Snap is somewhat less so.

1. Clear the workspace and add a cube.

2. Select Grid Snap, if it's not already on. If the Grid Snap property panel isn't open, right-click on the Grid Snap tool.

3. Open the Object Info panel by right-clicking on the Object tool.

4. Note that the cube's size is 2 × 2 × 2 meters. What if you want to halve its dimensions exactly? Obviously, you could simply enter new values in the Object Info panel, but you are using interactive tools in this exercise. Set the property panel settings to .5 and then drag the mouse to the lower left using both buttons. Try it now. What happened? Instead of being reduced by half, the cube has shrunk only by a third, with the new size being 1.33 meters cubed.

5. Let's try the opposite direction. Press and hold both mouse buttons and drag to the upper right. First the cube goes back to 2 meters cubed, then to 3, and then to 4.5; a 50 percent enlargement every time.

This phenomenon is due to another of trueSpace2's little peculiarities. The ratio as set in the Grid Snap panel is being *added to 1*, then multiplied by or divided into the object's size. So, when the cube was 1.33 meters cubed, that size was a result of dividing 2 by 1.5, then rounding off. And going up from 2 to 3 was a result of multiplying by 1.5. Knowing this, can you determine the setting needed in the property panel to halve or double the cube's size? How about to quadruple the cube, or to shrink it to one-fourth the original size? Think about this for a bit.

If you came up with 1 and 3, you get a gold star. Go ahead and try these scaling operations now to prove the theory.

TIP: You can also use Grid Snap to change the view in specific increments. Try it by turning on Grid Snap, then using the Eye Move, Eye Rotate, and Zoom tools. Note that the default values are exactly half of those for Object Move, Object Rotate, and Object Scale.

 TIP: You can change the measuring system used by the Grid Snap function for manipulation of both objects and the view by selecting a different one from the Object pop-up menu in the Object Info panel.

LESSON 2: ADDING POLYGONS WITH GRID SNAP

Let's see how using trueSpace2's Grid Snap feature can help when placing points for polygons. You'll make a simple letter B, as shown in the left side of Figure 7-3.

1. Clear the workspace, set the main window to Top View, and zoom out so you can see at least eight grid squares in the screen's vertical dimension.

2. Now, with Grid Snap off, try to create a letter B. Select the Polygon (not the Regular Polygon) tool.

3. Click at a grid intersection a couple of squares down from the top of the screen, near the horizontal center of the screen.

4. Click at the grid intersection four squares below the first point.

5. Click at the grid intersection two squares to the right of the second.

6. Click at the center of the grid square whose lower-left corner you just clicked on.

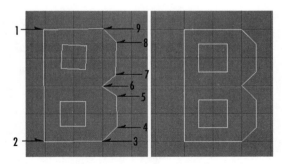

Figure 7-3 Letter B drawn with Grid Snap off (left side) and on (right side)

7. Click at the center of the grid square immediately above the one you clicked on previously.

8. Click in the upper-left corner of the grid square you just clicked in the middle of.

9. Repeat Steps 6, 7, and 8.

10. Right-click to close the B outline.

11. Select the Regular Polygon tool and, in the Poly Modes panel, select Subtract mode and set the number of sides to 4.

12. Draw two square polygons inside the B for the cutouts. Start the upper one at the grid intersection to the lower right of the B's top-left corner. Start the lower square poly at the grid intersection to the upper right of the bottom-left corner. (Because this is just an exercise, it's not a very fancy B.) Unless you're very talented or very careful, you'll likely end up with an out-of-kilter letter like the one on the left side of Figure 7-3.

13. Select the Object tool, delete the B, then select the Grid Snap and Polygon tools again and repeat Steps 3–12 above. This time, you should get a result more like the one on the right side of Figure 7-3. As you can see, it's a snap with Grid Snap!

Try changing the Grid Snap property panel settings and creating more polygons. Note that the setting has no affect on drawing polygons with Grid Snap on; the vertex always snaps to points at the grid intersection or half a square away, or the center of a grid square.

Try drawing a spline polygon with Grid Snap on and note that Grid Snap does not affect this process at all.

DynaUnits, an option in the Object Info panel that is fully explained in the trueSpace2 Help file, can implement a "local" independent unit measuring system for each object. This also pertains to Grid Snap. If the DynaUnits function is turned on via the Object Info panel, then an object's Grid Snap settings for movement use the same measuring system as the object.

LESSON 3: ROTATING OBJECT AXES

As you learned in Chapter 4, Navigation: Getting Around in truSpace2, each object's own set of axes comes into play when the object is manipulated in the Object coordinate system. (The Object coordinate system is the default for rotation and scaling.) You can use the Axes tool in the Utility group to make an object's axes visible, as well as to manipulate them directly. This latter capability is useful for a number of purposes. You can orient the axes so that the z axis is aligned with the "nose," or whichever part you want to point "forward" when using the Look At and Look Ahead tools. By moving the axes, you can change the "hinge" or "pivot" point on which the object rotates, for example, during an animation. Let's look at one application for rotating the axes first.

1. Start trueSpace2 or clear the workspace and add a sphere primitive.

2. Select the Point Edit: Faces tool.

3. Select a face near the vertical center on the right side of the sphere and right-button drag it to the right to move the selected face out from the sphere's surface, creating a "nose" (see Figure 7-4).

4. Select the Object tool, which automatically activates the Object Move tool. Drag the sphere to the right side of the workspace.

5. Use the Primitives panel to add another object, say a cone.

6. Select the sphere.

7. Activate the Look At tool, third from the left in the Animate group (see Figure 7-5), and click on the cone. This causes the part of the sphere that's aligned with its z axis to point at the cone and dynamically reorients the sphere to maintain this relationship if you move the sphere.

8. Move the sphere to the front of the workspace, then to the left side, and observe how the Look At function works. Unfortunately, you can see that it's not the sphere's nose that stays pointed at the cone, but rather the "top of the head." Let's see how to fix this.

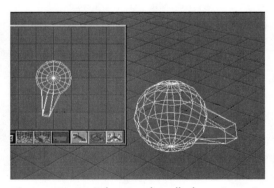

Figure 7–4 Sphere with pulled-out "nose"

Figure 7–5 The Look At tool

9. Select the Axes tool (refer back to Figure 7-1). This makes the sphere's set of axes visible. It also causes the sphere's wireframe mesh to turn orange (deactivated). Navigation functions performed on the object now apply only to the Axes object.

10. If you want the sphere's nose to stay pointed at the cone while you are using the Look At function, you must align the sphere's z axis with the nose. To do this, rotate the axes object a quarter-turn on the x axis. Select the Object Rotate tool and turn off y-axis rotation via the Y button on the Help bar.

11. The sphere is now on the left side of the workspace. The z and y axes are visible, but the x axis is hard to see because it's aimed right at the point of view. No matter; it's the z axis you're interested in. Right now it's pointing toward the cone; you want it to point at the nose. Left-button drag a short distance leftward in the workspace to rotate the Axes object a quarter-turn around the x axis. The z axis should now be roughly aligned with the nose (see Figure 7-6); if it isn't exact, that's okay, because this is just an exercise.

12. Select the Axes tool again to turn off the Axes object and reactivate the sphere.

TIP: If, for whatever reason, you'd like the Axes object to remain visible but become inactive, you can select another object. Or, to keep the sphere selected, simply press the ⊕ key on the keyboard. (I'll explore further use of the cursor keys for hierarchical navigation later on in this chapter, in the section on the Glue tool.) Later, if you want to disable display of the Axes object, select the sphere and then select the Axes tool twice.

Figure 7–6
Sphere's axes
rotated to align z
axis with nose

13. Select the Object Move tool. Then left-button drag in the workspace to move the sphere around. Note that, as soon as it starts moving, the sphere "jumps" to a new orientation in which the nose points at the cone, and continually adjusts itself to stay pointed at the cone no matter where you move it (see Figure 7-7). If it's not pointing exactly at the cone, you may have to rotate the sphere's axes slightly on the y axis.

LESSON 4: MOVING OBJECT AXES

As mentioned at the start of the previous lesson, the main reason to move an object's axes is to change its pivot point. This is primarily useful in animation. I'll demonstrate this by creating a simple door and altering its axes' location so it hinges correctly. You won't actually animate the door, but you can easily simulate animation by rotating it in real time.

1. Start trueSpace2 or clear the workspace and add a cube primitive.

2. Select the Object Scale tool. Scale the cube down quite a bit on the x axis, and by a small amount on the y axis. Once the proportions are correct, you might want to make it bigger, keeping the proportions, by dragging to the right with *both* buttons held down and all axes enabled (see Figure 7-8).

3. To simulate opening the door, rotate the object on the vertical axis. Select the Object Rotate tool and right-button drag in the workspace to rotate the door. As you can see, rotating on its center won't do, unless you want to make a revolving door by replicating the door, rotating the copy a quarter-turn, and gluing the two together.

4. Select the Axes tool to make the door's axes visible (see Figure 7-9).

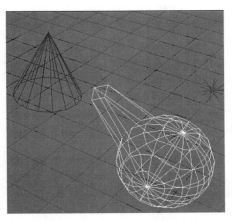

Figure 7-7 Sphere nose "looking at" cone

Figure 7–8 Cube repropor-
tioned to resemble a door

Figure 7–9 Cube with axes
in original position

5. Select the Object Move tool and click the X button on the Help bar. Make sure the Y button is selected.

6. Left-button drag rightward in the workspace until the Axes object is lined up with the door's right side. You'll probably find it helpful to switch between Front and Side views while doing this, or to open new windows with those views.

7. A hinge is attached to the door's edge, not its side, so another move is in order. Turn off the y axis, turn on the x axis, and drag leftward until the z axis is lined up with the door's edge (see Figure 7-10).

Figure 7–10 Cube with axes
in hinge position

8. Activate the Axes tool again and then click Object Rotate.

9. Right-button drag to the right, then to the left, to see how this door would properly open and close. If you were to install it in a house, you would build a frame to "stop" it from swinging "outward"—that is, clockwise from its original position.

NOTE: As you'll see later on in this chapter, moving an object's axes to change the hinge point is very useful in setting up hierarchical jointed characters for animation.

LESSON 5: WORKING WITH THE NORMALIZE TOOLS

The Normalize tools in trueSpace2 let you automatically return objects to their original orientation, location, and/or size. Using the Normalize tools is easy and straightforward—just select an object, invoke the command, and it's done. You can look at all three Normalize tools in a single quick tutorial.

1. Start trueSpace2 or clear the workspace and add a cone primitive.

2. Select the Object Move tool and drag the cone over to one side of the workspace.

3. Select Object Rotate and left-button drag to change the cone's orientation.

4. Select Object Scale and left-button drag to change the size and proportions.

5. Now reverse all three changes in a different order from which they were made. Start by selecting Normalize Rotation, the default Normalize tool in the Utility tool group (refer back to Figure 7-1). The cone is restored to its original orientation.

NOTE: The Normalize Rotation tool simply aligns the object's axes with the World axes, rotating the object itself by the same amount. If you had rotated the object axes with the Axes tool, the object's "normal" orientation would be different from that of its original orientation.

6. Click and hold on the Normalize Rotation tool to display the pop-up icon menu. Drag the mouse cursor over the Normalize Scale tool (refer back to Figure 7-1). Release the mouse button, and the cone is back to its original size and proportions.

7. Finally, open the pop-up menu again and select the Normalize Location tool (refer back to Figure 7-1). This returns the cone back to the center of the workspace.

NOTE: Normalize Location always returns an object to the location X=0, Y=0, Z=0, no matter where the object was created.

If you're thinking it would have been a lot easier just to invoke the Undo function three times, you're right—in this instance. However, Undo doesn't remember everything; in fact, its memory is often rather erratic. With complex scenes and many changes, it's usually best to use Normalize if you want to "start fresh" with an object's location, orientation, or size.

Using the Center Axis Tool

You may have noticed there's another tool in the Normalize pop-up. This one is Center Axis (sic). Its function is to reposition an object's axes at the geometric center of the object. Most objects' axes in trueSpace2 start out at their center, especially those created originally in 3D, such as the primitives. However, the axes of swept polygons and text remain in the plane of the original polygon. For example, say you're creating a flying logo animation and you want the text logo to swivel about its center as it moves toward the camera. Let's see how to set up the object so it rotates correctly.

1. Start trueSpace2 or clear the workspace.

2. Open the Primitives pane and select the Add Vertical Text tool.

3. Type a short word or phrase, such as `Hello`.

4. Select the Sweep tool to extrude the text.

5. Select the Object tool and then the Object Rotate tool.

6. With either the right or left button held down, drag the mouse in the workspace to rotate the text in various directions. Notice that it rotates around its lower-left corner, which is where its Axes object is placed by default.

7. From the Normalize pop-up, select the Center Axis tool (refer back to Figure 7-1). Instantly, the Axes object is moved to the exact geometric center of the 3D text, ready for manipulation with the object navigation tools.

8. Click the Axes tool to return the object to its normal status.

9. Try rotating the text again. It now rotates about its center.

As with many of the Utility functions, this is one you won't be using every day, but it's quite handy to have around when you need it.

LESSON 6: COMBINING NORMALIZE AND AXIS MANIPULATION

A popular 3D animation effect is the Univeral Pictures logo treatment, which has a company name circling the globe. Here's how to do it, using techniques you've already picked up in this and other chapters.

1. Start trueSpace2 or clear the workspace. Open the Primitives pane and add a sphere.

2. Select the Add Vertical Text tool. The text cursor appears in the center of the sphere, so click in front of and to the left of the sphere so you can see what you're typing.

3. Type the word Hello.

4. Click the Sweep tool to extrude the text. Then right-button drag upward to decrease the extrusion width.

5. Open new Top and Left view windows and move them into the upper-left and upper-right corners of the screen.

6. When trueSpace2 creates text, it places the object's axes at the lower-left corner, but you want them to be at the center so you can properly line up the two objects. From the Normalize pop-up menu, select the Center Axis tool. Then select the Axes tool to return the object to its normal selection state.

7. Use the Normalize Location tool on *both* the sphere and the text. This places both at the center of the workspace, or origin, so the two objects are truly concentric.

8. Select the Object and the Object Move tools and set the coordinate system to Object (use the pop-up near the right end of the Help bar).

9. Select the text, if necessary, and then right-button drag downward in the main window to move the text forward, away from the sphere's center. Stop when it's about a grid square diagonally away from the origin, as viewed from the top (see Figure 7-11). The text is centered vertically with respect to the sphere.

Figure 7-11 Text centered,
then moved away from sphere

Did you notice that right-button dragging the text did not move it vertically? This is because text is a special case: When trueSpace2 adds text, it places the text object's z axis perpendicular to the text face, because that's the axis along which the Sweep tool works. The y axis becomes the vertical axis.

NOTE: Here's another special aspect of text: It's created as a hierarchical object. You'll learn more about object hierarchy in the Edit tools section of this chapter, where you are introduced to the Glue brothers. For now, suffice it to say that a hierarchy is a way of combining objects so they can be manipulated as a whole, yet optionally be manipulated independently.

10. Press the ⊡ key on the keyboard to move downward into the hierarchy. Note that the H in Hello is now highlighted in white and the rest of the letters are in nonactive orange.

11. Each member of an object hierarchy has its own axis. When trueSpace2 creates a hierarchy, it automatically aligns the subobjects' axes with the main object's. Thus, each letter has a vertical y axis. Now rotate the letters to give the text a curved look. Select the Object Rotate tool and turn off x-axis rotation via the Help bar.

12. Left-button drag leftward in the workspace to rotate the H on its vertical axis. Watch the Top view as you do so, and stop when the H's front surface is almost aligned with the World x axis (see Figure 7-12).

13. Press the ⊡ key to select the next letter, which in this example is the e. Rotate this letter about half as far as you did the H, using Figure 7-12 as a guide. Don't worry about extreme precision; just get used to the techniques.

14. The first l is the "anchor," and thus won't be rotated. Press the ⊡ key twice to select the second l, then rotate it to the right by about the same amount as you rotated the e to the left.

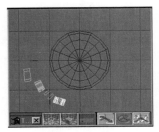

Figure 7-12 Letters reoriented

15. Press the ▣ key again and rotate the o to the right so its front surface is almost aligned with the World y axis.

16. As shown in Figure 7-12, although the letters are rotated correctly, they're not lined up very well. Select Object Move and, in the Top view, move the outermost letters until their inner surfaces (facing the sphere) form a curve that roughly matches the sphere's (see Figure 7-13).

17. You might also want to adjust rotations at this point.

TIP: You can select the different letters simply by clicking on them, which is probably easier in this case than using the ▣ and ▣ keys.

18. Press the ▣ key to return to the top level of the text's hierarchy, that is, the entire word.

19. The final step is to place the text's axis at the sphere's center so you can cause the text to "orbit" the sphere simply by rotating it around its vertical axis. Select the Axes tool, then Normalize Location, and note that the text's axes are now at the origin, coinciding with the sphere's center.

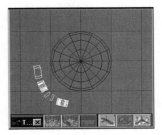

Figure 7-13 Letters moved to form curved outline

176

20. Reselect the Axes tool and then the Object Rotate tool. The x axis should still be turned off, so you can left-button drag to the right and left for the full orbital effect.

21. Use the File/Scene/Save command to save this scene as LOGO-ORB.SCN. You'll learn techniques for animating it in Chapter 11, Animation.

LESSON 7: USING THE QUAD DIVIDE AND TRIANGULATE OBJECT TOOLS

Now let's start in on the rightmost pop-up menu in the Utility group, which contains eight tools loosely related to modifying polygons. The first three (starting from the bottom of the pop-up)—Quad Divide, Smooth Quad Divide, and Triangulate Object—are closely related, so I'll cover all three in a single lesson.

From their names, you might suspect the Quad Divide tools are used to subdivide polygons into four smaller polygons. In general, you'd be correct, because most polygons in trueSpace2 are four sided. However, the more general rule is that the tools subdivide polygons with *n* sides into *n* polygons (e.g., a 10-sided polygon would be divided into 10 polygons). Let's explore these tools.

1. Start trueSpace2 or clear the workspace and add a cube primitive.

2. Smooth Quad Divide is the default tool in its pop-up (refer back to Figure 7-1). Select it now—nothing happens. You'll find out why in a moment.

NOTE: The other tools in the Quad Divide pop-up, including Mirror and Reverse Normals, are covered later in the chapter.

3. From the pop-up, select Quad Divide (refer back to Figure 7-1). Now you get a fairly predictable result: All the cube's polygons have been divided into four. This is the exact same object you'd get by creating a primitive cube with a resolution of 2.

4. Undo the last action (press CTRL-Z or select the Undo tool). Then select Smooth Quad Divide again to make it the default tool in its slot. Of course, nothing happens again. This is getting monotonous! Let's see how you can get some action out of Smooth Quad Divide.

5. Right-click on the Smooth Quad Divide tool. This opens its property panel (see Figure 7-14), which is labeled Subdivision and contains a setting for Angle.

Figure 7-14 The Smooth
Quad Divide property panel

6. The current Angle setting is 80. This means only polygons that meet each other at angles less than 80° can be subdivided with Smooth Quad Divide. To prove this, set the Angle value to 90 and select Smooth Quad Divide again. Again, nothing happens (last time, I promise!).

7. Set Angle to 91 and click Smooth Quad Divide. There—you now have a nice geodesic-looking spheroid (see Figure 7-15). Try rendering it to see how it looks as a solid. To make it even more spherical, simply click Smooth Quad Divide again.

One of the nice things about the Quad Divide tools is that they can be used on specific faces to add resolution to an object only where it's needed. Let's try subdividing only one of the cube's faces.

8. Start by pressing CTRL-Z twice to return the cube to its original pristine state. Then select the Point Edit: Context tool and click the cube's right front side.

9. Select the Quad Divide tool and note that only the selected face is subdivided.

10. Because you're still in Point Edit mode, select the new vertex in the center of the side, then right-button drag to pull it out to a point—about a meter or so.

11. Render the object to see how trueSpace2 handles the four nonplanar polygons you just created. You can see that the new side facing you seems okay, but its two neighbors look a bit strange.

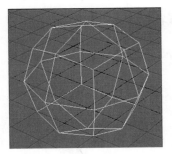

Figure 7-15 Smooth
Quad Divided cube

Let's see if you can fix this with the Triangulate Object tool. This tool is for subdividing faces into triangles. Note that the name is Triangulate *Object*; it works on an entire object at one time.

12. Select Triangulate Object now from the Quad Divide pop-up menu. The result is that every face on the former cube has been subdivided into triangles.

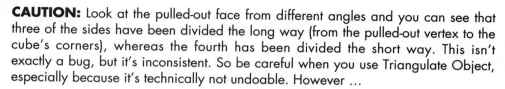

CAUTION: Look at the pulled-out face from different angles and you can see that three of the sides have been divided the long way (from the pulled-out vertex to the cube's corners), whereas the fourth has been divided the short way. This isn't exactly a bug, but it's inconsistent. So be careful when you use Triangulate Object, especially because it's technically not undoable. However ...

TIP: Here's an undocumented way to "undo" a Triangulate Object operation. Add an object and position it so it's not overlapping the triangulated object. Select the object that was triangulated. Activate the Object Subtraction tool and select the second object. This is just one of the many useful tricks from the friendly folks on the trueSpace Internet mailing list (see Appendix A, Additional Resources).

LESSON 8: USING DECOMPOSE

The Decompose tool (refer back to Figure 7-1) has nothing to do with rotting organic matter—it's for use mainly with objects created in other 3D programs and imported into trueSpace2. Decompose is especially useful for objects made with computer-aided design (CAD) programs that build objects in layers. It creates a hierarchy out of such objects, based on the object's layered structure and the surface types defined within the model. This is helpful for separating out parts of the model or for creating hierarchical animation with it.

You can simulate a layered object by creating a Boolean union of two physically separate objects. Let's try it.

1. Start trueSpace2 or clear the workspace. Then use the Primitives panel to add any two objects, say two spheres.

2. Use the Object Move tool to separate the two spheres so they're not touching each other. Then select the Object Union tool from the Boolean pop-up and click on the unselected sphere.

3. You've now created a single nonhierarchical object from the two spheres. Test this by pressing the ⊞ key. Nothing happens.

4. From the Quad Divide pop-up, select the Decompose tool. The wireframe objects blink slightly, but there's no visible change.

5. To see what happened, press the ⊞ key. You can see that a hierarchy has been created from the formerly monolithic object.

6. Use the ← or → key to select either of the spheres. You'll find out how to dissolve the hierarchy later in this chapter.

NOTE: Typically, objects suitable for treatment with the Decompose tool are in the DXF format created by Autodesk AutoCAD. In some cases, these objects automatically decompose upon loading; this is evident when the Down Arrow icon in the Navigation group becomes active. If the icon does not become active upon loading a DXF-format object, try using the Decompose tool. You can find many examples of objects in this format at file repositories on the Internet. And, although arrangements were not formalized at this writing, there's a good chance you'll find some on the CD-ROM that accompanies this book.

LESSON 9: CREATING REFLECTIONS WITH THE MIRROR TOOL

The Mirror tool in the Quad Divide pop-up simply flips an object about its own axes, reversing its structure in relation to the World x axis. If the object is parallel to the x axis, it seems to flip front to back, and if it's parallel to the y axis, it flips left to right. But it's basically the same thing, because rotating the object subsequently about its vertical axis resolves any differences.

Because so many objects are symmetrical right to left, this can save a lot of work when you're constructing, for example, human bodies. Just build one side, make a copy, mirror it, Boolean-union the two halves together, and voilà. You've created a perfectly symmetrical object with very little effort.

In this exercise, I'll illustrate a somewhat different use of Mirror. Say you want to create text that looks chiseled out of an object, using Boolean subtraction. The text doesn't necessarily have to be reversed. You can just extrude it and then subtract the "rear end" from the object. But if you want a *beveled* chisel, which looks much nicer, this technique doesn't work. You might think that you could create the text, perform a Sweep, move the swept faces behind the original ones, and then perform a bevel and move those surfaces toward the rear as well. You're welcome to try it, but you'll find that you can't move beveled faces behind the ones from which they're extruded during the beveling operation. Fortunately, the dilemma is easily solved with the Mirror tool.

1. Start trueSpace2 or clear the workspace.

2. Let's try something a bit different. It would be nice to have text start out parallel to the grid so you don't have to rotate it. (Text is always created parallel to the active Perspective view plane.) You want to flip the text front to back, so set the view to be parallel to the x axis. Activate the Eye Rotate tool (fifth from the left in the main window View tool group) and turn off x-axis rotation.

3. Left-button drag rightward in the workspace until the grid lines parallel to the x axis (the ones that run between screen lower left and upper right when you start the program) are running left to right. Get them as straight (no jaggies) or as near to straight as you can (see Figure 7-16).

NOTE: Interestingly enough, if you click in a Top view window before entering text, text is automatically created parallel to the x axis (you can't create text in Left and Front view windows). However, because you want to have a good view of all operations in this exercise, I have you go to the (slight) extra trouble of rotating the Perspective view.

4. Open the Primitives panel and select the Add Vertical Text tool.

5. For best results, use a fairly substantial font size—say, 24 points or so—and set it to Bold. Enter the word `Motion`.

6. Sweep the text. You needn't shorten it—in fact, when using text in Boolean subtraction, it's nice to have some extra length.

7. Select the Bevel tool. It's the one in the Sweep pop-up that looks like a green and orange circle. Use the default setting for now.

8. From the Quad Divide pop-up, select the Mirror tool (refer back to Figure 7-1). Now the text has been flipped front to back and is still legible from your viewpoint. However, if you rotated the view or the object so the beveled side were facing you, it would be as if you were reading it in a mirror.

9. Open a new Top view window and move it up and out of the way.

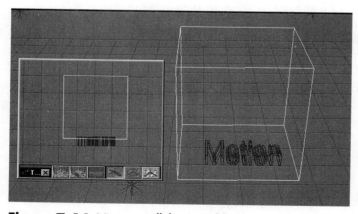

Figure 7–16 View parallel to World x axis

10. Add a cube primitive. Scale it up so it's at least a couple of meters wider than the text and move it so it's slightly overlapping the back side of the text as seen from the top (refer back to Figure 7-16).

11. Activate the Object Subtraction tool. In the Top view, select the part of the text that's sticking out from the cube.

12. Voilà! Render it from various angles to admire your handiwork (see Figure 7-17). It may be difficult to see some of the edges, which demonstrates the importance of proper lighting. You'll learn about that in Chapter 8, The Importance of Lighting.

LESSON 10: USING THE REVERSE NORMALS TOOL

The Reverse Normals tool isn't used very often, but it can come in handy now and again. Polygons in most 3D programs, including trueSpace2, face in a particular direction—normally, outward. But if a polygon is facing inward and the program doesn't account for that, you won't be able to see the polygon. When trueSpace2 renders objects, it renders both sides of all polygons, which is one reason it's not as fast as some other programs.

For expediency, the 3D technology as implemented in trueSpace2's Solid Render Display mode renders only polygons' front faces. A *normal*, by the way, is an imaginary line perpendicular to a polygon's "front." If you use 3D with an object whose normals are reversed—that is, its polygons are facing inward—the object appears inside out, because the polygons on the sides facing you are invisible. The polygons that they would normally be blocking, on the surfaces that are out of your view, are facing you.

This is easy to observe. Select Solid Render Display mode and add a cube primitive. Select the Reverse Normals tool (refer back to Figure 7-1) from the Quad Divide pop-up. You'll see only the cube's rear and bottom faces. Then render the cube, and it looks fine.

LESSON 11: WORKING WITH THE DIMENSIONING TOOL

CAD is a class of software used in architecture, engineering design, and other exacting applications. Although trueSpace2 is not a CAD program, it has a CAD-like feature in the Dimensioning tool.

If you're making a model from the real world or for the real world, it's often handy to be able to measure parts of the model. The Dimensioning tool doesn't permit measurement of arbitrary distances. Instead, it creates a pseudo-object consisting of a pair of lines sticking out from two of a model's vertices, connected at their endpoints by a line

Figure 7-17 Rendered chiseled text

containing text that shows the distance between the endpoints. The measurement remains visible on the object, whether or not the object is selected, unless you remove the measurement via the Dimension tool control panel.

Its use is straightforward:

1. If you're still in Solid Render mode from the Reverse Normals exercise, return to Wireframe Display. Select or add an object to measure, such as a sphere.

2. Select the Dimensioning tool from the Quad Divide pop-up (refer back to Figure 7-1).

3. Click on any two points, and the dimension measurement appears. You may need to rotate the object or view to see the measurement if it's edge-on to the view. If you alter the object's size or proportions, the measurement value changes dynamically. If you rotate the object or view to show the object's opposite side, the text flips so that it is always right side up and reads left to right.

4. To add another dimension measurement, reactivate the Dimensioning tool and select another pair of points. The active measurement, normally the most recently added one, is bright yellow. The others are darker yellow. However, in Figure 7-18, I've made them both black for visibility.

When you select the Dimensioning tool, the Dimensions control panel appears (see Figure 7-19). The two upper icons enable deleting the active measurement or all measurements. The lower arrow buttons let you activate the next or previous measurement, respectively.

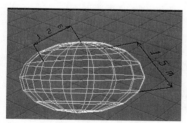

Figure 7–18 Object with two Dimension measurements

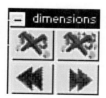

Figure 7–19 The Dimensions control panel

THE EDIT TOOLS

The first three commands in this group correspond to the same-named functions in the Edit menu. The fourth pop-up contains the tools for building and breaking down object hierarchies. The Edit tools (see Figure 7-20) are as follows:

- Undo and Redo
- Erase
- Copy
- Glue as Child, Glue as Sibling, and Unglue

LESSON 12: UNDO AND REDO

You've already used Undo liberally in the lessons so far. Let's take a quick closer look at this eminently useful Utility function, as well as its sibling, Redo.

1. Start trueSpace2 or clear the workspace. Then add a primitive object, say a sphere.

2. Move the object, then rotate it, and then scale it. It doesn't matter how you do it; you're just establishing a sequence of actions.

3. Select the Undo tool (or press CTRL-Z) three times. Note that your actions in Step 2 reversed, one step at a time, and you end up with the sphere exactly as it started. Undo is reasonably reliable, although it doesn't work with certain functions, including Triangulate Object.

4. From the Undo pop-up menu, select Redo three times. (Of course, after you select it the first time, it becomes the default tool and you no longer need to activate the pop-up to select it.) The sequence of manipulations from Step 2 is re-created precisely.

5. So far, so good. Redo can be recalcitrant, though. To see this, choose any Point Edit tool, select an entity on the sphere, and pull it out to change the object's shape.

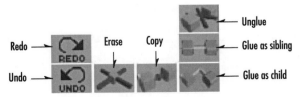

Figure 7-20 The Edit tools

6. Select Undo. Again, so far, so good; the entity is back where it began.

7. Select Redo. No dice! This behavior occurs with many operations. Fortunately, Redo is needed far less often than Undo, so it's really not much of a problem.

8. To redeem itself, Redo has the unique capability of repeating an operation an unlimited number of times for a cumulative effect. Move the object and use the Undo function. Then select Redo. The object moves back to its original position, as you expected.

9. Select Redo again. This time the object moves an equal distance to and in the same direction as in Step 8. Continue selecting Redo; each time the object will move the same distance in the same direction. Unfortunately, this facility would be more useful if it were applicable to different objects (i.e., Undo a manipulation of one object, and then apply the Redo to another one). This would let you, for example, place a series of objects at equal distances around the circumference of a circle.

Undo's Options

Let's take a look at the Undo function's options.

1. You should still have a sphere in the workspace from the previous tutorial. If not, add one from the Primitives panel.

2. Move the sphere a short distance.

3. Select the Zoom tool from the main window's View tool group and left-button drag upward in the workspace to magnify the view.

4. Move the sphere another short distance.

5. Select Undo three times and watch what happens. First the sphere moves back, then the view zooms back out, and finally the sphere is replaced at its original position.

You can see that Undo works equally well for changing the view as for manipulating objects. (This is a relatively rare capability—in most 3D graphics applications, the Undo function, if it exists, does not apply to modifications of the view.) This facility, however, isn't always desirable. In many cases, you will want to keep the changed view and undo only object changes. This is easy with the Undo Options panel.

6. Select Redo three times so you're back at the position you were in Step 4.

7. Right-click on the Redo tool to open the Undo Options panel (see Figure 7-21).

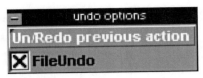

Figure 7-21 The Undo
Options panel

8. Notice that the pop-up menu item in the upper part of the panel reads **Un/Redo previous action**. This tells you that the Undo and Redo tools apply to all actions (well, most actions). Click and hold on this box, drag to the other menu item—Un/Redo object only—and release the button.

9. Click Undo twice. This time, instead of zooming out on the second Undo operation as before, the program simply skips to undoing the previous movement, restoring the sphere to its original position.

TIP: You can save yourself a lot of annoyance by remembering this facility for isolating Undo operations to object manipulations when you're performing a complex series of operations involving both object manipulation and view changes.

The panel's FileUndo option, which is the default, allows reversing destructive operations, such as Erase and Booleans, by creating a temporary file. There's no reason to disable this option unless your computer is very slow or disk space is extremely limited.

ERASE AND COPY

These tools work only on objects, not entities. They do exactly what their names sound like, and there isn't a whole lot more to say about them. Read the descriptions in the trueSpace2 Help file.

THE GLUE BROTHERS

No, I'm not talking about Elmer and Super. In trueSpace2, *glue* is used to describe the process of combining objects into hierarchical models. Of course, you've already learned one method of combining objects—Boolean addition—but its drawback is that the resulting model's parts are no longer independently manipulable. With hierarchical models, on the other hand, you can manipulate the model as a whole or you can go down into the hierarchy and work with the components individually. You can even animate parts of a hierarchical model while moving the whole thing around, combining multitudes of motion for sophisticated results such as character animation.

There are two Glue variants—the Glue as Child tool and the Glue as Sibling tool—as well as an Unglue command for breaking down hierarchies. Let's start with the simpler command: Glue as Sibling.

LESSON 13: USING GLUE AS SIBLING

When, in creating an object hierarchy, you want to place two or more objects at the same hierarchical level, use the Glue as Sibling tool. This tool is also useful if you want to unify some objects temporarily and don't particularly care about the hierarchical structure.

1. Start trueSpace2 or clear the workspace. Add four different primitive objects—a cube, a cylinder, a cone, and a sphere.

2. Use Object Move to line up the objects left to right, in the same order as listed in Step 1. When you're finished, select the cube.

3. Open the Glue pop-up menu from the rightmost icon in the Edit group. Select the Glue as Sibling tool (see Figure 7-20).

4. Move the mouse cursor into the workspace and watch it change to an inverted glue bottle.

Starting to Build the Hierarchy

1. Select the cylinder; both objects are now selected. You're still in Glue mode, as indicated by the cursor's appearance.

2. Choose any of the object navigation tools, such as Object Rotate, and manipulate the cube and cylinder to demonstrate that the two essentially constitute a single object.

3. Press the ⬇ key once to enter the hierarchy (you can also click the Down Arrow icon in the Navigation group). At this point, the Down Arrow icon in the Navigation group changes to an Up Arrow icon to indicate that you're at a lower level in the hierarchy. Both arrows are always available from a pop-up, although one or both may be ghosted (unavailable), depending on where you are in the hierarchy.

4. Then press the ➡ and ⬅ keys repeatedly. Note that only one of the objects at a time is selected and the other is orange in appearance. You are now at the lower level of the simple hierarchy you've just created. At this point, you can manipulate only the highlighted object.

5. Use the same navigation tool as in Step 2 to manipulate one object, then the other. In addition to using the cursor keys, you can simply click on the nonhighlighted object to select it.

6. Press the ⬆ key or click the ⬆ icon in the Navigation group to return to the top level of hierarchy.

Adding to the Hierarchy

Let's go ahead and add the remaining objects to the group.

1. Activate the Glue as Sibling tool again and then click on the cone and sphere objects in that order (left to right). All four objects are now selected. Use the Rotate Object tool to demonstrate that they act as a unit.

2. Again press the ⊡ key to enter the hierarchy, then the ⊡ and ⊡ keys to move between its members. Because you selected the objects in left-to-right order, the selection order is logical: Pressing the ⊡ key selects to the left, and pressing the ⊡ key selects to the right. Also, the selection order wraps around, so if the cube is selected and you press the ⊡ key, the sphere becomes selected. The same goes for the sphere and the ⊡ key.

3. As before, only the highlighted object is manipulable. Demonstrate this by rotating the various individual objects in different directions.

Dissolving the Hierarchy

It's time to break up that old gang of yours.

1. With any single member of the group highlighted, select the Unglue tool (refer back to Figure 7-20) from the Glue pop-up. The tool takes effect immediately, removing the highlighted object from the group and deselecting it and highlighting the next object. Select Unglue twice more to dissolve the hierarchy entirely.

Have you noticed that Unglue is a single-usage tool? After you invoke it, trueSpace2 returns to the tool that was active beforehand. Therefore, you need to select Unglue every time you want to use it. If one of the Glue tools is active when you use Unglue, the Glue tool remains the default, so you need to keep returning to the pop-up when you want Unglue. If you're using another tool, such as Object, then Unglue becomes the default tool until there are no more objects to unglue. At that point, the most recently used Glue variant is restored as the default.

2. The order in which you add objects to the hierarchy affects the order in which the cursor keys select them. Select the cone, then select Glue as Sibling, then select the objects in this order: cube, cylinder, sphere.

3. With all objects selected (i.e., at the upper level of the hierarchy), try to activate the Unglue tool. It can't be done. The program is smart enough to let you use Unglue only when you're down into the hierarchy and can indicate objects you want unglued by highlighting them.

4. Press the ⊡ key. The cone—the first object selected—is highlighted.

5. Press the ⊡ key three times to highlight the remaining objects in the same order that you selected them. Then press the ⊡ key repeatedly to highlight objects in the reverse order of selection. This is like pressing the cursor keys in the workspace to select objects in the same order you added or loaded them.

TIP: Remember: If you glued things in a weird order, you can always use the mouse to select hierarchy members.

6. Use the Unglue tool again to restore the objects to their original ungrouped status.

Creating Multiple Hierarchical Levels

So far, you've created only a single hierarchical level. Let's see how to use Glue as Sibling to create multiple levels.

1. Select the cube and glue it to the cylinder.

2. Press the ⊡ key to enter the hierarchy, and then the ⊡ key to select the cylinder.

3. Glue the cone to the cylinder. Then again press the ⊡ key followed by the ⊡ key to select the cone.

4. Glue the sphere to the cone.

5. Here's where things start to get complex. Let's explore your new multilevel hierarchy from the top down. Press the ⊡ key twice to return to the highest level of hierarchy, that of the entire group. Press the ⊡ key, then press the ⊡ or ⊡ key a few times. Notice that, at this level of hierarchy—one down from the top—you can select either the cube or the group consisting of the other three objects.

6. With the three objects selected, press the ⊡ key again. Now, using the ⊡ and ⊡ keys, you can select either the cylinder or the cone/sphere group, but not the cube. You are now two levels down from the top.

7. With the cone and sphere selected, press the ⊡ key once more. Now you're at the lowest hierarchical level and can select only the cone or the sphere—the last two glued objects.

8. If you're not going to continue on to the next lesson right away, return to the top level of hierarchy and save the object as HIERARCH.COB.

Here's some information that may help you understand the trueSpace2 hierarchy paradigm. If you've built hierarchical objects in some other 3D program, you know that a single object is considered the "parent" in the hierarchical object, with the objects below it in the hierarchy regarded as its "children." When you manipulate the parent, the kids come along for the ride; but when you manipulate the children, the parent remains steadfast. In trueSpace2, the parent is the *group of objects* or, rather, an invisible node "above" that group.

Yes, it's kind of confusing at first. Spend time experimenting, moving between the various levels and gluing groups of objects together in different ways, and you'll soon become familiar, if not comfortable, with Caligari's nonintuitive scheme for hierarchical object construction and manipulation. This aspect of modeling in trueSpace2 is one of the program's weak spots, and many of the program's users hope that Caligari will come up with an improved scheme in future versions. One of the unfriendliest aspects of hierarchical construction in trueSpace2 is the lack of a "tree" diagram or other outline of object hierarchies that helps you see the relationships between all members at a glance.

LESSON 14: USING GLUE AS CHILD

You're now going to re-create the same multilevel hierarchy you made at the end of Lesson 13, but in a somewhat more straightforward way, using the Glue as Child tool.

1. If you're not continuing from the previous lesson (Glue as Sibling), you'll need to load the HIERARCH.COB object you would have saved in the last step of that exercise.

2. Dissolve the hierarchy using the Unglue tool.

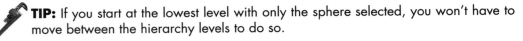

TIP: If you start at the lowest level with only the sphere selected, you won't have to move between the hierarchy levels to do so.

3. You may recall, in the last part of Lesson 13, that you used Glue as Sibling to build a multilevel hierarchy from the top down. You will now rebuild the hierarchy from the bottom up, so select the sphere object to start.

4. Select the Glue as Child tool (see Figure 7-20).

5. Select the remaining three objects in right-to-left order: first the cone, then the cylinder, and finally the cube.

6. Use the cursor keys to maneuver between the various hierarchy parts to verify that the object structure is indeed the same as the one built at the end of Lesson 13.

The key to understanding how Glue as Child works is simply this: The child is the one selected *before* the gluing operation. You started out with the sphere at the lowest level of hierarchy, then created a parent "node" consisting of the cone and sphere. You then created another node one level higher, with the parent node consisting of the cylinder and the cone-sphere group. Finally, you created the highest node, consisting of the cube and the cylinder-cone-sphere group.

LESSON 15: BUILDING A CHARACTER

Let's build a robot! In this lesson, you'll combine the two gluing methods you've learned so far to make an animatable character: a stick-figure mechanical being constructed from cylinders. Then, in Chapter 11, you'll make it walk!

1. Start trueSpace2 or clear the workspace and add a cylinder primitive.

2. Use the Copy and object navigation tools to construct the robot as depicted in Figure 7-22. It should have a head, a neck, a long horizontal cylinder for the shoulders, a larger cylinder for the torso, and two cylinders each for arms and legs. *Hint*: Open new Top and Side views to help line things up. Also, when rotating the cylinder(s) for the head and/or shoulders, use Grid Snap and disable the y axis.

NOTE: This step is good practice, but if you'd rather skip it, load the scene file ROBOT.SCN from the TUTORIAL\CH7 directory on the CD-ROM that accompanies this book.

Planning Ahead

Before starting to build the hierarchy, think about the kind of structure you want to create. When you walk, you lead with your torso and the rest of your body parts come along for the ride. If you bend your neck, the head moves too, but you can move your head without moving the neck (much). Also, you can move your arms without moving your shoulders, but if you move your shoulders, the arms move too. Likewise, you can move your legs without moving the rest of your body. So ideally, you'd place the torso at

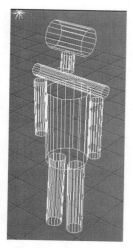

Figure 7–22
Robot made from
cylinders

the highest level of hierarchy. Its direct children would be the legs assembly, the shoulders/arms assembly (with the shoulders parent to the arms), and the head/neck assembly (neck parent to head). However, because of trueSpace2's nonstandard method of hierarchy construction, you'll have to make some compromises. Figure 7-23 depicts the actual structure you'll use. Notice that the actual body parts appear only at the end of each chain; all the upper chain members are nodes, or groupings of body parts.

1. Start by building the two sibling groups: the arms and legs. Select one leg, then select the Glue as Sibling tool, then select the other leg.

2. Repeat Step 1 for the arms.

 CAUTION: Select the Object tool before clicking on an arm, or you'll end up adding it to the leg group. Alternatively, you can leave the Glue as Sibling tool active and use the ⬅ or ➡ key to select the first arm.

It's All About Relationships

1. Now start creating the parent-child relationships. The arms are already selected, so select the Glue as Child tool and then select the shoulders. Remember, when using Glue as Child, the object selected first is the child. So the arms become subordinate to the shoulders—that is, the node consisting of the shoulders and arms. If you enter that hierarchy, you can manipulate the shoulders independently of the arms (one of the unnecessarily confusing aspects of trueSpace2's hierarchy paradigm).

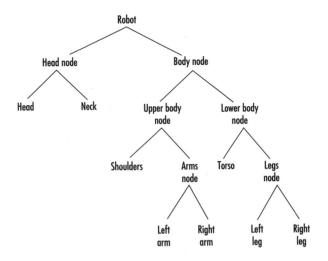

Figure 7-23 The robot's hierarchical structure

2. Now that the shoulders and arms are combined, make that assembly a child of the torso. With Glue as Child still active, select the torso.

3. Make the legs active (use the Object tool or the ⬅ or ➡ key, not the Glue as Child tool). Then click on the torso.

4. Make the head active and then glue it as a child to the neck.

5. Glue the head/neck group to the rest of the body.

6. You're done with the robot! Before exploring the hierarchy, save the object as ROBOT.COB. As mentioned above, you'll use it to learn character animation in Chapter 11.

Exploring the Hierarchy

1. You're now at the top hierarchy level. Press the ⬇ key once to enter the second level. The head-neck assembly remains highlighted, and the rest of the figure is orange.

2. Press the ⬅ or ➡ key once to activate the lower part of the body. Now the legs are highlighted. Press the ➡ key again to highlight the torso assembly, then the ⬇ key to enter that part of the hierarchy.

3. Continue navigating around in the hierarchy with the various cursor keys to familiarize yourself with the structure, using Figure 7-23 as a "map." Note that you must often move up and out of a substructure to work in another substructure.

Posed for Action

Before I close this chapter, let's look at posing the figure.

1. Activate the legs structure. Then press the ⬇ key to highlight either of the legs.

2. Select the Object and the Object Rotate tools and turn off the x axis.

3. Left-button drag back and forth in the workspace to rotate the leg forward and back. Wait a minute—something's not right! The leg is rotating at the knee, rather than the hip.

4. How do you fix this? In the discussion of the Axes tool earlier in this chapter, I said that the axes' location determines the pivot point. With this in mind, you can probably figure out what to do. Simply use the Axes tool to move the leg axes up to where the leg "connects" to the torso. Try it now and then rotate the leg again for proper movement.

5. If you like, set all subobject axes to logical pivot points. (Note that subassemblies have their own axes, independent of their component objects' axes. If you set trueSpace2 to Solid Render Display mode, you can see the axes for the active object or assembly.) Set the head-neck assembly's axis to the bottom center of the neck. I'll show you how to set all the axes in Chapter 11, Lesson 4, in preparation for animation.

WHAT NOW?

The more you know about utilities, the better off you'll be. There's a lot more good material about these tools in the Help file—in fact, most of the Help information is identical to what's in the trueSpace2 reference manual. So read up whenever you get a chance, or when you need a little more detail about a tool's function.

8

THE IMPORTANCE OF LIGHTING

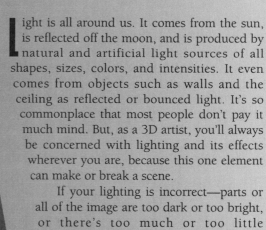

Light is all around us. It comes from the sun, is reflected off the moon, and is produced by natural and artificial light sources of all shapes, sizes, colors, and intensities. It even comes from objects such as walls and the ceiling as reflected or bounced light. It's so commonplace that most people don't pay it much mind. But, as a 3D artist, you'll always be concerned with lighting and its effects wherever you are, because this one element can make or break a scene.

If your lighting is incorrect—parts or all of the image are too dark or too bright, or there's too much or too little contrast—it doesn't matter how carefully you've sculpted and placed your models and textured their surfaces. The resulting images won't be quite good enough and won't achieve the recognition they deserve. Every scene is different: Some work well with a single light source, but most require several—and placement is crucial. Lighting in 3D graphics is often a trade-off between the need for *spot* (i.e., small-area) *lighting* in many different parts of a scene and

197

acknowledgment of the limitations of the technology. The more lights, the longer required to render the scene.

One of the best things you can do to improve your 3D artistry is to learn lighting craft, and one of the best ways to do that is to study photography. Go to the library and take out as many books as you can find about general photography and photographic lighting. Also, talk to photographers about their lighting experiences. If you have the time, offer to help a studio photographer with his or her lighting arrangements. You'll gain invaluable experience.

WORKING WITH TRUESPACE2'S LIGHTING LIMITATIONS

The trueSpace2 program offers a special benefit in its use of 3DR technology—to display lighting effects and changes in real time. But 3DR involves many compromises, some of which I'll cover in this chapter, so you should always render your scenes conventionally for more accurate results.

Even standard rendering has some serious limitations. Chapter 12, Rendering, talks about trueSpace2's ability to use ray tracing to simulate specular reflections, or reflected images in shiny surfaces. However, one thing trueSpace2 or most other 3D applications, for that matter, cannot do is render *reflected* light, which helps even out the lighting in many real-world scenes. That's why a 3D scene often needs more light sources than an equivalent setup would in reality. Some programs have a global ambient light setting, which simply raises the overall illumination level—a crude and usually unsatisfactory approximation of bounced lighting. Though trueSpace2 doesn't have this, it does incorporate a component of ambient light into each material, giving you the ability to set "general" lighting on a surface-by-surface basis. (Chapter 9, Materials Part 1: Basic Surface Attributes, examines this in its discussion of basic materials.) Some programs, to which you can export your trueSpace2 objects, do simulate bounce lighting using a technique called *radiosity*. The most notable of these is Lightscape, a high-end application for Windows NT and SGI workstations from Lightscape Technologies. You can find out more about the program at the company's World Wide Web site: http://www.lightscape.com.

Although light's effects are, of course, visible in trueSpace2, neither the light "rays" nor the light sources can be seen directly. Thus, several highly popular photographic lighting effects are not supported. These include visible light sources and beams, lens flare, and lens reflections. You can simulate some of these, but the compromises don't work as well as if the effects were built into the program.

Another limitation found in most programs, including trueSpace2, is the inability to simulate a diffuse light source, such as a fluorescent panel, sometimes called an *area light*. All light sources in trueSpace2 are points, so the only way to simulate an area light is to place several lights next to each other.

Finally, trueSpace2 does not offer a "projector" function that lets you map a still image, animation, or video to a light source so that it projects the image onto a surface.

Now that I've listed what trueSpace2 *can't* do with lighting, let's take an in-depth look at all the nifty things it *can* do. In the lessons of this chapter, you'll examine the various default lighting setups, look at the types of lights, and see how shadows work. You'll also learn how to make a spotlight beam visible. (Hint: It's a trick.)

VARIETIES OF LIGHTS

There are three types of light sources in trueSpace2: Infinite lights, Local lights, and Spotlights. (I'll explore the differences between these shortly.) When the program starts, the default lighting setup, as indicated in the Preferences panel, consists of three local lights colored white, orange, and blue. These are the red, star-shaped objects that usually appear when you start the program or use the Scene/New command. Let's begin with a quick exercise to examine this setup and the two alternative default arrangements.

LESSON 1: WORKING WITH DEFAULT LIGHTING SETUPS

When you're first setting up a scene, depending on your needs, you can quickly get a nice general lighting effect with one of trueSpace2's default setups, available in the Preferences panel.

1. Start trueSpace2 or use the Scene/New command to clear the workspace and restore the initial default lighting setup. You can probably see two of the three local lights at screen left and screen right, and perhaps a bit of the third light near the center of the top of the screen.

2. To move the camera up so you can see all three lights, select the Eye Move tool from the main window View group, fourth from the left. Then right-button drag a short distance upward in the workspace. Now you can see the third light, positioned near the rear of the workspace.

3. Click on the rightmost light source. The Lights panel appears (see Figure 8-1), which shows and lets you adjust the selected light's color, intensity, fall-off options, and shadow setting. Subsequent lessons will look at these. For now, note that the light's color is white.

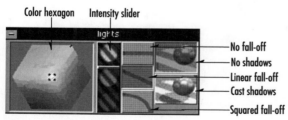

Figure 8-1 The Lights control panel

4. Select the leftmost light. The Lights panel's color hexagon shows that it's colored orange. Then select the rear light and note that its color is blue.

5. Use the Primitives panel to add a sphere object.

6. Use the Render Current Object tool (View tool group, second from left) to render the object. Note that the variation in coloration reflects the lighting setup, with white shading on the sphere's right side, orange on the left, and blue on the rear surface.

7. Now let's take a look at the alternative default lighting setups. Select the File/Preferences menu function. The Preferences panel (see Figure 8-2) lets you change the default lighting setup.

8. In the panel's lower-right corner, the Default Lights setting is Colored Lights. Click and hold the left button over the Colored Lights box, and in the pop-up menu, drag to White Lights and release. When the confirmation requester appears, click on the Yes button or press the (ENTER) key to accept the default response.

9. Take a look at the workspace. The three star-shaped Local lights are gone. In their place are four arrow-shaped Infinite lights, grouped at the center of the workspace and each pointing in a different direction (see Figure 8-3). You'll probably be able to see only three of them, because the fourth is pointed directly at you. Although the lights are colored red on your screen, I have colored them white in Figure 8-3 for better visibility.

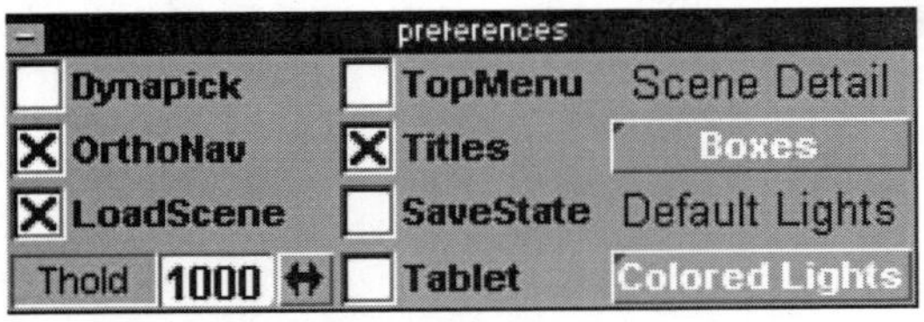

preferences		
☐ **Dynapick**	☐ **TopMenu**	Scene Detail
☒ **OrthoNav**	☒ **Titles**	**Boxes**
☒ **LoadScene**	☐ **SaveState**	Default Lights
Thold **1000** ↔	☐ **Tablet**	**Colored Lights**

Figure 8-2 The Preferences panel

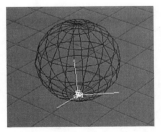

Figure 8-3 The White Lights default lighting setup

10. Render the sphere again to see how the lighting has changed. The sphere's natural white color is obvious now, and its surface appears to be divided into four quadrants, each lit by a different Infinite light.

11. Finally, in the Preferences panel's Default Lights pop-up, select the No Lights item. Confirm the change and rerender the sphere. It's pitch black. Use this option to create your own lighting setup without having to delete each of the default lights individually.

NOTE: To disable or enable the display of all light objects, right-click on any of the Add Light tools in the Primitives panel to open thex Visibility panel, and then click in the box next to Lights. You can also use this panel to toggle visibility of camera objects and freestanding deformation lattices.

NOTE: If you check the Preferences panel's SaveState option, the program uses the last default lighting setup you used; otherwise, it always defaults to Colored Lights.

LESSON 2: LIGHTING LOCALLY—THE BASICS

Local lights are called that because they're used for lighting the immediate area around their position. The real-world light source most similar to the Local light is a light bulb—hence its icon in the Primitives panel—which provides roughly the same lighting in all directions. In fact, the Local light is the only omnidirectional light type in trueSpace2, and though it can be rotated, it doesn't make sense to do so. Let's try some exercises using Local lights.

1. Start trueSpace2 or clear the workspace. Set the program to Wireframe Display mode if it isn't already. For best results, set your display to 24 bits, if available. Otherwise, use at least 16 bits (65,000 colors).

NOTE: This is the recommended mode/display setup for the exercises in this chapter.

2. In the Preferences panel, set the No Lights option in the Default Lights pop-up menu to delete all lights from the workspace. Confirm the deletion.

3. Select the Regular Polygon tool and, starting in the center of the workspace, draw a hexagonal polygon a bit larger than half the size of the workspace.

4. Open the Primitives panel and click the light-bulb tool to add a Local light source. It appears in the center of the workspace, as do most other objects added via the Primitives panel.

5. Select the Object Move tool and right-button drag the light source straight up a few inches (see Figure 8-4).

6. Select the hexagon and render it (see Figure 8-5). Kind of dim, isn't it? That's because trueSpace2's default setting for illumination from newly added lights is relatively low. Let's see how to remedy this.

Figure 8–4 Light testing setup

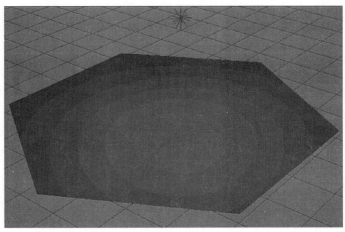

Figure 8–5 Default Local light illumination

7. Select the light source and take a look at the vertical Intensity scale in the center of the Lights control panel. Note that the slider (the horizontal bar) is about a third of the way up. Right-click on the slider or on the color hexagon at the left side of the panel to open the numeric settings requester (see Figure 8-6). The current Intensity setting is 0.5.

8. Click at the top of the Intensity scale, so the value is about 2.

9. Select the polygon again (the Lights panel goes away when you do so) and render it. A little better, right? Actually, it's too bright, so let's try to achieve a compromise.

Select the light again and set Intensity to about 1.0, slightly above the center of the Intensity scale. Then reselect and rerender the hexagon (see Figure 8-7). Ah, that's more like it! You now have a good dynamic range. A nice bright white in the hexagon's center, directly below the light source, falls off to a reasonably dark gray near the edges, which are farther away from the light. (In the next lesson, you'll see how to manage illumination fall-off.)

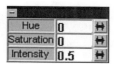

Figure 8–6 The Lights numeric setting panel

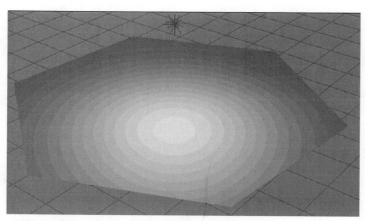

Figure 8–7 Improved Local light illumination

10. Select the light again and right-click on the left side of the Lights panel to get the numeric settings. Click in various parts of the color hexagon to see the numeric Hue equivalents of the various colors. Try clicking on various points along a straight line between the center and any edge or corner, and watch the Saturation value increase as you move farther from the center. The Hue doesn't increase, though (well, unless you're *very* accurate, it will change a little). You can see that the higher the Saturation setting, the purer the color; the lower the value, the more white (or gray, depending on the Intensity setting) the color contains.

11. Try rendering the hexagon with the light set to various colors to see the effects. When you're done, set the Hue and Saturation back to 0 and Intensity to 1.0.

12. The next lesson starts with the same setup, as does another later, so whether or not you're moving ahead right away, use the File/Scene/Save menu command and save this scene as LOCALITE.SCN.

LESSON 3: EXPLORING FALL-OFF

In this lesson, you will look at the differences between rendering with 3DR and standard rendering, as well as the fall-off settings in the Lights control panel.

1. If you're not continuing from the previous lesson, start trueSpace2 and use the File/Scene/Load menu command to load file LOCALITE.SCN. Set the program to Wireframe Display mode and set your display to 24 bits or 16 bits (65,000 colors).

2. Open a new Top view window and move it into one of the upper corners. If necessary, zoom the window's view out so you can see the entire hexagon.

3. In the Top view window, move the light source to the hexagon's leftmost corner.

4. Select the Copy tool or press CTRL-C to duplicate the light. In the Top view window, drag the copy to the opposite corner (see Figure 8-8). Close the Top view window.

5. Open the Preferences panel and then the Scene Detail pop-up menu in the panel's upper-right corner. Select the Render All option, if it isn't already selected. This forces 3DR to render all objects as solid, whether or not they're selected. Close the panel.

6. Using the leftmost pop-up in the View group, choose Solid Render Display mode (the 3DR icon). Note that the polygon renders with a white line between the two light sources, falling off to gray at the upper and lower edges (see Figure 8-9). If the polygon is solid white, lower both lights to about half their current height.

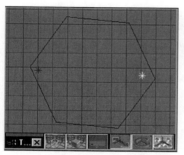

Figure 8-8 Two-light setup
from Top view window

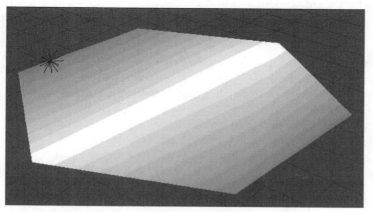

Figure 8-9 Two-light setup rendered with 3DR

7. This is a decent approximation of the effect of two lights, but it isn't very realistic. To prove this, select the hexagon and render it with the Render Current Object tool. As shown in Figure 8-10, this is much closer to the true effect, with two circular hot spots directly below the lights and circular fall-off areas around them. Of course, the fall-off isn't as distinct as with one light, because each light is illuminating the other's fall-off area.

8. To best learn how lights work in trueSpace2, you need better than this somewhat haphazard accuracy. Continue to use the Render function to see the results of changes. Set the display back to Wireframe.

Okay, let's see what fall-off is all about. First, a few words of explanation. In the real world, a light source's illumination normally decreases with distance. That is, the farther a light source is from the surface it's illuminating, the lower the illumination. In the Lights

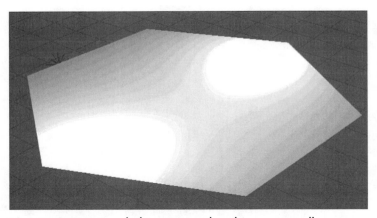

Figure 8-10 Two-light setup rendered conventionally

panel, the three buttons to the right of the Intensity slider let you set fall-off to No fall-off (the default), Linear, or Squared. Actually, "No fall-off" is something of a misnomer, because if there were no fall-off, the light would illuminate the entire scene evenly and, as you observed in Lesson 2, Step 10, it doesn't.

Now let's look at the other two fall-off settings. Linear fall-off sets up a linear correspondence between the amount of illumination and the distance. In other words, if one object is twice as far from a light source as another, all other factors being equal (e.g., the angles between the light and the surfaces), the first will receive half as much illumination as the second.

9. Select the closer or leftmost of the two lights; then select the Linear fall-off setting in the Lights panel. (The Linear icon is a diagonal blue line crossing the button from top left to bottom right.)

10. Select the hexagon object again and render it. Notice that the areas directly below the two lights are still illuminated at full brightness, but the fall-off around the more distant light is now clearer. That's because the closer light's illumination is decreasing with distance at a greater rate.

11. Select the closer light again, and in the Lights panel, choose Squared fall-off (the bottom icon, with the curved blue line). This is how real-world lights act, with the illumination falling off with the square of the distance. With one surface twice as far from a light source as a second, the farther surface receives one-fourth the illumination that the closer one does.

12. Render the polygon again. Now the fall-off under the farther light is quite distinct. If you have trouble seeing this, reduce the lights' intensities and rerender the polygon.

Here you have learned to illuminate most of a scene with omnidirectional lights, thus simulating the use of light bulbs, using the No fall-off setting. For small-area lighting, where the light source should affect only objects in its immediate vicinity, use Squared fall-off. For in-between situations, use the Linear setting. In most circumstances, especially with complex scenes containing many elements, a combination of fall-off types, which you can determine only by experimenting, works best.

LESSON 4: USING THE INFINITE LIGHT

In trueSpace2, the Infinite light source has these identifying characteristics:

It illuminates the entire scene evenly.

Its location is immaterial. It can be inside an object and still illuminate the object and the rest of the scene.

Only its angle makes a difference in how the scene is lit.

The real-world light source to which the Infinite light source can be most closely compared is the sun. Although the sun does have a specific location, it is so far away from the objects it illuminates that it always illuminates every object in a scene the same way. The Infinite light is probably used less than any other of trueSpace2's light sources. However, it comes in handy for outdoor scenes when you need sun-like illumination.

Let's take a look. This lesson demonstrates all the Infinite light's characteristics.

1. Start trueSpace2 or clear the workspace. If there are any light sources present, delete them. The easiest way to do this is by setting the Preferences panel's Default Lights option to No Lights.

2. You'll do your study of the Infinite light by comparing it to the Local light. Open the Primitives panel. Add a sphere and then add a Local light. The light is automatically placed at the center of the sphere.

3. Select the sphere and use the Render Current Object tool to see the lighting effect. The sphere renders as black—there is no lighting effect! That's because the Local light's rays are hitting only the sphere's inside surface, which you cannot see.

4. The rays from the Local light do, however, penetrate the sphere's surface. Demonstrate this by adding another sphere, moving it slightly northeast of the first one (see Figure 8-11, left side). Render the second sphere and you'll see that it is illuminated by the Local light.

5. Now let's see how the Local light affects the two spheres when it lights both simultaneously. Select the Local light, then select the Object Move tool and right-button drag upward in the workspace until the light is an inch or so above the first sphere (see Figure 8-11, right side).

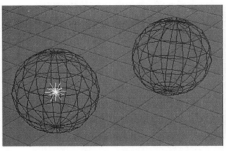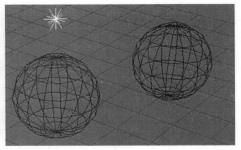

Figure 8–11 Two spheres, with Local light inside the first and with raised-up Local light

6. Here's where the use of 3DR really starts to pay off. To render both spheres simultaneously, you would normally have to first combine them, with either the Glue or the Boolean Union function, and then use the Render Current Object tool. Or you could render the entire scene, which would waste time by also rendering the blank background. The path of least resistance is simply to turn on Solid Render mode. Do so now.

7. You can see that the Local light illuminates the two spheres differently (see Figure 8-12). To make this more visible, raise the Local light's intensity to 1.0 or so. The closer sphere's "hot spot," or area of greatest illumination, is on top, whereas the other's is on the side. Obviously, the variance is due to the different angles between the light source and the two spheres.

8. With the Local light selected, press the (DELETE) key or select the Erase tool to remove it from the workspace.

Figure 8–12 Two spheres rendered with raised-up Local light

9. Open a new Perspective window so you can see Wireframe and Solid Render views at the same time. Move this window up into the corner and out of the way of the main view. In the small Wireframe view, zoom in on the two spheres so they fill the view, or use the Eye Move tool to get closer.

10. From the Primitives panel, select the Add Infinite Light tool. It's immediately to the right of the Add Camera tool and looks like a thin diagonal line. This places an Infinite light object in the center of the left-hand sphere. Set its intensity to about 1.0.

Now you're ready to examine the features of the Infinite light. First, note in the Wireframe view that it resembles an arrow with a pyramid-shaped tip, pointing straight down. This tip indicates the light's direction. In the Main view, both spheres are illuminated exactly the same way, as from above—even though the light is "inside" one of them and is above neither (see Figure 8-13). This demonstrates how the Infinite light's position is irrelevant to its effect. Its illumination "wraps around," starting in no particular place and continuing through the scene infinitely (hence the light's name).

11. Next, use the Object Move tool to reposition the Infinite light in the horizontal plane and vertically. Once again, no matter where you place it, the lighting does not change.

12. Finally, try rotating the Infinite light. Select the Object Rotate tool. In the small window, left-click and drag slowly in various directions, watching the solid-rendered spheres in the main window. As the light rotates, the illumination angle changes to conform to the light's orientation. If you rotate the light so it's pointing up, the illumination appears to be coming from below (see Figure 8-14). You can see that the light's angle does have significance, unlike its placement.

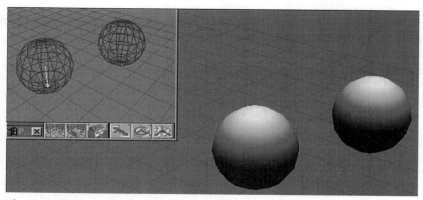

Figure 8-13 Two spheres with an Infinite light pointing down

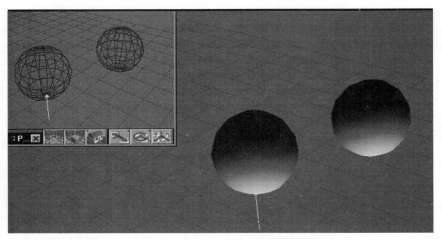

Figure 8–14 Two spheres with an Infinite light pointing up

LESSON 5: PUTTING OBJECTS IN THE SPOTLIGHT

The Spotlight in trueSpace2, as in most 3D programs, is for casting a circular "spot" of light in a specific area—just as it does in the real world. (Other programs also have a rectangular-beam option with Spotlights, which simulates the "barn door" shutters used with real-world spotlights.) The Spotlight has a position, like the Local light. But the Spotlight also has a direction, like the Infinite light. Let's see how it works.

1. Start trueSpace2 or clear the workspace. If there are any light sources present, delete them. Make sure you're in Wireframe Display mode.

2. Add a fairly large regular polygon in the center of the workspace.

3. Open the Primitives panel and click on the Add Spotlight tool (the cone-shaped one). The Spotlight appears near the center of the workspace, raised up off the "ground" by 1 meter.

4. Like other light sources in trueSpace2, the Spotlight starts out as a rather dim bulb. In the Lights control panel, set the Intensity to about 1.5.

5. It would be nice if you could use 3DR to show the Spotlight's effects, but it doesn't work very well with this type of lighting projected onto a flat surface, so use conventional rendering. Select the polygon and render it. Most of the polygon is black, but directly below the Spotlight there's a white circle of light with a slightly fuzzy edge. The edge is called a *penumbra*.

6. Press the right or left cursor key on the keyboard to reselect the light. Activate the Move Object tool and position the mouse cursor anywhere in the workspace *except* on the Spotlight. Right-button drag upward to raise the light up a couple of inches.

7. Render the polygon again. This time the illuminated circle is bigger, and so is the penumbra. That's because, by increasing the distance between the two, both the spot and the penumbra have more room to spread out before hitting the polygon.

8. Let's examine a different way of changing the spot size. Select the Spotlight; then select the Object Scale tool. Again, position the mouse cursor anywhere in the workspace *except* over the light object. Left-button drag leftward to make the cone narrower and rightward to make the cone wider. You can achieve the same results respectively by right-button dragging downward and upward.

NOTE: If you right-click on the Object tool, then make the cone as wide as you can, you'll see that the maximum size on the z axis is 5.671. This is probably an arbitrary number. The important thing is that if the cone were any wider, it would be a flat circle, which wouldn't make any sense.

9. Render the polygon with the Spotlight at various sizes. You can see that it's kind of difficult to tell just how large the spot will be from eyeballing the cone width. To gauge this coverage more effectively, you can use the handy View from Object function (you're already way ahead of me, aren't you?).

10. First, use the New Perspective View tool to open a new view window. Move the small window into the upper-left or -right corner, out of the way.

11. Select the Spotlight object and, in the small window, activate the View pop-up menu. Drag all the way to the top of the View from Object tool, which looks like a camera, and release the mouse button. You're now seeing things from the Spotlight's point of view. The white outer circle indicates the overall coverage, and the blue inner circle shows the location of the penumbra's inner edge.

12. In the main window, scale the Spotlight again in both directions while watching the small window. As you're scaling down, at the point that the white circle fits just inside the window, the view starts zooming in to indicate the narrower angle of coverage. When scaling up, the view zooms out.

NOTE: When you're zooming out by scaling up, the circles start expanding at a certain point until they're no longer visible in the small window. This doesn't make a whole lot of sense—the view should continue to zoom out. So if you need to set a wide angle of coverage interactively using the View from Object function, it may be better to move the Spotlight higher instead of making it wider.

13. Scale the light so you can see both circles in the small window.

Aiming the Spotlight

1. Let's try aiming the Spotlight. Select the Object Rotate tool.

2. Click away from the light object in the main window and left-button drag to change the light's angle of view. Notice how handy it is to be able to see the light's exact coverage in the small window. If things get disorienting in the small window (the view can easily turn upside down), right-button drag to rotate the light about its z axis.

3. Rotate the Spotlight so a polygon edge is approximately in the middle of the light's coverage (see Figure 8-15).

4. Select the polygon and render it. As with a real spotlight, the penumbra starts small at the point closest to the light source and spreads out on both sides (see Figure 8-16).

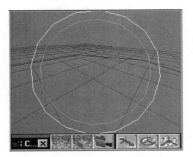

Figure 8-15 View from Spotlight rotated to project past polygon edge

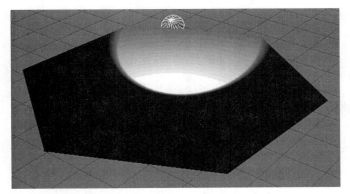

Figure 8-16 Light cast from angled Spotlight

5. Try rotating the light to different angles and rendering the polygon each time to get a feel for how the angle affects the light's coverage.

NOTE: To cause a Spotlight to reorient itself continually to stay aimed at an object during an animation, use the Look At function, which is covered in Chapter 11, Animation.

Adjusting the Penumbra Size

1. Let's see how to change the penumbra's relative size. Select the Spotlight and position the mouse cursor over the blue circle inside the cone. You can do this in either the main window or in the small one from the light's view (the latter is probably easier).

2. Left-click and drag leftward to make the circle smaller, increasing the penumbra's relative size, and rightward to make it larger, decreasing the size.

This effect applies no matter where you click on the blue circle, so for the most intuitive response, it's best to click on the circle's right side. Also, note that you can do this even though you're in Object Rotate mode. You can change penumbra size in Object Move and Object Scale modes as well. This is why, when manipulating the Spotlight, it's best not to click directly on the light object, which may inadvertently activate this feature.

3. Make the penumbra relatively large and render an image (see Figure 8-17, left side), and then make it relatively small and render another image (see Figure 8-17, right side). Notice the difference: In most cases, the default setting looks most realistic.

NOTE: Penumbra adjustment is a one-time setting and cannot be animated. Also, there is no numeric equivalent for the penumbra setting; you have to make this adjustment visually.

Figure 8–17 Spotlight with large penumbra (left) and small penumbra (right)

CASTING SHADOWS

You've probably seen 3D images in which the objects all looked very realistic, but something was missing that you just couldn't put your finger on. In all likelihood, the problem was that there were no shadows. Shadows are ubiquitous in the real world—you probably are aware of them only if they're missing. Like any optional aspect of 3D rendering, shadows take extra time to create, and some artists neglect them in the interest of getting faster results. Don't make that mistake.

3D applications use two methods for implementing shadow casting: ray tracing and shadow mapping. Both are available in trueSpace2. Chapter 12, Rendering, examines ray tracing a bit more closely when it covers rendering.

Shadow mapping, to oversimplify somewhat, involves drawing an outline of the shadow-casting object from the light's point of view onto the surfaces that are to receive the shadow. Unlike some other programs, which allow shadow mapping only with Spotlights, trueSpace2 allows shadow mapping with any light source type.

NOTE: Another feature found in some programs, but not trueSpace2, is the ability to enable/disable shadow casting and receiving object by object. This can make rendering more efficient. All programs that allow shadow casting let you toggle shadow casting for each light source individually, but some also provide a global shadow switch. That way, you can save time in preliminary renderings by temporarily turning off shadow casting for all lights and then, for the final image, turning it back on. Unfortunately, trueSpace2 does not have such a control.

Here are the most important differences between ray-traced and mapped shadows that you should know about:

Ray tracing takes longer but consumes less memory.

Shadow mapping is faster but consumes more memory.

Ray-traced shadows always have sharp edges, which tend to look surreal.

Mapped shadows can have fuzzy edges, but they may also look blocky, which is even more distracting than sharp edges.

LESSON 6: WORKING WITH SHADOWS

Because, as stated above, all light sources in trueSpace2 can cast shadows of either type, use the Local light setup from Lesson 2 to learn about shadows. Load the LOCALITE.SCN file you saved in the last step of Lesson 2. If you didn't save it or can't find it, set up a scene with a large hexagon in the center, with a Local light set to 1.0 Intensity a couple of meters above it. Make sure you're in Wireframe Display mode.

Start with ray-traced shadows.

1. Select Object Move and drag the light to the right so it's over the polygon's right-most corner.

2. Add a sphere from the Primitives panel. It appears in the center of the hexagon (see Figure 8-18).

3. Select the light object. When the Lights control panel appears (refer back to Figure 8-1), take a look at the two icons on the right side. Position the mouse cursor over each in turn and read the Help bar descriptions. The upper icon, selected by default, causes the light to cast no shadow. The lower icon enables shadow casting.

4. Select the lower icon now to set the light to cast a shadow.

5. Because trueSpace2 creates shadows only when rendering a scene, and you want to save time, do your rendering in a small window. Open a new Perspective view window, move it up and out of the way, and zoom in so it shows a close-up of the hexagon/sphere setup (see Figure 8-19).

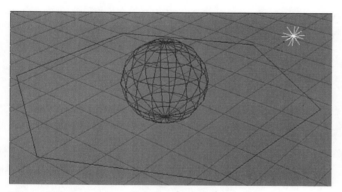

Figure 8-18 Setup for shadow lesson

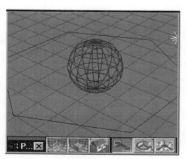

Figure 8-19
Small window setup

6. From the Render pop-up in the small window, select the Render Scene tool (second from the top). In the rendered image, the lighting seems to be fine, but there is no shadow.

7. To find out why not, right-click on the Cast Shadow button in the Lights control panel. This opens the Shadows property panel (see Figure 8-20). The first selection in the panel, labeled Shadow Type, is set to Ray. That means that the light casts shadows only if the scene is ray traced. This is the default setting for Local lights, as well as for Infinite lights (the default for Spotlights is Map). However, trueSpace2 does not ray trace scenes by default, so you've got to turn this feature on to see the ray-traced shadow.

8. To turn on ray tracing, right-click on the Render Scene tool to open the Render Options panel and click in the white box in the panel's upper-left corner, next to Raytrace.

9. Render the scene again. This time you get a nice, inky shadow on the polygon opposite the light source. In fact, it's too dark. To remedy this, add a second Local light, set it to Intensity 0.4, and position it on the left side of the scene. This is called a *fill light*, so named because it's used to fill in the shadows, allowing some detail to be seen.

10. Render the scene again (see Figure 8-21). That's more like it! From this simple demonstration, you can begin to see the benefits of using multiple lights.

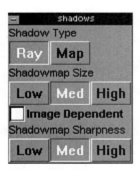

Figure 8–20
The Shadows property panel

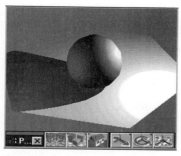

Figure 8–21 Ray-traced shadow with fill light

NOTE: By the way, you may notice jagged edges on the shadow. This is the result of a phenomenon called *aliasing*, known for its distracting stair-step look on distinct edges, especially at lower display resolutions. You'll learn how to deal with that in Chapter 12.

TIP: If you are wondering why I didn't set the fill light to cast shadows, it's because the extra shadow isn't really necessary, and in fact it could be distracting. Give it a try and you'll see what I mean. Professional photographers often go to great pains to remove excessive shadowing in their studio shots, so it's nice to be able to do it automatically, here in your virtual studio.

Working with Shadow Mapping

Okay, let's look at mapped shadows.

1. Select the first light and, in the Shadows property panel, select the Map option for Shadow Type. In the Render Options panel, turn off Raytrace and then close the panel.

2. Render the scene in the small window again. There's a short initial delay, while the message Generating Shadow Maps appears in the Help bar. During this period, the program draws the shadow outline as projected onto the poly surface and saves it in memory. Then it renders the scene, incorporating the shadow.

3. Note that the shadow outline is fairly rough. Let's see how to smooth it out. In the Shadows property panel, under Shadowmap Size, select the High option. Render the scene again in the small window. The shadow looks better, but it still suffers from aliasing. (The shadow looks pretty bad at the Low size setting, so don't even try it, although you might want to keep it in mind for low-memory situations that might arise.)

4. Can you make the shadow outline a bit softer, as most real-world shadows are? That's a job for the Shadowmap Sharpness setting in the property panel. Choose the Low option, then render the scene again. There's not much difference. Because shadow mapping is a compromise, intended to save rendering time over ray tracing (although it doesn't always work that way), its results are typically less satisfactory.

Experiment with various combinations of Shadows settings and observe the results closely. Try the Image Dependent option, too. According to the Help section, it sets up a direct correspondence between the shadow map size and the final output resolution. In my experience, the shadows created with this option turned on don't look very good, even at high resolution.

Also try using shadows with the other two types of light sources. You'll find that using Spotlights in combination with shadow casting can create some very dramatic lighting effects.

LESSON 7: SIMULATING A SPOTLIGHT BEAM

Whenever you view a scene lit with Spotlights—in the movies or in real life, such as at the circus—the beams cast by the Spotlights are visible from the side, creating an attractive lighting effect. This phenomenon is caused by dust particles in the air reflecting light. In 3D graphics, however, the air is pretty clean, so there are no dust particles to reflect the Spotlight beam. Therefore, you must simulate the beam. It's actually pretty simple to do.

1. Start trueSpace2 or clear the workspace. If there are any light sources present, delete them. Make sure you're in Wireframe Display mode.

2. Add a fairly large regular polygon in the center of the workspace.

3. Open the Primitives panel and select the Add Spotlight tool. Raise the Spotlight object straight up by a couple of meters and set its Intensity to about 1.5.

4. Open new Side and Top view windows. Move them into the upper screen corners and adjust them as necessary for good views of the light object and polygon.

5. Use a cone to simulate the actual spotlight in the scene. Add a primitive Cone object. Move and scale it so it's at about the same size and position as the Spotlight object.

6. In the Primitives panel, right-click on the Add Cylinder icon. In the Cylinder property panel that appears, set Top Radius to 0.3.

7. Left-click the Add Cylinder button to create a conical cylinder. At this point, things should look pretty much like Figure 8-22. Starting to get the picture?

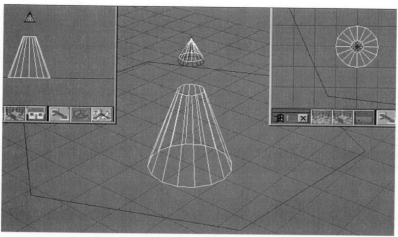

Figure 8–22 Setup with Spotlight, polygon, small cone, and cylinder

8. Enter Point Edit: Faces mode and select the cylinder's top face. Using the Point Move and Point Scale tools in the Point Navigation panel, move the face up (right-button drag) and scale it (drag with both buttons) so it's in about the same place and is the same size as the cone's bottom face.

9. Activate the Object tool and then the Paint Face tool. In the Material Color panel (with the color hexagon), set the Intensity slider on the right side to the highest position. In the Shader Attributes panel, set the leftmost vertical slider (Set Ambient Glow in the Help bar) to its highest position. Also in the Shader Attributes panel, set the fourth slider from the left (Set Transparency) to near the top, so the sample sphere in the Material panel is barely visible.

10. With the conical cylinder selected, use the Paint Object tool from the Paint pop-up menu.

11. That's pretty much it for the initial setup. Render the scene and you'll probably get something similar to Figure 8-23. Obviously, some adjustment is required.

The cylinder's bottom face needs to be scaled up (or the Spotlight scaled down), more lighting needs to be added, and it's probably a good idea, once you have the cylinder's top and bottom faces at the right size, to delete them. I'll leave all that up to you—it's good exercise for your modeling mind. It's also a good idea because you'll learn how to animate this setup in Chapter 11 (not specifically, but I'll give you the tools), and you don't want to show a goofy-looking animation to your friends, now do you? When you're done, save this scene as SPOTLITE.SCN.

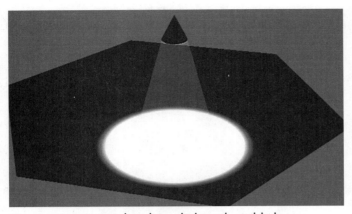

Figure 8–23 Rendered Spotlight with visible beam

WHAT NOW?

You can never pay too much attention to the lighting in your 3D scenes. Nor will I make the mistake of trying to give you general guidelines for lighting every one of your scenes. The more experience you get with lighting, the better idea you'll have of what's necessary when you build a scene. Don't stop experimenting, though. Who knows? If the 3D graphics profession keeps growing at its current rate, there may be a growing need for virtual gaffers, and there you'll be—ready and waiting to charge healthy fees for your skills!

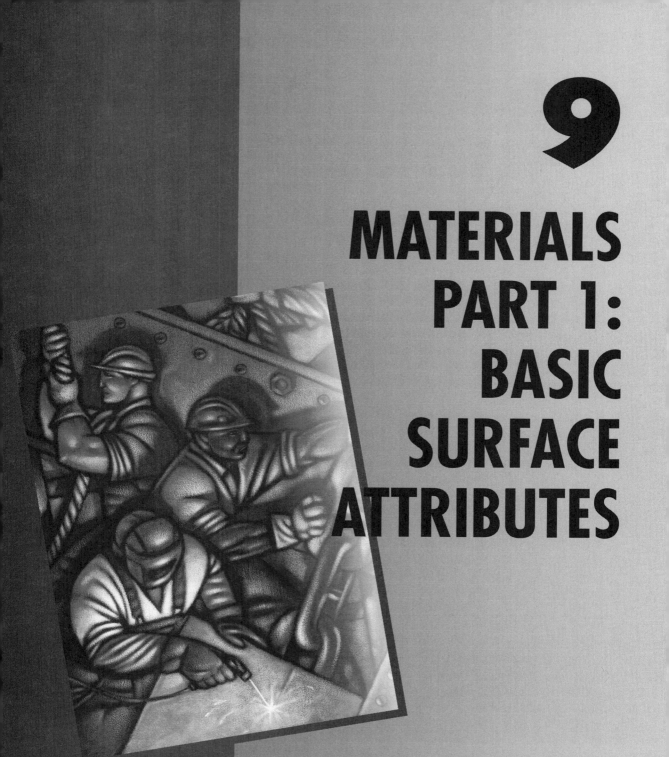

9

MATERIALS PART 1: BASIC SURFACE ATTRIBUTES

Take a look around you at the objects in your environment. Try to disregard the shapes, but pay careful attention to the surface of the objects. Note that each object has its own set of characteristics. A metal object may be painted, but even so, it's hard to mistake the metal surface for a different material. Glass is usually fully transparent, but it can also be colored, as in stained glass windows; translucent, as in frosted glass; or almost opaque, like a green lampshade. Observe the highly varied characteristics of materials such as wood, plastic, rubber, fabric, and paper. An important skill for a 3D artist is the ability to accurately re-create in virtual worlds the multitude of real-world surface characteristics—and maybe even to create new ones.

THE TRUESPACE2 MATERIAL SETTINGS

The Render tool group of trueSpace2 offers a wealth of methods for altering an object's appearance. In this program, a set of surface attributes is called a *material*. You designate material attributes in a group of panels associated with the Paint tools, found in the first pop-up in the Render group. Then you use the Paint tools to apply the material to all or parts of the object.

The basic material components in trueSpace2 consist of color, smoothness, shaders, and attributes such as shininess and transparency. This chapter covers these fundamental components, and Chapter 10, Materials Part 2: Advanced Surface Attributes, moves on to the more advanced attributes, including texture and bump mapping. The Paint tools are also covered here, and the Render group's other tools are covered in Chapter 10.

Resetting Material Defaults

As you work through the exercises in this chapter, you'll sometimes need to restore material settings to program defaults. Unfortunately, trueSpace2 does not have a function for automatically returning material settings to the ones that were in place when the program began. Therefore, if at any time you want to return the Material panels to their original settings, you can use several different methods.

- Simply quit and restart the program. This is the only way to ensure that *all* settings are returned to their defaults.

- Start the program, add an object, save it, and then load it and use the Inspect tool, which makes that object's material settings current (discussed in Lesson 6 in this chapter).

- Perhaps the most straightforward method is to start the program and then immediately open the Material library by clicking the Material Library icon in the Libraries group. Then click on the arrow in the bottom-left corner of the Library panel to add the current material. Whenever you want to restore the current material settings to this default, click on the white sphere in the Material library.

The latter two methods reset only the *current shader's* attributes to program defaults, however. (Shaders are covered in Lesson 3.) For example, if you change the attributes for a Metal-shaded material and then load a default Phong-shaded material, the attribute settings for the Metal shader remain as they are.

LESSON 1: LOOKING AT COLOR

The most basic element of an object's appearance, and the thing you usually notice first, is its color. Let's see how to set color in trueSpace2.

1. Start trueSpace2. You can be in either Wireframe or Solid Render mode for this exercise.

Figure 9–1
The Paint Face tool

2. Open the Primitives panel and select the Add Cylinder icon, to place a new cylinder primitive in the workspace. This makes the Paint tools available. (You don't really need the cylinder for this lesson, except to get at these tools.)

3. The Paint Face tool (see Figure 9-1) is the default tool in its pop-up, so it currently appears in the leftmost slot in the Render group. Select it now. The four panels for setting material attributes appear in the workspace.

The two Materials panels you're concerned with right now are Material Color and Material (see Figure 9-2). The latter contains a sphere, called the Sample Sphere, that reflects the changes to the current material as you make them. I'll cover the other panels later in this chapter and in Chapter 10.

You saw the Material Color panel briefly in Chapter 3, Quick Start Tutorial: A Guided Tour of Major Features, and its equivalent for setting a light source's color in Chapter 8, The Importance of Lighting. Now let's look more closely at how the Material Color panel works. Recall that, in Chapter 8, when you right-clicked on the color hexagon in the Lights control panel, another panel opened, containing numerical settings for the Hue, Saturation, and Intensity values. In most graphics programs, this color-adjustment system, or *color space,* is called Hue, Saturation, and Value, or HSV for short. Because trueSpace2 uses the term "Intensity" instead of "Value," I'll go with HSI.

Hue, of course, is another word for color. Back in your junior high (or middle) school art class, you probably learned the acronym ROY G BIV for the members of the color spectrum. It stands for Red, Orange, Yellow, Green, Blue, Indigo, Violet. If you start at the rightmost corner of the color hexagon in the Material Color panel and move around the edge in a counterclockwise direction, you'll see these colors.

Next is Saturation, which determines the "purity" of the hue. Consider a pair of blue jeans. When you first buy them, they're deep blue. But, over time, the color eventually fades, showing more and more of the white cotton fiber from which the pants are woven. Technically, the color is becoming less and less saturated as the dye is washed out. The same thing happens if you trace an imaginary straight line from any outermost pixel in the color hexagon to the center. The closer you get to the middle, the greater the white (or

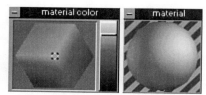

Figure 9–2 The Material Color
and Material panels

gray, if Intensity isn't at its highest setting) component, and the less of the original color there is—in other words, the lower the saturation. When you get to the center, it doesn't matter where you started: The color ends up as "pure" white or gray, with the Saturation value at 0.

4. By clicking anywhere on the color hexagon, you can set both a material's Hue and Saturation simultaneously. Click at various spots on the hexagon now and observe the color as rendered on the Sample Sphere in the Material panel.

There's another way to set a material's color. To see it, right-click on the color hexagon. This time you get a Red-Green-Blue (or RGB) panel (see Figure 9-3). You can set the red, green, and blue components of the material color by clicking in the horizontal color bars, by clicking and dragging on the sliders, or by clicking in the number boxes and entering new values from the keyboard. As usual, you can press [TAB] to move between fields and [ENTER] to quit keyboard entry.

5. Try setting different colors in the color hexagon to see their RGB equivalents. Also try setting some colors using the RGB panel.

6. Getting back to the Material Color panel, try the third component of the HSI color space, Intensity. It's set via the vertical slider to the right of the color hexagon. Open the RGB panel if it isn't already open and set the RGB colors to the default light gray, R=G=B=210 (set R, G, and B to 210). Click in various places in the Intensity scale and note the effect on the RGB values and the color hexagon.

The RGB values stay in roughly the same proportional relationships. Also, the entire color hexagon gets darker or brighter when you lower or raise Intensity. This tells you that all the colors visible in the color hexagon at any time have the same value. At any given time, there are 256 Hues × 256 Saturation values accessible from the color hexagon; then factor in the 256 levels of Intensity available in the slider, and you get 16,777,216—the full complement of colors available in the 24-bit color spectrum.

 TIP: For setting colors in the HSI color space, the color hexagon and Intensity slider work best. But if you want to set a color to pure blue, say, or a medium gray of R=128, G=128, B=128, the RGB panel may be preferable. Choose the color system that works best for you; it's nice to have a choice.

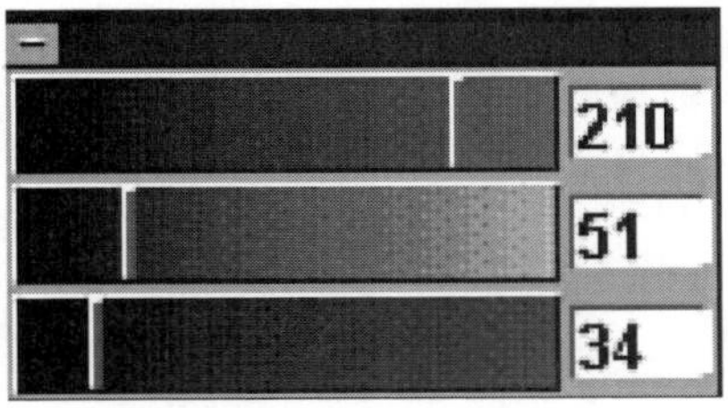

![The RGB panel showing values 210, 51, 34]

Figure 9-3 The RGB panel

7. Before you move on, experiment with the interactive aspect of the Sample Sphere in the Material panel. Click on it now with either mouse button. The sphere is replaced with a square plane. This is especially handy when mapping textures onto flat surfaces. Chapter 10 covers texture mapping.

8. Click again to return to the sphere.

Lesson 4 covers the remaining basic attributes.

NOTE: Newly added objects inherit the current material settings. Keep this in mind when editing materials while adding objects.

LESSON 2: SMOOTHING

Most rounded objects in the real world have smooth, curved surfaces. But in trueSpace2, as you've learned, roundness must be approximated by a series of straight line segments, in the case of edges, or flat polygons, in the case of surfaces. Fortunately, trueSpace2 incorporates methods for rendering the latter as fully smoothed surfaces. This lesson covers the leftmost column of the Shader/Maps panel, which contains three smoothness settings.

1. If you're not continuing directly from Lesson 1, start trueSpace2 or clear the workspace. You should be in Solid Render Display mode for this exercise. Add a Cylinder primitive and then select the Paint Face tool to open the Material panels.

2. Next to the Material panel is the Shader/Maps panel (see Figure 9-4). Move your mouse cursor slowly over the three icons in the leftmost column, while watching the Help bar. From top to bottom, the icons are described as Faceted, AutoFacet, and Smooth.

3. Click on the Faceted icon and note that the Sample Sphere's surface is now made up of flat polygons.

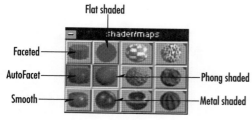

Figure 9–4 The Shader/Maps panel

4. Next, click on the Smooth icon, followed by the AutoFacet icon. You probably can't see any difference between the two in terms of their effect on the Sample Sphere's smoothed surface.

This bears some explanation, but don't worry: I'll keep it short and painless. As you learned in the chapters on modeling, all objects in trueSpace2, and in fact in most other 3D programs as well, are made up of flat polygons. In general, when you render these objects, the sharp edges between some of the polygons are smoothed over with mathematical averaging techniques. The smoothness settings in trueSpace2 give you some control over how this happens on a material-by-material basis.

5. Set the current material to the default light gray, R=G=B=210, and then click on the Faceted icon.

6. From the Paint tool pop-up menu, select the Paint Object tool (see Figure 9-5) to apply the current material to the cylinder's entire surface. You can now see the individual polygons in the cylinder's vertical surface (see Figure 9-6). With a Faceted material applied to an object, trueSpace2 performs no smoothing at all when rendering the object.

TIP: When experimenting with material editing, you'll probably be using the Paint Object tool often. You usually have to select it from the pop-up each time you need it. (It sometimes becomes the default tool after you use it, but usually not.) To save time, set (and remember to use) a keyboard shortcut. I recommend the Ⓞ key for Paint Object (the Ⓟ key is already used for the Animation Play function). Invoke the

Figure 9–5 The Paint Object tool

Figure 9–6 Cylinder with Faceted smoothing

Paint tool pop-up, drag the mouse cursor to the Paint Object tool, press and hold ⌃CTRL⌝-⌐F1⌐, and release the mouse button. The object is painted and rendered and then the Key Shortcuts dialog appears. Click on the New Key button, press the Ⓞ key (or whatever one you want to use), and, finally, click the Done button. Unfortunately, this key shortcut sometimes doesn't work, in which case you must resort to clicking the icon.

7. Now select the Smooth icon in the Shader/Maps panel's lower-left corner and again use the Paint Object tool. This time (see Figure 9-7), *all* the edges are smoothed—even the circles around the top and bottom, which to most eyes look better as sharp edges. Use the Smooth setting to force all edges to be rounded over, even those of 90 degrees or more. Unless you're very careful, however, this can lead to rendering artifacts like the ones visible on the top surface of the cylinder in Figure 9-7.

8. The default AutoFacet smoothing setting, applied to new materials when you don't choose something else, is a useful compromise between the Faceted and Smooth settings. Select AutoFacet now and reapply the material to the cylinder (see Figure 9-8). That's more like it! Now you have the sharp edges on top, with smoothing around the side, for a natural-looking cylinder.

Figure 9–7 Cylinder with Smooth smoothing

Figure 9–8 Cylinder with default AutoFacet smoothing

Examining AutoFacet

9. Let's take a closer look at how AutoFacet works. Right-click on the AutoFacet icon to bring up the Autofacet Angle panel (see Figure 9-9).

NOTE: The Autofacet Angle setting is similar to the Smooth Quad Divide Subdivision property, which Chapter 7, Utilities and Edit Tools, looked at, in that it lets you set the maximum smoothing angle for edges between polygons. However, AutoFacet isn't quite as straightforward. For example, the cylinder's side polygons meet the end surfaces at a 90-degree angle. I discovered through experimentation that, to get edge smoothing between the sides and the ends in Solid Render mode, the Autofacet Angle value must be set to at least 63.

10. Set Autofacet Angle to 63, use Paint Object, and note that all edges are rounded.

11. Set Autofacet Angle to 62 and use Paint Object again. This time the edges are sharp.

12. Actually, what you've just witnessed is due to inaccuracies in 3DR rendering. Set trueSpace2 to Wireframe Display mode, set Autofacet Angle to 89, and paint the object. Now the smoothing is correct.

13. Set Autofacet Angle to 90 and paint the object again. The 90-degree corners are rounded.

By the way, in some 3D programs, you have to set smoothing for groups of polygons, or you can set it only on an object-by-object basis. So trueSpace2's AutoFacet feature is a nice convenience. In most cases, the default Autofacet Angle value of 32 works well. You may need to adjust this from time to time, however, especially when importing objects with a wide variety of angles between polygons, such as human and animal figures. If you see faceted areas that should be smooth, increase the Autofacet Angle setting; if corners that should be sharp are rounded, decrease it. And keep in mind that, because your final output uses trueSpace2's renderer rather than 3DR, you'll need to check smoothing by rendering in Wireframe Display mode.

Figure 9–9 The Autofacet Angle panel

LESSON 3: APPLYING SHADERS

In the world of 3D graphics, the type of shading used in a surface is an important factor in determining how light interacts with that surface. Shading is implemented in a variety of ways in different programs. For example, in many applications, the Faceted smoothing option you used in Lesson 2, in which each polygon is shaded with a single color, is called Flat shading. In what trueSpace2 calls *Flat shading*, however, the entire surface to which the material is applied receives the single color. Other types of shaders in trueSpace2 include Phong, which uses standard shading with optional smoothing and specular highlights for a realistic look that's useful in most types of surfaces. Metal is a special-purpose shader best used for metallic and glass surfaces. You can see all three of trueSpace2's shading types in Figure 9-10. Let's take a quick look at them.

NOTE: A common shading type used in many programs, but not trueSpace2, is Gouraud (pronounced g'ro). With Gouraud shading, smoothing is performed, but no reflection or specular highlights are possible. Because it's significantly faster than Phong shading, Gouraud is used most often in applications that require real-time 3D rendering, such as games for the Sony PlayStation.

Flat Shading

1. Start trueSpace2 or clear the workspace and choose either Wireframe or Solid Render mode. Add any primitive. Select the Paint Face tool to open the Material panels.

2. In the Shader/Maps panel (see Figure 9-4), position the mouse cursor, in turn, over each of the three icons in the second column from the left. They're named, from top to bottom, Flat-shaded, Phong-shaded, and Metal-shaded.

3. Select the Flat-shaded icon and note the change in the Sample Sphere. Instead of a rounded sphere, it appears to be a flat disk, with no shading at all.

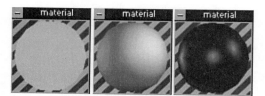

Figure 9-10 Sample Sphere with Flat, Phong, and Metal-shading

Any part of an object painted with a material set to this type of shading will always appear two-dimensional. There aren't many applications for Flat-shading, but here are a couple: Because Flat-shaded objects, especially more complex ones, render somewhat more quickly than Phong- or Metal-shaded objects, and trueSpace2 can't render wireframe animation files, Flat-shading is a way of testing animation setups, where you're more concerned with object motion than appearance. Also, for compositing animations, especially with video, you can use a Flat-shaded object as a matte, or placeholder, for the composited image. Typically, an object used for this purpose would be colored black.

4. For comparison, select the Phong-shaded icon and then select the Metal-shaded icon. The Sample Sphere is now black with white highlights.

5. Try changing the Color and Intensity settings and note that these affect primarily the highlights.

You may have noticed changes in the Shader Attributes panel settings as you selected the different Shader icons. That's because there are strong connections between the two settings groups. I'll explore these in the next lesson.

LESSON 4: THE SHADER ATTRIBUTES

You now come to the five settings in the Shader Attributes panel. Let's examine how these interact—with one another and with the other material components you've learned about so far—to create a wide variety of effects.

1. Start trueSpace2 or clear the workspace, and choose either Wireframe or Solid Render mode. Add any primitive. Select the Paint Face tool to open the Material panels.

2. In the Shader/Maps panel, make sure the default AutoFacet smoothing and Phong shader are selected.

3. Take a look at the Shader Attributes panel (see Figure 9-11). Pass your mouse cursor slowly over the five sliders and watch the Help bar. The five sliders are named, from left to right, Ambient Glow, Shininess, Roughness, Transparency, and Index of Refraction. Spheres depict the settings near the opposite extremes and at the center on each slider.

4. First, let's look at the attributes' numeric values. Right-click on any of the sliders to open the numeric equivalent of the panel (see Figure 9-12). The two panels are linked; if you change a slider setting, the corresponding numeric setting changes automatically, and vice-versa.

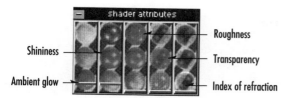

Figure 9-11 The Shader Attributes panel

shader attributes		
Ambient	0.1	↔
Shine	0.1	↔
Rough	0	↔
Opacity	1	↔
Refract	1	↔

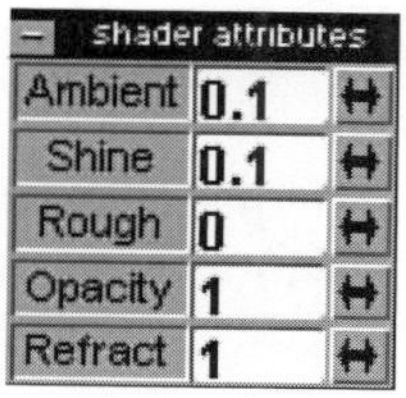

Figure 9-12 The Shader Attributes numeric settings panel

NOTE: The names of the attributes in the two panels are roughly equivalent, except for Transparency, which is called Opacity in the numeric panel—an unfortunate inconsistency.

Ambient Glow

5. Let's start at the left side Shader Attributes panel, with the Ambient setting. Click at the top end of the slider (Ambient=1.0); the Sample Sphere is completely white. Now click at the bottom end of the scale slider (Ambient=0) and note that the only lighting present is from the three Local lights used to illuminate the sphere. Click in other parts of the scale and watch the changes in the brightness of a simulated, pervasive light source. This is known as *ambient lighting*.

NOTE: In most programs, ambient lighting is a global setting and affects all objects in a scene, but in trueSpace2, you can set a different value for each material.

6. Set Ambient back to its default value of 0.1 and then try changing the Intensity setting in the Material Color panel. Near the upper end of the Intensity slider, the effect is similar to using a high Ambient setting, but the values in the lower half of the scale go much darker than is possible with the Ambient setting alone. Set Intensity back to its default value, near the top of the slider.

Shininess

7. Click near the top of the Shininess slider. The specular highlights, or illuminated bright spots, remain at their current intensity, but the rest of the Sample Sphere gets darker. Now it's easy to see that the Sample Sphere is lit by three lights: one near the front, one from the upper right, and one on the left.

8. With Shininess still set high, experiment with various combinations of the Ambient and Intensity settings. With Ambient at about half strength and Intensity about two-thirds of the way up, you get a nice semigloss, pewter-like finish.

NOTE: Shininess also determines reflectivity. Lesson 5 looks at that property.

Roughness

9. Just in case things aren't complex enough, let's add another variable. Without changing the settings from Steps 7 and 8, click near the top of the Roughness slider. Note that the sphere actually looks glossier. "Roughness" is something of a misnomer, because the material finish is least rough looking at the higher settings. Think of it as a "Glossiness" setting instead.

10. Lower Shininess down to about 0.15 to make the Sample Sphere look more natural.

11. Experiment with different Roughness settings. Notice that higher Roughness settings cause the specular highlights to become smaller, and vice-versa. This is an accurate model of the real-world phenomenon, in which glossy objects such as pool balls have small specular highlights, whereas objects with duller finishes, such as the aforementioned pewter, tend to spread the light out somewhat before reflecting it, causing larger highlights.

Transparency

12. Click in the middle of the Transparency slider (Opacity in the numeric settings) and watch the Sample Sphere fade out about halfway (see Figure 9-13).

Figure 9-13 Transparency with Phong shading

13. Click near the top of the slider. Now you can hardly see the sphere! It's pretty much invisible, as a fully transparent object should be. Note that the Opacity numeric values range in the opposite direction of the other scales. The default value is 1.0, which is fully opaque, and the opposite end of the scale is 0, which indicates full transparency.

Glass Surfaces

You might be thinking, "Why doesn't the transparent sphere look like glass?" In this section, you'll learn the secret of creating realistic glass surfaces.

1. In the Shader/Maps panel, select the Metal shader. All the Shader Attributes settings change instantly. These are the defaults for the Metal Shader, which are stored independently of the Phong attributes. (You might want to place a copy of this default material setup in the Materials library for easy recall while experimenting.)

An identifying characteristic of many, if not most, metal surfaces is that they're highly reflective of their surroundings. In fact, without that reflectivity, they're fairly dark. This is what you're seeing in the Sample Sphere right now. You can simulate reflectivity only during the rendering process, so you'll have to take it on trust for the moment that these default settings make for a good-looking generic metal surface.

2. Take a few seconds to experiment with the Ambient setting; then return it to its default.

3. You may recall that, with the Phong shader, you couldn't lose the specular highlights by changing Shininess—it only made the surrounding surface darker or lighter. Note that Metal's Shininess is set to a high value by default. Lower the Shininess values and watch the highlights get dimmer, rather than the background. (You may be able to see this phenomenon better by raising the Ambient setting a bit.)

4. The Roughness setting, on the other hand, works the same with the Metal shader as it does with the Phong shader. Take a few seconds to confirm this by altering Roughness to various levels and observing the changes in the Sample Sphere.

5. Now you get to the good part. Set the Ambient, Shininess, and Roughness settings back to their defaults, more or less. Then set Transparency all the way up. See the difference? (Compare Figure 9-13 to Figure 9-14.) Mainly, the transparency is greatest in the center, blending to opacity at the very edges, just like real curved glass.

6. Select a different color, such as red, and notice that this affects the highlights only. Set the color back to white.

7. Actually, this "glass" is unrealistically dark. For a more familiar appearance, set Ambient about halfway up or higher (see Figure 9-15).

Spend some time experimenting with the various settings, especially Roughness. You'll see you can get a great variety of interesting-looking glass types.

Also, try making some glass objects, such as beveled text, and render them—they probably won't look that great. For glass to look realistic, it must have images to reflect and objects behind it to show through. You have to render the entire scene with an appropriate background. Alternatively, you can create false reflections with trueSpace2's Environment Map capability, which is covered in Chapter 10.

Figure 9–14 Transparency with Metal shading

Figure 9–15 Glass-like material

NOTE: When a real-world glass object casts a shadow, its shadow is transparent as well. In trueSpace2, for a glass object's shadow to be transparent, the scene must be rendered in Raytrace mode. If the glass is colored, this color also shows up in the shadows.

LESSON 5: REFRACTION

Finally, let's explore the fifth setting in the Material Attributes panel: Index of Refraction. Take a moment to examine the rightmost vertical scale in the Material Attributes panel. Toward the top of the scale, the background diagonal stripes that are visible through the small spheres grow more distorted. The Index of Refraction setting determines the degree to which light bends as it passes through a transparent object. Refraction is a special case, because it requires rendering a scene with a background in Raytrace mode to be visible. Let's take a look.

1. Start trueSpace2 or clear the workspace. Use Wireframe mode for this exercise.

2. One of the best ways to show refraction is by placing an object with a simple, repeating texture behind or under the refracting object. Do this by adding a primitive plane and then texture mapping it with a grid image. Open the Primitives panel and select the Add Plane icon. Use Object Scale and drag with both mouse buttons to enlarge the plane to about 8 meters square.

3. Select the Paint Face tool. In the Shader/Maps panel, left-click the Use Texture map icon, which looks like a checkered sphere. Then right-click the same icon to open the Texture Map property panel.

4. In the Texture Map panel, click the rectangular button to the right of the small checkered-sphere image (it should say Checker). In the file requester that appears, navigate to the CD-ROM that comes with this book. Open the TUTORIAL directory, then the CH10 directory, and select the file named GRID512.BMP.

5. Select the Paint Object tool to apply the grid texture to the plane. If you don't wish to wait for the rendering, press ⌨ESC to abort it.

6. In the Primitives panel, select Add Sphere to place a new sphere in the center of the plane.

7. Activate the Paint Face tool and set the following values: high Intensity, Metal shader, no texture mapping. In the Material Attributes panel, set Ambient about two-thirds of the way up, between the top two spheres. Set Shininess, Roughness, and Transparency near or at the top of their respective scales.

8. Right-click on the Material Attributes panel and note that the Refract number is set to 1. This is the default Index of Refraction, which causes light to pass straight through transparent objects without bending. Set it to 1.08. Use the Paint Object tool to apply the refractive glass texture to the sphere.

9. Because you're going to start getting into fairly lengthy rendering now, minimize the waiting time by isolating the area you're interested in and making it fairly small. Open a new Perspective view window and use its Zoom and Eye Move tools to fill most of the view with the sphere. Go ahead; you should be fairly familiar with this process by now.

10. From the small window's Render pop-up, select the Render Scene tool. It should render fairly quickly and look like Figure 9-16. Where's the refraction?

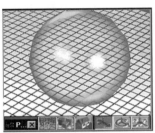

Figure 9–16 Refracting glass sphere rendered normally

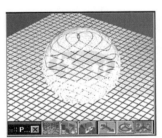

Figure 9–17 Refracting glass sphere ray traced

Ray Tracing for Refraction

11. As mentioned at the beginning of this lesson, the scene must be rendered in Raytrace mode to see the refraction effect. Right-click on the Render Scene tool; in the Render Options panel, click in the small white box in the upper-left corner, next to Raytrace.

12. Render the scene again in the small window. Rendering proceeds much more slowly this time, due to the many complex calculations required to simulate refraction accurately. You should get something more like Figure 9-17. Note that, even with a fairly low setting, there's considerable bending of light, resulting in the straight grid lines looking curved. Also, the curvature is greatest near the sphere's edges, with relatively little at the center, where light passes straight through. If you set the Index of Refraction much higher, lines visible through the sphere curve quite a bit; it's an unrealistic effect.

13. Speaking of unrealistic, it's interesting, although not terribly useful, to note that you can set the Refract number to values between 0 and 1. This level doesn't occur in nature. (The slider is limited to values between 1 and 2.) Try setting the number to some low values, remembering to use Paint Object each time, and rendering the scene in the small window to see how it looks.

Reflecting the Scene

14. You may have noticed that it's difficult to see the grid lines through the bottom part of the sphere. That's because another ray tracing phenomenon is occurring: reflection. To get a better look at this, set Transparency and Ambient all the way off, use Paint Object, and render the scene in the small view again (see Figure 9-18). This time, because the program doesn't have to render light rays passing through the sphere, the rendering goes much more quickly. (Note that the Index of Refraction setting is ignored if the object is opaque.) You can easily see the reflection of the grid in the bottom of the sphere.

15. The degree of reflectivity, by the way, is controlled with the Shininess setting. Try various values to see how this works. Also try placing other objects beside the sphere (they don't have to be visible in the render window) and rendering to see the reflections (see Figure 9-19).

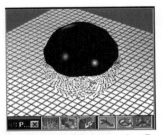

Figure 9-18 Metal reflective sphere ray traced

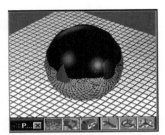

Figure 9-19 Metal sphere reflecting cone and cylinder

Nothing beats ray tracing for the accurate simulation of reflection and refraction, and trueSpace2 has both built in. The cost? Rendering time, of course. But whatever the cost, if you need the utmost in realism (or surrealism, when you use extreme Refract settings), the results are worth it.

LESSON 6: WORKING WITH THE PAINT TOOLS

You've been using the Paint Object tool regularly in this chapter to apply new materials to entire objects. The other tools in the Paint pop-up menu let you paint materials to parts of an object and bring material settings from an object into the Material panels. These tools are straightforward, so I can cover them fairly quickly.

Let's start with Paint Face.

1. Start trueSpace2 or clear the workspace and get into Wireframe mode. Make sure the current material uses the default settings. Add a sphere primitive and then select the Paint Face tool (refer back to Figure 9-1) to open the Material panels.

2. In the Material Color panel, click in the rightmost corner of the color hexagon to set the color to red. Make it a glossy red by also setting Ambient, Shininess, and Roughness to the center of the topmost sphere in their respective sliders.

3. Move the mouse cursor over the sphere; it changes to a paintbrush. Left-click once, anywhere near the top of the sphere. The face currently under the cursor is rendered with the new material (see Figure 9-20).

4. Render the sphere and note that only one face has changed.

5. The Paint Face tool also lets you paint an entire area in one stroke, sort of like in real-world painting. Simply left-button drag over the area to paint. Try it now, painting a different part of the sphere, but don't paint any of the faces next to the first one you painted (you'll see why in a bit). When you're done, rerender the sphere, eliminating the outline artifact around each face (see Figure 9-21). It's but a coarse approximation of real-world freehand painting, though, because you can paint only on a face-by-face basis.

6. Turn on texture mapping by selecting the checkered-sphere icon in the Shader/Maps panel. Paint a few more faces to demonstrate that applying a texture-mapped material with this tool works just like applying a solid color.

7. The other tool that lets you paint on parts of an object is, as far as I know, unique to trueSpace2. It's called Paint Vertices. Its icon looks like a cube with the corner painted. Select it now and change the Material Color setting to blue (or any other color you like).

Figure 9–20 Sphere with single face painted

Figure 9–21 Sphere with several faces painted

8. Left-button drag the mouse cursor over any part of the sphere to paint a few vertices (see Figure 9-22). The material is applied only to vertices, blending into the existing material in each surrounding face. Note that the Paint Vertices tool ignores the texture map; it works only with solid colors.

9. Say you decide to use a different material where you paint the first texture. That's where the two other Paint tools—Inspect and Paint Over—come in handy.

10. Use the Inspect tool to set the current material to the values of the part of the sphere to be changed. Activate the Inspect tool (the magnifying glass) from the Paint pop-up. The mouse cursor changes to a magnifying glass. Click on any sphere face that contains the texture map and watch the Material panels return to the previous settings.

11. Replace the previous material with a bumpy one. Click on the Texture Map icon to turn off texture mapping and click on the Use Bump Map icon immediately below it, to enable the default orange-peel bump map. (Chapter 10 examines bump mapping in greater detail.) Also, change the color to green, or some other color not previously used in this exercise.

12. From the Paint tool pop-up, select the tool that looks like a paint roller, which is called Paint Over and is described in the Help bar as Paint over existing Material. The mouse cursor changes to a paint roller. Click anywhere over the part of the sphere that contains the texture map. The entire sphere is rerendered, showing the new material wherever the texture map existed previously (see Figure 9-23).

Figure 9–22 Sphere with several vertices painted

Figure 9–23 Sphere with texture map changed to bump map

13. Of course, the faces' original texture maps were all contiguous. Let's demonstrate that the Paint Over tool also works on noncontiguous polygons. Recall that, when you applied the first red material with the Paint Face tool, you painted two separate parts of the sphere: first a single polygon, then a group. Click now on any face containing the red material; every face that was red is now green and bumpy. Also, note that the painted vertices are not affected by this. The Paint Over tool works only on faces, not on vertices.

LESSON 7: PAINTING A WINDSHIELD

With what you've learned about materials and painting so far, adding the glass windshield to the space fighter from Chapter 6 should be easy. Here's the procedure:

1. Load the FIGHTER.COB object you saved in Chapter 6, Advanced Modeling, Lesson 7. If your version isn't handy, you can find the file on the companion CD-ROM in the TUTORIAL/CH6 directory.

2. Rotate the object or the view so the top front surface of the fighter is accessible. Render the object.

3. Activate the Paint Face tool. Set the material to a nice shiny glass: Choose the Metal shader, set Ambient about two-thirds of the way up, and set Shininess, Roughness, and Transparency near the top of their sliders.

4. Paint a few polygons near the fighter's nose, wherever you think the cockpit should be. Render the object again. If you like, add the glass material to a few more polygons, or, if you went too far, use the Inspect tool, followed by the Paint Face tool, to restore the polygons to their former material.

You may want to add a small object inside the cockpit to demonstrate the windshield transparency (see Figure 9-24). To see both, you'll need to either glue the two objects together or render the scene.

Figure 9–24 Space Fighter with glass windshield

WHAT NOW?

Try loading some of the objects from the CD-ROM that comes with this book and applying new materials with the various tools you've learned about in this chapter. Then continue to the next chapter to see some of trueSpace2's more advanced material editing capabilities. They give you amazing power to control the appearance of objects.

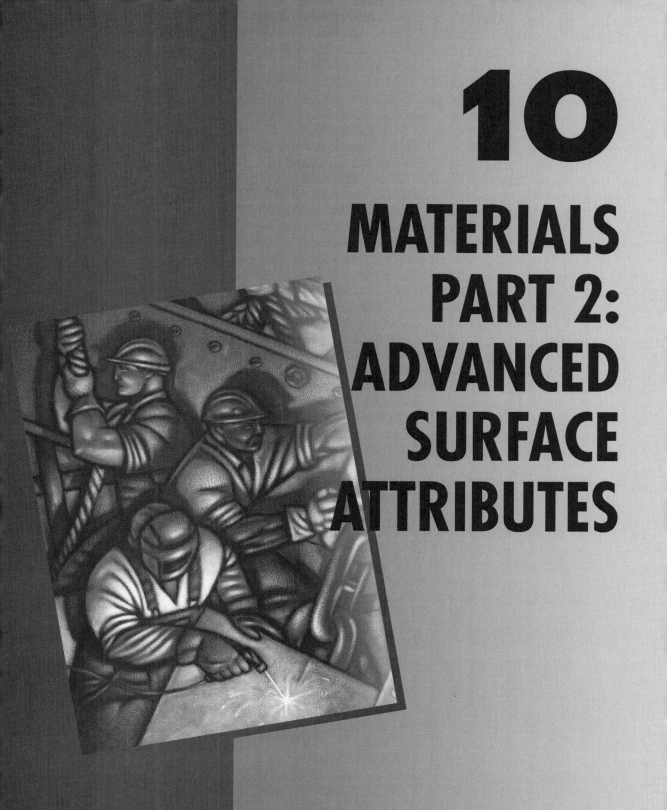

10

MATERIALS PART 2: ADVANCED SURFACE ATTRIBUTES

10

At the beginning of Chapter 9, Basic Surface Attributes, I asked you to look around your real-world environment and take note of the surfaces of the various objects present there. I want you to do that again, but this time, imagine that the surfaces contain no other visual information. That is, picture them with color, with shininess/ reflectivity or roughness, with transparency—but nothing else. Without its visual pattern, a rich wood grain would simply be brown. Without texture, plaster walls would be absolutely flat, and even your skin would have no pores, lines, or wrinkles (sort of like Odo in *Star Trek: Deep Space 9*). Sounds pretty dull, doesn't it? Textures and patterns aren't necessary in 3D graphics, but without them, your scenes would be flat and lifeless. (Not to say that Odo is, although there's something distinctly "unreal" about him ...)

Adding Images in trueSpace2

Image mapping simply means incorporating photographs, images from other programs, and the like in materials applied to objects in your scenes. There are three ways to do this in trueSpace2:

Texture mapping, in which the imported image's colors replace a material's color

Bump mapping, where luminance information from the image is translated to irregularities in the material surface

Environment mapping, which uses an image to simulate reflections without ray tracing

The trueSpace2 program sets up default images for each of these, but you can easily change them, as you'll see shortly.

In addition, trueSpace2 offers three built-in procedural textures that use mathematical formulas instead of images to simulate wood, marble, and granite. All the calculation is done by trueSpace2; you need only provide parameters (or use the defaults).

In this chapter, you'll learn how to use all these techniques. You'll also see how to set the mapping "space" with the UV Projection tool and work the unique Material Rectangle feature. Also covered here are the image utilities and Adobe Photoshop plug-ins.

First, the chapter reviews the Material library, where you will save and recall your work from this chapter.

THE MATERIAL LIBRARY, TAKE 2

The Material library is a panel for storing and retrieving materials. You can also use it to rename materials and to save and load library files. Chapter 3, Quick Start Tutorial: A Guided Tour of Major Features, covered the Material library pretty thoroughly, so this section is primarily a refresher.

To open the Material library, select its icon from the Libraries tool group (see Figure 10-1). This opens the Material Library panel, as shown in Figure 10-2.

The main section of the panel, containing a row of spheres representing the library's materials, lets you select any of its materials by clicking on it. This has two results: A thin red bar appears underneath the selected material and its parameters replace those of the current material. (You cannot undo this action.)

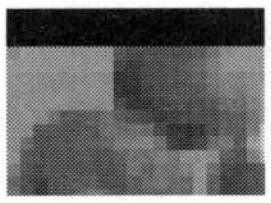

Figure 10-1 The Material Library icon

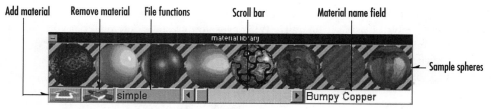

Figure 10–2 The Material Library panel

The rest of the Material Library controls are arrayed below the sample spheres. As shown in Figure 10-2, from left to right, these controls are as follows.

Add Material to Library

Selecting this icon adds the current material to the library, creating a new sample sphere or sample plane (whichever is currently displayed in the Material panel) to the right of the current one.

Remove Material from Library

Click this icon to remove the currently selected material and its representative sphere from the library. This action is permanent and cannot be revoked.

Load/Save Material Library

Clicking once on this button, which contains the file name of the current library, opens a pop-up menu. The menu has options to clear the current library (New), to load another library from disk, and to save the current library to disk with the current file name or under a different file name (Save As). When saving a file, the .MLB file name extension is automatically made for you. At start-up, if a Material library file with the name SIMPLE.MLB exists in the main trueSpace2 directory, it is loaded automatically.

Scroll Bar

This is a standard Windows scroll bar for moving horizontally through the library. Click on the arrows to scroll one material at a time or click in the scroll bar to move in larger increments, or you can click and drag on the slider.

Material Name Field

This displays the name of the current material (as selected in the library). When you first add a new material to the library, its name is Untitled. Although it seems selected, the name doesn't appear until you click on the newly added sample sphere. To rename a material, select it and click in the name field, and use standard editing methods to change the name. Press the (ENTER) key when you're done.

The Material library is a wonderfully convenient facility in trueSpace2, and if you're smart, you'll make a habit of using it liberally. Whenever you create a new material you like, add it to the library. If you change your mind, you can always delete it later. If you're building a scene with a lot of special materials, create a new library especially for that scene and use it to store all its materials, to keep them handy.

 NOTE: For a material that uses an image file, the Material library does not store the image file itself, but only the name and location of the file. If the image file is located on a removable storage medium such as a floppy disk or a CD-ROM, the medium must be present when its material is used. (Alternatively, the image file can be in the same directory as the library.) Similarly, if an image file used in a material is located on a hard disk drive and the file is moved or deleted, trueSpace2 will no longer be able to find the file. You can edit the material using the techniques you'll learn in Lesson 1, below, to locate the file.

WORKING WITH IMAGES

Image mapping in trueSpace2 lets you apply a single image to an object surface. This lets you create, for example, a leopard-skin coat without killing the cat. You can make something as mundane as a sign or as flashy as a yellow polka-dot bikini. You can map literally any image—imported or created with the computer—onto an object. The possibilities are truly mind boggling. Potential sources for images include graphics programs (including trueSpace2 itself!), scanned images, photo CD-ROMs, clip-art collections, or even faxes, if you use a fax modem.

TIP: If you use a lot of real-world imagery in your materials, consider investing in a good color scanner—you'll find it extremely useful.

Among the options available with image mapping are *tiling*, in which an image is repeated on the surface to which it's applied, and the ability to apply an offset, which lets you fine-tune where the image is placed. You can also use the image's alpha channel, if any, for transparency or overlay. Even animations can be applied as an image map.

Functions related to image mapping are UV Projection, which lets you determine the "mapping space" in which the image is applied, and Material Rectangle, which lets you apply multiple "decal" images to parts of an object. Before I get to those, however, I'll look at basic texture mapping, which is very easy to understand and accomplish.

LESSON 1: TEXTURE MAPPING

This introductory tutorial covers the fundamentals of image mapping. You'll learn how to incorporate an image in a material, how to multiply the image using repetition, and how to move and scale the image with the Offset parameter.

1. Start trueSpace2. You can be in either Wireframe or Solid Render mode for this tutorial. If you use Solid Render mode, right-click on the 3DR icon. In the Render Quality panel, turn on Textures (the checkered sphere) and set the Texture Resolution pop-up to 128×128 or 256×256.

2. Add a primitive plane object.

3. Select the Paint Face tool. In the Material Color panel, click in the color hexagon's top-right corner to make the current color yellow. Raise the intensity if you like.

4. Use the Paint Object tool to paint the plane object yellow.

5. In the Shader/Maps panel (see Figure 10-3), right-click on the Use Texture Map icon (another checkered sphere, in the top row). This opens the Texture Map panel (see Figure 10-4), where you set the texture map image file and its parameters.

6. In the Texture Map panel, click on the box that currently reads checker (the name of the default texture map). In the file requester that appears, click on the box under List Files of Type. Scroll through the list. You'll see that trueSpace2 can use files in these formats: Targa (*.tga), Windows bitmap (*.bmp), JPEG (*.jpg), Windows video (*.avi), and a special type called RPlus texture (*.txr), which you'll study in the Image Utilities section of this chapter. Go back to the top of the list and select All Textures. This lists all files of any of the above types in the current directory.

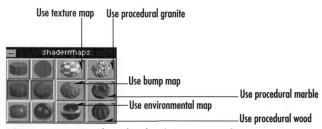

Figure 10–3 The Shader/Maps panel

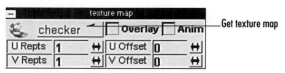

Figure 10–4 The Texture Map panel

7. The best way to learn about texture mapping is with a simple, recognizable image, and I've created one for this exercise. It's shown in Figure 10-5. Use the file requester to load the file named TEXT-MAP.BMP from the CD-ROM that came with this book. You'll find the file in the TUTORIAL/CH10 directory. In the Texture Map panel, the name "checker" is replaced by "TEXT-MAP."

8. Now turn on texture mapping by left-button clicking the Use Texture icon in the Shader/Maps panel. You'll see the sample sphere in the Material panel change to show the image. You won't be able to see the entire image because it's wrapped around the sphere. This is where the Material panel's other view mode comes in handy. Click on the sample sphere to replace it with a sample plane, which shows the full texture map image.

9. Save this material in the Material library. Give it the name Text Map and save the library.

10. Use the Paint Object tool again to paint the plane object with the new material, as shown in Figure 10-6. The image, with its blue and red text and border, plus white background, completely replaces the object's basic yellow color and has been fitted perfectly to the surface.

Figure 10–5 TEXT-MAP.BMP

Figure 10–6 Primitive plane painted with texture map

Notice that the image faces the upper-left corner of the screen. The easiest way to fix this, of course, is by rotating the object (you needn't do that now). That's fine for this very simple object, but it doesn't always work with more complex shapes, where you want the image map to be laid onto the surface in a specific orientation. You'll learn more about this when you look at UV Projection, later in this chapter.

NOTE: The trueSpace2 program doesn't have a built-in facility for viewing image files. Applying the image as a texture map to a plane object and then rendering it is a convenient way to get a quick look at a file without having to use another program.

11. Try scaling the plane object to change its proportions and then rendering it. You'll see that the texture map scales right along with the object. Use Undo to return it to the original square shape.

Repeating the Texture Map

Let's see how to tile the map. Say you want to have the image repeat four times across the plane's width and twice along its height. That's what the U Repts and V Repts settings in the Texture Map panel are for. U is computer graphics shorthand for Horizontal, V stands for Vertical, and Repts is short for Repetitions.

1. Set U Repts to 4 and V Repts to 2. As you can see in the Material panel, the image has indeed been repeated four times across its width and twice along its height.

2. Use the Paint Object tool to apply the modified texture to the plane object. It may be hard to read, so if you like, zoom in and rerender to get something like Figure 10-7.

3. Repetition settings don't have to be whole numbers. You can set them to be any decimal number, with accuracy to the hundredths place. Try, for example, setting U Repts to 1.33 for one and one-third repetitions and V Repts to 3.5. Notice that the "point of reference" for where the repetitions start is the image's lower-left corner.

Figure 10-7 Primitive plane mapped with 4x2 repetitions

4. You can magnify the image by setting U and V Repts to less than 1.0. For example, with U Repts at 0.25 and V Repts at 0.5, the image is magnified four times in the horizontal dimension and two times vertically. Try these and other values. When you're done experimenting, set U and V Repts back to 1.

Offsetting the Texture Map

Let's look at U and V Offset, to the right of the Repts settings in the Texture Map panel. The Offset setting determines the distance by which the texture map is moved from its default starting point.

NOTE: For this part of the tutorial, the results are easy to see in the Material panel sample plane, so you don't need to keep reapplying the material to the plane and rendering it.

1. As you can see, the default values for U and V Offset are both 0. Set both to 1.0 and then to -1.0. Note that the result with both settings is the same. This is the full range for both settings: -1.0 to 1.0.

2. Set both Offsets back to 0 and then change U Offset to 0.33. The image now starts a third of the way to the right of its initial starting point and "wraps around," so the left-hand third of the plane is occupied by the rightmost third of the image (see Figure 10-8).

3. Now that you know how horizontal offset works, vertical offset shouldn't be much of a shocker. Change the V Offset setting to 0.25. Now the texture map image starts a third of the way over and a quarter of the way up, and wraps around on both the left side and the bottom.

4. Try negative values for both Offsets and various combinations of negative and positive values for each.

Figure 10-8 Texture map offset by one-third

The principle at work here is easy to see: Positive offsets move the image up and/or to the right, and negative offsets move the image down and/or to the left. Also, the settings are essentially percentages of the image's width, if you throw away the decimal point or multiply by 100.

Here's a quick pop quiz: With what you've just learned about the Repts and Offsets settings, see if you can apply the Text-map image to the sample plane so that you can see all the text but none of the border. (Need a hint? You need to magnify the image slightly while simultaneously moving it down and to the left by a small amount.) I won't give you the answer, but before you give up, load the Material library file named TEXT-TUT.MLB from the TUTORIAL/CH10 directory on the CD-ROM and check out the single entry.

5. Before continuing, set both U and V Repts back to 1.0 and U and V Offset to 0.

Mapping with Transparency

Now let's take a look at the Overlay setting. This lets you tell trueSpace2's texture mapping how to use the transparency in 32-bit images that contain *alpha channel* information. In computer graphics, alpha channel refers to an optional 8 bits (256 levels) of *transparency information* contained in some images. In trueSpace2, such information is recognized only in images in the Targa and RPlus formats. Alpha channel information can be created in 32-bit paint programs, such as Adobe Photoshop, and within trueSpace2 via the Image Utilities section, which I'll examine later in this chapter.

1. Use the Get Texture Map file requester from the Texture Map panel to open the file TEXT-MAP.TGA from the TUTORIAL/CH10 directory on the CD-ROM.

2. The sample plane in the Material panel is now fully transparent, except for the areas containing colored pixels. Use Paint Object to apply it to the plane object in the workspace, with the same result (see Figure 10-9). The Targa-format image you're using as a texture map has all background (white) pixels set to full transparency.

Figure 10–9 Texture map using transparency in nonoverlay mode

3. In the Texture Map panel, click in the check box for Overlay to enable this setting. Note the immediate change in the sample plane's appearance. The texture map's colored pixels remain the same, but the yellow basic material now shows through from underneath the transparent background pixels. Thus, the nontransparent portions of the texture map are *overlaid* on top of the basic material.

4. To verify the Overlay effect, paint the plane object with the new color.

The remaining setting in the Texture Map panel, the Animation check box, is explained in Chapter 11, Animation.

You can see that there are many ways to use texture maps, even on a simple plane. When you examine the UV Projection functions later in this chapter, you'll see how to apply texture maps to three-dimensional objects.

LESSON 2: BUMP MAPPING

Bump mapping is similar to texture mapping, but instead of supplying color and/or transparency information, the bump map image provides *relative surface displacement information* (i.e., bumpiness). This facility is of substantial benefit in that it creates the appearance of an uneven surface without requiring a greatly subdivided mesh object. On the other hand, the surface bumpiness created by bump mapping is illusory, and thus can be seen head on but not in profile. By default, the bumps are higher where the image is lighter and lower where it's darker, but this can be reversed. In other words, only the image's luminance information is used to create the bumpiness; color information is ignored.

1. Start trueSpace2. Because 3DR doesn't render bump maps, use Wireframe Display mode for this tutorial.

2. Add a primitive sphere object.

3. Select the Paint Face tool.

4. In the Shader/Maps panel (see Figure 10-3), select the Use Bump Map icon, second from the right in the middle row. The sample sphere in the Material panel now has a bumpy appearance, much like that of an orange peel.

5. Right-click on the Use Bump Map icon to open the Bump Map panel (see Figure 10-10), and note that the default bump map file is indeed named orange.

6. Let's play around with the default bump map for a bit. The settings for U and V Repts and Offset work the same as in texture mapping. The Amp setting, which stands for Amplitude, controls the bumps' maximum height or depth. Default amplitude is 0.2. Try changing it to 0.5; this makes the sample sphere's bumpiness more pronounced (see Figure 10-11).

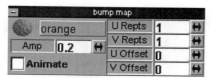

Figure 10-10 The bump map panel

Figure 10-11 Orange bump map with high Amplitude

7. Set Amp to a fairly high number, such as 6. Now you have a crater-like appearance (see Figure 10-12). Use Paint Object to apply this material to the sphere in the workspace and observe how the multicolored lighting brings out the sphere's 3D surface texture.

8. Just for kicks, set Amp to its maximum value of 10. Pretty craggy, right? In general, the more useful Amp settings occur at the lower end of the scale. But try this: Keep the same Amplitude setting, but use only a small portion of the bump map by setting both U and V Repts to 0.2. The sample sphere gives you some clues as to how the surface looks (see Figure 10-13), but for a better look, apply the material to the workspace sphere (see Figure 10-14). Again, the colored lighting brings out the dimensionality.

TIP: Can you see the bump map's "seam," where the edges meet, running between the sphere's top and bottom points and pointing toward the lower left? This is a constant concern in texture mapping, because it detracts from the realistic appearance. It's why "seamless" texture maps—images whose edges match perfectly—are desirable in 3D graphics. One of the best sources of original seamless textures is Texture Explorer, part of Kai's Power Tools from MetaTools. Appendix C looks at this excellent set of graphics programs.

9. Before going on, set Amp back to 0.2 and set both U and V Repts back to 1.

Figure 10–12 Orange bump map with very high Amplitude

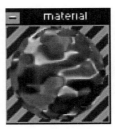

Figure 10–13 High-Amplitude bump map stretched out

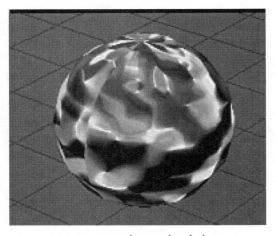

Figure 10–14 High-Amplitude bump map stretched out and rendered

Using an Image as a Bump Map

1. In the Bump Map panel, click on the Orange button to open the Get Bump Map file requester. Scroll down to the file that starts with "orange." As you can see, it has a .TAB file name extension. This special file format is used exclusively for bump mapping with trueSpace2 (I'll talk more about it in the Image Utilities portion of this chapter), so it's impossible to see it as a straight graphical image.

Check under List Files of Type; in addition to the .TAB format, all the same file formats accepted for texture mapping can be used for bump mapping as well.

2. Let's continue the exploration of bump mapping with the same image used in the first part of Lesson 1. Use the file requester to navigate to the CD-ROM included with this book (make sure it's in the drive!) and open the TEXT-MAP.BMP file from the TUTORIAL/CH10 directory.

3. After a moment or two, you'll see the image applied to the sample sphere as a bump map, as in Figure 10-15. You can see only a small amount of the word Texture on the top part of the sphere. For a better look at the total effect, click in the Material panel to change the sample sphere to a sample plane (see Figure 10-16). Now it's plainly evident that the text and border are "etched" out of the plane's surface. This happens because the text is darker than the background, so trueSpace2 treats the background as the higher area, using the default positive value for Amplitude.

4. Use the Paint Object tool to apply the material to the workspace sphere's surface (see Figure 10-17). In addition to the "carved-out" text, you can see a wedge-shaped depression on the sphere's front-left side where the left and right sides of the border meet. There's a circular depression on top, created by the border's top edge. The top border looks relatively small because it's mapped onto a small part of the sphere, whereas the text is spread out because it's mapped onto a larger part of the sphere. You can clearly see this effect in the area where the side borders meet. You know they're the same width from top to bottom, yet when mapped onto the sphere, they appear to change in width between the "poles" and the "equator."

5. How can you get the text and borders to "stick out"? You guessed it—by changing the Amplitude to a negative value. Try it now: Set Amp to -1, notice the change in the sample plane, and then apply the material to the workspace sphere (see Figure 10-18). The part of the text that coincides with the sphere's edge does not actually protrude outward, and thus does not change the profile. This may be a bit hard to see due to the sphere's angularity, which you can fix by using the Smooth Quad Divide tool once. After doing so, rerender the sphere and check out the edges. If you like, set Amp to higher values and reapply to the sphere. The edges don't change.

Figure 10–15 TEXT-MAP.BMP
applied as bump map to sample sphere

Figure 10–16 TEXT-MAP.BMP
applied as bump map to sample plane

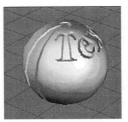

Figure 10-17 TEXT-MAP.BMP
applied as bump map to mesh sphere

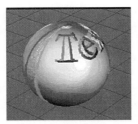

Figure 10-18 TEXT-MAP.BMP applied
as bump map with negative Amplitude

6. For an interesting look at how the same image can be used as both a texture map and a bump map, set Amp back to 1. Then activate the Use Texture Map tool and make TEXT-MAP.BMP the texture map. Click on the sample sphere to see how it looks mapped onto a plane. Also, try mapping this material onto a plane in the workspace and zoom in for a better look.

That's about all the technical information you need to get started with bump mapping. Again, U and V Offset work the same as in texture mapping; Chapter 11, Animation, covers the Animation switch for all the image-mapping tools.

Making the Most of Bump Mapping

Bear in mind that, although you've used fairly overt examples of bump mapping in this tutorial, the technique can be used very subtly to good effect. Most "flat" real-world surfaces, such as windows and walls, are not perfectly flat. Especially with reflective surfaces, such as glass and metal, you can lend a fair bit of realism by using a small bump applied with a relatively low Amplitude setting to simulate a slight unevenness. Such a bump map can come from almost anywhere. For example, you could use a small portion of a digitized image by setting low values for U and V Repts. However, the entire image would still be consuming precious memory. You'd be better off loading it into a paint program such as Adobe Photoshop, cutting out a 20×20-pixel (or so) swatch, and saving it as a separate file to use as the bump map.

One of the best sources for original bump maps is a paint program such as Photoshop. Work in grayscale mode to conserve memory. Set the image size fairly small and paint some black pixels at random locations. Then use the Blur and/or Blur More filters repeatedly on the entire image to create nice gradients between the black pixels and the white background. You'll find an example file created this way on the companion CD-ROM, in the TUTORIAL/CH10 directory, named Sampbmp1.bmp.

LESSON 3: ENVIRONMENT MAPPING

As you learned in Chapter 9, trueSpace2 can render accurate reflections on object surfaces by means of ray tracing. But ray tracing exacts a penalty in terms of the extra time required to render reflective objects, especially when transparency is involved. In *environment mapping* (also called *reflection mapping*), you use an existing image file to fake a reflection, thus saving rendering time. The image file can be in any of the formats already mentioned, except for the nonstandard .TXR and .TAB formats. Or it can be in either of two special formats: .T1D (one-dimensional environment) or .E2D (two-dimensional environment). Included with trueSpace2 are several sample .T1D files and one .E2D file. You can also make your own with the Image utilities, covered in Lesson 7.

Environment mapping is different from texture mapping mainly because the image isn't applied directly to the surface. Rather, it's applied to the inside surface of an implied sphere surrounding the scene, and then the reflections are calculated. Thus, there are no settings for U and V Repts or Offset, and when you modify the object, the reflection isn't directly affected. For example, if you rotate the object, the reflected image doesn't rotate with it, but stays in the same place relative to the scene.

Ready? Let's try some reflection mapping!

1. Start trueSpace2. Because 3DR doesn't render environment maps, get into Wireframe Display mode for this tutorial.

2. Add a primitive sphere object.

3. Select the Paint Face tool.

4. In the Shader/Maps panel (see Figure 10-3), select the Use Environment Map icon, second from the right in the bottom row. Look at the sample sphere in the Material panel; you can see a faint rainbow-like reflection around its center.

5. Of course, you're more accustomed to seeing reflections in metallic objects, so let's turn the sample sphere to steel. In the Shader/Maps panel, select the Metal Shaded button, immediately to the left of the Use Environment Map tool. Now the sample sphere looks very much like the icon on the Use Environment Map tool (see Figure 10-19). This default environment map, RAINBOW.T1D, is a one-dimensional map that consists of a vertical stack of single pixels that normally form one or more gradients, but actually can be of any value. Because the file is in a special format, you can't examine it directly, so use the Paint Object tool to apply the material to the workspace sphere (see Figure 10-20). The rainbow now seems to be around the

top part of the sphere, rather than the middle. That's because you're looking down on the sphere from above.

7. Open a new Front View window and render the sphere in that window. Now the reflection is around the middle of the sphere. Try setting the small window to Perspective view and use Eye Rotate to change the view to different angles on the vertical axis. Render with each new angle to see how the viewing angle affects the reflection. Also, try rotating and then rendering the sphere, and observe that this has no effect on the reflection's location. When you're finished, close the small window.

2D Environment Mapping

1. Let's look at the two-dimensional environment map that comes with trueSpace2. Right-click on the Use Environment Map button to open the Environment Map panel (see Figure 10-21). It's much smaller than the others, because the only functions are for designating the image file and toggling animation.

2. Click on the Get Environment Map button, which currently reads Rainbow. The file requester opens to the TRUSPACE/ENVIRMNT directory, which contains only .T1D files and the single .E2D file.

3. Load the WASTELAN.E2D file and then apply the material to the workspace sphere (see Figure 10-22).

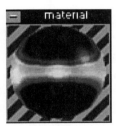

Figure 10–19 Sample metal sphere with Rainbow environment map

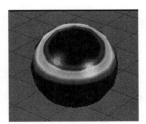

Figure 10–20 Mesh sphere in workspace with Rainbow environment map

Figure 10–21 The environment map panel

Figure 10–22 Mesh sphere in workspace with Wasteland environment map

Things have suddenly gotten much more interesting. Instead of a simple gradient, you now have the reflection of a seemingly real environment, with the sky above and mountains all around. Try rendering the sphere as viewed from various angles, high and low, and note the differences. You can see that from lower angles the sky is more prominent in the reflection, and from above the sky reflection is smallest. Think about the way light rays are reflected in rounded objects, and you'll understand why this is so. Or, if you have access to a large chrome ball, take it into various environments and view the reflection from different angles.

4. Try revolving the camera eye around the sphere in the workspace, rendering it from different sides. Notice that the 2D environment map seems to be seamless, with no noticeable edges.

While you're in the TRUSPACE/ENVIRMNT directory, take a look at the other available one-dimensional environment maps. They're quite useful, and you should always try to be aware of the varied resources available to you. You'll learn how to create 1D and 2D environment files in the Image Utilities section of this chapter.

Using a Standard Image as an Environment Map

Finally, let's take a look at using an actual bitmap image as an environment map.

1. In the Environment Map panel, load the TEXT-MAP.BMP file you used in the first two tutorials.

2. Apply the material to the workspace sphere.

3. It's probably difficult to see the reflection map on the sphere's surface, so use the Eye Rotate tool to orbit around the sphere on the World y axis, rendering as you go until you see something like Figure 10-23. You can see that the reflection is backward, as reflections are supposed to be.

Figure 10–23 The TEXT-MAP.BMP
file as a reflection map

NOTE: One thing that's really cool about the three mapping techniques you've just learned is that they can be combined in any way. As you've seen, you can use the same image for a texture map and a bump map, or you can use two different images. You can combine texture mapping or bump mapping with environment mapping, or use all three together. Let your imagination run away with you; the more creative you are with texture mapping, the more your work will mark you as a true 3D artist!

PROCEDURAL TEXTURES

Up to this point, you've learned about applying images to object surfaces for color, bumpiness, and reflections. But trueSpace2 has another trick up its sleeve for adding variety to objects' appearances called *procedural texturing*. Instead of using preset textures, in procedural texture mapping you use mathematical formulas to add colored patterns to object surfaces.

There are advantages and disadvantages to using this technique. On the positive side, you save memory, because a mathematical formula consumes far less than a bitmap—in fact, it uses hardly any memory at all. Another benefit is that there are never any seams with this method. On the other hand, you don't have the flexibility of image maps; you're pretty much limited to the textures the program gives you, although you can vary the effects a great deal by playing around with the parameters. And back on the plus side, procedural textures can be animated for some interesting effects not easily obtainable otherwise.

There are three procedural textures: Granite, Marble, and Wood.

LESSON 4: APPLYING THE PROCEDURAL GRANITE TEXTURE

1. Start trueSpace2. Because 3DR doesn't render procedural textures, use Wireframe Display mode for this tutorial.

2. Add a primitive sphere object.

3. Select the Paint Face tool.

4. In the Shader/Maps panel (see Figure 10-3), select the Use Procedural Granite Texture icon in the top-right corner. You can see the default look of the Granite texture on the sample sphere (see Figure 10-24).

5. Try changing the basic material color in the Material Color panel's color hexagon. There's no change in the sample sphere's appearance. Like texture maps, a procedural texture's colors completely supplant the material's fundamental color.

6. Granite is a fairly detailed texture, so it's kind of hard to see in the tiny Material panel. Let's get a better look. Use the Object Scale tool to make the sphere significantly larger; then use Paint Object to apply the material to the workspace sphere (see Figure 10-25). You can see that the material has been scaled up along with the sphere and is a crazy quilt of larger blotches and tiny specks in different shades of gray.

Figure 10–24 The default Granite procedural texture on the sample sphere

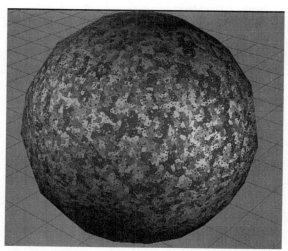

Figure 10–25 The default Granite procedural texture on a large sphere

265

7. Right-click on the Granite Texture icon to open the Granite Settings panel (see Figure 10-26). Among the texture parameters are four color components, each with its own Amount setting, plus overall Scale settings for the x, y, and z axes and a Sharpness setting.

8. The easiest way to see what the different parameters do is to reduce the number of colors, then work your way back up the complexity ladder. Start by setting all the Amount settings to 0 except Amount 1. (You can easily tell by experimenting that the full range for these settings is 0 to 1.) You don't need to apply this to the large sphere, because it's readily apparent in the Material panel that you simply have a solid light gray sphere.

9. Set Amount 2 to a low value, say 0.2 or so, then apply the material to the large sphere with Paint Object. Increase it gradually, repainting the sphere each time, until you reach the maximum value of 1. You can see that Amount is a pretty good descriptor for this parameter, because it sets the relative quantity of the various-sized speckles of each color.

10. Let's look at the Scale factors, starting with X. First, check out the range. To use the "spinner," press and hold the left mouse button on the double-headed arrow to the right of the Scale X setting and drag left until the number doesn't change any more. Then drag right until the setting again stops changing. The range of possible values is 0 to 10.

11. Set Scale X to 0 and paint the sphere. The speckles are spread out parallel to the x axis (see Figure 10-27, left side).

granite settings					
color 1		amount 1	1	scale X	3
color 2		amount 2	1	scale Y	3
color 3		amount 3	1	scale Z	3
color 4		amount 4	1	sharpness	1

Figure 10–26 The Granite Settings panel

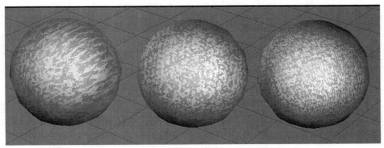

Figure 10–27 Granite spheres with Scale X settings of 0, 3, and 10

12. Set Scale X to 10 and repaint the sphere. Now the speckles are compressed, parallel to the x axis (see Figure 10-27, right side), but the effect is more subtle.

13. Try various values of Scale X, repainting the sphere each time. The differences between the higher values are hard to see, but if you do a side-by-side comparison, as in Figure 10-27, they're fairly evident. When you're finished, set Scale X back to 3.

14. Let's look at Sharpness. You might expect that lowering this would give the speckles fuzzy edges, but that's not the case. The range is 0 to 1. Set the value to 0 and look at the sample sphere. As in Step 7, the result is a blank sphere, consisting only of Color 1's light gray.

15. Experiment with increasingly higher values for Sharpness. From 0 to 0.5, the secondary color fades in, and from 0.5 to 1, the speckles break up so their size varies more and more (see Figure 10-28). Before proceeding, set Sharpness back to the default value of 1.

16. Finally, try changing the color. In the Granite Settings panel, click on the medium light gray color box (Color 2). This opens the Granite Color 2 panel, shown in Figure 10-29.

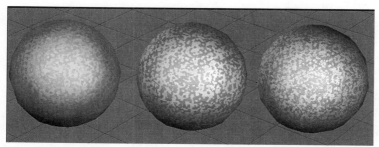

Figure 10–28 Granite spheres with Sharpness settings of 0.2, 0.5, and 1

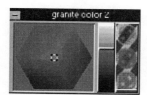

Figure 10–29 The Granite Color 2 panel

17. This panel combines the Material Color panel's color hexagon and Intensity slider with the Shader Attributes panel's Transparency slider. You already know how to manipulate these settings, so go for it!

 TIP: One interesting aspect of this interface: If you open a color panel and then move it, and then open a panel for a different color, the first one doesn't go away, as it does if you *don't* move it. Keep moving panels after opening them, and you can get all four available at once.

Here's an interesting combination to try: blue, red, yellow, and green, with Scale X, Scale Y, and Scale Z all set to 1 and all transparencies about halfway up.

Now that you've conquered Granite, the other two procedural textures—Marble and Wood—should be child's play. You can get explanations of all the parameters in the Help file.

Bear in mind that you are by no means limited to using procedural textures in materials for which they're named. For example, you can use Marble for clouds or lightning. The Wood texture with a low Density setting on a sphere creates a weird-looking eye. Use your imagination!

UV PROJECTION

I've mentioned the UV Projection tool several times in this chapter, and now you'll finally get to discover what it's all about. Basically, it lets you control how trueSpace2 takes images used in texture maps and bump maps and "wraps" them onto an object's surface, horizontally and vertically. When you create an object with trueSpace2, the program applies a default UV projection that depends on the type of object.

The program's three basic projection methods are planar, cylindrical, and spherical. As you might expect, the program uses the planar method with planar objects such as the primitive plane you used in Lesson 1, as well as with polygons and text. The cylindrical method is used for the primitive cone and cylinder, and the spherical method is used for the primitive sphere, as seen in Lesson 2. But with other shapes, trueSpace2 applies special-case projection methods.

LESSON 5: WORKING WITH UV PROJECTION

Because the cylinder is a sort of "hybrid" object, combining the plane's flatness with the sphere's rotundity, I'll use it to examine the three fundamental projections. Then I'll look briefly at some of the special cases.

1. Start trueSpace2 and choose Solid Render Display mode. Right-click on the 3DR icon; in the Render Quality panel, turn on Textures and set the Texture Resolution pop-up to 128×128 or 256×256. Close the panel.

2. Add a primitive cylinder object.

3. In Lesson 1, you created the Text Map material and saved it in the Material library. Make sure the companion CD-ROM is in your drive, and select that material from the Material library.

4. Use the Paint Object tool to apply the material to the cylinder.

5. Activate the Object Rotate tool and rotate the cylinder about its vertical axis using the right mouse button. You can see that the texture map wraps nicely around the cylinder's circumference like the label on a can, as shown in Figure 10-30. This is how cylindrical projection works.

6. From the Render tool group, select the UV Projection tool (see Figure 10-31, left side). This causes the UV Map panel to open (see Figure 10-31, right side).

In the UV Map panel, you can see three icons corresponding to the three projection types—from left to right, planar, cylindrical, and spherical. Planar is selected by default when you first select the UV Projection tool. If you change the projection method, the most recently selected method becomes the default.

7. Take a look at the cylinder in the workspace. Positioned over its top is a wireframe plane with a line projecting down from one corner. This shows the default positioning of the planar mapping method. In the UV Map panel, select the Apply button to apply the planar projection method. This automatically rerenders the object (see Figure 10-32), but only in Solid Render Display mode.

Figure 10–30 Cylindrical projection

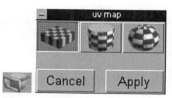

Figure 10–31 The UV Projection tool and UV Map panel

Figure 10–32 Cylinder with planar projection

Figure 10–33 Cylinder bottom with planar projection

8. You can see that the texture map image is now mapped onto the flat top surface, with its lower-left corner positioned where the wireframe plane's projecting line was. The parts of the image map that coincide with the edges of the cylinder's top surface project down through the cylinder's length—as does, in fact, the entire image. You can confirm this by selecting the Object tool (if it's not already selected), then select Object Rotate and left-button drag upward in the workspace to reorient the cylinder so its bottom surface is facing you (see Figure 10-33). The image on the cylinder's bottom is a mirror image of the texture map.

Moving the Projection Wireframe

1. Undo the rotation so the cylinder returns to its original vertical orientation. Then select the UV Projection tool again, and note that the Object Move tool is selected. This must mean you can move the projection wireframe around to reposition where the image is flat mapped onto the object surface, right? Give it a try. Drag in any direction in the workspace with either mouse button held down. Nothing happens!

2. In fact, to reposition the projection wireframe, you must use the Object Rotate tool. Select it now. Then you can right-button drag horizontally in the workspace to rotate the wireframe about the cylinder's vertical axis. Say you want to have the image facing you. The line projecting out from the wireframe indicates the image map's lower-left corner, so rotate the wireframe until the line is pointing southwest. (Think of the cylinder's top surface as a compass with north pointing directly away from you.) Click the Apply button.

3. Again select the UV Projection tool. The wireframe has returned to its initial default position.

NOTE: There is no equivalent of the Inspect tool for UV Projection. That is, you cannot directly observe and manipulate an object's current UV projection type. However, the Material Rectangle tool, discussed in the next lesson, offers an indirect method of displaying on object's UV Projection.

4. This time, left-button drag downward to rotate the wireframe so it's facing you (see Figure 10-34). Well, that's pretty interesting! The wireframe has actually been enlarged so that it fully encompasses the cylinder's extents.

NOTE: This is a standard side effect of rotating the projection wireframe, one over which you have no control. In fact, there is no provision for changing the projection's size; the Object Scale tool has no effect.

5. Click Apply to see the current projection's effect.

Continue rotating the UV Projection tool to various positions on the cylinder and then applying it. Try isolating the x and y axes and changing the coordinate system; all these functions are in full effect here.

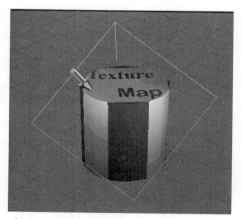

Figure 10–34 Cylinder with planar projection wireframe rotated toward viewer

NOTE: Undo doesn't work with repositioning the projection frame; the best you can do is select the Cancel button and start over.

Exploring Cylindrical and Spherical Projection

Let's look briefly at the other projection methods, cylindrical and spherical.

1. Start by selecting the UV Projection tool; in the UV Map panel, choose Cylindrical UV Projection. The cylinder in the workspace is now enclosed by a cylindrical projection wireframe.

2. Now try manipulating the projection. Select the Object Move tool first and left-button drag rightward a few inches in the workspace. You can see that the wire-frame actually does move a short distance, but much more noticeable is the fact that it grows larger on the side toward which you dragged.

3. Apply the projection and then rotate the cylinder. Observe how the sides of the texture map have been enlarged, whereas the center is reduced. (This isn't a terribly useful trick, but it is occasionally useful for adding a bit of unevenness to a texture map.)

4. Select the UV Projection tool again. As noted earlier in this lesson, the Cylindrical UV Projection button remains active. However, as you can see, the projection has returned to its original size and position. Now try Object Rotate and right-button drag to rotate the wireframe around the cylinder. This, of course, sets the texture map's start/end point and thus the seam's location.

This is useful with an object that must be in a certain position, but whose seam should not be visible. Try left-button dragging, and observe that you get the same continuous size adjustment as with planar projection. Again, there's no scaling of the cylindrical projection wireframe.

5. Now apply the default spherical UV projection to the cylinder (see Figure 10-35).

Figure 10–35 Cylinder with default spherical projection

Because spherical projection mode expects a gradual decreasing of an object's radius toward the top and bottom (as with a sphere) rather than an abrupt one (as with a cylinder), it increases the texture map's size around the center and decreases it at the extremities. As you can see, this doesn't look very good on the cylinder. However, it may be useful for other types of nonspherical objects, including human figures. In general, when working with irregular imported models, it's best to experiment with both the projection type and the texture map. I'll get to that shortly.

6. Finally, try moving and rotating the spherical projection wireframe. It works pretty much the same as with cylindrical projection.

Special-Case Projections

Let's look at some of the custom projection types trueSpace2 uses. These projections cannot be modified, but it's good to know about them to understand trueSpace2 fully.

1. Clear the workspace and make sure the Text Map material is active (select it in the Material library).

2. Add a cube primitive. You can see that the top-center portion of the image is flat mapped onto the cube's upper surface.

3. Rotate the cube and try to figure out how trueSpace2 mapped the rest of the image onto the different faces. Not too easy, is it? I'm just as much in the dark on this one as you are.

4. Try the other projection types on the cube.

5. Delete the cube and add a torus primitive. Rotate it to see how the image is mapped onto its surface. This one's much more logical. The torus is treated as a tube, with the image wrapped around from top edge to top edge and then curved into the donut shape.

6. Try a couple more objects, then you can move on. Clear the workspace and add a regular polygon. As you can see, the image is flat mapped onto its surface.

7. Select the Sweep tool. Right-drag upward to increase the depth of the extrusion (see Figure 10-36). Now you can see that two different projection types are at work: planar on the ends and cylindrical on the sides. Keep this in mind for the next lesson, where you'll learn how to map multiple images onto a single object.

8. Delete the swept object. Then select the Polygon tool and draw a simple outline for lathing, such as the one in Figure 10-37. Add the points in the order shown in the illustration.

Figure 10–36 Swept polygon
displaying custom hybrid projection

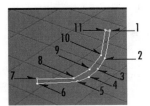

Figure 10–37 Lathe template
for bowl object

9. Lathe the outline 360° around the lower-left edge to create a bowl. As you can see, the mapping is sphere-like, starting at the lathed shape's first vertex and ending at the next-to-last vertex, and it follows the bowl's contours.

MULTIMAPPING WITH THE MATERIAL RECTANGLE

With the techniques learned so far, you can apply materials to an entire object or to specific polygons. The Material Rectangle is a special tool that permits the application of one or more materials to arbitrary parts of an object's surface. It also offers a means of indirectly observing an object's UV projection type, as noted in Lesson 5.

LESSON 6: USING THE MATERIAL RECTANGLE TOOL

In this lesson, you'll experience the mystery of the cube primitive's default UV Projection type. Along the way, you'll learn the basics of the highly useful Material Rectangle tool.

1. Start trueSpace2. If the program is already running, it's probably best to quit and restart, so as to make sure all material settings are at their defaults. For learning about the Material Rectangle tool, I recommend staying in Wireframe Display mode.

(Although you can use the tool in Solid Render Display mode, feedback can be quite slow unless you're using a very powerful machine.)

2. Add a primitive cube. If you've just started the trueSpace2 program, this object should be in the default light gray material. If you're not sure, render it and, if necessary, set the material to off-white (R=G=B=210) and paint the object.

3. Use simple materials for exploring Material Rectangle so it's easy to tell what's going on. Make the first one plain red. Select Paint Face and set the current material to red.

4. From the Render group, select the Material Rectangle tool (see Figure 10-38, left side) to open the Material Rectangle panel (see Figure 10-38, right side). Right now, all its controls are ghosted except the New button and the two large icons.

5. Select the New button. This places a new Material Rectangle across the cube's front corner (see Figure 10-39). It's depicted as a square, white outline with two blue lines running across it vertically and horizontally. The white outline shows the Material Rectangle's extents; the blue lines are merely visual aids.

6. Click the Render Object tool to render the area covered by the rectangle. The rendered area is red, whereas the surrounding area remains white. Just as with new objects, new Material Rectangles use the current material.

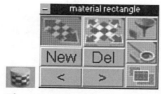

Figure 10–38 The Material Rectangle tool and Material Rectangle panel

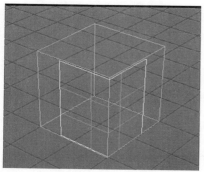

Figure 10–39 Cube with Material Rectangle visible

Moving and Scaling the Material Rectangle

1. In the Material Rectangle panel, position the mouse cursor over the upper-left icon, which is selected. As shown in the Help bar, this is the Move Material Rectangle button. Because it is already selected, you can reposition the rectangle by left-button dragging the mouse (the right button doesn't do anything in this case).

2. Now for the mystery. Drag left and right to move the rectangle horizontally in both directions. Then drag in either direction until the leading edge of the rectangle meets the cube's rear corner, and keep dragging a small distance more. As you drag, you're moving the rectangle through the cube's custom mapping space. You can see that the farther you drag, the more of the rectangle disappears. Where does it go? Nobody really knows, but I hear rumors from time to time of the "bit bucket" or the "Material Rectangle Twilight Zone" (do-de-do-do do-de-do-do)...

3. Bring the rectangle back to near its original position; then try dragging vertically. Watch it wrap around the left-front top and bottom edges nicely, but not so well with the right-front (and left-rear) top and bottom edges. If you try to move the rectangle vertically past the right-rear top and bottom edges from either direction, or past the left-rear top and bottom edges from the upper or lower surface respectively, it again disappears.

4. You can isolate horizontal and vertical movement by right-clicking on the Move Material Rectangle tool, which opens a small panel with U and V buttons. These work like the X, Y, and Z buttons on the Help bar, in that turning off U disables horizontal movement and turning off V disables vertical movement. Spend some more time experimenting with the various types of movement. Then enable both the U and V buttons and return the rectangle to its original position.

5. Select the Scale Material Rectangle tool, just to the right of the Move Material Rectangle tool. Now you can scale the rectangle up and down horizontally and vertically via corresponding mouse drags, with the rectangle's lower-left corner acting as anchor point. Again, you can isolate the scaling direction with the U and V buttons in the small panel. In this case, the U/V panel does double duty for both moving and scaling—there aren't separate settings.

6. Move and scale the rectangle so it's centered on the top surface and about half its size, as shown in Figure 10-40.

7. Exit the Material Rectangle tool by selecting the Object tool or pressing the ⊕ key. Render the cube. You have a nice red rectangle right where you'd expect.

8. If you like, to demonstrate that the rectangle doesn't go "through" the cube (as with planar projection), rotate it so you can see the bottom surface, then render again. Return the cube to its original position.

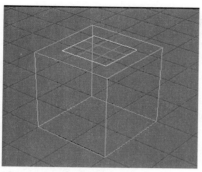

Figure 10–40 Material
Rectangle centered on cube top

Working with More Than One Material Rectangle

You can apply as many Material Rectangles to an object as memory allows, and cycle their selection forward and backward using the (and) buttons in the Material Rectangle panel.

1. Add a second rectangle, using a different material. Click the Paint Face tool and set the current material color to yellow. Then select the Material Rectangle tool again.

2. You can see that the original Material Rectangle is highlighted and ready to be manipulated, but just leave it be for now. In the Material Rectangle panel, select the New button. Another rectangle appears in the same initial position and size as the first. Move it up so it partially overlaps the first rectangle. You won't be able to see the latter, so just eyeball it.

3. Return to Object mode and render the cube. You can see that the second rectangle's yellow material indeed covers part of the first rectangle's red material.

4. Look at the panel's other controls. Select Material Rectangle again and note that the first rectangle is once again selected. Click on the (and) button at the bottom of the panel to cycle through the rectangles.

5. Select the small red rectangle. You'll now move it to the top of the "stack." In the Material Rectangle panel, position the mouse cursor over the icon in the lower-right corner. The Help bar now reads Bring Material Rectangle to Top. Click the button. This not only brings the rectangle to the top, but it renders a rectangular area around it, so the change is easily discernible.

6. Go to Object mode again and immediately reselect the Material Rectangle tool. You can see that the default rectangle is the one you placed second, which is now at the bottom of the stack. The selection order is from low to high in terms of layering.

7. Click the (or) button to switch to the red rectangle. Then open the Material library and select any material you like.

8. In the Material Rectangle panel, click the upper-right button, which looks just like the Paint Object tool. The red material has been replaced with the new one from the Library.

9. Go ahead and experiment with the remaining two buttons: Del to delete the current rectangle and the one that looks and acts like the Inspect tool.

10. Try applying cylindrical and spherical UV projections to the cube and then moving the rectangles around. In particular, note that with cylindrical projection, you cannot move the rectangles onto the top and bottom surfaces.

TIP: Say you want to apply an entire image exactly to one polygon of an object. You could use a Material Rectangle, but it might be difficult to position and size it accurately. A better way is to create the material first. Then select the polygon and detach it with the Separate function; then recombine the parts with the Glue function. Finally, move down into the hierarchy, select the face and material, and use the Paint Object function.

Mapping an Imported Object

Before you push on, one final experiment, in which you import a 3D object from another program and apply trueSpace2 mapping to it.

Delete the cube. Then, from the TUTORIAL/CH10 directory on the companion CD-ROM, load the file named Poserguy.cob. (This is a model created with Fractal Design Poser, a stand-alone 3D figure design program that can output its models in DXF format. Poserguy.cob is already converted to trueSpace2's native format for you.)

Activate the Material Rectangle tool. In the panel, select New. What's this? An error message appears, saying, "This object does not have a UV space." Usually, when trueSpace2 imports an object from another program, it does not automatically apply a UV projection type. You must do this yourself. In fact, if you import a model that does not have a UV space, then apply a texture map, and then render the object, trueSpace2 will not complain—but it will not render the texture map properly.

Try this. Select the UV Projection tool, choose a projection type, create a Material Rectangle, and move it around the figure. Very often, if the figure is going to be viewed from only one angle, using a planar projection perpendicular to the angle of view works best. But if the figure or point of view is to be moved, you'll need to use a more flexible projection type.

NOTE: Unfortunately, neither cylindrical nor spherical projection gives very predictable results with a shape as complex as the human body. What trueSpace2 needs is a more "organic" mapping capability, in which the UV space conforms to the model's shape.

THE IMAGE UTILITIES

As mentioned in Lesson 1, texture mapping automatically incorporates transparency from images that contain alpha channel information (created in 32-bit graphics programs, such as Adobe Photoshop). But even if you don't have access to a 32-bit paint program, you can still easily create transparency within your bitmaps, using trueSpace2's Image Utilities functions, available through the Edit menu. The Image utilities also let you create 1D and 2D reflection maps from existing images and trueSpace2 scenes, respectively.

LESSON 7: USING THE IMAGE UTILITIES

In this lesson, you'll recreate the texture map with the transparent background that was used in Lesson 1. Then you'll take a brief look at the process of making the two different types of reflection maps.

1. Start trueSpace2. Set the display mode to Wireframe. From the Edit menu, select Image Utilities. This opens the Image Utilities panel, as shown in Figure 10-41.

2. Let's begin with the Input Image box, which is currently empty. Select it to open the Get Texture Map file requester. Make sure the companion CD-ROM is in your drive, and open the TEXT-MAP.BMP file from the TUTORIAL/CH10 directory. The file name now appears in the box.

3. Under Alpha Conversion, the box says None. Click and hold on this box to view the pop-up menu of conversion methods, which determine how the transparency is to be set in the output image. The None option is for when you simply want to convert an image to the .TXR or .TAB formats (see Step 4). Drag to the White menu item and release. This conversion method sets all white pixels in the input image to be fully transparent. For details on the other conversions, consult the trueSpace2 Help file under Render Group/Image Utilities/Alpha Conversion.

4. Now select the Convert Image box to open the Save Converted Image As file requester. Scroll down to the Targa File *.tga file format and select it. In the File Name box, type TEXT-MAP.TGA and press ⌷ENTER⌷ or click OK.

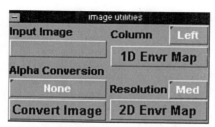

Figure 10–41 The Image Utilities panel

NOTE: The default output file format (under List Files of Type:) is Mipmap *.txr (actually, that should be MIP map). A MIP (*multum in parvo*—Latin for "many things in a small place") map is a special type of filtered bitmap image that looks better from various distances than a standard bitmap does but requires more disk space and memory. The format list also includes MipMap Bump Table *.tab, for images that work only as bump maps; they render faster than standard images used as bump maps. I'll leave you to experiment with these formats on your own.

5. You've just created an exact duplicate of the transparency-containing texture map used in Lesson 1. Try incorporating it into a material with a nonwhite-based color and see how it looks on the sample sphere or plane. Try it with the Overlay option in the Texture Map panel both on and off.

Try converting some of your own images to transparency-containing texture maps, in either the Targa or .TXR format, using the various Alpha Conversion methods. Note that, even with the Intensity conversion method, the image's colors are retained in the output image, so if you actually want to use only the source image's intensity, convert it to grayscale first with a paint or image-processing program.

Making One-Dimensional Environment Maps

Let's look at how to make 1D environment maps. You'll make three different maps from a single image file. First examine the source image that's to be converted.

1. Add any primitive object; then select the Paint Face tool. Activate the Use Texture Map icon and right-click to open the Texture Map panel. From the companion CD-ROM, load the GRADIENT.BMP file from the TUTORIAL/CH10 directory as a texture map. Click on the sample sphere to make it a sample plane, and you'll see a diagonal gradient (created with KPT Gradient Designer from MetaTools). From this image, take vertical strips from the left edge, the center, and the right edge as 1D environment maps.

2. If the Image Utilities panel isn't displayed, open it via the Edit menu. Choose the GRADIENT.BMP file as the Input Image.

3. Select the box that says 1D Envr Map and, in the Save Environment Map file requester, save the file as GRD-LEFT.T1D, preferably in the TRUSPACE/ ENVIRMNT directory on your hard disk.

This Image Utilities function takes a vertical strip of pixels from the input image to make the environment map. To the right of Column in the panel is a box that says Left. By default, the utility uses the leftmost column of pixels from the input image. This is as good a place as any to start.

4. Click and hold on the Left box. In the pop-up that appears, select the column of the input image to use. As you can see, the other choices are Middle and Right. Select Middle and save the file as GRD-MID.T1D. Then select Right and save the file as GRD-RT.T1D.

5. Take another look at the sample plane. Knowing what you do now about the 1D environment conversion utility, can you predict the appearances of the three environment maps you just created? Test your theory by loading each in succession as an environment map into a material, using the Metal shader, and displaying them on a sample sphere. You may notice that the order of the colors is flipped vertically; that's how the utility works.

Creating Two-Dimensional Environment Maps

Now you've come to the most complex of the Image utilities: the 2D environment map creator, which lets you simulate reflection without requiring ray tracing. It's actually pretty easy to use. Basically, it renders six small images of a selected object's environment from the object's point of view; then it combines them into a 2D environment map (actually, it's more like a cube surrounding the object) that you apply to the object.

1. Start by clearing any objects from the workspace. Set up a scene with a red cube, a yellow cone, a blue cylinder, and a metal-shaded sphere. Arrange them as shown in Figure 10-42.

2. Open a small Perspective View window and zoom in on the scene. Render the scene in the small window. Make a mental note of the length of time it takes.

3. Right-click on the Render Scene tool and, in the Render Options panel, click in the box next to Raytrace in the upper-left corner.

4. Render the scene again. It will take a bit longer than before, and this time you'll be able to see reflections in the sphere of the three outlying objects.

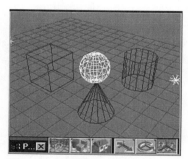

Figure 10–42 Scene setup for 2D environment map

5. Turn off the Raytrace option and close the Render Options panel.

6. Make sure the sphere is selected and open the Image Utilities panel.

7. Click and hold on the Med box next to Resolution. (The other choices are Low and High.) For this experiment, medium resolution is fine, so release the mouse button.

8. Select the 2D Envr Map button in the panel's lower-right corner. In the Save Environment Map file requester, navigate to the TRUSPACE/ENVIRMNT directory and enter the file name E2D-SCN.E2D. Note that, because trueSpace2 creates the environment file from scratch, any file name in the Input Image field is ignored.

9. Click OK or press ENTER and watch the screen carefully. The program quickly renders six small images, showing the view from the sphere's front, rear, sides, and straight up and down (not necessarily in that order).

10. When the rendering is done, select the Paint Face tool. In the Shader/Maps panel, select the Environment Map icon first with the left mouse button and then with the right. In the Environment Map panel, set the image file to be the E2D-SCN.E2D file you just created.

11. Use Paint Object to apply the modified material to the sphere.

12. Render the scene in the small window from several different angles. As you can see, the sphere's environment map accurately simulates a reflection of its surroundings from any point of view.

The 2D environment map is fast and easy to produce and works quite well in many circumstances, especially with symmetrical objects such as the sphere. But it may not be as effective with certain irregular objects, in which case you may need to resort to ray tracing. This may not seem much of a burden, because in the above tutorial, ray tracing the scene took hardly any more time than rendering it the standard way. Ray tracing can, however, really slow down processing of more complex scenes containing several reflective objects, as well as objects with higher polygon counts. And, of course, when you're creating an animation, you have to render the scene once for each animation frame, so even a small delay is magnified many times.

The general rule for a scene requiring reflective objects is this: Try using 2D environment maps first, and if the results are not satisfactory, use ray tracing (after removing the environment maps, of course). There's no way to fake refraction, though, so if you need that, you must use ray tracing.

PLUG-INS

Adobe Photoshop is well known as a professional graphics tool for computer artists. One of its principal claims to fame is the pioneering of plug-ins to extend software. Quite a few plug-in image-processing programs can be used within Photoshop for a wide variety of effects. If you use Adobe Photoshop (or a compatible program) and have some third-party plug-in filters, you're in for an extra treat. Even if you don't, you can have a lot of image-processing fun with the five cool filters from MetaTools (formerly HSC Software) included with trueSpace2. You can apply up to four plug-in filters in sequence to rendered scenes as a "post" (after rendering) effect. (Photoshop-only filters, such as those included with Photoshop, don't work.)

LESSON 8: IMAGE PROCESSING WITH PLUG-INS

The trueSpace2 program comes with five free plug-in filters: PixelWind, Diffuse More, Sharpen Intensity, Find Edges (Soft), and 3D Stereo Noise. You'll use Diffuse More in this tutorial because its effects are easy to see. The options for plug-in usage are fairly well covered in the trueSpace2 Help file (see Render Group/Plug-ins), so I won't go into all the particulars.

1. Start trueSpace2 in Wireframe Display mode.

2. Add a cylinder primitive. Give it a nice blue coat of paint.

3. Open a small Perspective View window and zoom in on the top half of the cylinder.

4. You'll find the Plug-ins tool (see Figure 10-43, left side) at the right end of the Render tool group. Select it now to open the Plug-in Setup panel, as shown in Figure 10-43, right side.

5. When you first select the Plug-ins tool during a trueSpace2 session, you see the Select a Filter Plug-in from your Plug-in directory file requester. Navigate to the TRUSPACE/PLUGINS directory on your hard disk and select any of the .8bf files shown. Click OK or press the ENTER key.

6. Take a look at the four rows of the Plug-in panel. In this tutorial, you'll use only the first row, but you can have trueSpace2 apply up to four plug-in filters to rendered scenes, in the order shown in this panel.

7. Click once on the (None) field in the first row. A drop-down menu shows you the names of the five plug-in filters. Select the Diffuse More entry. Notice that the sample sphere is now heavily diffused, to the point that it's barely recognizable.

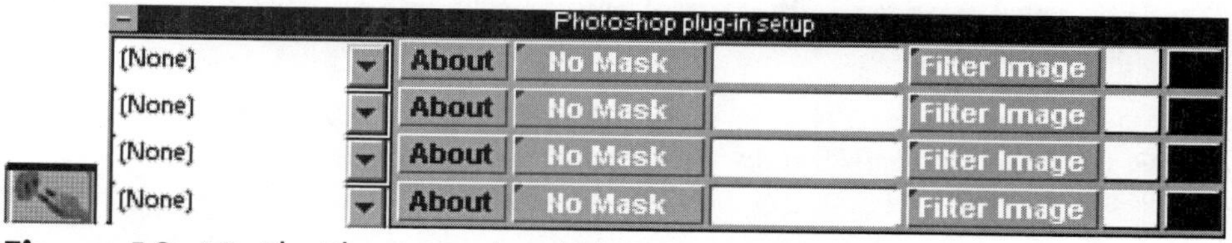

Figure 10-43 The Plug-ins tool and Plug-in Setup panel

8. Use the small window's Render Object tool to render the cylinder. It looks perfectly normal. Why? Recall from the introduction to this tutorial that plug-in filters are applied to rendered *scenes*.

9. Now use the small window's Render Scene tool, and you'll see the background and the cylinder rendered, followed by the application of the diffusion filter. Pretty dotty, isn't it?

10. What if you want to decrease the effect? Right now, the filter is using its medium setting of 5; the full range is 1 (low) to 0 (high). (Think left to right on the keyboard; in this case, 0 is a stand-in for 10.) To change the setting, you must press the appropriate number key on the keyboard *when the filter is called*. Render the scene again, and just before the initial rendering is finished, press and hold the ① key. When the processing is finished, you'll see that the diffusion effect is quite subdued. To see the other end of the scale, render the scene again and press and hold the ⓪ key any time before the rendering is finished.

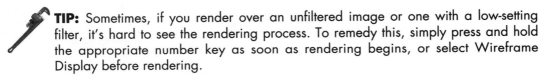

TIP: Sometimes, if you render over an unfiltered image or one with a low-setting filter, it's hard to see the rendering process. To remedy this, simply press and hold the appropriate number key as soon as rendering begins, or select Wireframe Display before rendering.

NOTE: Not all filters are controlled by pressing a number key. When in doubt, check the Help file for the particular filter. To access the Help file, click the About button in the Plug-in panel and then click the Help button in the dialog that appears.

11. Render the scene again without pressing any number key. As you can see, changing the filter's setting affects all subsequent renderings. Set the diffusion value back to the default value by rerendering the scene with the ⑤ key held down. (Because the ⑤ key is a shortcut for Path Library, the library panel may open, but this doesn't affect the filter setting; just close it when you're done.)

12. Let's look briefly at the panel's other settings. Click and hold on the No Mask button and look over the menu of different values for masking. Try the Obj Mask setting and note that the name of the current object—cylinder—appears in the space next to the setting.

13. Render the scene again. This time, the diffusion is applied only to the object mask—that is, the area encompassed by the cylinder's outline as originally rendered.

As mentioned above, the other options available in the Plug-In Setup panel are documented in the trueSpace2 Help file. Spend some time reading it over and then experiment with the filters and their options. Once you become familiar with the filters' effects, try using combinations of filters. You probably won't have much need for this facility in day-to-day rendering, but filters are a great solution when you need a particular special effect.

WHAT NOW?

You've covered *a lot* of territory in this chapter, but it's all fairly straightforward stuff. If you've followed all the tutorials, you should have the basics down—but, as always, practice makes perfect.

And now, on to animation and animated texture maps. See you in the next chapter!

11
ANIMATION

11

Building 3D objects and using them to populate a scene, adding visual interest with texture mapping, and then bringing objects to life by adding motion each involve very different sets of functions and skills. More and more people have taken up 3D graphics as a vocation or hobby, and many are specializing in modeling or animation. But as one who is just starting out on this entertaining and fascinating journey, you should explore all the various paths you can take, including animation. And trueSpace2 is an eminently suitable vehicle for this.

You'll see in this chapter that trueSpace2's implementation of animation, although very good, is by no means perfect. For example, trueSpace2 provides no way to perform *morphing* animation, in which objects transform magically into vastly differing shapes. The program's ability to animate object deformation goes a long way to make up for this, however. Other shortcomings keenly felt by character animators are the program's lack of *inverse kinematics* (IK), in which figures can be controlled from their extremities rather than in the top-down fashion required by trueSpace2, and the awkward implementation of hierarchical control.

This chapter illustrates basic 3D animation techniques in the light of trueSpace2's considerable capabilities, covering all the various ways to animate in the step-by-step tutorials.

BASIC KEYFRAME ANIMATION

Keyframe animation is an easy concept to understand, but producing it requires a certain amount of advance planning. An animation, such as a movie or video, is a sequence of still images or *frames*. To create an action, such as changing an object's location, that is to occur over several frames, you go to the frame at which the action is to start, set a *key* for that object and action, and then set more keys at critical points in subsequent and/or previous frames. How do you set a key? Simply by manipulating the object in the *keyframe*. The program then creates in-between positions, rotations, and so forth in intervening frames. This process is called *tweening*. Let's explore how it works.

NOTE: Remember—a key is set for a specific object as the result of a particular type of manipulation, such as moving or rotation. A keyframe is the frame in which the manipulation occurs.

LESSON 1: ANIMATING MOVEMENT WITH KEYFRAMES

You'll start your exploration of keyframe animation by creating an elementary two-stage motion. As usual, you'll use a simple object to illustrate the concepts, bearing in mind that the same principles can be applied to any object or hierarchical subobject, no matter how complex.

1. Start trueSpace2. Unless you're using a very fast machine, stay in Wireframe Display mode for fast response when playing back animations.

2. Add a cube primitive.

3. Select the Object Move tool and drag the cube to the left side of the workspace. This is the starting point for the cube in the animation.

4. Select the Animation tool to open the Animation panel (see Figure 11-1). You've now set the first key.

NOTE: In the Quick Start tutorial in Chapter 3, QuickStart Tutorial: A Guided Tour of Major Features, you opened the Animation panel first and then placed the object for its first key. For this exercise, I have reversed the procedure to demonstrate that the order of these two steps is immaterial.

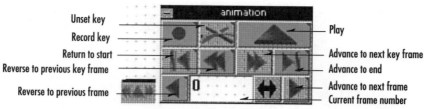

Figure 11-1 The Animation tool and Animation panel

Unset key
Record key
Return to start
Reverse to previous key frame
Reverse to previous frame

Play
Advance to next key frame
Advance to end
Advance to next frame
Current frame number

5. Go to frame 15 by setting the current frame number to 15. You can either click on the Current Frame Number field, type 15, and press (ENTER), or drag rightward on the double-headed arrow until the field displays the number 15.

6. Now set the second key: Drag the cube to the front center of the workspace. This automatically sets a key for the cube's new position at frame 15.

7. Go to frame 30.

8. Drag the cube to the right side of the workspace, about halfway up the screen. Release the mouse button, and you've just set a third keyframe for the cube's movement. In doing so, you've extended the animation's total length to 30 frames, or 1 second.

9. To view the animation, select the Animation panel's Play button. Watch the cube travel a rounded path between the first and third points, because trueSpace2 automatically creates a spline curve for the animation path. You'll learn how to edit this path in a bit.

10. Save this object as CUBE-ANI.COB. You needn't save the scene, because trueSpace2 saves animation information in object files.

LESSON 2: ANIMATING ROTATION AND SCALING

Now you'll make the animation slightly more complex, first by adding rotation during the second half of the animation and then by adding scaling during the first half.

1. If you're not continuing directly from Lesson 1, start trueSpace2 and load the CUBE-ANI.COB file.

2. Select the Animation tool and play the animation by clicking the Play button in the Animation panel.

3. When you play an animation in trueSpace2, you're left at the last frame, no matter which frame you were in when you started. In this case, the last frame is where you want to be right now. Let's introduce rotation. Select the Object Rotate tool and right-button drag to the right to rotate the cube about half a turn on its vertical axis.

4. Play the animation. This time, as it travels throughout the entire animation, the cube rotates.

What if you want it to rotate only during the second half of the animation?

5. Select the Undo tool; then play the animation again to confirm that the cube is no longer rotating.

6. Go to frame 15. You can do this using either of the methods mentioned in Lesson 1, Step 5. Another way is to select the Object Move tool and then click the Animation panel's Reverse to Previous Key Frame button (see Figure 11-1). Selecting Object Move is necessary because there is no *rotation* key at frame 15, only a *move* key.

7. If you used the latter method in Step 6, you now need to reactivate the Object Rotate tool. Do this, and notice that the Animation panel's Unset Key button, which was available in Object Move mode, is now grayed out. This indicates that there is no key for the current object navigation mode at this frame.

8. In the Animation panel, select the Record button. This sets a rotation key for the cube's current (i.e., starting) orientation in this frame. The Unset Key button again becomes available.

9. The next keyframe is also the final frame in the animation, so go to frame 30 by selecting, in the Animation panel, either Advance to Next Key Frame or Advance to End.

10. Again, right-button drag rightward to rotate the cube about 180°.

11. Play the animation. This time, the cube rotates only during the second half of the animation. Because it has to rotate the same amount as before but in only half the time, the cube rotates twice as fast.

12. Finally, make the cube start out small and grow to full size in the first half of the animation. In the Animation panel, select the Return to Start button. The Current Frame Number field reflects that you're now at frame 0.

13. Select the Object Scale tool. Scale the cube down in all three dimensions by pressing and holding both mouse buttons and dragging downward in the workspace. Make the cube fairly small—about one-fourth the size of a grid square.

14. This time, try a different way of playing the animation. Instead of pressing the Play button, click and hold on the Animation panel's double-headed arrow. Drag rightward slowly to play forward, then leftward to play backward. This way you can interactively control the playback speed and direction. If you keep dragging right-ward after frame 30, the numbers continue to increment, but the action stops because there are no keys after that frame. As you can see, the cube stays small throughout the animation.

15. Remember that you want the cube to grow in size in the first half of the animation. If you've figured out that you have to set another scaling key at frame 15, you're ahead of the game. Go to frame 15 now.

16. You could manually scale the cube up or do it with numbers in the Object Info panel, but there's an easier way. Remember the Normalize Scale tool? (It's in the Utility group's third pop-up.) Select it now to return the cube to its original size. This also sets a scale key for frame 15.

17. Play the animation again. Now the cube moves and grows in size between frames 0 and 15, and moves and rotates between 15 and 30.

18. Select File/Save Object to store the cube object on disk as CUBE-ANI.COB.

TIP: If you want to experiment with object manipulation during animation setup without recording every action as a key, right-click the Animation panel's Record button. In the small Set Keyframe panel that appears, turn off the AutoRecord function. When you're ready to return to animation recording, remember to turn it back on.

LESSON 3: ANIMATING MULTIPLE OBJECTS

This next tutorial demonstrates the use of the Animation Parameters panel for determining how trueSpace2 plays back an animation incorporating more than one object. You'll also examine various other settings in the panel.

1. Start trueSpace2. You can be in either Wireframe Display or Solid Render mode for this tutorial.

2. Add two primitive spheres. Both appear in the same spot, so there appears to be only one. (If you're in Solid Render mode, you can see the first sphere's bounding box surrounding the second's solid shape.)

3. This step is for Solid Render Display users only; if you're in Wireframe Display, skip ahead to Step 4. Let's set nonactive objects to display as wireframes. Select the File/Preferences panel. From the Scene/Detail pop-up, choose Wireframe. In Solid mode, this causes the other sphere to be redrawn as a wireframe, although you may not be able to see it at this point. Close the panel.

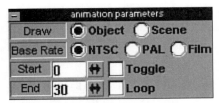

Figure 11-2 The Animation Parameters panel

4. Open the Animation panel and set the current frame to 30.

5. Select Object Move and drag the active sphere to the right side of the workspace.

6. Select the other sphere. This resets the frame counter to 0, because this sphere has key information only at frame 0 (automatically set when you created the object). (In Lesson 14, you'll learn how to edit a scene so an object's animation doesn't have to start at frame 0.)

7. Again set the current frame to 30; then drag the selected sphere to the left side of the workspace.

8. Play the animation. Only one sphere moves.

9. Select the other sphere and play the animation again. Again, only the selected sphere (this time, the first one you moved) is animated. What's going on here?

10. To find out, first right-click the Animation panel's Play button. This opens the Animation Parameters panel (see Figure 11-2).

11. In the top row, next to Draw, the Object item is selected. With this setting turned on, trueSpace2 plays only the animation associated with the current object whenever you click Play. The same rule applies to the other Animation panel controls (Return to Start, and so forth). To change this setup, click the Scene radio button. This causes *all* objects in the scene to move, rotate, and the like when the animation is played.

The default setting for Draw is Object, because with complex animation setups, you're typically concerned with the behavior of only one object at a time. If *all* objects were redrawn for each frame, animation playback would slow down considerably. During final setup, however, especially when objects will interact while moving (for example, crashing into one another), it's important to have the option to animate the entire scene.

12. Play the animation again. This time, both objects move along their respective paths simultaneously, but considerably more slowly than before.

Here's something that's important to know about: Even with the Draw parameter set to Scene, the Advance to End function applies only to animation of the *current* object. By the same token, so does Return to Start. Let's demonstrate this.

13. Go to frame 60 and move the selected sphere to set another key.

14. In the Animation panel, select Return to Start to go to frame 0, and then Advance to End to go to frame 60.

15. Now select the other sphere. Click again on the Return to Start and Advance to End buttons. This time, they go between frames 0 and 30 only.

16. Before moving on, let's look at the Animation Parameters panel's other options. Click in the check box next to Toggle to turn this option on. Then play the animation. The animation plays forward, then backward. This lets you examine the action in both directions.

17. Turn off Toggle (uncheck the box) and turn on Loop instead. Play the animation again. This time, the animation plays forward only; when it gets to the end, it starts over. Press [ESC] to stop. If you like, you can combine Toggle and Loop by checking both boxes. Try it and see what happens. When you're done experimenting, turn off both the Toggle and Loop options.

18. When you're developing a long, complex animation, you don't always want to see the entire animation when you click on Play, but rather just the part you're working on at the moment. That's what the Start and End (frame) parameters are for. Type or dial up 10 in the Start field and 20 in the End field, and play the animation. As you might expect, the animation starts at frame 10 and ends at frame 20.

The Base Rate Parameter

I skipped over the Base Rate parameter in this panel because it's not often used. The default setting, NTSC, refers to the video system used in the USA, Japan, and many other countries. It causes animations to be played back at the rate of 30 frames per second. Often, however, the computer isn't able to play back that fast because of the computation required between frames. But with a reasonably fast video subsystem, that's the standard playback speed for a rendered animation. The PAL video system, used in Great Britain, uses a frame rate of 25 per second. If you're working on an animation that will be transferred to film, you'll want to set Base Rate to Film, which displays 24 frames per second.

LESSON 4: SETTING UP FOR WALKING THE ROBOT

Remember the robot you made out of cylinders in Chapter 7, Utilities and Edit Tools? At the end of that chapter, I suggested that you set the robot's axes to logical pivot points. If you did so and then saved the object, you can skip ahead to Lesson 5, but you might want to read through this lesson anyway to make sure you did it right.

1. Start trueSpace2 or clear the workspace. I recommend Wireframe Display mode for this exercise.

2. Load the file ROBOT.COB from the TUTORIAL/CH12 directory on the CD-ROM. This is the robot object as created in Chapter 7, Lesson 15, with all axes in their original positions.

3. Start with the arms. To swing naturally, their axes should be at their upper ends, just below the shoulders. Right now, the entire robot structure—that is, the topmost node—is selected. Press ⊡ once to move down one hierarchical level. This selects the head-neck subassembly.

4. Press either ⊡ or ⊡ once to select the lower part of the robot.

5. Press ⊡ leaving only the shoulders/arms subassembly selected.

6. Press ⊡, and then either ⊡ or ⊡ , and once again ⊡. This leaves only one of the arms selected.

7. Select the Axes tool to display the arm's axes.

8. Activate the Object Move tool; then right-button drag upward in the workspace until the axes appear at the upper end of the arm (see Figure 11-3).

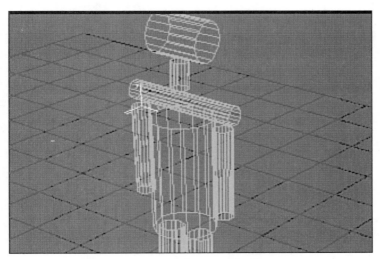

296   **Figure 11-3** Axes positioned at top of robot arm

9. Select the Axes tool again to make the axes disappear and reselect the arm.

10. Press either ⊡ or ⊡, or simply click on the other arm to select it.

11. Repeat Steps 7-9 with the second arm (you needn't select Object Move again).

12. Use the arrow keys to navigate through the hierarchy and select one of the legs. Here's the key sequence, just in case, arbitrarily using ⊡ (in this case, because there are no more than two subobjects in any of the relevant hierarchical levels, ⊡ would work just as well): ⊡, ⊡, ⊡, ⊡, ⊡, ⊡.

13. Repeat Steps 7-9 for the selected leg, then again for the other leg.

14. Press ⊡ four times to move back to the hierarchy's top node. (If you want to bend the head and/or neck in the animation, you'll need to set those, too. In this animation, though, you'll move only the limbs.)

15. Save the robot object now. You don't want to have to go through that again! But just in case anything happens, you can load this object as the file ROB-AXES.COB from the TUTORIAL/CH12 directory on the CD-ROM.

LESSON 5: WALKING THE ROBOT, PART 1

In this lesson, you'll create the first half of a simple walking motion cycle for your robot.

1. If you're not continuing directly from Lesson 4, start trueSpace2 and load the ROB-AXES.COB file from the TUTORIAL/CH12 directory on the CD-ROM.

You'll begin by animating the robot's limbs, with rotational keys for the arms and legs. Then, in the next tutorial, you'll complete the limb rotation and create translation keys for the entire structure to simulate walking. But first, get up and walk around, swinging your arms as you go. Observe how your right arm and left leg swing forward more or less at the same time, as do your left arm and right leg. Because you want to create a walk *cycle*, not just a single movement, you'll need to start with the left arm and the right leg swung forward and the other two swung back.

2. Open the Animation panel and also open a new Top View window to get a better idea of how things are moving. Position the window out of the way in an upper screen corner.

3. Navigate back down through the hierarchy to the left arm. (Assuming that the robot is facing toward the lower left, this would be the arm closer to you.)

4. Select the Object Rotate tool and turn off x-axis rotation at the right end of the Help bar.

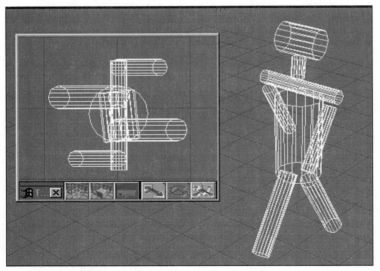

Figure 11–4 Robot object at start of walk cycle

5. Left-button drag rightward in the workspace to rotate the arm forward about 30º or so. This is just a test, so the actual amount isn't crucial.

6. Select the other arm (the right one) and left-button drag leftward to rotate it back by the same amount (30º or so).

7. Use the keyboard arrow keys to navigate to the left leg and rotate it back a little less than the right arm.

8. Select the right leg and rotate it forward about the same degree to which you rotated the left leg back. The robot should now look like Figure 11-4.

9. Now for the second phase of the character animation. Use the Animation panel to go to frame 30.

10. Rotate the right leg, which is still selected, back to the same angle as the left leg.

11. Select the left leg. The Current Frame Number field is reset to 0.

NOTE: This resetting of the frame number happens because the newly selected object has no keys at any frame other than 0. It's always a good idea to keep an eye on Current Frame Number, because it can jump around when selecting different objects, depending on which frame you left the object in.

12. Set Current Frame back to 30 and rotate the left leg forward to the right leg's original angle.

13. Navigate back up to the left arm and reverse both arms' positions as you did for the legs. Remember to set Current Frame back to 30 both times, if necessary.

14. Navigate to the top of the hierarchy and play the animation. Watch the left leg and right arm swing forward while the right leg and left arm swing back.

15. Save your work as ROB-ANI.COB.

You'll continue to teach the robot to walk in the next lesson.

LESSON 6: WALKING THE ROBOT, PART 2

With trueSpace2's Keyframe Monitor feature, you'll easily bring the robot's walking action full circle. Then you'll combine it with a forward motion to propel it across the workspace.

1. Start trueSpace2 if necessary. Make sure ROB-ANI.COB, saved in Step 15 of Lesson 5, is open.

2. If Current Frame isn't set to 0, click Return to Start in the Animation panel.

3. For each limb's third key, you want to come back to the original position. You could do this manually, but there's an easier way using the Keyframe Monitor (Figure 11-5). Open it now by right-clicking on any Animation panel button except Record or Play.

The Keyframe Monitor is a special panel for editing keyframes for objects (top row of buttons), materials (middle row), and scenes (bottom row). This panel is fairly well documented in the trueSpace2 Help file, so I'll demonstrate only basic functionality here. You can experiment on your own.

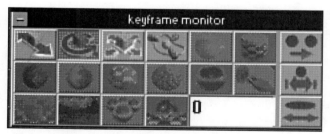

Figure 11–5 The Keyframe Monitor

4. Navigate down through the hierarchy to either arm. As soon as the arm is selected, the Rotate Key Frame button is highlighted and available (it's the second from the left end in the Keyframe Monitor's top row). This indicates that there's a rotation key at frame 0 for the arm.

5. In the Keyframe Monitor, select the Copy Key Frame (sic) button at the right end of the top row.

6. In the Monitor panel's numeric field, which now reads 0, enter the number 60 (don't forget to press (ENTER)). This copies the initial rotation key to frame 60. Thus, the arm swings forward during the first 30 frames and back to its original position in the next 30.

7. Click Play in the Animation panel to see the arm swing forward and back.

NOTE: Due to an anomaly in the Keyframe Monitor's operation, you may see only the first half of the motion. If that happens, press ⊕ once and click Play again. This time you'll see the forward-and-back motion.

8. Return to frame 0 in the Animation panel.

9. Select the other arm and repeat Step 6.

10. Do the same for both legs.

11. Navigate to the top of the robot's hierarchy and play the animation. This is a basic walking cycle. As you'll see in Lesson 14 in this chapter, this cycle can easily be repeated during lateral movement of the entire figure to make it walk as long as you like.

12. Let's have the robot come walking toward you from the upper-right side of the workspace. Return to frame 0 in the Animation panel, activate Object Move, and drag the robot up and to the right (see Figure 11-6).

13. Set Current Frame to 60.

14. Drag the robot down and to the left, so it's near the center of the workspace (see Figure 11-7).

15. That's it! Play the animation and watch your robot strut toward you as if it's alive!

16. Save this object as ROB-ANI2.COB. You'll use it in subsequent lessons to explore trueSpace2's other animation tools.

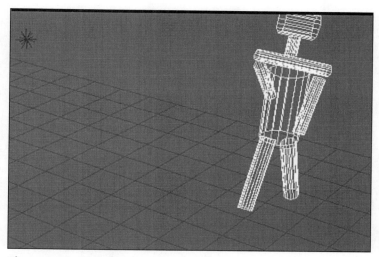

Figure 11–6 Robot at start of walk

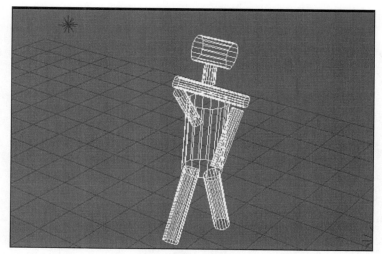

Figure 11–7 Robot at end of walk

ANIMATING OBJECT SHAPES

Just as an object's position, rotation, and scale can be keyframed for animation, you can also animate shape changes wrought with the Deform tool. In addition, you can use the Primitive panel's free-standing deformation objects for special animation effects. In this section, you'll explore each of these techniques in turn.

LESSON 7: ANIMATING DEFORMATION, PART 1

Once you understand the basics of keyframe animation in trueSpace2, it's a snap to animate object shapes using the Deform Object tool.

1. Start trueSpace2. Use either Wireframe Display or Solid Render Display for this tutorial.

2. Add a primitive sphere. Subdivide its mesh by selecting the Smooth Quad Divide tool once.

3. Select the Animation and the Deform Object tools.

4. Advance to frame 30.

5. With the left mouse button, click and drag downward and to the right on the deform grid intersection facing the lower-right corner of the workspace. Pull out an extension of the sphere as shown in Figure 11-8.

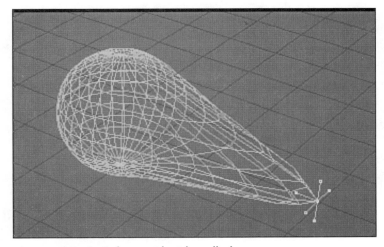

Figure 11-8 Sphere with side pulled out

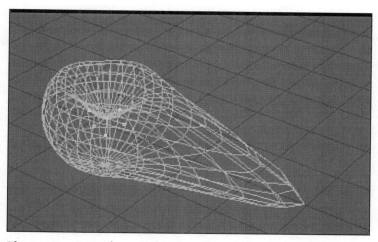

Figure 11-9 Sphere with side pulled out and top pushed in

6. Play the animation to see the extension stretch outward.

7. Let's add some complexity. Right-click on the top of the sphere and drag downward to create a depression (see Figure 11-9).

8. Play the animation again. Unlike animating multiple objects (Lesson 3), in this case you don't need to change any settings to see multiple deformation animations on a single object.

9. Clear the workspace, add and subdivide another sphere, and then try a similar deformation experiment with the Sculpt Surface tool.

 CAUTION: You'll find that you can play back the animation while a deformation's handle is active, but the results will be unpredictable. Even worse, once you create a new deformation or exit the tool, the animation information is lost. The Sculpt Surface tool really doesn't work for animation.

LESSON 8: ANIMATING DEFORMATION, PART 2

Using trueSpace2's free-standing deformation tools to affect polygon mesh objects, you can easily create magical animation effects that are difficult or impossible to do with most other programs. In this exercise, you'll make a sphere squeeze itself through a small hole.

1. Start trueSpace2 in Wireframe Display mode.

2. Add a small Front View window and position it up and out of the way.

3. Add a primitive sphere and subdivide it once.

4. From the Primitives panel, select the Add Free-Standing Pipe for Deformation icon in the center of the rightmost column. The pipe appears in the exact center of the workspace, with its center plane coincident with the ground plane.

5. Use Object Scale to make the pipe about 10 percent larger.

6. Activate the Object Move tool. Move the pipe straight up, right-button dragging in the Main window while watching the Front View window, until the bottom end of the pipe slightly overlaps the sphere's top (see Figure 11-10). You might want to raise the eye in the the Main window to see this better.

7. In the Deformation Navigation panel, select the Stretch tool (the top-right icon) and select the pipe's center green ring.

8. Hold both mouse buttons and drag leftward to scale the center ring down to a fairly small size (see Figure 11-11).

9. Activate the Object tool and then the Object Move tool.

10. Select the sphere and right-button drag it upward "through" the pipe. Notice there's no effect on the sphere's shape. That's because you've neglected a crucial step: telling the program that the two objects are to be linked.

11. Use the Undo function to return the sphere to its original position.

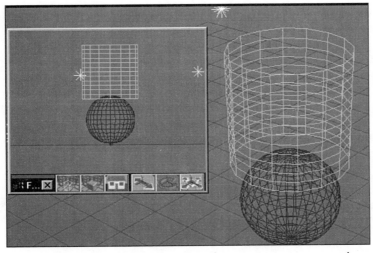

Figure 11-10 Deformation pipe object in position over sphere

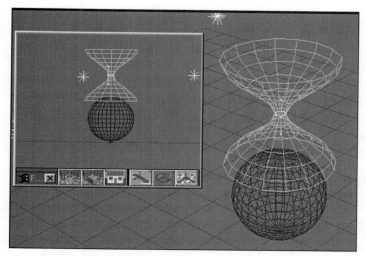

Figure 11–11 Deformation pipe object with center ring scaled down

12. Click and hold on the Deform Object tool. When the pop-up appears, select the topmost tool, labeled in the Help bar as Start Deforming by Stand-Alone Deformation Object.

13. Move the mouse cursor, which now resembles an inverted bottle, away from the tool. The Help bar is now telling you to pick a deformation object. (If you had selected the pipe before the tool, the message would be telling you to pick an object to deform. The order isn't important.)

14. Select the deformed pipe object. You won't see any indication of change, apart from the return of the mouse cursor's appearance to the default arrow. If you had clicked anywhere but on a deformation object, the program would not exit this mode until you selected one or another tool.

15. Again, right-drag upward to move the sphere through the pipe. Go slowly so you can see exactly what's happening. As the sphere approaches the pipe's center, its top end begins to narrow. As it passes through the small opening, it squeezes and then expands, from top to bottom (see Figure 11-12). Pretty cool, huh?

16. What's even cooler is that you can animate this. Move the sphere back to its original position under the pipe. Then open the Animation panel, set the current frame to 30, and move the sphere to the top of the pipe so that it's no longer deformed.

17. Play the animation. The sphere moves upward through the pipe under its own power, squeezing itself as it goes.

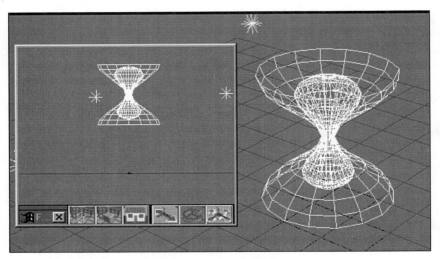

Figure 11-12 Sphere squeezed by deformation pipe

18. Unfortunately, the reverse of this effect does not hold true. That is, you can't deform an object in place by moving a linked free-standing object over it. The object must move through the deform object, not vice-versa.

 NOTE: When you select a free-standing deformation object, it's automatically placed in deformation mode, where you can change its shape by moving, rotating, and scaling its green grid lines. You can manipulate the entire object by selecting the Object Move, Rotate, or Scale tool. If you select the Object tool (the white arrow icon), which you must do before you can select another object, the entire deformation object's wireframe turns blue, which means it's still selected but not deformable. When not selected, its wireframe is red.

Try animating the deformation object's grid lines. In frame 30, select the pipe and rotate its top end so it's facing to the side instead of straight up. You'll need to select Draw: Scene in the Animation Parameters panel to see both objects animate.

CAUTION: Be particularly careful when using this technique. If any part of a deformed object strays outside its deformation object's volume, it snaps back to its original shape.

To make this animation look really magical, you need to create some sort of object with a hole in it for the sphere to squeeze through. I'll leave this as an extra-credit assignment for you.

The Stop Deforming by Stand-Alone Deformation Object tool, immediately above the Start Deforming… tool, lets you break the link between an object and its deformer. Both tools work on an all-or-nothing basis; that is, they work throughout the entire animation. You can't start deforming at a certain frame, then stop deforming at another.

I haven't covered the Free-Standing Deformation Plane or Free-Standing Deformation Cube tools in the Primitives panel. Their operation is similar to that of the Free-Standing Pipe. Use them with objects of approximately those shapes (planes and cubes).

NOTE: Of course, all these deformation objects can be used without animation, but for those tasks, you generally get better control with the Deform Object tool.

ANIMATION OF SURFACE ATTRIBUTES

There are two ways to animate an object's appearance. First, you can keyframe a material's attributes. Second, you can use an animation file as a texture map. You'll look at both of these in the next two tutorials.

LESSON 9: KEYFRAMING MATERIAL ATTRIBUTES

Get ready for endlessly fascinating results when you animate a material's settings. You can animate any or all of them, and the procedural textures lend themselves particularly well. The process is the same as keyframe animation, except that you must use the Paint Over tool to set a key.

1. Start trueSpace2 or clear the workspace. You'll be using procedural textures, which 3DR does not render, so you might as well be in Wireframe Display mode.

2. Add a primitive sphere.

3. Select the Paint Face tool.

4. Try animating the Procedural Marble texture. In the Shader/Maps panel, select the Procedural Marble icon (rightmost column, second one down), first with the left mouse button, then with the right button, to open the Marble Settings panel.

5. Start the animation with the default settings. Select the Paint Object tool to apply them to the sphere.

6. Open the Animation panel and advance to frame 30.

7. Change the predominant color. In the Marble Settings panel, click on the Stonecol color box. In the Marble Stone Color panel, click on the color hexagon's upper-right corner to make the color yellow.

8. While you're at it, animate a few other settings. Click on the Veincol color box. In the Marble Vein Color panel, click at the top of the vertical transparency scale on the right side.

9. Back in Marble Settings, set Turbulence to 10 and Sharpness to 0.26.

10. Select the Paint Over tool—remember, it looks like a paint roller—from the Paint pop-up and click on the sphere. This sets a new key for the changed material.

11. Go to frame 0. The Marble settings and sample sphere change back to the initial settings.

12. Go to frame 10, then to frame 20, and finally to frame 30, observing the changes in the Marble settings and sample sphere.

13. Let's set another key at frame 60. Go there now and set the vein color to blue, the X, Y, and Z Scale values each to 3, and the Grain to X.

14. The Paint Over tool is still active. Click on the sphere again to set the third key.

Go to various frames between 30 and 60 and observe the changes in the sample sphere. In particular, notice the change between frames 59 and 60.

Because you set the grain direction to be around the x axis, you might expect to get a gradual rotation of the grain between frames 30 and 60, but alas, that value is not tween-able (i.e., it doesn't gradually change between the two keys). What happens is that the grain direction suddenly switches to the new value at frame 60.

As mentioned in the trueSpace2 Help file, a similar phenomenon occurs if you change the image used in a material's texture, bump, or reflection map at a keyframe; the material changes abruptly. In general, this is an undesirable effect, but it can come in handy for certain special situations.

15. Set Grain Direction back to Y and select the sphere again with the Paint Over tool.

16. Save this object as MAT-ANI.COB.

 NOTE: Before continuing, try rendering an animation. If you need to, review this process in the Quick Start tutorial in Chapter 3. Watch the second half of the animation and notice that the changes in the texture pattern are rather abrupt. I was unable to avoid this result, even by using smaller changes in the Scale settings.

CAUTION: If you're animating different materials on more than one object in a scene (or, for that matter, multiple materials on an object), you'll need to use the Inspect tool from the Paint pop-up to make the material settings current before setting new keys.

LESSON 10: USING VIDEO IN A MATERIAL

Anywhere you can use a still image in trueSpace2, you can also use an animation or video file fairly easily.

1. Start trueSpace2 or clear the workspace. This time you'll be using bitmap textures, which 3DR does render, so choose Solid Render Display. In the Render Quality panel, enable the display of texture maps.

2. Add a primitive cube.

3. Select the Paint Face tool.

4. In the Shader/Maps panel, select the Texture Map icon, first with the left mouse button, then with the right button.

5. In the Texture Map panel, click on the Anim box. This enables animation of video files applied as texture maps. Click the checker box next to the checkered sphere to open the Get Texture Map file requester.

 CAUTION: Always enable animation of texture maps before applying them. If you do so afterward, trueSpace2 ignores the setting.

6. Make sure the companion CD from this book is in your drive and open the VIDEO directory. Here you'll find a number of digital video sequences created especially for you. Use them freely in your animations for any purpose.

7. Open the file named CLOUDS.AVI.

8. Select the Paint Object tool to apply the animated material to the cube's surface.

9. Open the Animation panel and click Play. Nothing happens, because you haven't set any keyframes.

10. Select the Object Move tool.

11. CLOUDS.AVI is a 60-frame animation and the animation starts at frame 0, so set a key at frame 59 by clicking on the Animation panel's Record button.

12. Click Play again.

 NOTE: Depending on your computer setup, you may or may not see the video play on the cube's surface. In some cases, you may need to advance through the frames one at a time first using the Forward button in the Animation panel's lower-right corner.

13. Set another key at frame 119 and play the animation again. The video may play faster, because it was fully loaded into memory only during the first playing in Step 12. Again, this depends on your setup, and in particular the amount of available memory. Also, when the video reaches its last frame, it starts over at the beginning.

PATH ANIMATION

Whenever you create movement keyframes for an object during animation setup, an invisible animation path is created. You can make this path visible and edit it using the Path tool. You can also use it to draw an animation path with the mouse, and even substitute paths from the Path library for existing animation paths.

LESSON 11: USING PATHS FOR ANIMATION

In this exercise, you'll take the cube animation from Lessons 1 and 2 and use trueSpace2's path-related functions to mangle it beyond all recognition.

1. Start trueSpace2 and load the CUBE-ANI.COB file from Lesson 2.

2. Select the Path tool, second from the left in the Animation group. The path you created in the first eight steps of Lesson 1 appears (see Figure 11-13).

3. Play the animation to see the cube follow the path as it enlarges and then rotates.

4. Change the path's shape. Instead of coming forward as it moves, you want the cube to move away and up, then down again. Select the path's center point, and left-button drag upward so the point moves straight back toward the rear of the workspace.

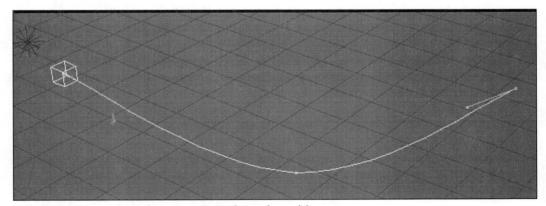

Figure 11–13 The cube's motion path made visible

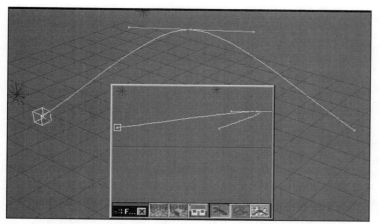

Figure 11–14 Path with center point moved back and up

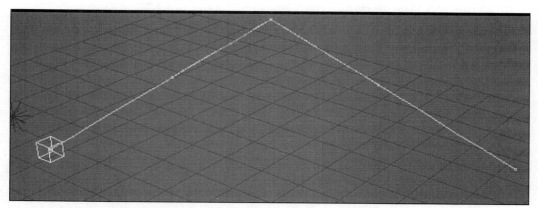

Figure 11–15 Path with center point made into a sharp corner

5. Right-button drag upward a few inches to raise the path's center point above the ground plane, as in Figure 11-14. I've added an extra Front View window so it's easier to see that the path is now three dimensional.

6. Play the animation and watch the cube steadfastly follow the altered path, first away and upward, and then closer and downward.

7. You can use other spline-editing tools to alter the cube's path. Instead of rounding the bend at the center point, have it turn a sharp corner. Right-click on the Path tool, and in the Spline panel that appears, choose the Sharp Corner tool in the upper-left corner. The path instantly changes in appearance (see Figure 11-15).

8. Play the animation again to see the change in movement.

Note: You can use the spline-editing tools to modify only movement along the path. Although the path does contain rotation and scaling information, such keys must be modified using the keyframe methods outlined previously (as in Lesson 2).

9. You can extend the path by adding new nodes, just like drawing a spline polygon. In the Draw Path panel, activate the Draw New Spline Point tool, immediately to the right of the currently selected Point Move tool.

10. An inch or two to the lower left of the rightmost path point, click once, and again an inch or two to the upper-left of the previous point (see Figure 11-16). Because the original path endpoint has "smooth corner" attributes, a smooth curve is created between it and the fourth point. But because the "sharp corner" settings remain current, there's a sharp angle between all subsequent path segments.

11. In the Spline panel, click either Smooth Corner or Very Smooth Corner. Place a few more points, noting the difference in the angles between the segments. Also, watch the Animation panel's current frame number: It increments by 10 each time you add a segment. That's because the Draw Path panel's Segments setting is 10. You can set the number of frames for added path segments by changing this setting.

12. Play the animation to see how the cube moves along the newly extended path.

13. In the Draw Path panel, click Delete Spline Point a couple of times. Each time you click, the most recently added path point is deleted and the previous one is selected.

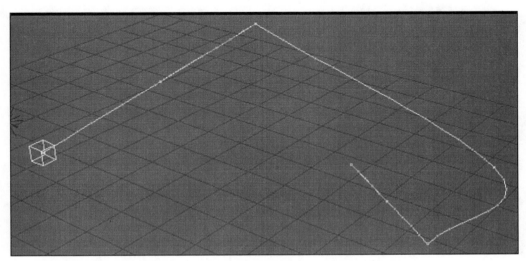

Figure 11-16 Path extended with Draw New Spline Point tool

14. Select Point Move; then select a path node other than the endpoint and select Delete Spline Point. Instead of creating a hole in the path, you now have two adjacent points that are directly connected. By the way, another way to delete the current path point is by selecting the Animation panel's Unset Key icon.

15. Select the Path Library tool. From the library list, choose one of the supplied paths, for example, Heart. The current path is instantly replaced by the one you selected from the library. Chances are it's not much bigger than the cube, if at all, so use the Object Scale tool to make it bigger. You can also use the Object Move and Object Rotate tools to manipulate the entire path.

16. Play the animation and observe the results.

17. Save this object as CUBEPATH.COB.

No doubt you've already realized that being able to use the same basic controls for drawing and editing spline polygons, extrusion paths, and animation paths is a trueSpace2 blessing. This saves you from having to remember unnecessary functions. Make these controls part of your basic repertoire and you'll be able to work that much more efficiently.

AUTOMATING YOUR AIM

Two handy functions in trueSpace2—Look At and Look Ahead—let you automatically aim an object during animation, either along its path of movement or at another object. You'll explore each of these operations in the next two tutorials.

LESSON 12: HERE'S LOOKING AT YOU, KID!

This lesson demonstrates the use of trueSpace2's Look At function to aim a camera or any other object at another object.

1. Start trueSpace2 and load the CUBEPATH.COB file from Lesson 11.

2. Select the Path tool and inspect the heart-shaped path. It should be fairly large, as shown in Figure 11-17. If it isn't, select the Object Scale tool and, holding down both mouse buttons, drag rightward to enlarge it.

3. Add a camera object from the Primitives panel. Use the Object Move tool to drag it to the upper-right side of the ground-level grid, and right-button drag upward to raise it up a couple of inches.

4. Add a new Perspective View window and position it in the upper-left corner of the screen.

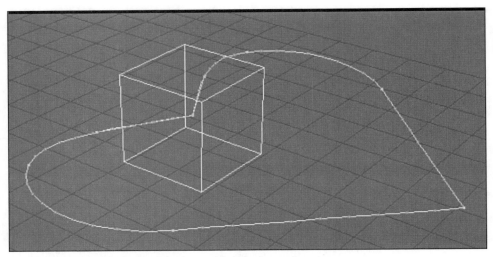

Figure 11–17 Cube with enlarged heart-shaped path

5. From the small window's View pop-up, select the View From Object item, which looks like a camera. Your setup should now look like Figure 11-18, giving you a good view of the cube in the small window. If not, adjust the camera position.

6. Open the Animation panel, select the cube object in the Main window, and play the animation. You can see it move in both windows. In the small window, it moves in and out of the camera view and is hard to follow.

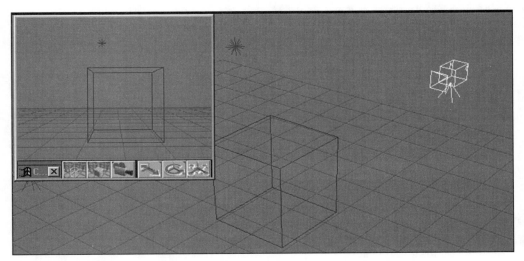

Figure 11–18 Setup with camera view

Figure 11-19 The Look At tool

7. Right-click on the Play button, and in the Animation Parameters panel, activate the Draw: Scene option.

8. Play the animation again. With Draw: Scene active, it plays only in the active (main) window, because animating all objects in all windows would be too slow.

9. Select the Return to Start button in the Animation panel.

10. You'll now implement the Look At action, forcing the camera to stay aimed at the cube as it moves so that it stays in view. In the Main window, select the camera object.

11. In the Animation tool group, select the Look At tool (see Figure 11-19), third from the left.

12. Move the mouse cursor into the Main window. It now resembles an inverted bottle, and the Help bar tells you to pick an object to look at. Click anywhere on the cube.

13. Play the animation, which runs in the Main window, and watch the camera. As the cube moves, the camera continually swivels toward it. Two objects are being animated now (which is why I chose the Draw: Scene setting).

14. Click in the small window and play the animation again. Watch as the view orientation constantly readjusts itself to keep the cube centered in the window.

15. Let's make the admiration mutual. Return to frame 0, and in the Main window select the cube. Next, select the Look At tool and click on the camera. Play back the animation in both views. It's easier to see in the Main view that the cube now rotates slightly as it moves to keep the same side toward the camera, just like the Moon as it orbits Earth.

16. Finally, at frame 60 (you're there now), move the camera to various parts of the workspace. The camera adjusts its aim in real time to stay pointed at the cube, whereas the small window continually updates itself. This real-time feedback greatly enhances experimentation with different camera angles.

17. When you've found a new location you like for the camera, play back the animation one more time. Now both objects move and simultaneously reorient themselves to stay pointed at each other.

In trueSpace2, you can supposedly set keys to enable the Look At function for parts of an animation, but I've found this to be unreliable. In general, always be sure you're at the first frame of the animation before selecting Look At. Also, to disable the function, go to the start of the animation, select the object to which Look At was applied, and then select the Look At tool.

TIP: If you want to create an animation in which the camera first looks at an object and then abruptly cuts to another object (or the same object from a different angle), do what professional cinematographers do: "Film" the action using multiple cameras and then splice the segments together with a video editing program. See Appendix C for more information on programs you can use. Of course, unlike real cinematography, you need to render only the animation segments you're actually going to use.

LESSON 13: LOOKING AHEAD

When a vehicle takes a turn in the road or track along which it's traveling, it rotates to stay pointed in a forward direction, rather than keeping the orientation it had before the turn. As you may have noticed, however, objects don't necessarily do this when moving on paths in trueSpace2. You can, of course, set rotation keys to simulate this effect. But the Look Ahead function automates this process, saving you a great deal of work.

1. Start trueSpace2. You can be in Wireframe or Solid mode for this tutorial.

2. Add a primitive cone to serve as an stand-in for a vehicle; call it the nose cone of a rocket car.

3. In the Animation group, select the Animation tool and then the Path tool.

4. Select the Path Library tool. Let's give the cone a figure-eight racetrack. In the Path Library panel, scroll down and choose the Eight item. Close the panel.

5. Select the Object Scale tool and, dragging with both buttons, enlarge the path so it's fairly big.

6. At this point, part of the path is probably outside the view, so use Object Move to move the path back and to the left so you can see all of it (see Figure 11-20).

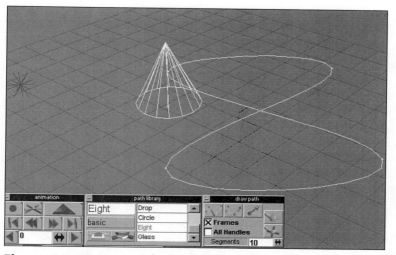

Figure 11–20 Cone with attached figure-eight path

7. Play the animation. The cone moves along the 40-frame figure-eight path, but remains pointed upward.

8. Return to frame 0.

9. Select the Look Ahead tool (see Figure 11-21) from the pop-up associated with the Look At tool. The cone's tip is now pointed forward.

10. Play the animation. Just as a real rocket car would, the cone continually adjusts its orientation to stay pointed forward on the track.

NOTE: This happens because trueSpace2 reorients the cone in each frame so that its z axis is aligned with the path. In the cone's case, the z axis happened to be aimed in the right direction initially. With some objects, you may need to reorient the axes so the z axis is aligned correctly with the object and points toward the object's front.

Figure 11–21 The Look Ahead tool

11. Let's set keys for this function to enable it and disable it at different points throughout the animation. Return to frame 0 and select the Look Ahead tool. This disables its application to the cone, although the cone does not return to its original orientation (you have to do that manually).

12. Select the Object tool and then the Object Rotate tool. Left-button drag to rotate the cone so the tip is pointing upward.

13. If you want to see the path, reselect the Path tool (though it's not necessary for this part of the lesson). Go to frame 15 and select the Look Ahead tool. The cone is again pointing forward.

14. Go to frame 25 and select the Look Ahead tool again to disable the effect from that point on in the animation.

15. Play the animation. At the start, the cone moves along the track while rotating until it's pointing forward at frame 15. The Look Ahead function remains in force until frame 25, at which point the cone stops adjusting its orientation and stays pointed in the same direction for the rest of the animation.

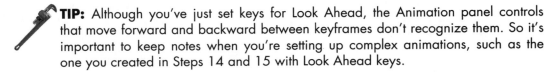 **TIP:** Although you've just set keys for Look Ahead, the Animation panel controls that move forward and backward between keyframes don't recognize them. So it's important to keep notes when you're setting up complex animations, such as the one you created in Steps 14 and 15 with Look Ahead keys.

ANIMATION EDITING

The trueSpace2 program has a built-in animation editor of limited functionality called the Animation Project window. In the following tutorials, you'll get a chance to see what it's useful for and what its shortcomings are.

LESSON 14: BASIC PROJECT EDITING

This tutorial describes the basic components of the Animation Project window and shows how to use them.

1. Start trueSpace2. You can be in either Wireframe or Solid mode.

2. Load the ROB-ANI2.COB file from Lesson 6.

3. In the Animation group, select the Animation tool. Then choose the Animation Project Window tool (see Figure 11-22, left side), which you'll find at the right end of the Animation tool group. This opens the Animation Project window, shown on the right side of Figure 11-22.

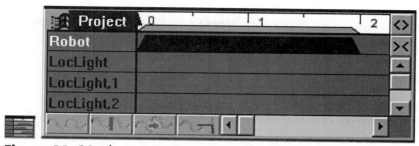

Figure 11–22 The Animation Project tool and window

Let's look briefly at the window's components. To zoom in so as to better see what's what, click a few times on the < > button in the window's top-right corner. The > < button just below it zooms back out.

Running down the left side of the window is a list of objects in the scene; in this case, the robot and three Local lights. To see them all, you may have expand the window vertically by dragging its bottom edge downward a bit. Click on each name in turn to select and highlight the respective object in the workspace. This is a good way to select objects by name—especially helpful with complex scenes. Finish by reselecting the robot.

At the top of the window, to the right of the word **Project**, is a scale showing animation time in seconds, at 30 frames per second. At the left end of this scale, a black triangular pointer indicates the current frame (at frame 0 you can see only the right half of the pointer). Left-button drag this pointer slowly to the right and the animation advances while the robot goes through its paces. This is a convenient way of quickly reviewing part of an animation.

In the bottom half of the time scale is a blue bar that indicates the active frames for playback of the current object's animation. This represents the numerical Start and End settings in the Animation Parameters panel. Currently it shows that the robot object's animation starts at time 0 and ends at 2 seconds, or 60 frames.

You can drag the left and right ends of the blue bar to adjust the starting and ending frames, respectively. You can also click near the bar's center and drag it to adjust both the start and end frames simultaneously, without changing the total length. Try these operations: Right-click on the Animation panel's Play button to open the Parameters panel and play with the blue bar while you watch the changes in the numeric Start and End fields. Make several changes and play the animation each time to see the results. Then set the Start and End frames back to 0 and 60. The easiest way to do this is by clicking on the name of one of the lights in the Project window list and reselecting the robot.

Next, you have the black bar that indicates the actual animation frames for the current object. Because only one object in the current scene is animated, there's only one black bar. Let's add a second "dummy" object for comparison purposes.

4. Make sure you're at frame 0 and add a primitive cube.

5. Select the Object Move tool, go to frame 90, and move the cube to the left-front area of the workspace. The moment you start to move it at frame 90, a second black bar appears in the Project window and the blue bar expands to encompass 3 seconds, or 90 frames. You may need to zoom the Project window out slightly to see this.

6. Click on the robot's name in the Project window list on the left (*not* on the black bar). The blue bar returns to its previous length and position.

7. In the Parameters panel, select the Draw: Scene option. Then go back and alternately select the cube and robot. This time, because Draw: Scene is active, playback uses the frames of the object with the longest animation—that is, the blue bar uses frames 0 to 90.

8. Play the animation with either object selected. Much as you might expect, the robot stops moving at frame 60, whereas the cube continues on to frame 90.

9. Okay, now you're ready to look at the black action bar. Click in the center of the robot object's action bar and drag it to the right until it's centered with respect to the cube's bar. The robot's Start frame should be around 0.5 second, and the End frame around 2.5 seconds.

10. Play the animation. This time, the robot performs the same one-cycle walk, but waits to start until half a second into the animation and finishes a half-second before the end of the animation.

By the way, you could have done this without adding the cube. Even in Draw: Scene mode, though, and if you manually extended the playback frame extents (that is, the blue bar's length), the program would have played only the actual animation frames (from 0.5 to 2.5 seconds). In other words, there would be no initial delay in the robot's movement. If you wanted to create a scene with only one object and delay its starting movement, you'd have to set an additional key in the frame where you wanted the movement to start.

11. Now drag the robot's action bar rightward until its right end is at about the 4-second mark. When you release the mouse button, the blue bar automatically extends its right end to encompass the increased total animation time.

12. Play the animation. This time, the robot starts at the 2-second mark and keeps walking for a second after the cube stops moving. No surprises there.

13. Drag the robot's action bar back to frame 0.

14. Say you want the robot to perform the same action, twice as fast. Of course, you could go back and reset all the keys, but as usual, there's a better way. Just as you can adjust the animation playback length by dragging the ends of the blue bar, so too can you adjust an object's animation by dragging the ends of its action bar. Click on the very right end of the robot's action bar and drag it leftward to the 1-second mark. The bar is now one-half its original length.

15. Play the animation again. This time, the robot performs the same one-cycle walk but does it twice as fast.

16. Save the scene under the name ROB-BOX.SCN.

What if you want the robot to keep walking forward, continuing the cycle as it moves along its path? That's a good question, and I have an answer for you in the next tutorial.

LESSON 15: REPEATING AND COPYING ACTION

You have now come to the mysterious-looking buttons lined up along the Project window's bottom edge. I'll cover the first three—Repeat Action, Stop Repeat Action, and Copy Action—in this tutorial.

1. Unless you're continuing directly from Lesson 14, start trueSpace2 and load the ROB-BOX.SCN scene file.

2. Open the Animation panel and Animation Project window.

3. Open the Animation Parameters panel and set the Draw mode to Scene, if necessary.

Now to tackle the question posed at the end of Lesson 14: How can you keep the robot walking forward at its accelerated pace throughout the animation? Because you originally created its animation starting at the middle of a walk cycle rather than standing still, all you need to do is repeat the action. Fortunately, trueSpace2's Animation Project window has a function that automatically does exactly that.

4. Select the Repeat Action button (see Figure 11-23) in the window's lower-left corner. Click on the robot's action bar and notice the gray repetition bars now extending from its right side. These bars go on "forever," meaning that no matter how long you make the animation, the robot will continue walking forward.

5. Play the animation. The robot's transition from the original walk cycle to its first repetition is seamless, as is the transition between the first and second repetitions.

6. When you edit a repeated action bar, the repetitions automatically follow suit. Try dragging the right end of the robot's action bar to the right and then to the left. Like the action bar, the repetitions first become wider and then thinner. You cannot, however, manipulate repetitions independently.

7. Return the action bar to its original length of 1 second.

Figure 11-23 The Repeat Action tool

Figure 11–24 The Stop Repeat Action tool

8. What? You want to know how to have the robot pause for a moment between the first and second repetition? I'm glad you asked. To the right of the Repeat Action tool icon is the Stop Repeat Action tool (see Figure 11-24), which looks almost the same but has a vertical gray bar through its center. Select this tool.

9. Click on the first diagonal line to the right of the robot's action bar. An additional diagonal line appears near it. Now create a break in the bar by left-button dragging rightward on the right-hand section of the repetition bar. As you drag, the gap widens. Leave a gap of about half a second in length.

10. Play the animation. The robot pauses at about the 2-second mark and then resumes its motion after a half a second.

11. You can create as many breaks in the repetition segment(s) as you like. To rejoin two repetition segments, thus eliminating the pause between, simply drag either segment toward the other until they meet. Try it now.

12. To eliminate a repetition segment entirely, right-button drag it out of the Project window. You won't see it move, but as soon as the mouse cursor exits the window area, the segment vanishes. Try this, too.

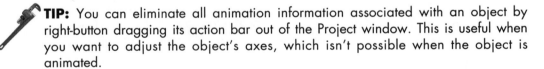

TIP: You can eliminate all animation information associated with an object by right-button dragging its action bar out of the Project window. This is useful when you want to adjust the object's axes, which isn't possible when the object is animated.

13. Before continuing, take a look at the Copy Action tool (see Figure 11-25), to the right of Stop Repeat Action. Select it and then select the robot's action bar. A second action bar appears immediately to the right of the first. Its length is 2 seconds, the same as the original before you reduced it. Unlike repetitions, when you copy action you can apply all the same editing functions to the copy that you can to the original.

Figure 11–25 The Copy Action tool

14. Play the animation. When it reaches the 1-second mark, the robot pops back to its starting position and repeats the action.

Copying is less useful than repetition, where the repeated action starts out from where the original or previous action left off, unless you originally animated the object with this capability in mind (e.g., the object moves cyclically rather than linearly). Copying does come in handy when you want to be able to use repetitions of varying durations.

LESSON 16: LOCALIZING ACTION

Confession time: When I showed you how to set up hierarchical animation in Lessons 5 and 6, I wasn't giving you the very best advice. Of course, those techniques worked fine for the immediate purposes, and as well for the illustration of Animation Project editing in Lessons 14 and 15. And now that you have the fundamentals down, you'll be able to employ them in this tutorial, which shows you how to use the Animation Project window's Make Action Local tool to create more controllable, hierarchical animation. By animating hierarchy members independently, you can apply different Project window controls to each individual part.

1. Start trueSpace2 or clear the workspace. For the best feedback, use Wireframe Display.

2. Load the version of the robot object you saved at the end of Lesson 4, or the ROB-AXES.COB object from the TUTORIAL/CH12 directory on the companion CD.

3. Before going into animation, reorient the robot's main axes to enable the use of the Look Ahead tool for path animation. Select the Axes and Object Rotate tools and turn off the x axis. Then left-button drag rightward to rotate the axes 90° on the y axis, so the z axis points forward (see Figure 11-26). You may want to open a Top View window temporarily as a visual aid.

4. Select the Axes tool again to turn off display of the axes.

5. Open the Animation panel and the Animation Project window.

For the next few steps, you'll be repeating Lesson 5's setup of the arms' and legs' animation—with two crucial differences. First, instead of setting up all the limbs' positions keyframe by keyframe, you'll work on each limb separately. Second, you'll use the Make Action Local tool after setting up each limb to separate its motion conceptually from the rest of the object. It's a little more work, but you'll reap significant benefits in the long run, as you'll see.

6. Navigate to the left arm and rotate it forward about 30°.

7. Go to frame 60 and, in the Animation panel, click Record. Cool shortcut, eh? Advance planning can save you loads of time!

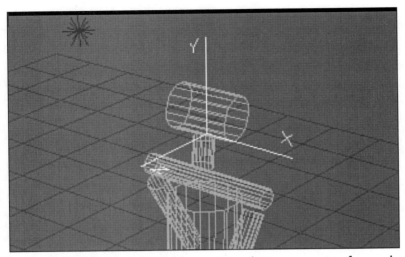

Figure 11–26 Robot's main axes rotated so z axis points forward

8. Go to frame 30 and rotate the arm back by 60 °.

9. In the Project window, select the Make Action Local tool (see Figure 11-27), at the right end of the row of icons along the window's bottom edge. Then select the action bar to the right of the Robot list entry. The bar moves down a slot and is now labeled Local1.

10. Play the animation to ensure that the action is still there.

11. Select the other (right) arm, and rotate it back at frame 0. Set a key at frame 60 and then rotate forward at frame 30.

12. Now make this new action local by again clicking Make Action Local and then selecting the Robot action bar. Like the first bar, the new one drops down a slot and is labeled Local2. (You might want to keep notes on which bars correspond to which limb, as there's no way to relabel the bars.)

13. Repeat the key-setting procedure for both legs. Rotate the right leg forward at frames 0 and 60, and then back at frame 30. Rotate the left leg back at frames 0 and 60, and forward at frame 30. Remember to make each action local as you go.

Figure 11–27 The Make Action Local tool

14. Navigate to the top of the hierarchy and play the animation to verify that you've set the keys correctly. If not, navigate back down, make the necessary corrections, and then navigate back up.

15. Save this object as ROB1LOCL.COB.

16. Let's take little Robby for a walk. Return to frame 0, select Object Move, and position the robot where you'd like it to start.

17. Activate the Path tool from the Animation group and, in the Draw Path panel, set Segments to 60. This way, the robot will go through a complete walk cycle for each path segment.

18. Draw a path by clicking on five or six locations around the workspace.

19. Play the animation. The robot performs the walk cycle in the first path segment and then glides through the rest of the path. You know what to do about that, right?

20. To stop the action before it gets to the end of the path, press the (ESC) key. Then return to frame 0.

21. In the Project window, select the Repeat Action tool and then the Local1 action bar. Continue selecting the tool followed by each of the other local action bars until all are repeated.

22. Play the animation again. This time, Robby keeps walking along the entire length of the path—but he doesn't turn to face the way he's going. This, too, is easily fixed.

23. Return to frame 0 and select the Look Ahead tool.

24. Now play the animation and watch Robby behave as naturally as such an abstract automaton can.

You may notice that the limbs' pivoting action slows down in midcycle. Unfortunately, there's not much to be done about that, other than setting additional keys. This must be done during initial setup, because once you make an object's action local, you can no longer edit its animation.

The benefit of making an object's action local is that you can control subobjects' animation individually using all the Project window's tools. For example, you could have the walking robot stop swinging one or both of its arms in midstride while continuing to pump its legs. Or, for a helicopter that suddenly breaks down, the rotor could stop spinning as the chopper begins its downward trajectory.

WHAT NEXT?

Caligari has given you the tools and I've shown you how to use them. Now it's up to you to put your imagination to work and come up with original animations to wow your friends and relatives—and possibly even get you some lucrative work. In the next chapter, I'll cover trueSpace2's rendering functions, for getting your work out into the world.

12
RENDERING

12

My American Heritage dictionary offers 12 definitions for the word *render*. In the context of 3D graphics, definition 6b, "To represent in a drawing or painting, especially in perspective," might, at first blush, seem most appropriate. (It sure ain't definition 11—melting down fat!). But definition 8, "To express in another language or form; translate," also has the ring of truth to it. In 3D graphics, rendering is the process of taking a scene that's represented as numbers in the computer, and on the screen (generally) in the abstracted form of a wireframe, and expressing that scene as a fully fleshed-out photo-realistic still or moving image. As you've no doubt experienced by now, the dramatic difference between a scene depicted skeletally in wireframe form, and the same scene rendered with lighting, backgrounds, smoothing, textures, and so forth, can take your breath away.

Rendering in trueSpace2 is often quite straightforward: Invoke the command and the computer does the rest. But there's actually quite a bit more to it than that, particularly when rendering scenes and especially when rendering animations. In this chapter, we'll explore trueSpace2's rendering options, along with the special effects and options available only when rendering to a file.

SOLID VERSUS WIREFRAME

It was a rarity just a couple of years ago, but today more and more 3D graphics applications can display solid objects *as you work with them*, not just after using a special render function. You've already seen the trueSpace2 optional Solid Render Display mode at work, which uses Intel's nearly obsolete 3DR technology to render objects on-the-fly. In certain circumstances, such as when working with lighting, Solid mode has significant advantages over Wireframe Display. Nevertheless, it is a disappointing solution—because of its rendering inaccuracies, the lack of support for transparency, bump mapping, shadows, and so on, and its skimpy hardware support (currently, the only trueSpace2/3DR hardware support is provided by the Matrox Millennium card under Windows 3.1).

At this writing, Intel seems to have abandoned 3DR and Microsoft is ballyhooing its just-released Direct3D technology as the ultimate for real-time 3D graphics. Caligari, meanwhile, has announced that the next version of trueSpace will support Direct3D. But 3DR is here now, and it works in a variety of circumstances, so use it whenever appropriate. A good rule of thumb is to try to work in Solid mode, and if reaction time slows down too much or you're just not getting the right type of feedback, revert to Wireframe Display mode and render only when necessary.

THE RENDER TOOLS

Attached to each window in trueSpace2 is a pop-up menu of rendering tools (see Figure 12-1), of which Render Current Object is the default in the slot. The variants are Render Scene and Render Scene to File (see Figure 12-1). If you right-click on any of these, the Render Options panel opens, as shown in Figure 12-2.

In the next few lessons, I'll examine the various options presented here.

Figure 12-1 The Render Current Object, Render Scene, and Render Scene to File tools

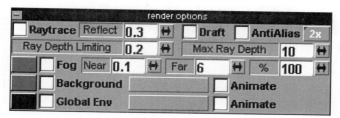

Figure 12-2 The Render Options panel

Ray Tracing

The Raytrace options are in the first two rows of the Render Options panel (not including the Draft and AntiAlias check box options). The Raytrace settings affect how trueSpace2 handles ray tracing. In Chapters 9, Materials Part 1: Basic Surface Attributes, and 10, Materials Part 2: Advanced Surface Attributes, you used what trueSpace2 calls the Raytrace option to render with shadows, reflection, and refraction. According to the book *Computer Graphics: Principles and Practice* (Addison Wesley, 1990, p. 701) by Foley, van Dam, Feiner, and Hughes, "Ray tracing…determines the visibility of surfaces by tracing imaginary rays of light from the viewer's eye to the objects in the scene." Because of the way this rendering method works, it's ideal for accurately simulating shadows, reflection, and refraction. But it's computation intensive, and when you render complex scenes with ray tracing, you may see your machine slow down to a crawl.

LESSON 1: USING THE TRUESPACE2 RAYTRACE OPTIONS

The first ray tracing option is the Raytrace check box, which lets you turn ray tracing on and off. The others—Reflect, Ray Depth Limiting, and Max Ray Depth—are numerical settings that affect how ray tracing is done. (The latter two were added in version 2.01.)

Reflecting Your Environment

Let's start by looking at the Reflect setting.

1. Start trueSpace2 in Wireframe mode.

2. Add a primitive sphere. Then add a primitive cube and move it to the right of the sphere.

3. Paint both objects with a material that uses the Metal shader.

4. Open a small Perspective window and zoom in on the sphere and cube.

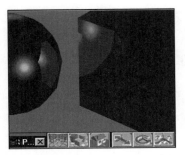

Figure 12-3 Sphere and cube reflecting each other

5. In the small window, select the Render Scene tool from the pop-up menu (second from the left). Both the sphere and the cube render as dark metallic solids.

6. Right-click on the Render Scene tool to open the Render Options panel. In the panel, select the Raytrace option.

7. Render the scene again. This time you can see the cube's reflection in the sphere and vice-versa. In fact, you can even see the sphere's reflection of the cube in the cube's reflection (see Figure 12-3).

8. Right-click on the Shader Attributes panel to display the numeric equivalents of the Attributes settings. Shininess (Shine), which determines reflectivity, is set to 0.9.

Because the Reflect value determines the Shine threshold value below which objects won't reflect, first set one of the objects' Shine setting to a lower value, and then set Reflect to a value between the two objects' Shine settings.

9. Set Shine to 0.5 and apply the altered material to the sphere.

10. Render the scene again. You can still see both reflections.

11. Set Reflect to 0.6 and render the scene again. This time, the cube reflects but the sphere doesn't.

According to the trueSpace2 documentation, if an object's shininess is below the Reflect value, the object won't reflect, but this isn't precisely true. For example, if you set Reflect to 0.7, neither object reflects, even though the cube's Shine setting is well above this, at 0.9. Thus, if you want to have a ray traced scene in which some shiny objects reflect their surroundings and others don't, you'll have to experiment with the various settings.

Bouncing Off the Walls

The Max Ray Depth setting determines how trueSpace2 generates rays for tracing.

Normally, in these tutorials, I have you do all the scene setup because it's a good way to learn the program. In this case, I'll have you load the scene already set up, to save some time.

1. Load the scene file MIRRORS.SCN from the TUTORIAL/CH13 directory on the companion CD-ROM.

This scene contains two mirrors facing each other—one with a blue border and the other with a yellow border—with a blue sphere and a camera between them. The small window shows the view from the camera, which is pointing at the blue-bordered mirror.

In case you're interested, I created the mirrors by drawing a four-sided polygon, then subtracting a smaller one from its center to make the border. I then drew another polygon with the Union option, inside the border. I set the border to yellow and set the inside rectangle to the default metal-shaded material. Then I copied the mirror and changed the copy's border color to blue.

2. Render the scene in the small window (see Figure 12-4). You can see the reflection of the yellow mirror in the blue one, and inside that the reflection of the blue, and inside that another reflection of the yellow, and so on—the reflection-bouncing goes on for a while. In fact, it's difficult to see just how far down the reflections go.

3. Right-click on the Render tool to open the Render Options panel. Set Max Ray Depth to its lowest value of 1. If you click and drag on the double-headed arrow, you can see that this setting uses integers only. It determines the number of times trueSpace2 bounces rays before rendering.

4. Render the scene again. Now there's only one reflection of the yellow mirror. You don't need to do this, but if you flipped the camera half a turn on the vertical axis and rendered the other mirror, you'd still see one reflection.

Figure 12-4 Multiple reflections in the mirror

5. Set Max Ray Depth to 2 and render the scene. This time you see two reflections.

Continue raising the Max Ray Depth setting and rerendering the scene. You can see that there's a one-to-one correspondence between Max Ray Depth and the number of reflections. Also, notice that, the more bounces required, the longer the rendering takes. (It might not be that obvious with a scene as simple as this one.) In general, if you're ray tracing a scene that doesn't require "deep" reflecting, you can save time by lowering the Max Ray Depth setting.

NOTE: According to the text file that comes with trueSpace2 2.01, Ray Depth Limiting is used to prevent the creation of many insignificant rays in a scene. If this is set to 1.0, you get minimal ray tracing. Setting it to 0.0 will result in up to Max Ray Depth rays getting spawned, as successive reflective surfaces are encountered, even if the contribution of the spawned rays will be insignificant. Thus, you can use this to limit ray tracing to important reflections and the like. Be careful of setting it too high because this can unnecessarily waste CPU time.

NOTE: The Reflect parameter can be animated, although Ray Depth Limiting and Max Ray Depth cannot. To animate Reflect, make sure you have Draw: Scene turned on in the Animation Parameters panel and set keys as usual.

DRAFT AND ANTIALIAS

These two settings on the Render Options panel are related only in the sense that they affect *jagginess*—the stair-step artifact often seen on object edges. They're pretty straightforward, so I can quickly cover both in a single lesson.

LESSON 2: ELIMINATING THE JAGGIES

1. Start trueSpace2 in Wireframe mode.

2. Add a primitive cube object.

3. Use Render Current Object to render the cube. Take a close look at the edges. They're pretty smooth.

4. Right-click on the Render tool and click in the box to the left of Draft to turn on Draft mode.

5. Render the cube again. It's noticeably faster—but, though the sides look the same, the edges have taken on a distinct stair-step look (see Figure 12-5).

Here's what happened: When you render in Draft mode, trueSpace2 halves the output image's vertical and horizontal resolution, thus having to render only a fourth as

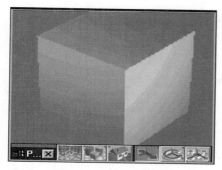

Figure 12-5 Cube with the jaggies, rendered in Draft mode

many pixels. Then, when drawing the image, each pixel's size is doubled so that it takes up as much space as four pixels would have originally.

Draft mode is useful for testing lighting, object overlap, textures, and so on when you don't need to see fine details.

Slow and Smooth

The AntiAlias setting helps eliminate the jaggies. *Aliasing* occurs in computer graphics when the screen resolution isn't high enough to draw smooth diagonal lines. The result is a stair-step look on lines drawn at certain angles.

1. Turn off Draft mode.

2. Delete the cube and add a primitive torus object.

3. Open a new Perspective View window and move the eye in fairly close to the torus.

4. Render the scene in the small window. The aliasing on the object's lower edges, both inside and outside, is fairly evident (see Figure 12-6, left side), but most of the other edges look okay. In general, the least aliasing occurs on vertical and horizontal

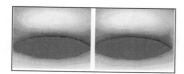

Figure 12-6 Magnified edge of torus rendered without (left) and with (right) antialiasing turned on

335

lines and 45° diagonals, because they're aligned with the grid of pixels making up the screen display.

5. In the Render Options panel, click the check box next to AntiAlias. This turns on *antialiasing*, which fills in the corners of the stair-stepped edges with pixels whose color values are between that of the object and its background. The eye is fooled and you perceive a smoother edge.

6. Render the scene again. (For antialiasing to work, you must render the entire scene, not just the object, because the background color(s) must be blended with the foreground objects' edge pixels.) This time, the edges appear considerably smoother, as shown in the right-hand image in Figure 12-6.

7. Look closely and you'll still see some remnants of the jaggies. In the Render Options panel, click on the 2X button in the upper-right corner to see the other available settings for AntiAlias—3X and 4X. Try one or both of these and see if you can notice the difference.

Figure 12-7 is an enlargement of the edge of a white sphere, rendered against a black background, with antialiasing set to 4X, showing the intermediate gray pixels.

LESSON 3: FOGGING IT UP

The Fog setting in trueSpace2 creates a somewhat realistic effect of a scene gradually fading out as the distance from the viewpoint increases. You don't get the swirling, wispy characteristics of real fog, but you can animate the effect.

One of the best ways to illustrate fog is with a line of objects receding from the point of view. You'll also use a camera to see how the distance settings affect the fog.

Fog Extents

1. Start trueSpace2 in Wireframe mode.

2. From the Primitives panel, add a camera object. It appears aimed toward the lower left.

Figure 12-7 Antialiasing of white sphere on black background (enlarged)

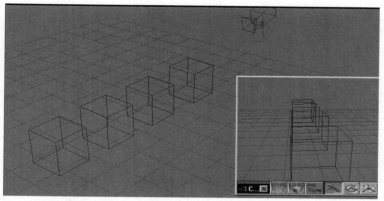

Figure 12-8 Scene setup for testing Fog settings

3. Move it back along the x axis so it's positioned near the upper-right corner of the workspace. Also, raise it up by about 2.5 meters; use the Object Info panel, if you like.

4. Add a new view window of any type and set it to show the view from the camera.

5. Add a primitive cube object, scale it down to about 1 cubic meter, and position it in front of the camera.

6. Copy the cube (CTRL-C) and move the copy about 1 meter behind the first.

7. Repeat the copying and moving operation until you have four cubes. See Figure 12-8.

8. Select the camera and use the Look At function to aim it at the second cube. Your setup should now resemble Figure 12-8.

9. Open the Render Options panel and check the Fog option to turn it on. Using the default settings, render the scene in the small window. Not much difference, is there? Let's see why not.

10. Examine the Near and Far settings next to Fog in the panel. These are known as *extents.* The Near setting is where the fog starts, and the Far setting is where the fog fully obscures all objects at and beyond that distance. Because the cube farthest away is a good deal closer than 50 meters—the default Far setting—the effect isn't visible. The fog's greatest density is way behind the rearmost cube (from the camera's point of view).

11. The distance between the camera and the midpoint of the row of cubes is about 6 meters (depending on your setup). Set the Far number to 6 and render the scene again. Quite a difference, isn't there? Now only the two closest cubes are visible, and even they are kind of fogged out.

12. This is a good time to experiment with the fog color. Open the Fog Color panel by clicking on the gray box to the left of the Fog check box.

13. Try creating a bright yellow fog by turning red and green all the way up, and then render this somewhat bizarre scene. Often the most fun you can have using a 3D program is with effects that aren't possible in the real world.

14. Try a few other colors if you like; finish by resetting red, green, and blue to 128.

15. Let's play with the distances a bit more. You can make the fog boundary more abrupt, so the two rear cubes are still invisible but the first two are completely clear. Set Near to 6.0, Far to 6.2, and render the scene. No problem there.

16. But what if you want a nice, gradual fade, so all the cubes are visible but there's a noticeable increase in the fog with each successive cube? Set Near to your estimated distance from the camera to the front of the nearest cube, and Far to the distance between the camera and the rear of the farthest cube. In this scene, 2 and 9 work well.

17. Save this scene as FOG.SCN. You can use it again in the next exercise.

NOTE: The fog fadeout is always perpendicular to the camera plane. You cannot simulate a fog that decreases with vertical height, using this facility.

Fog Intensity

The third Fog setting is %, which determines the fog's overall density. By default it's set to 100%, so let's look at a few other settings.

1. Set Near back to its default of 0.1 and Far to 6.0.

2. Render the scene for a point of reference.

3. Set the % value to 50 and render again. This time there's a little fog, but it's barely noticeable.

4. Try intermediate values and see what looks best. Remember, you're the final judge of your output, so make a point of getting familiar with the full range of available tools.

TIP: In the real world, there's always a certain amount of mist (water vapor) in the air, even on clear days. By adding a small amount of fog to your outdoor scenes, you can make them look more realistic. This technique adds depth cueing, which helps the viewer determine how far various objects are from the camera. Be sure to match the fog color to your background color or to a background image's predominant color (such as light blue for a sky).

Animating Fog

To animate trueSpace2's fog effect, simply set keys, like animating any other attribute, after turning on Draw: Scene mode.

1. Set up your scene.

2. In the Animation panel, right-click on the Play button to open the Animation Parameters panel.

3. In the top row of the parameters panel, click in the circle next to Scene.

4. Go to frame 0 and set the starting values for Fog: Color, Near, Far, and percent.

5. Go to the next keyframe and change any values as appropriate.

6. Repeat Step 5 as many times as necessary.

 CAUTION: Unfortunately, as with most types of keys in trueSpace2, you cannot use the Animation panel's Reverse and Advance buttons to skip between fog keys, so keep careful notes.

BACKGROUND AND GLOBAL ENVIRONMENT

You've come now to the two final settings in the Render Options panel: Background and Global Environment. Background is a color or image that appears behind the scene. Global Env(ironment) is a color or image that's applied to all reflective objects as an environment map, whether or not ray tracing is enabled and in addition to any environment maps applied to specific objects. The settings for both are quite similar. You can set and animate different colors for each, or you can use an image, numbered image sequence, or an AVI-format animation.

The check boxes next to Background and Global Env are used to enable and disable the use of images. If selected without specifying an image file, Background defaults to the Mandrill image included with trueSpace2 and Global Env defaults to the Rainbow environment map. The Animate check boxes are for enabling the animation of image sequences or AVI files. There's more information about these options in the trueSpace2 Help file, under View Group/Render Tools/Render Options Panel.

Some Tips on Your Scene's Background

When rendering an image to be composited into another graphic, for example with Adobe Photoshop, do not use a background image if you want the background to be transparent. You can find more information about image compositing using background transparency in Appendix C.

Don't waste the effort to set up a complex scene for an animation in which the background is static and only foreground objects move and then render every frame that way. In such cases, as long as the camera view doesn't change, you can save a great deal of time by prerendering the background objects and then using the image as the background:

1. Set up your objects and animation and save the scene.

2. Remove all foreground objects and render the scene to a single image file (see Rendering to Files, below).

3. Load the original scene and remove all background objects.

4. Set the background image to be the file created in Step 2.

5. Render the animation.

This way, the background objects need to be rendered only once.

If the camera is to move during an animation, however, it's generally not a good idea to use a background image, because viewers will see the foreground changing while the background remains static. In such cases, create a large sphere surrounding the entire scene and map a background image to it.

RENDERING TO FILES

When it comes time to immortalize your creations, in the form of still-image files or animations, use the Render to File tool, which invokes the Render to File dialog (see Figure 12-9). Most of this dialog's settings are explained in the trueSpace2 Help file, under View Group/Render Tools/Render to File Dialog.

NOTE: When rendering an image or animation to disk, if you do not specify a file name extension, trueSpace2 creates a Targa-format file, no matter what the current entry is under List Files of Type. If you do specify an allowed file name extension, trueSpace2 uses that format, again disregarding any conflicting entry in List Files of Type.

Saving AVI Files

When you specify an .AVI file for trueSpace2 output, the next thing you see is the AVI Compression dialog. Its options are documented in the trueSpace2 Help file. In this section you'll find some additional guidance.

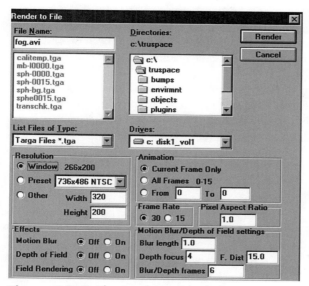

Figure 12–9 The Render to File dialog

First you must select a compression method for your output files. The latest cutting edge *codec* (**co**mpression/**dec**ompression technology) is Intel's Indeo Video Interactive. Optimal playback of videos using this compression method requires a lot of computing power, so if your machine (or your target) is not state of the art, this might not be the best choice. Intel's previous codec, Indeo Video R3.2, is a good all-around compression method. Cinepak is preferred by many animators for its versatility.

The best codec for a given situation depends on many variables, including the subject matter. If you have time, experiment with the various methods available, to determine which works best for your particular animation; otherwise, go for one of the tried-and-true codecs.

Certain codecs support the configuration options offered in the AVI Compression dialog. For example, Indeo Video Interactive has the widest range of configuration options, including switches for scalability and bidirectional prediction. These are useful when you're not sure what type of platform will be used to play the video and the intended usage of the video (such as reverse play).

NOTE: One of the best available resources for exploring compression methods for Windows video is a $130 CD-ROM from Doceo Publishing called *Video Compression Sampler.* It covers a range of codecs, including the three mentioned above, and provides extensive benchmarking facilities. Contact Doceo Publishing at One Meca Way, Norcross, Georgia 30093; phone 770-564-5545; fax 770-564-5528; e-mail jan@doceo.com. Doceo's Jan Ozer has also written a book entitled *Video Compression for Multimedia* (AP Professional, 1995), which includes a demo version of Video Compression Sampler.

After setting a codec in the AVI Compression dialog, use the slider to select the compression quality, which can range from 0 to 100. Higher values yield better quality, of course, but require greater amounts of disk storage space. The opposite can be said of the frequency of keyframes; use lower values for the best quality, but make sure you have extra free space on your hard disk.

Finally, use the Data Rate setting to optimize playback for a particular type of device. For example, the most common type of CD-ROM player is currently 2X, which uses the default data rate of 300KB/sec; but 4X drives, which use a 600KB/sec data rate, are growing in popularity. If an animation is optimized for a 2X drive, it may not play back as well on a 4X drive, and vice-versa.

MOTION BLUR

If you've ever seen a photograph of a fast-moving object, you may have detected some blurring around the edges. (Even if you didn't notice the blur, your subconscious did.) That and the subject's position are visual clues to how fast the object is moving. *Motion blur* is a common photographic artifact that occurs when a subject moves a significant distance while the camera shutter is open. It's even more common in movies and video, which typically use slower shutter speeds than still photography.

Because there's no such thing as shutter speed in 3D graphics, and because objects in a particular frame remain perfectly still for the entire rendering time, motion blur doesn't exist. However, trueSpace2 can be set to fake the effect automatically, by averaging an object's image over the course of several frames.

LESSON 4: BLURRING VIRTUAL MOTION

In this tutorial, you'll examine the use of trueSpace2's Motion Blur feature. To use this in either still images or animations, one or more objects must be in motion create the motion blur effect.

NOTE: If you'd rather skip the setup, load the SPH-ANI.SCN scene file from the companion CD-ROM's TUTORIAL/CH13 directory. Then start at Step 13.

1. Start trueSpace2 in Wireframe mode.

2. Add a primitive sphere and a new Perspective View window.

3. Zoom in on the sphere in the small window.

4. Select the Paint Face tool.

5. You want as much contrast as possible between the sphere and the background, to make the motion blur readily apparent, so set the current material to pure white by raising the Intensity slider in the Material Color panel all the way to the top. Then apply the material to the sphere.

6. Open the Preferences panel (File/Preferences). Set Default Lights to White Lights, confirm the change, and close the panel.

7. Open the Render Options panel by right-clicking on the Render Current Object tool. Set the background to black and close the panel.

8. Move the sphere leftward so that it's just outside the small window's left edge.

9. Open the Animation panel and go to frame 30.

10. Move the sphere rightward so that it's just outside the small window's right edge.

11. Play the animation, to confirm that the sphere moves quickly across the small window from right to left.

12. Go to frame 15.

13. From the small window's Render pop-up, select Render to File to open the Render to File dialog. Set Resolution to Other (320 × 200) and Animation to Current Frame Only (if necessary). Under Effects, set Motion Blur to On. Leave all other settings at their default values.

14. Enter a file name such as MBSPHERE.BMP and click the Render button.

15. In the Windows Bitmap Settings dialog, turn off the Begin frame numbers with 0 option if necessary and then click OK. The image is rendered six times, after which the six renderings are combined into a single motion-blurred image. This final image is visible for a moment during the combining process.

Use any BMP-compatible graphics program, such as the Paint program that comes with Windows, to view the image. The six steps will be noticeable, giving a somewhat unrealistic effect (left-hand image in Figure 12-10). For greater realism but longer rendering times, use a higher value for the Blur/Depth frames setting (right-hand image in Figure 12-10). Everything's a trade-off!

DEPTH OF FIELD

Depth of field is another photographic artifact that results from a lens' ability to focus only on a particular distance from the camera. Any objects closer or farther than the focus point are out of focus; as the distance increases, so does the blurring. If the lens aperture is wide open, this effect is more noticeable than if the lens is stopped down. Also, the effect is more pronounced with telephoto lenses than with wide-angle lenses.

In standard 3D rendering, all objects are always in focus, which can detract from a scene's realistic look, especially if you're going for a photographic effect. Using trueSpace2's Depth of Field option can help remedy this, but at a cost in rendering time. As with the Motion Blur option, trueSpace2 fakes depth of field by averaging several exposures, but taken from slightly different points of view rather than different points in time.

Figure 12-10 Motion-blur sphere with Blur/Depth frames of 6 (left) and 10 (right)

LESSON 5: USING DEPTH OF FIELD

1. Open the FOG.SCN scene file you saved in Lesson 3. (If it's not handy, load the file of the same name from the TUTORIAL/CH13 directory on the companion CD.)

2. Open the Render Options panel and turn off the Fog option. Close the panel.

3. Select the small window's Render Scene to File tool to open the Render to File dialog.

4. Set Resolution to Other (320 × 200) and Animation to Current Frame Only (if necessary). Under Effects, set Depth of Field to On and all other options to Off.

5. Take a look at the Motion Blur/Depth of Field settings section in the dialog's lower-right corner, particularly the Depth Focus and F. Dist. (Focal Distance) settings. Recall that in Lesson 3 you used Look At to aim the camera at the second cube. Because this key is still active, the F. Dist. setting is disregarded. This feature is very handy, because it saves you from having to guesstimate the distance from the camera to the focus point.

6. Make sure the other relevant settings, Depth Focus and Blur/Depth Frames, are at their default values of 4 and 6.

7. Enter a name such as DOF.BMP for the image file and click on the Render button.

8. In the Windows Bitmap Settings dialog, turn off the Begin frame numbers with 0 option if necessary and then click OK. The image is rendered six times, and then the six renderings are combined into a single image with depth of field. This final image is visible for a moment, during the combining process.

Use any BMP-compatible graphics program, such as the Paint program that comes with Windows, to view the image (see Figure 12-11, left side). The second box is sharp, the third is slightly out of focus, and the most distant and closest boxes are quite fuzzy. The artifacting caused by the combining of the six images is particularly noticeable in the front edge of the closest box. As with Motion Blur, you'll want to use a higher value for the Blur/Depth frames setting (see Figure 12-11, right side).

Figure 12–11 Depth of field with Blur/Depth frames of 6 and 10

Depth of field is a wonderful effect for adding photorealism to your renderings. As you've seen, the cost is a rendering time of 600% or more over standard rendering. As long as you're not under a tight deadline or rendering a complex ray traced scene, the results can be well worth it.

WHAT NOW?

The trueSpace2 Help file offers a lot of useful information on rendering. Read it over and print out the sections of greatest interest for handy reference. As usual, spend as much time as possible exploring the various available options and combinations.

In the next chapter, you'll take a whirlwind tour of the latest rage in online technology, as implemented in Caligari's Pioneer. This new program incorporates a subset of trueSpace2's capabilities for VRML authoring and browsing, letting you create and navigate three-dimensional worlds on the World Wide Web.

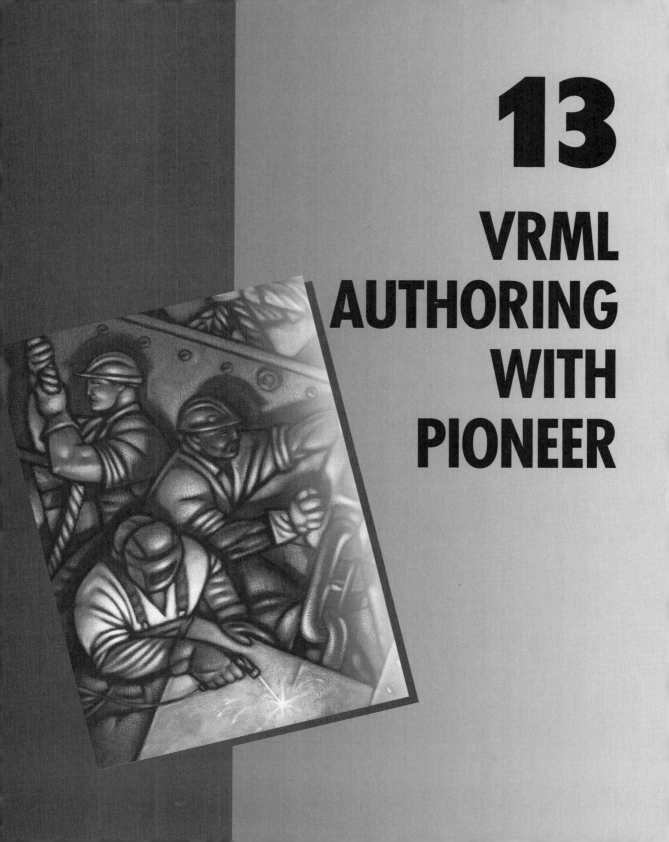

13
VRML AUTHORING WITH PIONEER

13

Until recently, we of the three-dimensional world have been limited to negotiating the exciting new world of cyberspace through the two-dimensional interface of HyperText Markup Language (HTML). Thanks to the ground-breaking work of visionaries such as Mark Pesce, a new standard called Virtual Reality Modeling Language (VRML, pronounced "vermul") has emerged as a way to put navigable 3D graphics on the Internet's World Wide Web. VRML has the potential to fulfill the promises of virtual reality. We'll be able to visit places and people not otherwise accessible, expanding our horizons in ways made possible by technology and vision.

Among providers of VRML authoring tools, Caligari has jumped to the head of the pack. Its new program called Pioneer is a scaled-down version of trueSpace that lets you create 3D worlds and add links to specific objects. With a single click on a linked object, users can jump between 3D scenes, much as they can surf the 2D Web now with the hypertext links between HTML documents. Pioneer can also be used as a VRML browser, either stand-alone or by linking it to an HTML browser such as Netscape Navigator. This chapter shows how to use Pioneer as a VRML authoring and browsing tool.

Although you perform most functions in Pioneer by pointing, clicking, and dragging, the underlying technology is VRML. However, you don't need to learn the specifics of VRML unless you want to. One of the best resources available is *VRML: Browsing and Building Cyberspace*, written by VRML co-creator Mark Pesce (New Riders Publishing, 1995).

Pioneer has much in common with trueSpace2, including many of the latter's navigation and modeling tools, as well as the ability to work in the 3DR real-time solid mode. With Pioneer's additional capabilities, such as adding hyperlinks to 3D objects, you can navigate among cyberspace locations with a click of the mouse. This program can also save and load scenes in the VRML standard WRL format. It can load 2D and 3D objects from many other programs, including Caligari trueSpace, 3D Studio, AutoCAD, LightWave, and WaveFront. Pioneer also supports Intel's 3D for working in real time with solid shaded objects instead of wireframes.

NOTE: The most important thing to know about Pioneer is that, to use it to browse 3D worlds on the World Wide Web, you need to have an Internet connection. If you have a working PPP, SLIP, ISDN, or other account with a direct Internet provider, you're all set. Also, if you plan to publish 3D worlds on the Web, you'll need to have a Web site. Contact your Internet service provider for details.

INSTALLING AND RUNNING PIONEER

You'll find full instructions for installing and running Pioneer on the companion CD-ROM. Use Program Manager (Windows 3.1) or Windows Explorer (Windows 95) to navigate to the PIONEER directory and double-click on the README.WRI file name. If you have a printer connected to your computer, print out the file for easy reference.

Once you have Pioneer installed, run it by selecting its icon from the Caligari Pioneer item in the Program menu (Windows 95) or by double-clicking its icon in the Caligari Pioneer program group (Windows 3.1).

GUIDED TOUR OF PIONEER'S INTERFACE

Pioneer has two different working modes that you switch between by clicking on the leftmost icon at the bottom of the workspace. When you first start the program, you're placed in World Browsing mode (see Figure 13-1), used for navigating within 3D worlds and between 3D worlds and 2D pages. The other mode, World Building mode, is for creating 3D worlds, mostly using the standard trueSpace2 functions you've become familiar with in previous chapters.

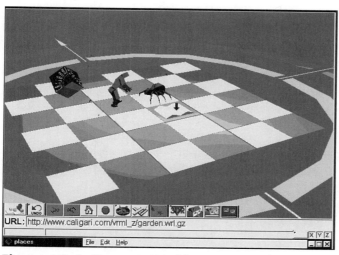

Figure 13–1 Pioneer in World Browsing mode

World Browsing Mode

Let's start with a quick tour of the program interface in World Browsing mode. Most of the screen is taken up by the workspace, a virtual 3D, full-perspective space mapped to your 2D display. Using simple mouse controls, you can navigate through this space in three dimensions and link to other worlds and/or HTML pages by clicking on objects.

Below the workspace are the program's tools, and below the tools is a Uniform Resource Locator (URL) line showing the Web address (or disk file location) of the current object (the one most recently pointed at). Below this, in the Help bar, is an optional text line describing the current object.

As in trueSpace2, Pioneer tools are represented by small icon buttons. On the opening screen, the leftmost tool is for switching between World Building and World Browsing modes. To its right is an Undo tool, and to the right of that are four tools for VRML browsing. The Back and Forward tools (left and light arrows) take you between Web locations in the order of selection. The Home tool (the house icon) takes you to the default Home scene, and the Stop tool (a red octagon) lets you halt a lengthy load while in progress. These buttons work like the Netscape Navigator buttons of the same names. As in Navigator, you can set the default Home scene to any on-line or local disk-based VRML file; this is done via the File/Preferences panel.

The next tool (a green disk with crisscrossing roads) is the Show Neighborhood button. The neighborhood is a collection of 3D objects that work like bookmarks in a Web browser. After first installing Pioneer, the neighborhood is the home file that's automatically loaded when you run the program. You can change the home file in the File/Preferences panel. When you're in a VRML space that you want to be able to recall readily, activate the Add to Neighborhood tool from the Show Neighborhood pop-up and then click on an easily identifiable object. This object and the URL from which it came are copied into your neighborhood collection of objects. After adding an object, use File/Save

351

Neighborhood to make the change permanent. To access your neighborhood, use the Show Neighborhood button.

The next icon (the yellow arrow) is the Publish tool. This tool allows files to be transferred via FTP to directories on remote machines, facilitating the exchange of WRL files in a common space. See the Help file for more information

The next pop-up contains tools for the four World Browsing methods: Fly, Walk, Encircle Selected Object, and Move to Selected Object. I'll cover these in more detail shortly. Finally, there's a View group that corresponds to trueSpace2's.

NOTE: For best results when following these tutorials—and when using Pioneer in general—you should use the Solid Render (3DR) display.

LESSON 1: BROWSING CYBERSPACE

When you first run Pioneer, it loads a default Neighborhood world containing a collection of objects, including a robot, a spider, and the Eiffel Tower, that link you to various virtual worlds on the World Wide Web. In this lesson, you'll learn how to use Pioneer's world-browsing tools.

1. Position the mouse pointer over the various objects, keeping your eye on the URL line near the bottom of the display. You can see the URL address of the location each object is linked to, as well as the location's description in the Help bar. You'll also notice that the mouse cursor changes to a small cube that says 3D when it's over a linked object.

2. Click on an object. If you're on line or are set up to go on line, this click loads the VRML file the object points to from the file's Web site. If you aren't on line, nothing happens. To return to the previous world, click the Back tool (left arrow).

When you start the program, you are using the Fly navigation method, as shown by the airplane icon next to the Publish tool, so let's explore how this type of navigation works.

3. Move the mouse cursor into the workspace, click the left button and hold, and roll the mouse forward. After a short distance, stop rolling but keep the mouse button held down. Your forward movement continues until you release the mouse button (but don't release it yet). This continuing motion is the identifying characteristic of the Fly navigation method.

4. Drag the mouse forward a bit more. The forward movement is accelerated.

5. To slow down, drag in the opposite direction. If you continue dragging toward you, you'll actually stop and then start flying backward! Try to return to your approximate starting location.

6. Left-button drag the mouse to the left, stop for a moment while still holding the mouse button, then drag back to the right. Instead of moving the viewpoint (as in trueSpace2), you're rotating it.

7. Release the mouse button to stop the "flying" movement.

8. Press and hold both mouse buttons and drag forward and back. This time you're changing your pitch, rotating the point of view up and down.

9. Next, release the left mouse button, press and hold the right button, and move the mouse forward and back. Now you're flying straight up and down in the air!

10. Try the Walk navigation method. From the Fly method pop-up menu, select the icon that looks like a pair of walking shoes. The Walk method works the same as Fly mode, but the motion ceases when you stop dragging the mouse.

11. Available from the same pop-up are the Encircle Selected Object and Move to Selected Object tools. To use these, you must first select an object. Do this in World Browsing mode by right-clicking on the object. Then try both these tools.

TIP: If you're working in the Wireframe Display and see objects disappearing, open the Render Options panel and turn off Constant Frame Rate.

12. Navigate around some more in the various modes and see if you can end up near where you started.

LESSON 2: BUILDING CYBERSPACE

In this tutorial, you'll create and paint a simple octagonal "house," using many techniques you already know from trueSpace2. Along the way, I'll point out a few differences between Pioneer and trueSpace2.

1. Earlier, I mentioned the difference between World Building and World Browsing modes. Right now, on the VRML scene, you're still in Browsing mode. Select File/World/New. This automatically places you in World Building mode (see Figure 13-2), where you can manipulate existing objects and create new ones. The URL bar goes away, the familiar reference grid or checkered floor appears, and several tool groups appear. You'll recognize most of these from trueSpace2. As in World Browsing mode, the Fly navigation method is still in effect.

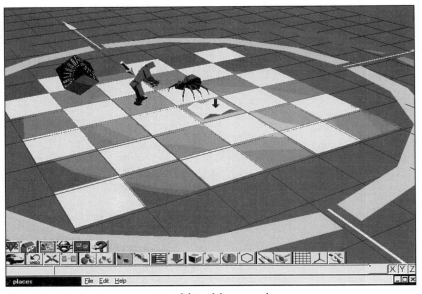

Figure 13–2 Pioneer in World Building mode

Let me take a moment to point out a few significant differences between the Pioneer and trueSpace2 interfaces. The Object tool is available from the Fly tool's pop-up (the airplane), as are the Walk, Encircle, and Move To tools. To the immediate right, the Object Move, Rotate, and Scale tools are combined in a single pop-up. There are no Eye Move, Eye Rotate, or Zoom tools; nor are there any orthogonal view tools. And because the current VRML specification does not support animation, there are no animation tools. One new addition is the Help tool (the question mark). To get information on another tool, click on the Help tool and then on the tool in question. Also new are the Task Tutorials, which you can access from the Help menu. I'll cover some of the other differences later on in this chapter.

You may find that the floor in Pioneer slows down your navigation somewhat, because it requires additional rendering. If this is the case, you can turn it off. Right-click the 3DR tool and, in the Render Quality panel, click the Toggle Shaded Grid icon. This changes the floor to a wireframe grid. By the way, notice that Pioneer's Render Quality panel contains several controls found in trueSpace2's Preferences panel, including the Texture Res, Scene Detail, and Default Lighting pop-up menus. Close the Render Quality panel by clicking the Close box in its upper-left corner.

Now let's start building the octagonal house.

1. Use the Regular Polygon tool to draw an octagon about 2 or 3 meters in diameter.

2. If you're working in Solid Render Display mode and have the checkered grid (solid floor) turned on, use the Object Move tool to raise the octagon up a short distance so it's visible.

3. Use File/World/Save As to save the scene as VRMLTUT1.WRL. Before saving the file, Pioneer presents you with an Export VRML File dialog. Ignore it for now and click OK to save.

4. Click the Sweep tool to extrude the octagon a short distance upward.

5. Let's make the extrusion higher. You're now in Point Move mode. Right-button drag upward in the workspace to raise the octagon's top surface so it's about 1 meter (1 grid square) high (see Figure 13-3). If you right-click the Sweep tool, you'll see that Pioneer does not offer trueSpace2's numeric equivalent panels.

6. Click the Sweep tool to extrude the octagon again, doubling its height. You now have a two-story building.

7. Select the Object tool.

8. Let's paint the entire object gold, then paint parts of it blue. Choose the Paint Face tool. Notice that the Shader/Maps panel is considerably simplified.

9. In the Material Color panel, click just to the lower right of the hexagon's top-right corner.

10. Now apply this color to your shape. Access the Paint tool pop-up menu; all trueSpace2's variants are present.

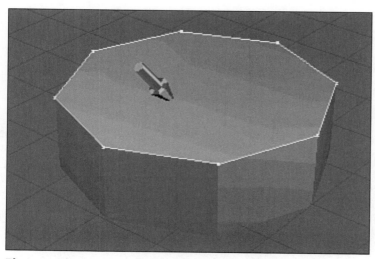

Figure 13-3 Octagon extruded to correct height

11. Select the Paint Object tool. If you're in Wireframe mode, all you'll see is the object's wireframe redrawn. Pioneer has no rendering capability other than that supplied by 3DR.

12. Change the current material to blue by clicking on the Material Color hexagon's lower-left corner.

13. Now paint four faces on the lower half of every other side face of the object. Move the mouse cursor into the workspace and notice that it changes to a paintbrush. Position it over the lower half of one of the building's sides facing 45° *away* from you (next to the side that's facing directly *toward* you) and click. The entire polygon is repainted blue.

14. Paint the lower half of the other 45° side. Your object should look like Figure 13-4.

15. Now rotate the building half a turn and paint the two polygons opposite the first two. Select the Object Rotate tool from the pop-up.

16. Right-button drag horizontally to spin the building about 180°. If you're not sure if it's 180°, rotate the object back until one of the blue polygons appears, then slowly rotate it away again until you're sure it's half a turn. That's one of the benefits of working in Solid Render mode; you can always see what's what in color!

17. Reselect the Paint Face tool and, again, paint the bottom half of the two sides facing 45° away from you.

Figure 13–4 Two polygons painted blue

18. To add a "roof" to the building, activate the Point Edit: Faces tool. (No variants available here.) Click the top surface of the building to select it.

19. Click and hold on the Sweep tool to bring up its variant menu; then drag upward to the Tip tool and release. This automatically creates a conical roof.

20. Raise the roof peak a bit by right-button dragging upward in the workspace.

21. Save the scene as VRMLTUT2.WRL.

Using the Camera in Pioneer

If you don't add a camera to your Pioneer scenes, upon loading them the program uses a default point of view that isn't the same as trueSpace2's. Create your own default viewpoint by adding and positioning a camera.

1. Load the VRMLTUT2.WRL scene file you saved at the end of the previous tutorial, even if you're continuing directly from there.

Instead of the previous view, angled down into the workspace, the point of view is at ground level. You can restore the standard trueSpace2 default view by selecting the Reset View tool from the Close All Panels pop-up. However, if you're going to be publishing VRML worlds on the Web, you don't know which browser will be used, so you can set a default viewpoint by adding and aiming a camera.

2. Activate the Reset View tool from the Close All Panels pop-up, just to the left of the Question Mark icon.

3. Open the Primitives panel and select the Add Camera tool to place a new camera object in the workspace.

4. Use the Object Move tool to position the camera where you'd like the default point of view to be.

5. Use the Object Rotate tool to aim the camera. (Pioneer lacks the Look At function.)

6. Use the View from Object tool, available from the Perspective View pop-up, to view the scene from the camera.

7. Save this scene as VRMLTUT3.WRL.

8. Load the scene and you'll see that the default viewpoint is from the camera.

VRMLIZING YOUR SCENES

A VRML file, which is what you create when you save a WRL-format scene in Pioneer, contains a number of entities called *nodes*. One of the most powerful types of node is called WWWInline.

Until now, when you've saved Pioneer worlds, you've saved all objects in the world explicitly as parts of that scene. When you specify an object as inlined and save the scene, the object is saved in a separate file that you specify, and the main scene then contains only a reference to that file. When the main scene file is loaded, Pioneer sees the reference and loads the inlined object file, too. The powerful aspect is that the inline object can be anywhere on the World Wide Web! Thus, you can build 3D worlds that contain objects from many different Web sites, not just objects you've created.

LESSON 3: INLINING AND LINKING

In this tutorial, you designate your building object to be inlined. Then you add a link so that, when you click the building, the link is executed.

1. Open the VRMLTUT3.WRL file. Make sure you're in World Building mode.

2. Select the house object.

3. Open the Object Info panel by right-clicking the Object tool, the Fly or Walk Mode tool, or the Switch to World Browsing Mode tool. To set the building to be inlined, click the Inlined check box. Then close the panel. Now, when you save the scene, the inlined object or objects will be saved as separate files.

4. Save the scene as VRMLTUT4.WRL—but before you click OK, let's take a brief look at the Export VRML File dialog (see Figure 13-5).

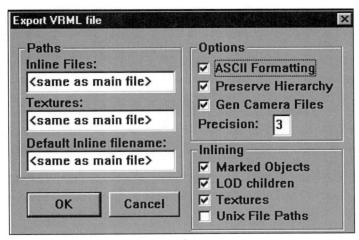

Figure 13–5 The Export VRML file dialog

In the Paths section on the left side, the Inline Files box gives the directory path in which objects specified as inlined are saved, and Default Inline filename shows the names under which those objects are saved. The defaults for both are <same as main file>. This means the inlined object files are saved in the same directory path as the main scene file, and they derive their names from the scene file's name. In the Inlining section of the dialog, Marked Objects is selected. This means objects marked as inlined get saved as separate files.

Now go ahead and finish the save by clicking OK. If you are curious about VRML programming, take a minute to look at the file. Otherwise, you can skip to Step 5. Use Windows multitasking to run a text editor or word processing application. Execute the File/Open command, navigate to the PIONEER directory, and find the file named VRMLTUT4.WRL. Open it and page to the end. You'll see something like the following at the end of the file:

```
DEF NoName_1 WWWInline {
     name    "vrmlt000.wrl"
     bboxSize 4.203 2.735 4.203
     bboxCenter 1.240 1.367 -0.862
     }
```

The above lines identify the object as inlined, give its file name, and specify the size and location of its bounding box.

When you're ready, quit and return to Pioneer.

5. Use the Scene/Open command and take a look at the directory. There is now a file named VRMLT000.WRL that was referred to in the main scene file. This is the inlined object file. Pioneer names the inlined object files using the first five characters of the main scene file's name, plus a three digit number, counting up from 000. Thus, if there were three inlined objects, their file names would be VRMLT000.WRL, VRMLT001.WRL, and VRMLT002.WRL. (You needn't open the inlined object file unless you're really curious.)

Linking Objects to VRML Scenes

The real power of the World Wide Web is in hypertext links. When you click on a highlighted word or phrase, you jump instantly to another location that may be halfway around the (physical) world. VRML has an equivalent function, which is quite easy to implement. In this tutorial, you'll link your building to a VRML world file on your hard drive or on the Caligari Web site.

1. Start Pioneer, load the VRMLTUT4.WRL scene, and select the building object.

2. Click the Attach URL tool (its icon looks like the Earth with a blue chain across it). The Attach URL Link dialog appears, with a text cursor in the URL to Jump To field.

3. Type the following, but don't press ENTER:

```
c:\pioneer\main.wrl
```

As you can see, the URL needn't be a Web address, as long as it uses a legitimate path and file name. (If you installed Pioneer on a drive other than C, you'll need to substitute that drive's letter for the first character above, and if you used a different path, enter the appropriate information.) The MAIN.WRL file is a VRML world file that comes with Pioneer.

Alternatively, if you're on line, you might like to link to the Web address of the same file on Caligari's site:

`http://www.caligari.com/vrml_z/main.wrl`

(This address was correct at the time of printing, but it may have changed since then.)

4. If you like, press TAB or click in the URL Description: field and type a description of the scene.

5. Press ENTER or click on the Attach button.

6. Save the scene as VRMLTUT5.WRL.

7. Enter Browse mode and position the mouse over the building object. The address and description you entered appear at the bottom of the screen.

8. Click on the building; after a few seconds, you'll see the main scene displayed on your monitor.

9. To return to your own scene, click the Back tool (Left Arrow icon). Couldn't be easier!

Linking Objects to HTML Pages

If you're on line and have installed an HTML browser such as Netscape Navigator, you can also link 3D objects to 2D HTML pages. You'll change the link so that, when you click the object, you're transferred to your HTML browser displaying Caligari's home page.

1. For best results, run your HTML browser and minimize it.

2. Run Pioneer, if necessary, and load the VRMLTUT5.WRL scene.

3. Go to World Building mode and select the building object. Again click the Attach URL tool. You'll see the previous link you entered in the dialog.

4. Change the link to the following:

`http://www.caligari.com`

5. Press ENTER or click the Attach button.

6. Save the scene file again.

7. Return to World Browsing mode and click the building. If your browser isn't already running, the Locate HTML Browser dialog appears, so navigate to your browser's directory and open the browser program. Your HTML browser is now loaded (if necessary) and brought to the front, and Caligari's home page appears. (This doesn't always work correctly if the browser isn't already running, which is why I recommend running it first.)

This is the end of the introductory tutorial section. You've learned most of what you need to know to use Pioneer. You know how to walk and fly around in World Browsing mode, how to get into World Building mode to create your own 3D scenes, and how to attach URL addresses to objects so you can link them to other scenes and pages.

NOTE: A new feature added just before this book went to press is the 3D sound function, whose tool is available from the Attach URL Link pop-up. This lets you attach sound files to objects, which activate within a certain distance range from the object. You can find more information on this feature in the Pioneer Help file, under World Building/Adding 3D Sound.

LEVEL OF DETAIL

You've covered quite a bit of ground in this chapter, but one vital concept remains. Level of detail (LOD) is an important part of VRML.

When you move around in the world, you don't see the same amount of detail viewing an object from a distance as you do when viewing it from close up. For example, imagine a high-rise office building construction site (the closest thing we have to wire-frame meshes in the real world). If you're several blocks away, you see only the large I beams and other principal elements. Up closer, you can see the smaller cross-beams. The thousands of rivets are visible only when you're practically standing on top of the thing.

Similarly, because of perspective in a virtual 3D world, faraway objects are drawn so small on the screen that there aren't enough pixels to resolve their full detail. Most 3D programs try to draw them in full detail anyway, wasting rendering time and slowing down the navigation process.

Fortunately, VRML lets you specify levels of detail at various distances for each object in your 3D world. You can set things up so a faraway object's structure is simple and quick to draw, but the same object, when viewed close up, is fully detailed. You can specify many levels of detail for each object, but usually you won't need more than three or four. To accomplish this, create versions of the same object, combine the versions into one multi-LOD object, and specify the distances from the user point of view at which each version is displayed.

Pioneer fully supports this LOD capability. For example, if you have people in a scene, you can tell Pioneer to represent the people at a significant distance with stick figures, but to draw the nearby folks with clothes, hands, headgear, and so on. Once you've modeled an object's various detail levels, it's absurdly easy to set up.

LESSON 4: ADDING LEVEL OF DETAIL TO A SCENE

In this tutorial, you'll create three levels of detail for the house object you worked on in the previous lesson. The simplest level will be a cylinder. The existing house is the second level. For the third level, you'll add some wings.

1. Start by modifying your octagonal house model. Run Pioneer if necessary and load the VRMLTUT4.WRL scene file.

2. If you're in World Browsing mode, enter World Building mode.

3. Select the octagonal building object. This is the LOD2 object—that is, the second simplest level of detail for the set of house objects.

You want to embellish the LOD2 object to add a bit of complexity, creating an LOD3 object. But because each level of detail must be represented by a separate object, make a copy of the LOD2 and modify that.

4. First, a name. Open the Object Info panel. Click in the box next to Name, change the name to HouseB, and press (ENTER). You can use any name you like, but it helps to use a descriptive one. Close the Object Info panel.

5. Now make a copy of the house. Select the Copy tool, which in Pioneer is on the Erase pop-up menu, or press (CTRL)-(C). You now have two identical copies in the same place, so there's no visible change.

6. Let's see what has actually happened to the database. Select the Object List tool, which resembles trueSpace2's Animation Project tool, to open the Objects window. In the list of items, you now have objects named HouseB and HouseB,1, and the latter one is selected.

7. Because you want to work on HouseB,1, keeping it in the center of the workspace, you want to move the other object out of the way. Select HouseB by clicking on its name. Close the Objects window.

8. Use the Object Move tool to position HouseB on the left side of the screen, not touching the copy.

9. Select the copy, HouseB,1, by clicking on it.

Adding Wings to the House

10. Now apply a Sweep operation to all four colored polygons to create wings for the house. Activate the Point Edit Faces tool and select one of the visible blue polygons. It's now outlined in green. Press and hold (CTRL) and click on the other visible blue poly. Now they're both highlighted.

11. Select the Object Rotate tool and right-button drag left or right to spin the house object half a turn, so you can see the two unselected blue faces. Press and hold (CTRL) again and select the other two blue faces so they're highlighted as well.

12. Select the Sweep tool. All four faces are extruded outward from the house's vertical center.

13. The house is now starting to look like a mansion, but the wings could stand to be somewhat longer. Right-button drag in the workspace to extend the wings by a meter or so.

14. Use the Object Move tool to position the "mansion" on the right side of the workspace.

15. Give the newly modified house a name. Open the Object Info panel, click in the space next to Name, and enter the name HouseC. This is the LOD3 object.

16. Use the Primitives panel to add a cylinder of longitude 8 to the workspace. Name the cylinder HouseA and scale it to be about the same size as the first house.

17. At last, you're ready to demonstrate LOD. Your workspace should resemble Figure 13-6. The cylinder object, which is closest to the center of the workspace, should be selected; if it's not, select it now.

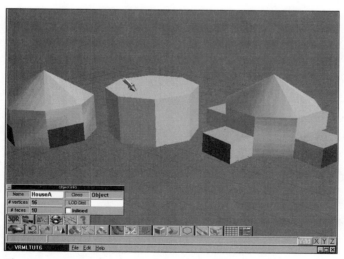

Figure 13–6 The three "house" objects before LOD grouping

One of the beauties of Pioneer's LOD function is that you needn't combine objects in any particular order. The program bases the combination of the order in which they appear, as distance changes, on the relative complexity or polygon/vertex count. In this tutorial, you'll use a specific order of grouping, because grouped LOD objects are combined at the first selected object's location.

18. From the Glue tool pop-up, select the Group LOD tool. (Its icon resembles a cone and a pyramid, connected by a blue line, and it's described in the Help bar as Group several objects together as Level of Detail Representations.)

19. Click on the original house object and then on the mansion.

When you select the first house object, it seems to replace the cylinder, and when you click on the mansion, that object seems to vanish. Actually, HouseA and HouseC are just hiding; you can see only one object at a time in an LOD grouping.

20. Let's check it out! Select the Fly or Walk Through World tool.

21. Click and hold the left mouse button in a blank part of the workspace and drag forward and backward; at certain points you'll see the LOD objects appear. Farthest away, you see the cylinder. As you get closer, you see HouseB. Finally, the most complex object, HouseC, appears when you're very close.

22. This also works when moving the object nearer and farther away with the Object Move tool. Try it now.

As you move the object nearer and then farther away, observe the changes in the Object Info panel. First, the LOD object has been renamed NoName,1. More important, the LOD Dist value changes with distance. The closest object's LOD Dist value is relatively meaningless, because the most complex object always appears when the distance is less than the second object's LOD Dist value. When the distance is greater than the third object's LOD Dist value, the cylinder appears. In this case, the original octagonal house appears at distances between 15 and 20 meters, and the other two objects appear outside that range.

23. Try manipulating the LOD Dist values for the second and third objects; then move in and out again and observe the differences.

24. If you want to go back and edit a member of an LOD group, you'll need to break up the group. Fortunately, that's easy to do in Pioneer. Select the house object and then, from the Glue/Group LOD pop-up, select the Ungroup Level of Detail objects as a Regular Scene objects tool. (It has a red cross between a cone and pyramid.) The objects are restored as discrete entities, but they all remain in the same place, so you may see parts of some of them poking out.

25. Spread the objects out and use the Inspect and Paint Object tools to apply the gold paint to the cylinder. Then recombine them. Now you get a more natural transition between the objects when you move in and out.

26. Save the scene as VRMLTUT6.WRL. This time, when the Export VRML File dialog appears, stop for a moment and take a look at the Options section.

The ASCII Formatting choice is also known as "pretty formatting." When this option is enabled, the saved VRML file is formatted with indents to make it more readable. If you don't care about readability and want to save disk space, turn off this option. Similarly, the Preserve Hierarchy option makes saved files easier to understand. Turn it off to save space. The Precision setting lets you determine to how many places floating-point values in your files are written out. The default value is 3. If accuracy to the thousandths place isn't necessary, set this this value to 1 or 2 to make your files smaller.

Most other Pioneer features are explained in the Help and Readme files. Bear in mind when using this program that Pioneer, like VRML itself, is a work in progress, so things may not always go as anticipated. You've got to be adventurous to work on the cutting edge!

WHAT NOW?

When using an advanced program such as trueSpace2, even experienced users need all the help they can get. In the appendices that follow, you'll find lots of resources for getting answers to specific questions, lists of frequently asked questions (FAQs) with answers, free object and texture files, a quick reference guide to the program, and information on using trueSpace2 in conjunction with other programs.

A
ADDITIONAL RESOURCES

You'll quickly outgrow the introductory material in this book and find yourself wanting to know more about how to use trueSpace2. A huge amount of helpful information is out there, and you can find almost all of it in that nebulous entity known as cyberspace. This appendix will help you locate online information as well as available sources in print. It also provides the names of some companies that sell collections of 3D models.

INFORMATION IN PRINT

At this writing, there are three U.S.-published print magazines dedicated to 3D computer graphics and animation. I highly recommend regular perusal of all these. Many of the articles are about programs other than trueSpace2, but the magazines often contain practical advice that is useful within the context of almost any 3D application. You should be able to find them in the computer magazine section of any well-stocked retailer of periodicals. If you're interested in contributing articles and/or submitting images to any of them, pick up a copy for general guidelines.

🛰 10 Tara Boulevard, 5th Floor, Nashua, NH 03062-2801

🛰 Editorial email 74674.1553@compuserve.com

🛰 Editorial phone 603-891-0123

🛰 Editorial fax 603-891-0539

🛰 Subscription inquiries email cary@pennwell.com, phone 918-853-3161 ext. 400, fax 918-831-9497, TDD 918-831-9566

Computer Graphics World, at 18 years and counting, is by far the longest-running member of this group. The emphasis in recent years has been on high-end professional applications of 3D graphics, as well as computer-aided design (CAD) graphics.

3D Artist

PO Box 4787, Santa Fe, NM 87502

Phone 505-982-3532

Fax 505-820-6929

Email editors@3dartist.com

Web site http://www.3dartist.com/

3D Artist, the only independent magazine listed here, is a small (in page count) but valuable publication loaded to the gills with practical information including how-to's, reviews, and advice. The company also publishes an electronic 3D graphics newsletter, available on its Web site, called *Tessellation Times* (*Tess,* for short).

3D Design

600 Harrison Street, San Francisco, CA 94107

Email kdove@mfi.com

Subscription information 800-829-2505 or 904-445-4662; fax 904-446-2774

3D Design is the newest and slickest of this in-print trio. It has regular coverage of a wide range of programs and applications. The publisher, Miller Freeman, also sponsors an annual 3D Design conference and trade show, the first of which was held in June 1996 in San Francisco.

GOING ONLINE

I bought my first computer, an Atari 800, in 1982. Shortly afterward, I got a modem (a 300 bit-per-second screamer), and I've been on line ever since—first with local bulletin board systems and friends, later on the commercial information service CompuServe, and most recently with the Internet (I'm also still on CompuServe).

As far as I'm concerned, a modem is as important a peripheral as a disk drive—perhaps even more so, because your modem and a phone line give you access to information from millions of computers (and computer users) all over the world. On the Internet today, most people can almost instantly get their hands on terabytes of digital data, for little more than the price of a local phone call.

Online, you'll be able to find a virtually unlimited supply of free and low-cost programs, 3D objects, and 2D images you can use in your 3D image making. All kinds of helpful tips and tricks are out there, as well as answers to just about any question you might have on using trueSpace2. And 3D online worlds are available in which you can explore with Pioneer and other VRML browsers. When you're ready to show your work to the world, you can contribute images to Web sites such as Caligari's, or even create your own.

If you don't have a modem, the most valuable advice I can give you is to get one as soon as possible. Get the fastest modem you can afford. Spend a few more dollars now, and you'll save time and money in the long run. Nowadays, 28.8Kbps modems are affordable, and that's the kind you should get.

Buy a name-brand modem, such as U.S. Robotics. You might think they're all the same, but they're not. The few dollars you might save on an off-brand modem won't be worth its potential for causing you hair-pulling frustration.

Internal or external? With an internal modem, as long as the connection is okay, there's no problem. But if the online service drops the carrier, which can and does happen, there are no LEDs to stop glowing and let you know that you have to reconnect. Internal modems can't be reset simply by turning them off and on again when a connection goes screwy—you have to reset the whole computer, which takes a lot more time. Another disadvantage is that you can't easily transport them between computers.

On the plus side, internal modems don't take up any desk space or serial port connections—assuming you have a free slot in your computer. They're cheaper; and they usually come with their own high-speed serial port chips. (Many PC makers, even today, save a few dollars by using older slow UARTs [serial port chips], and you need the high-speed chips to take advantage of faster modems.)

THE CALIGARI CONNECTION

Caligari has a forum on CompuServe (GO Caligari), but the company Web site at http://www.caligari.com is much more active and up to date.

Figure A-1 shows the Caligari home page as of this writing, although it will probably be different when you get there.

The trueSpace Mailing List

On Caligari's Web site, you'll find a number of interesting sections. One of the most valuable isn't actually on the site; it's a mailing list that you can subscribe to on the site. A mailing list is an ongoing discussion conducted via email, to which anyone can subscribe and contribute. New users often post questions about something that's puzzling them, and within a few hours several helpful answers are available from experienced trueSpace2 artists. List members often share useful information, such as a new 3D-related Web site or a source for free mesh objects. When members create their own Web sites, they often post that address to the list, and very often these pages contain links to other useful 3D-related sites.

Figure A-1 The Caligari Web home page

Caligari's Web Site

Here's a list of the various areas on Caligari's Web site, with brief descriptions of each.

Art Gallery

The Art Gallery is a showcase of trueSpace2-generated renderings submitted by users. All the images are represented as small pictures called *thumbnails*; click on a thumbnail to see the image full size. The Commercial section shows the use of trueSpace2 in professional software, such as the recent game Zapitalism, created by LavaMind. The Top 10 area (see Figure A-2) features thumbnails of 10 of the best recent images, both commercial and noncommercial. The Non-commercial area offers a range of images created by enthusiasts who work more for their own aesthetic satisfaction than for profit. This page links to the Picture library, which is a list of downloadable pictures in JPEG format with text files describing how they were made. This is a great place to go when you're seeking a little inspiration; all the images are of professional quality and many are quite stunning.

Caligari

The Caligari area offers a Company Backgrounder with information on the company's history and goals, job openings for those seeking employment with the company, and information on how to contact Caligari employees, where you can explore individual employees' home pages, and related files.

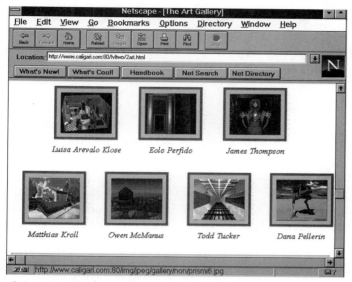

Figure A-2 The Gallery Top 10 area

VRML

The VRML area (see Figure A-3) provides information on VRML and Caligari Pioneer, as well as links to a number of online 3D worlds created with Pioneer. Here's the menu:

- Join worldBuilders mailing list
- Get info on Caligari Pioneer
- Download Pioneer
- Configuring your HTML browser
- Access VRML worlds, compressed using GZIP
- Access VRML worlds, uncompressed
- Get info on Caligari worldBuilder
- Access worlds created by Pioneer Users
- A VRML Primer
- What is VRML?

What does VRML do?

How does VRML compare with HTML?

Where can I learn more about VRML?

News

The News section covers product upgrades, offers special promotions and beta software, and has a list of recent press releases linked to the full text of each.

Support

The Support section gives information on how to contact the company, as well as how to subscribe (or unsubscribe) to the two Caligari-oriented mailing lists. There are separate frequently asked question (FAQ) lists for trueSpace SE, trueSpace2, and Pioneer. You can link to updates of Caligari software and support programs such as 3DR and Win32S. Also, there's a link to Caligari's File library, which has sections for trueSpace2, Pioneer, and utilities.

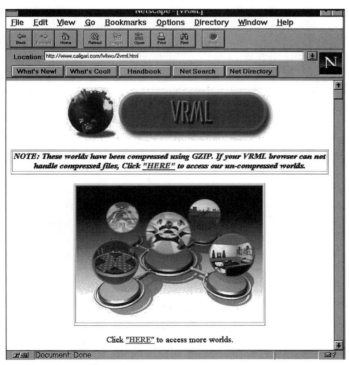

Figure A–3 The VRML area

Following is a list of files in the trueSpace2 section, with brief descriptions:

- ts1demo.zip truSpace 1 / SE Demo

- ts2trial.txt trueSpace 2 Trial Version instructions

- ts2trial.zip trueSpace 2 Trial Version (full distribution)

- ts2-1.exe trueSpace 2 Trial Version (part 1 of 4)

- ts2-2.exe trueSpace 2 Trial Version (part 2 of 4)

- ts2-3.exe trueSpace 2 Trial Version (part 3 of 4)

- ts2-4.exe trueSpace 2 Trial Version (part 4 of 4)

- 3dr_208.txt Info for version 2.0.8 of 3DR

- 3dr_208.zip Version 2.0.8 of Intel's 3DR

- 3dr_2014.txt Info for version 2.0.14 of 3DR (README!)

- 3dr_2014.zip Latest tested verion of Intel's 3DR

- vfw1_1e.zip MicroSoft Video for Windows 1.1e

- w32s1_25.txt Info about Win32s

- w32s1_25.zip Latest version of Microsoft Win32s

- bugform.txt Bug report form

- add_ons/ DIR Add on software

- animations/ DIR Animations created with trueSpace

- info/ DIR Tech Documents about trueSpace

- objects/ DIR trueSpace Objects

- pictures/ DIR Images created primarily with trueSpace

- scenes/ DIR trueSpace Scenes

- updates/ DIR trueSpace updates

Also in the Support section is a link to the Hot Links page, with the following list of Web sites of interest to trueSpace2 users:

- WebWorlds: A Modeling Approach to VRML with Caligari Pioneer

- The Unofficial trueSpace Tips page

- Dub's trueSpace F/X page, with downloadable files that let you create such sought-after effects as lens flare, smoke, explosions, star sphere, and animated bump-mapped ripples, plus links to other trueSpace2-related sites of interest

- Mark Jeffers' 3D Resource Page, with 3D objects, textures, tutorials on planet scenes, terrain and landscapes, radiant light sources, and more

- Destination: Cyberspace is an online game that requires a Java-capable browser

- Robots in 3D by Bob Fergusson combines Bob's interest in 3D computer graphics and animation with a childhood fascination with robots and "neat space stuff"

- LavaMind Games & Entertainment

- The kinte space is a poetry-oriented site that incorporates trueSpace2-rendered images

- Naked Hoof is Bill Anderson's home page, with glass and metal material libraries available for download

- RSS / trueSpace resource page: Reliable Software Solutions

- Kroll Graphics (German)

Products

A Products section provides descriptions of Caligari's software plus lists of awards and dealers, as well as a Library section that offers information on Caligari mailing lists, File formats, and downloadable trueSpace add-ons, such as Exploder, Intel Indeo for video compression, and Landscape Maker.

DAVID HENION'S RESOURCES LIST

If you subscribe to the trueSpace mailing list (highly recommended!), you'll regularly find mailing list member David Henion's compilation of useful information for trueSpace users in your electronic mailbox. A recent version is reproduced below. David's email address is david.henion@pobox.com and his Web page is at http://www.pobox.com/~david.henion.

Resources for trueSpace-Related Help and Information

by David Henion
This weekly post is a service provided to new users of trueSpace, and this mailing list is to guide you toward other resources to help answer your questions about trueSpace.

The TSML (trueSpace Mailing List) is a community of artists, designers, engineers, hobbyists, and all walks of trueSpace users. Posting your question here (or just reading the posts by other users) is a great way to learn about trueSpace and to find the answers to your questions.

However—there are many other places where you can find TS information! Before posting your question to this mailing list, you may want to check these other places first—sometimes you can find the answer to your question instantly instead of waiting for someone to answer your post.

FIRST: Check your manual: The manual for trueSpace2 is in two parts: a "User" manual and a "Reference" manual—CHECK THEM BOTH. Some subjects are covered in only one, some subjects are covered in both. Check both the table of contents and the index carefully. Some of the more complex subjects are discussed only very briefly—but if you read it carefully and experiment, most answers are there.

SECOND: Check the "trueSpace Tips" pages: David Campbell (a member of this mailing list) has collected many of the tips that have been discussed here and put them on his site. The URL is http://www.realtime.net/~dcampbel/ts_tips.html. Topics covered include: modeling, materials, lighting, rendering, animation, special effects, using TS with other tools, misc, and other resources. (See below for a listing of topics.)

THIRD: Check the mailing list archives at Caligari: The trueSpace Mailing List is maintained by Caligari. They also archive all posts which are viewable sorted by date, author, or subject. Chances are good that someone else posted the information you are looking for already. The URL is http://www.caligari.com/com/ml/tslist.html.

Other Information Resources

- Caligari's home page: http://www.caligari.com/

- Caligari's support page (contains links to the mailing lists, FAQs, file updates, and how to contact Caligari): http://www.caligari.com/lvltwo/2supp.html

- trueSpace related links: http://152.160.186.1/TS_links.html

- Caligari's FTP site: ftp://ftp.caligari.com/pub/

- The "netnet" ftp site: ftp://ftp.netnet.net/pub/mirrors/truespace/

- "Ultimate 3D Links"—a collection of links for objects, textures, modelers, tools, etc: http://www.portraits.com/web/3d/3df.htm

Other Useful Stuff

- "MS VidEdit"—an AVI editor: ftp the three "DISK" directories from ftp.microsoft.com in directory: /developr/drg/Multimedia/Jumpstart/VfW11e/ODK/DISKS/RETAIL/

- To UNSUBSCRIBE from the mailing list: Send mail to "truespace-request@caligari.com" with the word "unsubscribe" in the body of the message.

To get a list of all mailing list commands: Send mail to "truespace-request@caligari.com" with the word "help" in the body of the message.

For various Web "search engines" to find almost anything on the Web: http://home.netscape.com/home/internet-search.html.

THE TRUESPACE TIPS PAGE

As mentioned in David Henion's notes above, David Campbell is another active trueSpace mailing list member who maintains a Web page (http://www.realtime.net/~dcampbel/ts_tips.html). You'll find a vast assortment of useful tips from the mailing list that aren't available anywhere else (unless you spend hours poring through the list archives). To whet your appetite, reprinted below is David's introduction plus a condensation of the list, with the titles of all the tips.

Welcome to the unofficial trueSpace Tips page. The ideas listed here are ones that aren't explicitly covered in the trueSpace documentation. This page compiles the usage tips and tricks from the trueSpace Mailing List (TSML) since the list's inception in December 1994. Therefore, this page is actually owned and authored by many people.

Modeling Tips

Creating New Vertices
Creating New Edges Between Vertices
Deleting Vertices
De-selecting Vertices
Hiding Objects
Object Simplification
Stars
Splatters and Puddles
Fancy Text (TS2 only)
Neon Text
Modeling Humans
Sweeping a keyboard
Diamonds
Rope
Bending Text On A Circular Path
Creating Bent Poles

Materials Tips

Realistic Wood in TS1/TS-SE
Planet textures
Planet atmospheres
Realistic Metal

Object Painting
Glass
Enhancing Shadows with the Paint Vertices Tool
"Cool" Materials
Cloudy Gas (TS2 only)
Copying a Material Rectangle
Compact Disc Rainbow Texture
Texture for Clear Liquid Objects
Texturing Object Faces Using an Independent UV Mapping
Monitoring Materials Changes While Keyframing
BumpMaps Not Rendering
Shimmering Reflection On Flat Surface

Lighting Tips

Tricks with Lights
Aiming Spotlights
Visible Lights
Raytraced Shadows VS Shadow Maps
Light Gels—Projecting Images with Light

Rendering Tips

Transparent Object Showing Black
Render Limit Guidelines
Render "Notch Filter"

Animation Tips

Miscellaneous Animation Hints
Selecting Single Spline Points on an Animation Path
Animating Waves
Animating Events at Regular Intervals
Copying Animation Paths to Other Objects
Deleting Keyframes
Tunnel Run Animations
Orbit Animations
Animating Spotlights
Making Objects Appear or Disappear
Automatic Object Banking
Cut-away Animations

Special Effects Tips

Engine Exhaust Fire
The Ubiquitous Lens Flare

Using trueSpace with Other Tools

Miscellaneous Tips

Other Resources

MESH OBJECT VENDORS

Following is an alphabetical listing of companies that sell collections of 3D objects of all kinds. All collections are compatible with trueSpace2, thanks to its versatile object format conversion capabilities. Many of these companies are more than willing to create custom objects, too—often for a substantial fee, however.

- 3rd Dimension Technologies, 800-455-3558; Web http://www.3dt.net/3D-art/

- Acuris, 800-OK-ACURIS; Web http://www.acuris.com

- Cyberprops, 310-314-2171; fax 310-314-2181; email info@ywd.com; Web http://www.ywd.com

- Graphic Detail, voice/fax 502-363-2986; email michael@iglou.com

- Ketiv Technologies, 800-458-0690; fax 503-252-3668

- Viewpoint DataLabs, 800-DATA-SET; Viewpoint maintains a Web site at http://www.viewpoint.com, where you can find the Avalon collection of free 3D objects: Click on Site Directory and then on Avalon, or browse directly to http://www.viewpoint.com/avalon

- Visual Software, 818-883-7900; fax 818-593-3750

- Zygote Media Group, 800-267-5170 or 801-278-5934; Web http://www.zygote.com

B

TOOLS QUICK REFERENCE

Icon-based functions in trueSpace2 are known collectively as tools, even if they're used for other functions such as changing the view. This appendix briefly describes each of trueSpace2's tools with its icon, name, and associated keystroke, if any. If the tool is part of a pop-up, its entry also mentions whether it is the default tool in its slot or is available from the pop-up.

View Group

The View tool group is attached to the main window. It contains tools for viewpoint navigation, changing the view mode, opening new windows, and view-related utilities. A subset of the View group consisting of the Display Mode, Render, View Select, and View Navigation tools is also present in the smaller auxiliary windows opened with the New Window tools.

Display Modes

 Wireframe Display (default): Redraws the objects in the workspace as wireframes. Use it after rendering or to switch back from Solid Render Display mode. In this mode, a selected object is white, nonselected objects are dark blue, and nonselected objects in a hierarchy are orange.

 Solid Render Display (available from pop-up): Invokes the Intel 3DR library. In this mode, the selected object is always drawn as a solid when at rest and is indicated by a 3D arrow. Depending on its complexity and the Preferences panel's Threshold setting, the object may switch to a bounding box when being manipulated. Other objects may be drawn as solid, wireframes, or bounding boxes, depending on the Preferences panel's Scene Detail setting. Other Solid Render Display options can be set in the Render Quality panel, invoked by right-clicking the Solid Render Display tool.

Render Tools

 Render Current Object (default): Draws the current object as a textured solid, using trueSpace2's standard rendering mode. Not available with this function are ray-tracing-related effects—shadows, refraction, and true reflections—or motion blur and depth of field. Other scene-related effects—fog and global environment—are applied by this function.

 Render Scene (available from pop-up): Draws the entire scene contents plus the optional background as textured solids, using trueSpace2's standard rendering mode. Refraction, true reflections, and shadows are available with this function. Right-clicking this tool opens the Render Options panel.

 Render Scene to File (available from pop-up): Draws the entire scene contents plus the optional background as textured solids, using trueSpace2's standard rendering mode. Saves image or animation to disk. Refraction, true reflections, and shadows are available with this function. Right-clicking this tool opens the Render Options panel.

View Select Tools

 Perspective View (default): Sets the window to a Perspective view, looking at the scene from the point of view of an invisible "eye" that can be moved, rotated, and zoomed in and out.

 Front View (available from pop-up): Sets the window to an Orthogonal view from the front, looking down the y axis. The view cannot be rotated and can be moved only in the x-z plane.

 Left View (available from pop-up): Sets the window to an Orthogonal view from the left side, looking down the x axis. The view cannot be rotated and can be moved only in the y-z plane.

 Top View (available from pop-up): Sets the window to an Orthogonal view from the top, looking down the z axis. The view cannot be rotated and can be moved only in the x-y plane.

 View from Object (available from pop-up): Sets the window to a Perspective view, using the currently selected object as the "camera," looking down the object's z axis.

View Navigation Tools

 Eye Move: Enables viewpoint repositioning by dragging the mouse in the window. Right-click to open Coordinates property panel for setting coordinate system and enabling/disabling movement along specific axes.

Eye Rotate: Enables viewpoint reorientation by dragging the mouse in the window. The orthogonal Front, Left, and Top views cannot be rotated. Right-click to open Coordinates property panel for setting coordinate system and enabling/disabling rotation on specific axes.

 Zoom: Enables enlarging and reducing the scale of the view by dragging the mouse in the window. The view cannot be scaled along specific axes.

New Window Tools

These tools, used for opening smaller auxiliary views into the workspace, are found only in the main window's View tool group. No more than three auxiliary views can be open at once.

 New Perspective View (default): Opens a new auxiliary window in Perspective View mode.

 New Front View (available from pop-up): Opens a new auxiliary window in Front View mode.

 New Left View (available from pop-up): Opens a new auxiliary window in Left View mode.

 New Top View (available from pop-up): Opens a new auxiliary window in Top View mode.

View Utilities

 Close All Panels (default): Closes any open tool property or control panels.

 Dock All Panels (available from pop-up): Aligns any open tool property or control panels above (or below) the "floating" tool groups.

 Look at Object (available from pop-up): In Perspective View mode, rotates the viewpoint to look at the selected object. In Front, Left, and Top View modes, moves the viewpoint to center the selected object. Has no effect in View from Object mode.

 Reset View (available from pop-up): Returns Perspective, Front, Left, and Top View windows to their original positions.

Object Navigation Group

This group contains tools for selecting and manipulating specific objects and navigating through hierarchical objects' vertical levels.

 Object Tool (Space Bar): Returns to object navigation mode from use of other tools, such as Point Edit. Right-click to open the Object Info panel, which allows renaming objects, observing their statistics, and manipulating them via numerical settings.

 Object Move Ⓩ: Enables repositioning of the selected object by dragging the mouse in the workspace. Right-click to open the Coordinates property panel to set coordinate system and enable/disable movement along specific axes.

 Object Rotate Ⓧ: Enables reorientation of the selected object by dragging the mouse in the workspace. Right-click to open the Coordinates property panel to set coordinate system and enable/disable rotation on specific axes.

 Object Scale Ⓒ: Enables resizing of the selected object by dragging the mouse in the workspace. Right-click to open the Coordinates property panel to set coordinate system and enable/disable scaling on specific axes.

 Navigate Down (default at topmost level) ⊡: Select the first object in the first node below the current hierarchical level. Use the ⊡ and ⊡ keys to select other objects in the same node.

 Navigate Up (default at all levels below topmost) ⊡: Select the first object in the first node above the current hierarchical level. Use the ⊡ and ⊡ keys to select other objects in the same node.

Model Group

These tools are for creating and editing custom objects.

Point Edit Tools

The Point Edit tools allow selection of part(s) of the current object (i.e., vertices, edges, and/or faces) for further manipulation. Select multiple nonadjacent elements by holding ⌈CTRL⌉, and select adjacent entities by holding ⌈SHIFT⌉. Selecting any Point Edit tool opens the Point Navigation panel, with Move, Rotate, and Scale tools for manipulating the selected object part(s).

 Context (default): Enables selection of vertices by clicking on edge intersections, selection of edges by clicking on edges between intersections, and selection of faces by clicking on object away from edges and edge intersections.

Faces (available from pop-up): Enables selection of faces only.

 Edges (available from pop-up): Enables selection of edges only.

 Vertices (available from pop-up): Enables selection of vertices only.

 Delete Face (available from pop-up): Enables deletion of all faces clicked on when the tool is active, indicated by the mouse cursor's appearance as an arrow with a small rectangular cut-out and the letter F attached.

Sweep Tools

These tools enable creation of three-dimensional objects from the selected face(s). Faces may be stand-alone or may belong to an existing object.

 Sweep (default): Causes the selected face(s) to be extruded outward. Using the Sweep tool opens the Point Navigation panel, with Move, Rotate, and Scale tools for manipulating the extruded face(s).

 Bevel (available from pop-up): Creates a beveled extrusion, in which outer edges of the face(s) are swept inward and inner edges (i.e., edges of holes in the face(s)) are swept outward.

 Macro/Sweep (available from pop-up): When first invoked, attaches the default or most recently used sweep path to the selected face(s). Rotate the path by dragging the mouse in the workspace or select a different path from the Path library. Select the Macro/Sweep tool again to perform the path sweep.

 Lathe (available from pop-up): When first invoked, attaches the default or most recently used lathe path to the selected face(s). Edit the path by clicking and dragging on its various elements; then select the Lathe tool again to perform the lathe operation.

 Tip (available from pop-up): Sweeps the selected face(s) to a point.

Deform/Sculpt Tools

These tools enable manipulating object surfaces like clay or putty. The first three tools are all on one pop-up; the Sculpt tool occupies its own spot in the Model group.

Deform Object (default): Creates a deformation lattice around an object. Clicking and dragging enables moving, rotating, and scaling of the object surface underlying lattice intersections or cross sections, depending on the options selected in the Deform Navigation panel.

 Start Deforming by Stand-alone Deformation Object (available from pop-up): Creates connection between object and free-standing deformation object (created from Primitives panel). Used for animation; objects must be juxtaposed in space.

 Stop Deforming by Stand-alone Deformation Object (available from pop-up): Breaks connection between object and free-standing deformation object (created from Primitives panel).

 Sculpt Surface: Enables pushing/pulling of object parts with adjustable tool. Selecting this tool opens a panel that allows moving the deformation, adjusting its scope, and copying it to other parts of the object.

Boolean Tools

These tools let you apply Boolean operations to pairs of objects. You cannot use the Boolean tools with objects imported in the DXF format.

 Object Subtraction (default): Enables sculpting of an object by subtracting other objects. First position the two objects by overlapping their volumes. Select the object to be sculpted, then this tool, and finally the object to be subtracted. In some circumstances, can be used to eliminate unnecessary geometry in sculpted object by subtracting a nonoverlapping object.

 Object Intersection (available from pop-up): Creates a new object consisting of overlapping volume of two objects.

 Object Union (available from pop-up): Creates a new object consisting of combined volumes of two objects, which need not overlap.

Polygon Tools

These tools enable the creation of two-dimensional shapes that can be used for a variety of purposes, including as stand-alone flat objects.

 Spline Polygon (default): Allows point-by-point drawing of spline-based polygons, which can be added to a Path library at any point during creation. Right-click in the workspace to close the polygon. The Draw Path panel options allow adjustment of splines before finishing the polygon. Right-click on the tool to get the Spline panel, which allows further modification.

Polygon (available from pop-up): Enables point-by-point drawing of straight-edged polygons. Right-click in the workspace to close the polygon. Use the Poly Modes panel options to implement Boolean operations between polygons.

 Regular Polygon (available from pop-up): Enables click-and-drag, center-outward drawing of regular polygons. Use the Poly Modes panel options to set the number of sides and to implement Boolean operations between polygons.

Utilities Group

This group contains useful tools that don't fit into any other group.

 Grid Snap: Toggles stepwise adjustment of view and creation/manipulation of objects. Right-click to open the Grid panel for numeric adjustment.

 Axes: Toggles object axes' visibility. When the axes are visible, they can be manipulated using standard object navigation tools.

Normalize Tools

These variants set an object or its axes to its original status and center its axes.

 Normalize Rotation (default): Sets the selected object back to its original orientation by aligning its axes with World axes.

 Normalize Location (available from pop-up): Positions the selected object at the center of the workspace at position x=0, y=0, z=0.

 Normalize Scale (available from pop-up): Resizes the selected object to its original scale as created or loaded.

 Center Axes (available from pop-up): Positions a selected object's axes at the object's geometric center and selects axes. Click on Axes tool to return to normal arrangement.

Geometry Tools

These tools affect an object's geometry either directly or indirectly.

 Smooth Quad Divide (default): Subdivides all an object's polygons into quadrangles and/or triangles and adjusts new vertices' positions to smooth outline. Does not affect polygons whose angles to each other exceed Subdivision threshold. Right-click on tool icon to get the Subdivision threshold setting panel.

 Quad Divide (available from pop-up): Subdivides object's polygons without altering new vertices' positions.

Triangulate Object (available from pop-up): Subdivides all an object's nontriangular polygons into triangles.

 Decompose (available from pop-up): Breaks down the surface groups in certain imported objects into object hierarchy.

 Mirror (available from pop-up): Reverses object geometry along World x-z plane.

 Fix Bad Geometry (available from pop-up): Attempts to resolve incorrect geometry in imported objects.

 Reverse Normals (available from pop-up): Flips all an object's faces so that all polygons facing inward will face outward and vice versa. Useful for selecting nonaccessible faces "inside" an object or on a side not facing you.

 Dimensioning Tool (available from pop-up): Creates a nonrenderable "ruler" with dynamically updated measurement between two points on an object.

Edit Group

These tools replicate functions found in the Edit menu and enable building and destroying object hierarchies.

 Undo (default) CTRL-Z: Reverses most recent operation. In most cases, trueSpace2 remembers the most recent sequence of operations, so repeated use of the Undo function reverses each step, in reverse order. Right-click on the Tool icon to access the options panel.

 Redo (available from pop-up): Restores most recently undone operation. Repeated use of Redo applies the operation cumulatively.

 Erase DEL: Deletes selected object from the workspace.

 Copy CTRL-C: Makes an exact copy of the selected object in the same place as the original.

Glue Tools

 Glue as Child (default): Creates hierarchical structure. The object selected before clicking the tool becomes the child of the object selected after clicking the tool.

Glue as Sibling (available from pop-up): Combines objects at the same hierarchical level.

 Unglue (available from pop-up): Available only when subobject of a hierarchical structure is selected. Detaches selected object from structure.

Render Group

Despite the name of this tool group, its tools are actually used to create and modify materials and to apply them to object surfaces.

Paint Tools

Selecting any of these tools automatically opens the four Paint panels for setting material attributes.

 Paint Face (default): Applies the current material to any faces clicked on when this tool is active. Objects need not be selected first. Drag the mouse to paint adjacent faces.

 Paint Object (available from pop-up): Applies the current material to selected object. One-time use only.

 Paint Over (available from pop-up): Replaces the material clicked on in the workspace wherever it exists in that object with the current material.

 Inspect (available from pop-up): Sets the current material to the material clicked on in the workspace.

 Paint Vertices (available from pop-up): The current material, sans texture mapping, is applied to any vertices, blending into the existing material on adjacent faces.

 UV Projection: Enables applying planar, cylindrical, or spherical UV mapping space to an object, which determines how texture maps are "wrapped" onto its surface.

 Material Rectangle: Enables application of discrete rectangles of the current material to object surfaces. Rectangles can be layered, repositioned, and scaled.

 Plug-ins: Enables postrendering processing of rendered scenes with up to four Adobe Photoshop-compatible plug-in filters.

Library Group

These tools provide access to true Space2's Material and Path libraries and Primitives panel.

 Material Library: Opens the Material library, which allows storing, naming, selecting, and deleting materials, as well as viewing stored materials. Also includes functions for saving and loading library files.

 Path Library: Opens the Path library, which allows storing, naming, selecting, and deleting materials. Also includes functions for saving and loading library files.

 Primitives Panel: Opens the Primitives panel, which enables creation of six geometric primitives and stand-alone deform primitives, as well as the addition of camera, text, and light objects.

Animation Group

These tools allow animation setup and modification.

 Animation Tool: Opens the Animation panel, which gives access to basic animation functions including moving between frames and keyframes, recording keyframes, and playing animations. Right-click on the panel's Play button to access the Animation Parameters panel and on the Record button to access a control for toggling automatic animation recording. Right-click on any other button to access the Keyframe Monitor for editing keyframes.

 Animation Path: Enables drawing and editing spline paths along which objects move during an animation. Uses the same additional controls as the Spline Polygon tool.

 Look At (default): Forces an object to continually reorient itself during an animation to keep its z axis pointed at another object. Select the "looker" object first, then this tool, then the object to be looked at.

 Look Ahead (available from pop-up): Forces an object to continually reorient itself during an animation to keep its z axis pointed "forward" on the path along which it moves.

 Animation Project Window: Opens the Animation Project window, with animation editing functions.

C

USING TRUESPACE2 WITH OTHER PROGRAMS

Certainly trueSpace2 is a terrific program, but it cannot and does not do everything. Among the most frequently asked questions on the Internet trueSpace mailing list are ones about how to edit animations, how to add special effects, and how to augment animations with sound. This appendix covers some of the available programs for those functions and more.

You'll find copies of all the shareware programs described here in the SHARWARE directory on the companion CD-ROM. Demo versions of some of the commercial programs covered in this chapter may also be included on the companion CD—check in the DEMOS directory.

EDITING AND ADDING SOUND

Editing animations is much like editing film and video. You take existing footage and splice segments together for added dramatic and/or informational impact. For example, if you're re-creating an automobile accident for a forensic application, you might show the situation from a driver's point of view until just before the point of impact, and then switch to an outside view for the actual collision. You could do this in trueSpace2 by setting keys for the camera, but it's far more advantageous to render the collision from both viewpoints and then combine the separate animations with an editing application. That way, you have much more control over the exact point at which the cut occurs. Another benefit is that you can use the editing program to add sounds—a racing engine, the squeal of brakes, the crash of impact.

This appendix covers several Windows programs for editing animations—Adobe Premiere, Microsoft VidEdit, Autodesk Animator Studio, and Avid Elastic Reality. You should also be aware of the other good applications available, including Razor and Razor Pro from in:sync corporation, MediaStudio from ULead, and Digital Video Producer from Asymetrix. I've chosen to cover Premiere because it's the most popular video-editing program, VidEdit because it's free, Animator Studio because it's specifically designed for animation, and Elastic Reality because it's great for morphing and warping images.

NOTE: All these programs let you create animations from image file sequences, as indicated by consecutive numbers (with leading zeroes) at the end of the first part of the file name. This is important, because AVI files created directly by trueSpace2 are not always of the best quality. In many cases, you'll get significantly improved quality in your animations by rendering sequences of still image files and then compiling them into AVI files with the editing program. The drawback with this method is that it requires a great deal more disk space.

ADOBE PREMIERE FOR WINDOWS

Premiere is far more sophisticated than VidEdit in many ways. You can load several video and/or audio files at once (see Figure C-1) with Premiere. You can also create transitions between tracks and add special effects with filters.

Premiere starts with several open windows. Imported files are placed in a scrolling alphabetical list in the Project window, with graphics files represented by a thumbnail and descriptive information. The program can import the following:

- Still image files in Targa, BMP, JPEG, and other formats

- Movies and animations in AVI, QuickTime MOV, FLI, and FLC formats

- Numbered sequences of BMP, TIFF, and Targa stills

- Digital audio files in WAV and AIF formats

- Certain specialized formats such as title files

If you have the requisite hardware, Premiere can even capture audio and video from outside sources. You can build a movie by dragging items from the Project window to the Construction window, which can contain up to 99 video and 99 audio tracks, plus tracks for transitions and superimposed images. Video clips are shown as sequences of thumbnails.

For "cut" transitions, which make up the vast majority of edits, simply place clips end to end in the same track. To create a special effects transition between two video sequences, overlap them in two separate tracks and drag an icon from the Transitions window to the transitions track in between. Premiere automatically matches the transition duration to the overlap. You can preview the presentation, including transitions, at any

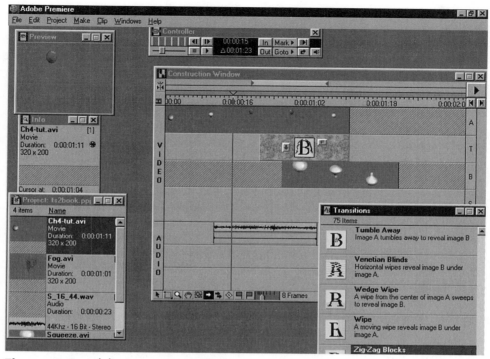

Figure C–1 Adobe Premiere interface

time without delay; simply drag a pointer in the Construction window's time track. But for actual speed playback using the Play button, you must create a preview, which can take a while to build and then runs in the Preview window. The program comes with 75 transitions such as Curtain, Fold Up, and Spiral Boxes, each depicted as a small cycling animation when the Transitions window is active. If that's not enough, you can add your own transitions using the Blend tool in Photoshop and create new mathematics-based transitions with the built-in Transition Factory. The Info window displays (as text) important statistics about the item currently selected in the Construction window, including start and stop time.

To change a video or audio clip's duration, simply drag either end in the Construction window; for greater precision, double-click on the window to open it into a Clipping window. Here you can set "in" and "out" points by a variety of methods, including numeric entry, and play the clip back using the current clipping settings. A Trimming window gives you ultimate precision by letting you add and subtract individual and groups of five frames, showing the exact frames that appear on each side of the edit point. This performs a "ripple" edit, automatically closing the gap and moving all subsequent clips forward in time by the clipped amount.

Premiere comes with 58 filters such as Blur and Lens Flare; their settings can be animated, changing over time, and filters can be applied to isolated parts of clips.

Premiere's new Filter Factory lets you create custom filters with mathematical expressions. Because of its plug-in capability, Premiere can use third-party filters and transitions. Another way to modify a presentation is by superimposing tracks such as titles, which can be created with the built-in Title window, essentially a limited paint program with text capabilities. There are 15 transparency options for superimposed tracks, including Chroma, Luminance, and various alpha channel variations. One extremely powerful and sophisticated feature lets you add motion paths to superimposed tracks, with options to rotate, zoom, distort, and temporarily hold them as they fly.

When it comes time to output the final project, you can specify such options as resolution and file format—AVI, FLI/FLC, or QuickTime movie, filmstrip, and numbered file sequence. With AVI and QuickTime, you can also define compression parameters, including codec, quality, frame, and keyframe rate and color depth. The manual section covering output is informative and includes advice for making movies for playback on CD-ROM. It also describes the Sequence window, useful for storyboarding and quick compilation of a series of clips.

There's much more, such as the ability to treat any segment of tracks as an independent "virtual" clip, giving you practically unlimited mixing capabilities. The manual's final chapter shows how to create such special effects as split edits (e.g., starting a clip's audio before its video) and playing a movie through a traveling matte (i.e., a moving window). In every way, Premiere 1.0 is an essential tool for anyone using video on Macs and Windows PCs.

The User Guide is organized according to functionality, starting with basic concepts. It then moves on to assembling, editing, and previewing movies; using transitions, filters, and motion settings; creating superimpositions and titles; compiling and videotaping movies; and capturing video, and it includes a final chapter on tips and techniques. There are tutorials throughout and an extensive index, plus comprehensive online help. What's more, the CD-ROM that comes with the program contains the User Guide in Acrobat Reader format, along with the Reader program, video tutorials, and several hundred megabytes of clip media.

VIDEDIT

VidEdit is a free Windows video-editing program that Microsoft created to show off its Video for Windows technology. It's included on several of Microsoft's software development kits (SDKs), and you can download it from various locations on the Internet, including ftp://ftp.microsoft.com/developr/drg/Multimedia/Jumpstart/VfW11e/ODK/DISKS/RETAIL/.

A VidEdit tutorial is presented below, but first let's go through a program overview. Though its functionality is more limited than Premiere's, VidEdit is also less memory hungry and therefore preferable for certain small jobs. It's easy to use: Start by opening a video/animation file in AVI or Autodesk FLI/FLC format or an image file sequence in DIB format. (DIB stands for device-independent bitmap and is for all intents and purposes the same as BMP.) You can open a BMP sequence by selecting the first file in the sequence and then choosing DIB Sequence in the Open Video File dialog. If you select a file other than the first one in the sequence, only that file and those with higher numbers are loaded.

After loading a file or sequence, the first frame appears in the center of the program display (see Figure C-2). The bottom line shows the current frame number and total number of frames, the current editing mode (Insert or Overwrite), and other information. At this point, you can play the animation, jump to different parts of the sequence, and set a frame range using the iconic controls underneath the image. The buttons in the upper part of the interface let you zoom in and out, copy and cut frame ranges, and do file operations.

Many other operations are available from the drop-down menus. Among the most useful for trueSpace2 animators is the File/Insert command. The tutorial that follows takes a closer look at this function. Also helpful if you have extra memory is the Video/Load File Into Memory function, which saves time spent reading the frames from disk every time you play the animation.

LESSON 1: EXPLORING VIDEDIT

The best way to learn VidEdit is by reading the Help file (it's very good) and experimenting with the program functions. This simple tutorial will get you started.

1. In trueSpace2, render an animation of 30 frames or so at 320x200 resolution. Name it TEST.DIB. The program will output a sequence of files named TEST0000.DIB, TEST0001.DIB, TEST0002.DIB, etc.

2. If you don't have any other animations on disk, create another short animation in AVI format at a different resolution—say, 400x300.

3. Quit trueSpace2.

4. Run VidEdit and select File/Open. (Look at the List files of type box. The Open function supports only a few different types of files.)

5. Load the first frame in the sequence. The program loads the entire sequence and displays the first frame.

Figure C–2 VidEdit interface

6. Click on the Play button in the lower-left corner of the interface to view the animation.

7. Drag the slider immediately below the image window and move to different parts of the animation. Finish by dragging it all the way to the right, or click on the Next Mark button (>|) to go to the last frame. As you can see, it's blank.

8. Select File/Insert. Scroll through the list List files of type and note the many different file formats that can be inserted.

9. If it isn't already selected, click on Microsoft AVI. Choose any AVI-format animation or video file, or the one you created in Step 2.

10. If the selected animation is in a different resolution than the one currently in memory, the program asks you if you want the new one stretched to fit. Of course, if the first one is smaller, then the second will be reduced in resolution. It's generally best to say Yes to this requester.

11. The new animation is loaded and inserted at the end of the first. Click on the Previous Mark button (|<) to return to the first frame and play the combined animation.

12. Now move part of the inital sequence to the end of animation. Go to the first frame and click on the Mark In: button under the track bar.

13. Drag the slider to frame 10 or so and click on the Mark Out: button. The leftmost part of the slider bar is now shaded, with its endpoints indicated by small triangles.

14. In the upper part of the window, select the Cut icon, which looks like a pair of scissors. The selected portion of the video disappears.

15. Go to the last frame and select the Paste icon, which resembles a clipboard with a small sheet of paper on it. It's difficult to see, but the cut segment has been inserted at the end of the video.

16. Return to the first frame and play the video. The second part of the initial animation plays, followed by the second animation, and finally the first part of the first animation. Video editing—it's that easy!

17. Add a simple soundtrack. Go to the first frame of the second segment. (Hint: You can move forward or backward one frame at a time using the two small arrow buttons at the right end of the track bar.)

18. Select File/Insert and, under List files of type, select Microsoft Waveform. This sets the file dialog to show only WAV-format files.

19. Navigate to the WINDOWS directory and load the TADA.WAV file.

20. Return to the first frame and play the animation. This time, when the second part begins, you're greeted by a trumpet flourish. Pretty neat, eh?

AUTODESK ANIMATOR STUDIO

For the past several years, a DOS program from Autodesk called Animator Pro (AP) has set the standard for PC 2D animation programs. Indeed, the program was almost single-handedly responsible for the popularity of the FLIC animation format used by trueSpace2 and many others. Unfortunately, because of limited graphics capabilities in DOS, such animations generally max out at 256 colors. This was okay a few years ago, because 386 processors (found in most systems at that time) can't handle deeper palettes. Today's processors, however, have dramatically increased power, and the AVI and QuickTime formats, with millions of colors and interleaved audio, are widely used. Premiere and other fine video-editing programs handle these formats; until now there have been no true animation programs that do so. Leave it to good old Autodesk to revamp AP into a truly awesome Windows animation program: Animator Studio (AS). The main program interface is shown in Figure C-3.

Animator Studio's Painting Tools

A worthy animation program needs a good set of painting tools, which AS has in spades. It's so capable, you could use it in a pinch as your sole bitmap editor. Selection tools, which let you isolate part of an image for processing, are Marquee, or rectangular; Lasso,

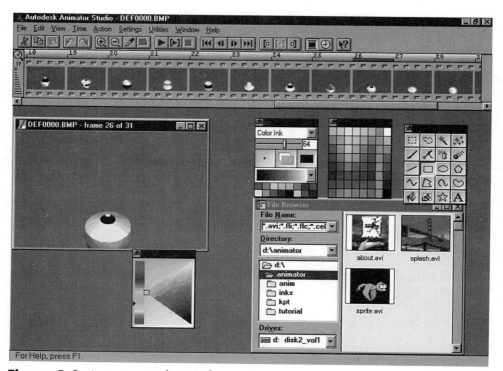

Figure C–3 Animator Studio interface

or freehand; Magic Wand, which selects similar pixels adjacent to the point you click on; and Separator, which selects similar pixels to the one you click on anywhere in the picture. The latter two are useful for automatically selecting odd-shaped image areas, such as someone's head.

Once you've selected an area, you can turn it into an animatable floating object. You can create and independently save and load *rubylith masks*, which protect parts of the image from being affected by drawing or processing. Rubyliths can be based on selection areas, background color, alpha channel, or even the lightness value of each pixel. With masks, animated objects appear to move "behind" other picture elements. As you work, you can turn masks and their visibility on and off.

The AS paint tools include Paintbrush for standard freehand drawing; Airbrush, which lets "ink" build up with successive strokes; and Spray, which randomly scatters the current brush footprint. If you have a touch tablet, you can achieve more expressive results with these freehand tools by letting such factors as brush size and ink strength vary with the stylus pressure. You can draw filled shapes and outlines with geometric tools, including Rectangle, Ellipse, Polygon (regular and irregular), and Curve (b spline). There are also Fill and Edge Fill tools, which base their effects on image colors. The freehand and outline tools work with different brushes, which can be round with partial transparency (there are 10 preset profiles, which you can alter), straight lines, or rectangles. You can even draw with single images and animations, called *sprites*.

There is a vast array of inks, which specify how your drawing affects the image. Some of these are Color, the default; Brighten and Darken; Clone, which replaces drawn-on pixels with those from a different "source" image, useful for creating custom transitions; Colorize, for selectively adding color to grayscale images; and Gray, which does the opposite. Special effects inks include Emboss, Engrave, Jumble, Lace, Pixelate, Sweep, Sharpen, Soften, and XOR. There's also Gradient, which can use a preset or custom color sweep in either the RGB or HLS color space. Unbuzz ink helps remove video flicker, and Unzag removes undesirable "staircase" edges. There's more, but now it's time to talk animation.

Animating with Animator Studio

When you draw, it can be on a single frame or "over time," that is, across a sequence of frames. This is where the magic really starts to happen. You can draw a line or series of lines or drag a sprite over a background, and the program will automatically match the drawing to the number of frames, which can be all or any subset of the animation. Normally, if you're using a freehand tool, the lines are shortest in the first frame and grow to full length at the final frame. But with the Time Action controls, you can set a Trail Length so the line "pulls in its tail," never growing past a specified percentage of the overall length. You can also set Fade In and Fade Out percentages. If drawing with a Sprite, the program normally places only one image per frame, but by setting Trail Length with optional Fade settings, you can create stroboscopic special effects. Another "over time" setting is the Action Envelope, which lets you graphically set variations in drawing speed. Preset envelopes include linear (the default), acceleration, deceleration, and zigzag (where the motion goes forward, then backward, then forward again). Like almost everything else in AS, these are eminently customizable.

You can also animate objects by setting start and end positions, sizes, angles, colors, and shapes and then letting the program do the tweening. If you set a motion path by dragging or multiclicking an object over the background, you can edit the path by moving, adding, and deleting control points before committing to it. Even if you do commit and then change your mind, there are multiple levels of undo and redo. Another cool animation feature is Text, which lets you draw titles letter by letter or scroll them in three dimensions, easily creating a *Star Wars*-type crawl, among other effects. Some users may find it inconvenient that they can't scroll text downward, only up and sideways.

The AS macro capability is a real labor saver. You can record a sequence of commands, then apply them as often as you like. So, for example, you can create an animation simply by repeatedly applying a special effects ink to a frame and then copying the frame, letting the program do the tedious repetition. You can save and load macros, but only one can be present in memory at a time.

Adding Sound

Of course, graphics are only half the story. Any animation worth its salt has a soundtrack, and AS makes it easy to create one. Actually, this is done with its companion program, SoundLab. This program is unique in that you can record an audio accompaniment in real time while your animation is playing. Of course, you can also load and synchronize a canned soundtrack, but that isn't nearly as much fun. SoundLab is a full-featured digital audio recording and editing application. It has cut, copy, and paste functions, as well as filters such as Reverse, Pitch & Tempo, Chorus, Reverb, and Volume. As in AS, envelopes can be used to modulate changes over time.

Another bundled program is Scriptor, which lets you string together several movies, add sound and playback controls, and save everything as a presentation.

Documentation

Autodesk hasn't stinted on documentation, either. The tutorial manual introduces you to nearly all the tools, although there could be somewhat more explanation. There's no reference manual, but the online help is the most versatile I've seen. In addition to using the standard methods of looking things up alphabetically and searching for keywords, you can create a custom table of contents via bookmarks, and you can add your own notes as well. Also, when you point at any icon, a text description of it and the equivalent keystroke appears at the bottom of the screen.

AVID ELASTIC REALITY

Even though trueSpace2 cannot create morphing animation between disparate objects, you can render the two objects into separate images and then create a magical-looking animation in which one smoothly changes into the other. You can do this with a 2D morphing program such as Elastic reality.

The term *morph* is derived from *metamorphosis*, which implies transformation. In film and video, it's become a popular animation technique for changing faces and other shapes, â la Michael Jackson's *Black and White* video. Morphing as a video special effect is considered by many to be old hat, partly because it's been applied in broad strokes by digital hacks, more as a means of catching the jaded viewer's eye than conveying any meaningful idea. That doesn't mean the technique can't be employed by true artists to real effect. It takes imagination, which is up to you, and good tools. You probably won't find a better one today than Elastic Reality from Avid, the digital video company.

How to Tween: The Fine Points

Elastic Reality uses *tweening* to save you lots of work. To transform an image, you specify start and end points and the program calculates and draws all the intermediate steps. Actually, you define areas via open and closed shapes. Say, for example, you want to create an animation in which someone's face shrinks while the head stays the same size. All that's required is to draw a large rectangle or oval just inside the face's edges and a smaller one that defines the face's final size, select both, and use the Join command. When you render the animation, the pixels defined by joined shapes move between them in straight or curved lines from frame to frame while "dissolving" between the two images.

Other drawing tools are Freehand, which lets you draw continuous open and closed Bezier curves, and Pen, with which you define an area via successive clicks of the mouse button. When you use Freehand, the program automatically places control points as necessary (you can define the precision) to follow your shape. The Reshape tool lets you modify a shape by moving control points and adjusting their tangents, which define curvature between points, as well as add and delete points. To encourage experimentation, there are multiple levels of undo and redo.

Another type of point is "correspondence," four of which are automatically created when you draw a shape. These are used to determine how pixels move between shapes. For example, in the above "face-shrinking" animation, if you move the smaller rectangle's correspondence points 90 degrees away from their starting positions, the face twists as it shrinks. (Alternatively, you could simply rotate the shape.) You can modify morphing precision by adding and deleting correspondence points and you can even combine shapes by connecting them.

Roll Away the Clips

Elastic Reality uses a metaphor found in film and video editing to set up morphs between different images. Load the "from" images into an *A-roll* sequence, and the "to" images into the *B-roll*. There's also a *Matte roll*, which contains images such as alpha channels to define transparency for compositing, and a *Background roll* to define the compositing "bed." You set these up in the Sequence Editor—essentially four horizontal strips into which you can load still and moving images in various formats. The program supports input and output of Alias, BMP, Cineon (Kodak DPX), FLI/FLC, GIF, IFF (Amiga), JPEG, PICT, QRT, Rendition, SGI RGB, Softimage, Sun Raster, Targa, TIFF, AVI, Wavefront, Xwindows, and Abekas YUV. The Sequence Editor gives you standard functions such as cut, copy, and paste of single images and ranges, as well as the ability to reverse and delete ranges.

To morph between two still images, simply specify corresponding areas between the two with the shape creation tools, then join each pair of shapes. To save drawing time, you can copy and paste shapes between images, moving and reshaping them on the destination as necessary. You can also define "barrier" shapes, used to restrict movement beyond certain parts of an image, and use shapes as mattes to define transparent and opaque areas in mattes. During shape definition, you can see the A-roll or B-roll image, or both superimposed, using a slider to fade between them. Unfortunately, there's no way to see both the A-roll and B-roll images side by side. Another slider lets you move instantly to any frame, where you can render a preview of the transition at that point.

Thanks to the A-roll/B-roll scheme, you can morph between image sequences, for example, to change from one face to another while turning the head. In such cases, however, you must set up corresponding shapes throughout the animation. Usually you can use keyframes to avoid having to do this on every frame. Elastic Reality's Groups window lets you create, rename, remove, hide, depth arrange, and edit groups of shapes for special effects, such as sliding body parts in front of or behind one another. The motion curve and transparency curve editors can be used to control acceleration of pixel motion and image mixing on a regional basis. You can create overshoot and undershoot motion for cartoon-like exaggeration, or clamp the motion curve to disallow these.

Elastic Reality's reference documentation is excellent, but the tutorial manual needs to be significantly expanded. Of particular interest is the reference manual's chapter on special effects, which covers the aforementioned "folding" parts of an image behind and in front of other parts, breaking an image into independently moving pieces, and creating special effects transitions. Suffice it to say, if you're looking to become a digital video wizard, Elastic Reality should be near the top of your bag of tricks.

PAINT PROGRAMS

For creating custom bitmaps for backgrounds and textures, compositing images, and other functions related to 3D animation, *Adobe Photoshop* and *Fractal Design Painter* are the acknowledged industry leaders. Both are third-generation, robust, and mature products. This section looks at each program's capabilities, then compares the two. But if you want it in one sentence, here goes: Photoshop excels at image manipulation and fine-tuning, whereas Painter offers practically unlimited creative freedom.

This section also covers *Strata MediaPaint*, a nifty new program that lets you paint special effects onto animations and videos.

Incidentally, using these paint programs brings home the inadequacy of 16MB of RAM. Almost every operation results in lengthy, frustrating disk accesses. For any serious graphics work on a PC or Mac these days, consider 32MB the minimum.

Adobe Photoshop

Take a look at Figure C-4. Photoshop's tools are represented as icons in a vertical toolbox palette. For isolating parts of images, there's a rectangular/elliptical marquee that can be drawn from the corner or center, a lasso for freehand selection, and a magic wand for selecting contiguous picture sections with similar colors. You can also open a special dialog for selecting color ranges anywhere in the image by clicking on a grayscale representation. In all cases, you can choose whether additional selections replace the original or are added or subtracted.

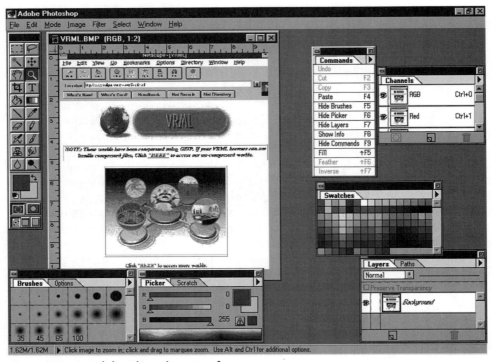

Figure C–4 Adobe Photoshop interface

The Move tool lets you reposition the selected part of an image. You can scroll around an image with the Hand tool (there are scroll bars too, of course), and the Zoom tool lets you focus closely on areas of interest. The Crop tool is for removing extraneous edges. Type lets you add text to an image, and the Paint bucket fills areas with color. Other tools create gradient fills, draw straight lines, sample colors from an image, and erase parts of the image. Painting tools include Pencil, Airbrush, Paint brush, and Smudge; Rubber stamp, useful for retouching, lets you paint onto an image from a different part of it or from another image. Image-processing tools are Blur/Sharpen and Dodge/Burn/Sponge, which lightens, darkens, or changes the saturation of an area. Each has a single-key equivalent, which is handy, and most have an options panel for additional settings. For example, the Paint brush tool's wealth of options includes various painting modes, such as darken, lighten, dissolve, behind, and multiply, as well as a transparency setting, pressure settings if using a tablet, and a wet edge option.

Selection Manipulation

When an area is selected, you can do plenty of interesting things with it. Naturally, there's cut, copy, and paste. You can rotate it, flip it, and scale it, and apply effects such as distortion and perspective. You can paste it into another selection on a different image, where it "shows through" the selection—useful for compositing images. For example, to make someone's face appear in a window, select the face in the source picture, then select the window panes in the destination, then paste the former into the latter—the face appears "behind" the nonselected window frame. But that's just the beginning.

One of Photoshop 3's most powerful features gives you a Layers palette, in which each element pasted into a composition maintains a separate identity and can be manipulated individually. This gives an "object" orientation to a bitmap program, resulting in the best of both worlds: the bitmap's photographic and/or painterly quality combined with the flexibility and versatility of an object-oriented drawing program. What's more, elements can be combined in various ways, with endlessly fascinating results. The number of available layers is limited only by memory.

Paths is another feature that adds "draw" functionality. With the pen tool, you can draw straight line and curved paths, useful for defining areas to fill or shapes that can be stroked using a painting tool. Because they use memory more efficiently than masks, paths are useful for long-term storage of selection areas, with the only limitation being that the outline must be fairly simple. Because they're defined by mathematical formulas rather than pixels, paths can be adjusted and scaled without losing resolution or quality. Paths can be imported from and exported to Adobe Illustrator.

For a glimpse of Photoshop's image-processing power, a list of some of the relevant commands is helpful. Under Map, Invert negates colors, Equalize creates an evenly distributed brightness range, Threshold converts images to high-contrast black-and-white, and Posterize lets you specify the number of tonal levels, creating large areas of flat color. Under Adjust, Levels gives you control over highlights, midranges, and shadows, whereas Curves gives you "micro" control, letting you set up to 16 points directly on a graph display, automatically creating a smooth curve between the points. The latter also lets you draw freehand on the graph for ultimate control. Other more generalized controls are Brightness/Contrast, Color Balance, and Hue/Saturation. There's also Replace Color, which lets you create a temporary mask based on color value for correcting hue, value, and saturation, and Selective Color, which lets you modify colors by adjusting the amount of "ink" used to create a specific color. If your original image is low in contrast, the Auto Levels function can instantly improve it by defining the darkest and lightest colors as black and white, then equally redistributing the colors between them. There are others I could list, but it's more important to state here that most of these functions can be applied to the image as a whole or individually to red, green, blue, and alpha channels, giving unparalleled image-processing control.

Plug-In Filters

Plug-in filters were pioneered by Adobe. New in Photoshop 3.0 is the Lighting Effects filter, which lets you add up to 16 light sources to an image with different colors, intensities, and angles. Also new are Dust & Scratches for retouching and Mezzotint for that hard-to-achieve engraved look. If none of the existing filters does exactly what you need, try Filter Factory. The Render filters create endless fractal clouds, add lens flare, and incorporate bump map images in Lighting Effects. The Distort filter set includes Displace, Pinch, Polar Coordinates, Ripple, Shear, Spherize, Twirl, Wave, and Zigzag. Other filter sets are Blur, Noise, Pixelate, Sharpen, Stylize, and Video. Unfortunately, most of these cannot be used directly with trueSpace2, but most of the many third-party filters available from MetaTools (formerly HSC Software), Alien Skin, and others are compatible.

LESSON 2: ALPHA CHANNEL COMPOSITING WITH TRUESPACE2 AND PHOTOSHOP

If you render a 32-bit image in trueSpace2, it's a snap to take it into Photoshop and use it for professional image compositing. Here's a brief example of how to do it.

1. In trueSpace2, create or load a simple object.

2. Open a small Perspective window and zoom in on or move the eye close to the object.

3. Use the small window's Render Scene to File tool and render a Targa-format image file named COMP1.TGA. When the Targa Settings dialog appears, accept the defaults of 32-bit image, compression, and frame numbering, and click OK.

4. Delete the object, add or load another, give it a glassy, semitransparent material, and render it to a file named COMP2.TGA.

5. Quit trueSpace2 and start Photoshop.

6. Use the New function to start an image of about 500x500 pixels in RGB Color mode. Draw something, or open an existing image such as a scanned photo.

7. Open the Layers palette if it's not displayed and use its menu to create a new layer. Accept the default settings.

8. Open the COMP1.TGA file from Step 3.

9. Open the Channels palette if necessary, and scroll down to last entry, labeled 4. This is the alpha channel, which defines transparency. As shown in its Channels palette entry, the background area is black, or fully transparent, whereas the foreground area is white, or fully opaque.

10. <ALT>-click on the image area in the alpha channel entry in the Channels palette. This selects the foreground section of the image.

11. In the Tools palette, click on the rectangular selection tool, which is the dashed-line rectangle in the upper-left corner.

12. In the COMP1.TGA image, left-button click and hold on the center of the object and drag it to the other image. Once the mouse cursor leaves the "from" window, you won't see anything, but when you release the mouse cursor, the object appears as a selection in the "to" window.

13. Click on the "to" window's background to deselect the object.

14. Add a new layer to the background image.

15. Close COMP1.TGA and open COMP2.TGA.

16. Again, <ALT>-click on the new image's alpha channel in the Channels palette to select the foreground and drag the selection to the main image. When you release the mouse button, notice that the object's translucency is preserved, so you can see through it to the background.

17. Deselect the selection by clicking in the background.

18. You now have a three-layer image "sandwich." It contains the background and over that, the first composited image and in the uppermost layer, the second composited image. You can manipulate each of these layers independently by selecting it in the Layers palette. First select the Move tool, which is the cross-shaped tool second from the top in the Tools palette's right-hand column.

19. The highest layer, containing the translucent object, is currently selected. Left-button drag anywhere in the main image to move the object around. Wherever you move it, you can see through it to the layers below.

20. Select the other layers in the Layers palette and try moving them around. You can also change a layer's priority or depth by dragging it vertically in the palette.

As you can see, combining alpha channel output from trueSpace2 with Photoshop's channel and layer operations opens up a whole new world of image-making possibilities, with near real-time feedback.

Fractal Design Painter

The first thing you notice about Painter (included on CD-ROM with this book), after the attractive and colorful interface (see Figure C-5), is the wealth of available tools. First there are the brushes: hairy, with simulated bristles; graduated, which can vary between two colors depending on tablet pressure; covered with soft edges; and the hard-edged penetration brush. Some others are oil, with variations such as Loaded Oils and Big Wet Oils; camel hair, with bristles that spread out if you paint slowly; and various watercolor brushes. Other painting tools include Artists such as Van Gogh and Seurat and liquid variants, which look like paint applied with a palette knife and can be used to distort images as though floating on a liquid surface. And even more: airbrush, pen and pencil, eraser, chalk, charcoal, crayons, felt-tip pens, and you can even paint with water! The manual uses 28 pages to document these.

Every brush can be customized in a variety of ways. Primary categories of methods include buildup, cover, eraser, and drip (or smear), each with subcategories of soft, grainy, flat, hard, and variable. You can change the brush's size, profile, angle, dab type (circular, 1 pixel, and bristly), and dab spacing. You can create multistroke "rake" brushes, use the Well palette to adjust how a brush interacts with a medium such as paint

Figure C–5 Fractal Design Painter interface, showing onionskin feature

or ink, and add randomness to such factors as dab placement and clone location. Cloning is a powerful technique that involves painting on one image using a different image as a source. The Expression palette gives tablet users lots of flexibility in stroke variation and lets mouse users emulate a stylus by dynamically modifying such factors as jitter, opacity, color, and grain according to input variations such as speed and direction. New in Painter 3 is the ability to use any selection as a brush. Custom brushes can be saved and loaded in libraries as any other resource can.

Art materials in Painter are organized into palettes. The Color Set palette gives you a rectangular grid of commonly used hues. You can use either provided set—Painter Colors or Pantone—or create your own. The Colors palette lets you choose any of 16 million colors via a hue ring around a saturation/value triangle. The Papers palette provides textured surfaces that can affect painting, adding to the "natural media" look. Then there's the Gradients palette, with linear, radial, circular, and spiral color ramps. The Weaves palette lets you use patterns such as plaid as fill textures.

Processing Images with Painter

Painter's image-processing capabilities are not to be sneezed at. The Equalize function works much like Photoshop's. You can adjust hue, saturation, and value for all colors or just the ones that you select in the dialog. There are also controls for Brightness/Contrast, Posterize, and Negative. You can set all colors to within safe limits for printing and video.

Under Surface Control, you can apply such effects as lighting, screens, surface texture, and color overlay. Focus controls include Glass Distortion and Motion Blur. Esoterica offers such intriguing functions as Apply Marbling and the amazing Auto Clone, which can turn photos into oil paintings. All these can be applied to the entire image or a selection, which can be rectangular, oval, freehand, straight lines, or Bezier curves. Selections can be stored into and retrieved from a palette and saved as disk files. You can also have a number of floating selections, equivalent to Photoshop's layers, giving you the same object-oriented compositional capabilities.

Unique to Painter and a potential boon to multimedia developers is the Sessions function. Say two artists are working on a project, but it's inconvenient for them to meet in person. One sends a killer image to the other, who wants to know how she got that other-worldly sheen on the alien's skin. She could try explaining, but a picture's worth a thousand words, right? All she has to do is record her movements into a session, then send the file to her colleague, who plays it back and can see the exact sequence that achieved the effect! You can also output a session as an AVI animation file or as a numbered file sequence.

In addition, you can load AVI files and numbered sequences, and the latter feature lets you select the start and end frames. You can paint on animations one frame at a time (not *over* time) with an "onionskin" feature that lets you see up to five frames superimposed. Painter's unique and eminently cool Image Hose lets you paint with an image sequence, and you can use it or any other tool to create seamless textures with a "wrap-around" painting feature. New multicolor brushes emulate the artist's technique known as "loading a brush." There's advanced modeling of physical brush bristles, and the ability to warp images interactively. The Gradation Composer gives endless control over color ramp creation, and Weaving lets you use a virtual eight-harness loom as a painting tool.

Painter or Photoshop?

Painter's key concept is virtual natural media. You want to draw with chalk on grainy cotton paper? You got it. You want to smear existing colors with a wet brush on a canvas consisting of random typewritten characters? Two clicks and it's yours. Of course, the program lets you do many things impossible with traditional tools, like randomly varying brush color, saturation, and/or value on the fly and using different sizes and styles of paper textures in the same picture. The variety of combinations is virtually unlimited. Just as with actual media, the tools can take weeks to get to know and years to master.

One the other hand, Photoshop's design philosophy is based on technical accuracy. You can work in any of a broad range of color spaces, including LAB, the device-independent model on which the others (such as RGB and CMYK) are based. You can adjust individual color channels and overall color using a scientific histogram (a graphic display of brightness distribution throughout an image).

Painter erases only to white or the original paper color, plus a darken option. Photoshop, on the other hand, can erase to the saved image, letting you easily restore small areas after a major operation without having to use cloning.

Painter can undo and redo as many as 32 operations, whereas Photoshop only has one level of undo/redo, but Photoshop has a "hidden" function to reset settings in some dialog boxes to their original values (accessed by pressing the <ALT> key).

Both programs come with excellent reference manuals with step-by-step procedures for most functions. Painter's is on the short, thick side to fit into the distinctive packaging (a paint can, complete with paint smell!), so there's more page flipping. Tutorial manuals are included with both, although Painter's could be better written and more comprehensive. Both have a CD-ROM packed with resources and information.

At the end of the day, Photoshop is for production work, whereas Painter users, to paraphrase a forgotten pop star, just wanna have fun. That's not to say that the roles can't be reversed; it's just that the programs seem to be designed that way.

So which one should you get? If you're serious about multimedia development, take my advice and buy both. Some capabilities overlap, but the overall functionality of each program is diverse enough to make both programs essential tools in your development armament. (Don't forget; business is war!)

Kai's Power Tools

If Kai's Power Tools (KPT) 3 from MetaTools (formerly HSC Software) doesn't get you excited about computer graphics, then nothing can. Take the eminently useful, if fairly staid Adobe Photoshop, plug in these innovative, unique filters, and you've got an incredibly fun pixel festival in your computer! Some members of the KPT toolbox are actually full-fledged, dedicated 2D design programs in the form of plug-ins, whereas others work much like standard filters. The KPT filters also work with other compatible programs such as Fractal Design Painter. Unfortunately though, being full 32-bit applications, they don't work as Photoshop plug-ins with trueSpace2. However, if you can find a copy of KPT 2, you're in luck—you'll be able to use its filters directly with trueSpace2.

Perhaps the two most useful programs in KPT 3 are Texture Explorer (see Figure C-6), which creates an unlimited variety of colorful and fascinating seamless textures, and Gradient Designer, which is probably the most versatile tool ever created for producing color gradients. Both have unique, super-friendly user interfaces, with large preview windows and several layers of tools under the surface. Texture Explorer now produces crystalline shapes as well as the previous versions' organic textures. Thanks to the larger preview window, there's room for 16 "cousins" surrounding the "mother" texture. The most important new feature in Gradient Designer is the ability to tweak hue, saturation, brightness, contrast, and blur in real time. Also, you can now adjust squeeze and rotate with the mouse instead of the keyboard and you have the ability to feather any effect.

If you know KPT 2, you'll recognize many of version 3's filters, including 3D Stereo Noise, which turns a selection into one of those dotty pictures you have to cross your eyes to see in 3D; Glass Lens; Page Curl; Vortex Tiling; Seamless Welder, which makes a smooth-edged pattern from your selection; and nifty new filters such as Planar Tiling, which makes a receding plane of tiled images; Twirl, with a Kaleidoscope option; and Video Feedback, which simulates aiming a video camera at its output monitor so you get an endlessly repeating image disappearing into itself. What's new about these filters is that, instead of working instantly and making you press number keys as you invoke them (What did the <5> key do again?), each now has its own user interface with real-time feedback. For instance, with Glass Lens, you change the lighting angle by dragging the mouse over the lens surface. Also, thanks to the interface, you have additional capabilities like being able to set the apply mode and opacity.

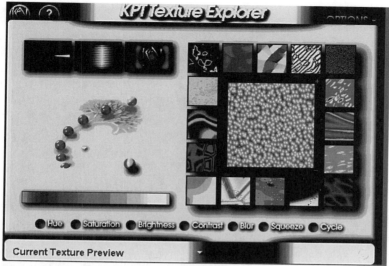

Figure C–6 KPT 3's Texture Explorer

Metatools also grouped KPT's pixel-based effects—Pixel, Gaussian, Noise, Edge, Intensity, and Smudge—together as Lens f/x, with a very cool new interface that works directly in Photoshop. The Lens f/x "precision instrument" looks like a scientific lens with dials and buttons around the edge that you can slide around anywhere in the Photoshop interface, viewing the filter effects as you go. The controls include Intensity, Opacity, Preview Mode toggle, Channel Operations, and Effect Modifiers.

The most exciting innovations in KPT 3 are the two new plug-in applications. Spheroid Designer lets you create ray-traced 3D spheres, refracting or opaque, with infinite variations. You can create, design, multiply, randomize, splatter, pack, build, stack, scatter, and even animate the spheres. The plug-in uses a truly gnarly looking interface to let you control up to four light sources and change lens curvature and opacity, light diffusion, bumping, mutation, and much more. The other new plug-in is Interform, which merges two Texture Explorer presets into a new static texture or even a QuickTime-format movie. Interform offers an animated preview with 22 different motion algorithms, including Manual Scoot, where you set the texture's speed and direction by clicking and dragging with the mouse, plus horizontal, vertical, and sometimes diagonal variants of PullMe, SineVibe, Rubber, Oscillate, and others. It would have been nice if these were documented somewhere, but I guess if a picture's worth a thousand words, then a moving picture must be worth even more. There are also 10 frame panels that let you set animation keyframes.

KPT 3 has something for just about everyone, and it gives you the tools to create endlessly fascinating images even if you can't draw a straight line. There's nothing else like it, and I recommend it highly to anyone who wants to fully exploit his or her computer's graphics capabilities.

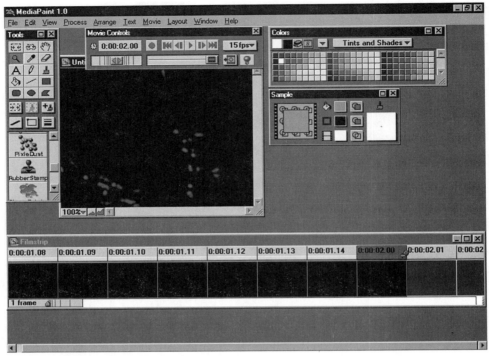

Figure C-7 MediaPaint interface

Strata MediaPaint

Strata MediaPaint has been available for Macintosh computers for about a year, but the Windows version was released only recently. A save-disabled demo version is included on the CD-ROM with this book, so you can try it out for yourself. To install it, run the SETUP program in the DEMOS/MEDIAPNT directory. Here's a brief overview.

MediaPaint looks a bit like Premiere or Animator Studio (Figure C-7), but it doesn't perform standard editing functions. Its main purpose is to let you paint special effects onto movies. It also lets you paint from one movie onto another. For example, one of the tutorials has you load two versions of a 3D animation, one rendered in wireframe and the other as a solid. By painting the latter onto the former, you cause the solid appearance to magically "flow" onto the wireframe object as it moves. You can load movie files and/or still images (but not an image sequence), or start from scratch.

To use MediaPaint, load a file or invoke the New function, select a painting tool, hit the Record button, and start painting. The Tools palette offers such standard painting tools as a brush, eraser, and pencil. But the real fun is in using the special customizable plug-in tools, found in a scrolling list in the bottom section of the Tools palette. These tools are listed on the following page.

Airbrush—paints a fine stream of paint with feathered edges

Blur—blurs the area you click and drag over

Burn—darkens pixels drawn on

Diffuse—causes the painted part of the image to appear fuzzy and randomized

Distort—lets you "push" portions of paint around the image

Dodge—lightens pixels drawn on

Fade in/fade out—increases opacity/transparency of painted area

Fine brush—permits customizing current brush's transparency and flow

Invert—creates color "negative"

Magic wand—creates selection by sampling a specific color range

Rubber stamp—lets you copy parts of the image to other parts

ShapePainter—lets you draw a small animation onto a movie

Sharpen—increases apparent sharpness by reducing gradients

Smear—causes colors to run together

Smudge—similar to dragging your fingers across a wet oil painting

There are also four spectacular particle-based tools, each with many settings.

BabyBoom—creates self-propagating particles that fly straight, spin, and have trails (shown in Figure C-7)

PixieDust—creates particles with trails that fly straight, but react to gravity and friction

SpinOut—creates particles with trails that spin wildly as they fly across the screen

Squiggle—creates worm-like lines that wriggle and squirm

MediaPaint is almost as much fun to use as trueSpace2, and it should be considered an essential tool for almost any animator.

Universe

Because outer space is a favorite milieu for 3D animation, the companion CD includes Universe, a shareware program by Jess Diard. This nifty little application is dedicated to creating cool-looking space images with star fields, globular star clusters, nebulae, and nearby stars with coronas. The output is ideal for using as backgrounds in your sci-fi epics.

When the program starts, you're presented with the black of deep space. To create your background, choose the drawing tool and adjust the settings as necessary. Then click (for star fields) or click and drag to draw the desired feature. Usage is pretty straightforward, but if you need help, see the README file.

NOTE: If you like this program, please register it (see About Universe in the Help menu). It's only $19.95, and doing so will encourage Jess to create even more cool software.

"PLUG-IN" PROGRAMS

One of the most popular topics in discussions on the trueSpace Internet mailing list is desired features for the next version of the program. Most list members agree that a plug-in architecture would be truly wonderful. This feature, found in many other 3D graphics programs, lets third-party developers extend an application's capabilities by adding such functions as procedural modeling and textures and ways to make advanced animation easier to accomplish. Although trueSpace2 does not currently accommodate plug-ins, the two programs in this section—Exploder and Landscape Maker—are so useful that they could almost be considered such.

A copy of Landscape Maker is included on the companion CD, in the SHARWARE directory. See the README file for installation directions. You can download Exploder from Caligari's Web site at http://www.caligari.com/ftp/pub/trueSpace/add_ons/.

Exploder

The Exploder shareware utility, expertly programmed by Rob Bryerton, adds limited particle animation capability to trueSpace2. It loads trueSpace2-format objects; then it creates and saves 3D animation files that you can load back into trueSpace2 and render. The animations are, of course, of objects exploding. You can explode objects into their constituent polygons, or particles defined by another object file, or both. Among the basic settings are minimum number of pieces, explosion distance, and number of rotations. You can also specify the world axes to which movement, rotation, and optional scaling are applied and create extremely cool special effects with a "stagger" option. Gravity-related options include the ground location, number of bounces, and a rebound scale.

NOTE: The most important thing to remember with Exploder is that the program does not read objects in the standard trueSpace2 format; they must be in ASCII COB format. To save an object in this format, check the ASCII box in the trueSpace2 Save Object file dialog.

Landscape Maker

Kevin O'Toole's Landscape Maker is another trueSpace2-dedicated shareware program that converts bitmap images to 3D landscapes in trueSpace2 format. Its operation is straightforward. Load a BMP-format image and save it as a COB-format trueSpace2 object. The settings let you determine which color scale is used to convert the input image's color pixels to height in the landscape object, as well as the landscape's vertex density and maximum height. One option that's available only if you register the program lets you output the landscape as a solid, which lets you perform Boolean operations with it.

WARNING: Landscape Maker creates nonplanar polygons. To avoid shading errors, triangulate landscapes before rendering them.

GAME DEVELOPMENT WITH TRUESPACE2

by Tom Marlin

Tom Marlin of Marlin Studios in Arlington, Texas, is a PC game developer, designer, 3D artist/animator, and writer. He is an active member of the Internet trueSpace mailing list. Tom has used trueSpace2 to create art and animation for several PC games and multimedia projects. His most recent accomplishment is creation of the art and animation for MVP Software's Rings of the Magi, *named ZD Net/Computer Gaming World 1996 Shareware Game of the Year (Puzzle and Logic category).*

Caligari's trueSpace2 is a great stand-alone 3D tool for modeling, rendering, and animation; but a good artist can take his or her work a step further by using trueSpace2 with other programs. It's been my experience that no single graphics program fills all the needs of any practicing graphics professional. Most 3D artists have a large suite of programs, each with some unique feature that makes it worth keeping on the hard drive. I find myself switching back and forth between four or five programs to create even the simplest 3D scene. Although many excellent programs are available, I'll describe the ones I'm most comfortable with and find most useful.

With Autodesk's Animator Pro or Animator Studio, you can bring your renderings to life by creating vivid texture maps and bump maps and adding finishing touches in post-production editing. With Macromedia's Director, you can include your trueSpace2-rendered art and animations in distributable games and presentations that include sound and music.

Autodesk's products are extremely versatile graphics and animation programs, with dozens of features that can be used in a variety of applications. Some of these features are useful with trueSpace2 renderings. These Autodesk products are mainly 2D programs, which means they are incapable of producing graphics with the depth or photorealistic quality provided by true 3D software such as trueSpace2.

Autodesk Animator Pro

Animator Pro is an 8-bit (256-color) DOS-based graphics and animation program. Although initially marketed as a presentation creation tool, the program has been used widely in the game business. The art and animation for many classic DOS-based 2D games were created with Animator Pro. Because most PC games are created in 8-bit, Animator Pro's features fit in nicely for the creation of game art. The program can complement trueSpace2 for any 8-bit art and animation you create.

Autodesk created the "flic" animation format, with its FLI format in 320x200 resolution and its FLC format for higher resolutions at 640x480 and above. Stills output from trueSpace2 can be dithered to 8 bits and trueSpace2 animations can be output in the FLC format, then imported into Animator Pro for postproduction editing. Autodesk's ANICONVERT utility will dither your stills for you, or you can use your favorite dithering program.

Animator Pro offers multiple "inks" (filters) that can be applied to one or all of your trueSpace2 animation frames. The more useful inks include OPAQUE for applying color from the existing 256-color palette; SOFTEN, UNBUZZ, and UNZAG for antialiasing; TILE for distributing a small texture over a large area; BRIGHT and DARK for changing scene lighting; GLASS for applying a color tint; H GRAD, V GRAD, R GRAD, and L GRAD for creating horizontal, vertical, radial, and linear gradients; and many others such as EMBOSS, for creating an embossed look.

Animator Pro also has good 2D animation tools in its OPTICS area; powerful palette manipulation capabilities; FLI and FLIC editing tools for changing animation speed; file format conversion capabilities with its ANICONVERT utility; the ability to save oft-repeated tasks with its POCO macros; a scripting language that allows you to add sound on a limited basis; and freely distributable animation players.

Animator Studio

Animator Studio takes most of the DOS-based Animator Pro features and ports them to a MS Windows 3.x/95 environment. In addition, many new features are added to facilitate 24- or 32-bit art and animation editing. Basically, you can do the same things in Animator Studio under Windows that you can with Animator Pro in DOS. Because most of the art and animation created in trueSpace2 is rendered in 24- or 32-bit formats, this program can be more useful. Its learning curve is a little steeper than Animator Pro, and it takes large system resources to make it work effectively. In other words, it takes a fast machine with lots of RAM to use all its high-end editing capabilities fully, but the type of machine you'll need to effectively use trueSpace2 will generally fill that need.

Whereas Animator Pro is limited to working within the confines of the 8-bit flic format, Animator Studio can handle flics, plus MS Video's AVI format and the Macintosh QT Movie format. The program also supports input and output of most Windows graphics file formats.

The inks in Animator Studio are extremely useful with trueSpace2. More inks and ink adjustments are available, allowing you to apply them on a level-of-intensity percentage. Their greatest use is in the creation of texture and bump maps. I think I turned the corner from amateur to professional 3D artist when I discovered the use of textures and bumps. By creating my own texture maps, rather than relying on standard maps that come with trueSpace2 or found on many CDs and online services, my renderings took on exactly the look I wanted. By creating bump maps to match many of these textures, my renderings came alive with exciting shadows and texture.

When working in trueSpace2, you can create textures and bumps in Animator Studio on the fly. While creating a trueSpace2 scene, you might find that a certain texture would enhance the object you're creating. Without exiting trueSpace2, you can switch tasks and open Animator Studio. There you can use the many filters and tools to create your texture, save it, then switch back to trueSpace2 and apply it. If it doesn't quite suit your needs, you can switch back to Animator Studio and alter the texture. If a bump map will further enhance your creation, you can switch back to Animator Studio and repeat the process for texture creation and application, then use the trueSpace2 Image utilities to create the bump map.

Animator Studio includes an improved scriptor program and animation player for distribution of your trueSpace2-created animations. It also includes Animator Sound Lab for creating, editing, and adding sounds to animations suitable for playing in a Windows environment. You can marvel at your smooth trueSpace2 animations, but when you add synchronized sound effects, the animation really comes alive. I mainly use the Sound Lab editor for creating game demos done in trueSpace2 and Animator Studio, but Sound Lab is such a versatile program, I also keep it around as my main sound editor. It's great for mixing, cutting, pasting, and applying a wide variety of special effects.

Macromedia Director

Although Animator Pro and Animator Studio do allow for adding sound to your trueSpace2 animations and distributing them with an animation player, their capabilities are not as sophisticated for these purposes as Macromedia's Director. Director is a true authoring program used in many of today's best-selling games and multimedia titles.

You can take your trueSpace2-created art and animations and import them into Director with its user-friendly graphics interface. There, you can alter speeds, splice in other animations, do some art and animation editing, and add two sound tracks. You can make a truly interactive program without typing lines of code. Director's LINGO scripting language can be as simple as you want it to be or almost as versatile as a C++ program, depending on how deeply you want to learn LINGO. You can define mouse "hot spots" (image maps), create dozens of scene transitions (fades, sweeps, etc.), add digital video, and wrap the whole thing up in a user-executable file, which can be distributed royalty free.

Director also offers 2D art and animation creation/editing capabilities, which can complement trueSpace2, Animator Pro, or Animator Studio.

The 3D logo in Figure C-8 was created with Caligari's trueSpace and Autodesk's Animator Pro. The letters were typed in trueSpace2, then extruded using the SWEEP function. The ocean and clouds were cropped from photographs using Animator Pro, then assembled as one background image. The whole scene was then rendered in trueSpace.

The scene in Figure C-9, from *The Roswell Omen—a Graphic Mystery Game* by Marlin Studios, was created with trueSpace2 and Autodesk Animator Studio. It comprises mostly 3D models, but the characters were cropped in Animator Studio from photos, then their backgrounds dropped out with an Alpha channel (making them transparent). The Alpha images were then converted to TXR files with the trueSpace Image utility and mapped onto two-dimensional planes. In postproduction, Animator Studio was used to add lens flares to the headlights and kleig lights.

Figure C–8 3D Logo

Figure C–9 UFO Crash

INDEX

Symbols

3D graphics
  career opportunities, 8-10
  creating, 5-7
  defined, 4-5
3D object vendors, 379
3DR, 7

A

Add Cube tool, 37
Alpha channel compositing, 404-405
Ambient Glow, Shader Attributes, 233-234
animation, 45-48, 289-326
  automatic aim, 313-318
  Base Rate parameter, 295
  career opportunities, 9
  characters, 296-301
  deformation, 302-307
  frames, counting, 44
  group tools, 44, 390
  keyframe, *see* keyframe animation
  localizing action, 323-326
  material attributes, 307-308
  movement, 290-291
  multiple objects, 293-295
  Paths, 310-312
  project editing, 318-320
  rendering, 48-50
  repeating/copying action, 321-322
  rotation/scaling, 291-293
  setting up, 7, 44-48
  tweening, 290
  video files, 309-310
Animator Pro, 413-414
Animator Studio, 397-399, 414-415
architecture career opportunities, 8
AutoFacet, 230
axes, 36, 54-62
  loading objects, 54-55
  locking, 56-58

axes (*continued*)
  moving objects, 56-59, 170-172
  object coordinate system, 116-119
  repositioning at center of objects, 173-176
  rotating objects, 58-61, 167-170
  scaling objects, 61-62
  tool, 167-172

B-C

Bevel tool, sweeping polygons, 108-109
Boolean tools, 5, 90-94, 152-158, 386
bump mapping, 256-261

Caligari's Web site, 370-374
camera, creating with Pioneer, 357
career opportunities, 8-10
Center Axis tool, 173-176
characters
  building, 191-194
  keyframe animation, 296-301
Close All Panels tool, 36, 44
coloring objects, 224-227
commercial design career opportunities, 8
cones, 5, 76
coordinate systems, 56-61
Coordinates property panel, 57-58
Copy tool, 186
cubes, 5 72-73
cylinders, 5, 73-75

D

Decompose tool, 179-180
Deform Object tool, 137-148
Deform/Sculpt tools, 385-386
deforming objects, 5, 136-148, 302-307
Delete Face tool, 129-130
dimensional promotion, 123-126
Dimensioning tool, 182-183
Director, 415
Display modes tools, 381
Displays, Solid Render, 24

417

Books have a substantial influence on the destruction of the forests of the Earth. For example, it takes 17 trees to produce one ton of paper. A first printing of 30,000 copies of a typical 480-page book consumes 108,000 pounds of paper, which will require 918 trees!

Waite Group Press™ is against the clear-cutting of forests and supports reforestation of the Pacific Northwest of the United States and Canada, where most of this paper comes from. As a publisher with several hundred thousand books sold each year, we feel an obligation to give back to the planet. We will therefore support organizations that seek to preserve the forests of planet Earth.

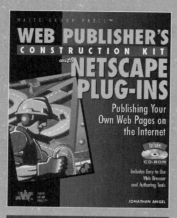

This is a legal agreement between you, the end user and purchaser, and The Waite Group®, Inc., and the authors of the programs contained in the disk. By opening the sealed disk package, you are agreeing to be bound by the terms of this Agreement. If you do not agree with the terms of this Agreement, promptly return the unopened disk package and the accompanying items (including the related book and other written material) to the place you obtained them for a refund.

SOFTWARE LICENSE

1. The Waite Group, Inc. grants you the right to use one copy of the enclosed software programs (the programs) on a single computer system (whether a single CPU, part of a licensed network, or a terminal connected to a single CPU). Each concurrent user of the program must have exclusive use of the related Waite Group, Inc. written materials.

2. The program, including the copyrights in each program, is owned by the respective author and the copyright in the entire work is owned by The Waite Group, Inc. and they are therefore protected under the copyright laws of the United States and other nations, under international treaties. You may make only one copy of the disk containing the programs exclusively for backup or archival purposes, or you may transfer the programs to one hard disk drive, using the original for backup or archival purposes. You may make no other copies of the programs, and you may make no copies of all or any part of the related Waite Group, Inc. written materials.

3. You may not rent or lease the programs, but you may transfer ownership of the programs and related written materials (including any and all updates and earlier versions) if you keep no copies of either, and if you make sure the transferee agrees to the terms of this license.

4. You may not decompile, reverse engineer, disassemble, copy, create a derivative work, or otherwise use the programs except as stated in this Agreement.

GOVERNING LAW

This Agreement is governed by the laws of the State of California.

LIMITED WARRANTY

The following warranties shall be effective for 90 days from the date of purchase: (i) The Waite Group, Inc. warrants the enclosed disk to be free of defects in materials and workmanship under normal use; and (ii) The Waite Group, Inc. warrants that the programs, unless modified by the purchaser, will substantially perform the functions described in the documentation provided by The Waite Group, Inc. when operated on the designated hardware and operating system. The Waite Group, Inc. does not warrant that the programs will meet purchaser's requirements or that operation of a program will be uninterrupted or error-free. The program warranty does not cover any program that has been altered or changed in any way by anyone other than The Waite Group, Inc. The Waite Group, Inc. is not responsible for problems caused by changes in the operating characteristics of computer hardware or computer operating systems that are made after the release of the programs, nor for problems in the interaction of the programs with each other or other software.

THESE WARRANTIES ARE EXCLUSIVE AND IN LIEU OF ALL OTHER WARRANTIES OF MERCHANTABILITY OR FITNESS FOR A PARTICULAR PURPOSE OR OF ANY OTHER WARRANTY, WHETHER EXPRESS OR IMPLIED.

EXCLUSIVE REMEDY

The Waite Group, Inc. will replace any defective disk without charge if the defective disk is returned to The Waite Group, Inc. within 90 days from date of purchase.

This is Purchaser's sole and exclusive remedy for any breach of warranty or claim for contract, tort, or damages.

LIMITATION OF LIABILITY

THE WAITE GROUP, INC. AND THE AUTHORS OF THE PROGRAMS SHALL NOT IN ANY CASE BE LIABLE FOR SPECIAL, INCIDENTAL, CONSEQUENTIAL, INDIRECT, OR OTHER SIMILAR DAMAGES ARISING FROM ANY BREACH OF THESE WARRANTIES EVEN IF THE WAITE GROUP, INC. OR ITS AGENT HAS BEEN ADVISED OF THE POSSIBILITY OF SUCH DAMAGES.

THE LIABILITY FOR DAMAGES OF THE WAITE GROUP, INC. AND THE AUTHORS OF THE PROGRAMS UNDER THIS AGREEMENT SHALL IN NO EVENT EXCEED THE PURCHASE PRICE PAID.

COMPLETE AGREEMENT

This Agreement constitutes the complete agreement between The Waite Group, Inc. and the authors of the programs, and you, the purchaser.

Some states do not allow the exclusion or limitation of implied warranties or liability for incidental or consequential damages, so the above exclusions or limitations may not apply to you. This limited warranty gives you specific legal rights; you may have others, which vary from state to state.

SATISFACTION REPORT CARD

Please fill out this card if you wish to know of future updates to
3D Modeling Construction Kit, **or to receive our catalog.**

First Name: _____ **Last Name:** _____

Street Address: _____

City: _____ **State:** _____ **Zip:** _____

E-mail Address _____

Daytime Telephone: (   ) _____

Date product was acquired: Month _____ **Day** _____ **Year** _____ **Your Occupation:** _____

Overall, how would you rate *3D Modeling Construction Kit*?

☐ Excellent   ☐ Very Good   ☐ Good
☐ Fair   ☐ Below Average   ☐ Poor

What did you like MOST about this book? _____

_____

_____

What did you like LEAST about this book? _____

_____

_____

Please describe any problems you may have encountered with installing or using the disk: _____

_____

How did you use this book (problem-solver, tutorial, reference...)?

_____

What is your level of computer expertise?

☐ New   ☐ Dabbler   ☐ Hacker
☐ Power User   ☐ Programmer   ☐ Experienced Professional

What computer languages are you familiar with? _____

_____

Please describe your computer hardware:

Computer _____ Hard disk _____
5.25" disk drives _____ 3.5" disk drives_____
Video card _____ Monitor_____
Printer _____ Peripherals _____
Sound Board _____ CD ROM_____

Where did you buy this book?

☐ Bookstore (name): _____
☐ Discount store (name): _____
☐ Computer store (name): _____
☐ Catalog (name): _____
☐ Direct from WGP   ☐ Other _____

What price did you pay for this book? _____

What influenced your purchase of this book?

☐ Recommendation   ☐ Advertisement
☐ Magazine review   ☐ Store display
☐ Mailing   ☐ Book's format
☐ Reputation of Waite Group Press   ☐ Other

How many computer books do you buy each year?_____

How many other Waite Group books do you own?_____

What is your favorite Waite Group book?_____

_____

Is there any program or subject you would like to see Waite Group Press cover in a similar approach?_____

_____

Additional comments?_____

_____

_____

Please send to: Waite Group Press
200 Tamal Plaza
Corte Madera, CA 94925

☐ **Check here for a free Waite Group catalog**

STOP!

BEFORE YOU OPEN THE DISK OR CD-ROM PACKAGE ON THE FACING PAGE, CAREFULLY READ THE LICENSE AGREEMENT.

Opening this package indicates that you agree to abide by the license agreement found in the back of this book. If you do not agree with it, promptly return the unopened disk package (including the related book) to the place you obtained them for a refund.